Seventh Edition

New Directions in Music

David Cope
University of California, Santa Cruz

WAVELAND
PRESS, INC.
Prospect Heights, Illinois

81378

For information about this book, contact:
Waveland Press, Inc.
P.O. Box 400
Prospect Heights, Illinois 60070
(847) 634-0081
www.waveland.com

CONTENTS

PREFACE

This seventh edition of *New Directions in Music* contains a number of significant changes from the sixth edition. The book has been reorganized to represent a more logical succession of ideas and developments. Analog Electronic Music and Digital Electronic Music have been combined into a single chapter: Electroacoustic Music. Extended Media has been moved to the chapter on Experimentalism. The chapters on serialism and atonality have been rearranged so that atonality and set theory precede serialism, reflecting what I feel is a more logical progression of ideas. Many other chapters also have been renamed to better reflect their content. For example, Minimalism replaces The New Conservatism, Timbralism takes the place of Instrument Exploration, and Integration replaces The Post-Avant-Garde. Chapter 9 on Algorithmic Composition (previously Automated Music) has been completely revised to reflect a more practical and less theoretical point of view. Also, a new section on Virtual Reality and the Internet, fast-growing areas of contemporary composition, has been included in the chapter on Experimentalism.

The chapter bibliographies have been moved to the end of the book to avoid breaking up important connections in the text. Each chapter bibliography is divided into two categories. The readings section includes books and articles relevant to the subject matter of the chapter (listed alphabetically by author). Each entry is linked to a parenthetical reference in the body of the text. Compact Discs, Recordings, and Publishers include record/CD/video numbers and publishers (when available) of works referred to in the chapter as well as other works I feel demonstrate chapter content (listed alphabetically by composer). New information on laser discs, websites, email addresses, and so on also has been included as appropriate. Over one hundred new bibliographic citings for reference and further study have been added. Though by no means all-inclusive, the bibliographies should be sufficiently comprehensive to provide readers with documentation and references for further study. This, combined with the updating of the composer biographies (Appendix II), the expansions of terms and their definitions (Appendix I), and the source addresses of Appendix IV, should make the music and reference material discussed more accessible. Composition or publication dates of works when mentioned in the text (if available) are included with the first appearance of the name of the work and not thereafter. The date is also included in the chapter bibliography under Recordings and Publishers.

Vectoral analysis is used for larger in-depth analyses in each chapter. This type of analysis provides an analytical approach in seven stages for understanding recent experimental music:

1. Historical Background includes information of relevance to the work including period of composition, school of composition (if any), inclusive dates of composition, country of origin, historical influences, and the composer's important teachers.

2. Overview, Structure and Texture includes general formal analysis and a careful look at musical structure (e.g., homophonic, monophonic, contrapuntal), general notational principles, rhythmic ideas, general compositional techniques influencing structure (e.g., mobile forms, graphic notation), and use of texts.

3. Orchestration Techniques covers basic timbral analysis, general instrumentation, unusual techniques (e.g., multiphonics, preparations), range extremes, unusual balance, and relations of timbre to form.

4. Basic Techniques includes pitch organization (e.g., tonal), motivic structures, and rhythmic detail.

5. Vertical Models presents samplings of significant vertical structures including chord roots and centers.

6. Horizontal Models includes samplings of significant horizontal melodic structures involving cadence, balance, and motion.

7. Style presents a summary of the stylistic parameters employed by the composer, any relevant material not discussed in parts 1 through 6, a general summation of harmonic, melodic, rhythmic, and formal techniques used, and their correlation.

Interviews or articles relevant to the chapter content have been added to each chapter. Most of these interviews or articles originally appeared in *The Composer Magazine* (quite separate and distinct from the British journal *The Composer*) which I edited from 1968 to 1981. Each issue of *The Composer Magazine* contained a number of often interrelated, high-quality articles, interviews, and reviews of new music. Controversial pieces often appeared, the risk of which, however, was offset by the extraordinary excitement that came from publishing articles or interviews that simply could not or would not be published elsewhere. *The Composer Magazine* was, therefore, never safe or predictable.

The three decades in which *The Composer Magazine* appeared represented some of the most significant years in the twentieth century. The Vietnam War grew in size and expired. Nixon was re-elected and then resigned. Men walked on the moon, and a space vehicle landed successfully on Mars. New music was equally dynamic during this time. The articles and interviews I have selected represent a mosaic of the special period in which they were published. Each interview/article is preceded by a brief introduction.

Directions in the avant-garde of the past fifty years seem as numerous and as diverse as the composers and their works. Yet these directions have historical motives and aesthetic values, traceable and uniquely observable due to their singularly radical nature. Electronic instruments and techniques, indeterminacy, adoption of scientific procedures, and theatrical participation, once held as highly controversial and innovative, have influenced a large number of current mainstream compositions. It was not always so. Berlioz's innovations in orchestration waited half a century for recognition and acceptance. Charles Ives's experiments took many years to be discovered and many more years to be considered musically viable.

The purpose of this book, then, is to explore the history, philosophy, composers, and works of the avant-garde since the late 1940s. Emphasis is placed on works which depart radically from tradition. Designed for music students at the undergraduate and graduate college levels, this text may be suitably integrated into any course covering aspects of twentieth-century musical forms, techniques, and/or philosophy. *New Directions in Music* should provide a valuable supplement to the well-rounded education of any serious musician. By virtue of the fact that many of the years discussed here have not yet become history in the academic sense, I have intentionally avoided the standard musicological approach and rhetoric in order to more aptly capture the essence of new directions in music.

Just as writing about Greek mythology does not make one either a Greek or a believer in myths, so writing about various types of avant-garde music does not necessarily make one an avant-garde composer. Therefore, do not assume that because I include something here, that I endorse it, just that I feel it worth knowing. Likewise, readers must weigh carefully the statement made in the Preface to the first edition of *New Directions in Music*:

> The lack of material herein related to more traditional (mainstream) techniques is not intended to reflect or suggest their unimportance (they are most important), but is rather due both to the fact that there is a wealth of material already available on these subjects, and to the necessarily limited scope of this text.

Whether one agrees or disagrees with the concepts, philosophies, and/or music discussed here is simply beside the point. This music exists and therefore deserves to be studied and performed.

David Cope

INTRODUCTION

As work neared completion on the fourth edition of *New Directions in Music*, I was struck with the idea of including an original John Cage mesostic (text aligned to create words simultaneously both vertically and horizontally). I wrote to John in New York half suspecting he would not even receive my letter before my publisher's deadline. Amazingly, he responded in less than ten days and promised to send a mesostic based on quotations from my book as soon as he could get around to creating it. Since I had thought to send a copy of the third edition of *New Directions in Music* with my request, I was overjoyed to think that he would now be able to contribute a mesostic for the new edition.

After a few days had passed, John phoned me from Oakland, California. He was quite apologetic. It seems that he had placed the third edition of *New Directions in Music* in a desk drawer in his apartment in New York City. When he went to retrieve the book for creating the mesostic, the drawer would not open. No subsequent prying would open it. John had called a carpenter but he had had to fly to Oakland before the carpenter arrived. So, the book remained locked in the drawer. I quickly mailed John a new copy of the third edition. Time was short, however, and my optimism was fast waning.

Finally, John wrote a note and attached the following correspondence. While nothing could surpass a personal Cage mesostic as far as I was concerned, these letters come close. The articulate dialogue here speaks for itself. It should provide readers with the spirit of inquiry necessary as they progress through *New Directions in Music*. Mr. Berry's kind permission to use his letters is gratefully appreciated.

1 November, 1982

Dear Mr. Cage,

What follows is the angry cry of a young composer demanding explanation and justification for what he perceives as folly in an older colleague. It is offered as a tossed gauntlet. I challenge you to defend yourself so I may understand you better. And be assured I sincerely prefer understanding over anger.

Mr. Cage: I accuse you for items 1 and 2, and hold you directly responsible for the situation described in item 3.

ITEM 1: You have systematically bastardized the art of music composition through the abuse of language. By redefinition of the word 'music,' in a way which says, 'anything and everything is music' you have made the word 'music' meaningless. If everything is music, then nothing is music. And therefore, composers can no longer exist . . . there is simply nothing left for them to do.

ITEM 2: You have declared, 'My purpose is to eliminate purpose.' You would have all composers eliminate beauty, sincerity, joy, compassion, expression, and love from their music. You would have all composers ignore these basic qualities in music which humanity has enjoyed for several thousand years.

ITEM 3: As a result of your nihilistic philosophy of music, and your pointless musical-sociological experiments, most young composers have been completely alienated from other musicians and from concert audiences. Concert audiences (in the U.S.) are for the most part completely disinterested in New Music, having been convinced there is no purpose or sincerity in the work of most twentieth-century composers. You have caused a near-total collapse of musical culture in this country, and left nothing for us (the young composers) to work with. We have no patrons, and our motives for composing music are constantly suspect.

I believe the Great John Cage, 'grandfather of modern music,' is a nihilistic comedian playing to an audience of indoctrinated sheep. His art is not art at all: it is blasphemy.

Sincerely,
Charles Berry

JOHN CAGE
101 West 18 Street (5B) • New York,
New York 10011

MESSAGE	REPLY
TO ⌐ Mr. Charles Berry 3571 Ruffin Rd. #238 San Diego, Calif. 92123 ⌐ DATE Nov. 21, 1982 It seems that what angers you are my writings, my ideas. I suggest you drop interest in them and focus on your own. Turn your attention to what you believe in. That is what I did. Thus I found alternative compositional means that would permit the introduction of noises and sounds available through new technology into musical works. I rediscovered the traditional purposes for making music	a) to imitate nature in her manner of operation, and b) to sober and quiet the mind thus making it susceptible to divine influences. Thus I was freed from self expression. Music became a discipline, a way of life. I have always noticed that very few people are interested in New Music. I was 50 years old before there was any supportive acceptance of my work. I am now much older but my work remains controversial as your feelings testify. Sincerely, *John Cage*

Detach and File for Follow-up

8 Dec 1982

Dear Mr. Cage,

Thank you for your letter. It has given me a much better understanding of the intent and substance of your ideas and your music. For the present I will take your advice and concentrate on my own creative instincts. However, I do feel compelled to study your work further.

At some future date I may, quite possibly, approach your work from a different perspective and find it refreshing and enjoyable.

Sincerely,
Charles Berry

In the preface I promised an article or interview would appear at the end of each chapter. While few readers would agree that this introduction qualifies as a chapter, the following article by Ben Johnston seems to me most appropriate at this point. This article has great merit and covers so much ground that attaching it to a single ideology, as suffixing it to a particular chapter would tend to do, seems unjust. "Art and Sur-vival" appeared in the 1971 Fall-Winter edition of *The Composer Magazine*. Interestingly, this piece seems as pertinent today as it did when it first appeared.

BEN JOHNSTON: ART AND SURVIVAL

The aims of avant-garde art show themselves in large part destructive: happily so, to be sure, but quite ruthlessly so. It is important that destruction not proceed indiscriminately, as well.

Most musical concerts are, without any need to parody them, a form of anti-art. Nevertheless, if concerts are to be destroyed, what then will be the occasions when we listen to music? On records and tapes only? In concerts which have become theater occasions? Solely in historical museums?

Some music is enhanced by the impersonal formality of conventional concerts, but much of it is stultified by this environment. Always to have such concert customs creates a stifling atmosphere which audiences may accept but which frequently bores them.

Harry Partch's "corporealism" is a protest against the dehumanizing abstraction of the concert occasion.

So, in its own time, was Franz Liszt's virtuosity; and so also in a much different social context, is Nam June Paik's reassertion of sex in concert music.

Formality is not the only trap into which concert-giving can fall, however. The utter informality of certain avant garde concerts, with people constantly entering and exiting, talking out loud, eating food and rattling paper, can destroy utterly everyone's ability to attend to any music which takes close and active listening. Obviously this custom, too, as an *a priori* condition for concerts, is severely limiting. The tyranny of the traditional concert could only too easily give way to a new tyranny of opposite aesthetic persuasion. Revolutions are well-known to be followed frequently by dictatorships, no matter what the contradiction of explicit revolutionary ideals.

For better or worse, we are in the midst of profound changes in our musical customs. One of the principal causes is technology, which is altering music from the ground up. There is far more electronic music today than any other kind if you include in the term phonograph and tape reproductions. This state of affairs has an adverse effect upon established customs of concert-going.

In addition, through mass media, the arts now reach millions of people, in sharp contrast to the aristocratic status quo of earlier times. This changes utterly the nature, the aims, the techniques of the arts. In most record companies the pop, rock and other mass-consumed music supports the "serious" music as a kind of prestige item. This has long been the case with music publishers. A.S.C.A.P. and B.M.I. have to operate on this basis.

The tradition of American public school music education up to now divides itself between a parade— and football—oriented band program and sundry adapted varieties of traditional concert music. Faced with the increasing self-assertion of youth and with the spectacular commercial success of youth music, which far outdoes any of the concert or educational varieties in popularity, some educators are playing with the idea that such music might make a superior basis for public school music programs. Since the performance training provided in public school music programs is a large part of the foundation of almost all advanced musical study in the United States, such a policy would precipitate a major shift in our artistic life.

When you consider also the economic straits in which nearly all United States symphony orchestras and opera companies find themselves today, it is evident that we are approaching a crisis in the musical life of our country.

We are rapidly approaching a time when those who value the artistic traditions of the past must search for a mutation which can survive in the changed conditions of contemporary life. Technology is trying to enable us to survive, if possible even to thrive in the face of overpopulation and its attendant mass culture. If the arts are to help us to maintain sensitivity and alertness of perception in these circumstances, they will need a great deal of help from all who understand what art is.

It has been pointed out by many philosophers that the arts are potent means for emotional education. No kind of education is more widely or more disastrously neglected today. Meaninglessness, lack of beauty, aimlessness, and boredom are as great causes of suffering as are hunger, disease, and exposure. The role of these and similar emotional factors in causing delinquency and mental illness is basic. The poor have no monopoly upon these ills. It is well known that the incidence of delinquency and mental illness in affluent segments of society is very high.

Much of the thrust of the avant-garde is toward erasing boundaries, whether between stage and audience, between socially proper and socially shocking, between black and white, or between nations and between cultures. Inhibitions and habits are under attack, along with prejudices. A crucial shift has occurred in many avant-garde works: they are no longer about experience, whether concrete or abstract: they *are* experience.

Paralleling the long-established trend away from representation in painting, twentieth-century music underwent early disenchantment with emotional expressivity. These trends have by now taken a full spiral turn, to the point that we now have a new kind of naturalism (consider, for instance, John Cage's insistence that the sound environment *is* music). The emphasis in much avant-garde art is not upon intellectual content nor is it upon emotional meaning: rather it is directly upon sense experience. Emotion itself, rather than emotional meaning, has re-entered some of the new art, and for its own sake, not as a symbol of life.

For example, in mixed media works, with electronic capability to inundate the senses with *power*, we get not only intermodal relations between different senses, but sometimes the Dionysian ecstasy itself. Information overload can produce an emotional intoxication similar to that induced by drugs, and sometimes almost as destructive. Small wonder that the varieties of psychedelia have at least an adjunctive relevance to avant-garde art of this type.

As Marshall McLuhan has observed, it is not only his nervous system which man has uttered (in the form of an all-pervasive communications network) but also his brain itself. In the absorbing exploration of the workings of artificial intelligence, it did not take artists long to get computers to simulate processes of artistic composition. In particular, Lejaren Hiller's experiments with computer-composed music have led to radical speculations about the nature of artistic creativity. Beside this there is widespread use of computers to synthesize musical performance. Consider especially the experiments of Max Mathews of Bell Laboratories.

Computers can also be used to discover and to exploit hitherto forbidding areas of complexity. Iannis Xenakis's use of the computer to produce a "statistical" music, in which only very large-scale, long-range decisions are made by the composer, is one such use. I am engaged at present with an associate, Edward Kobrin, in an extensive series of experiments to determine the nature of ratio-scale order and to exploit this in computer-composed pieces of music. I am convinced that the problem of order in music (and by extension in all aesthetic perception) can be approached fruitfully through the use of mathematics, provided the mathematics are sufficiently comprehensive and complex. The many failures and near-failures of such methodology in the past convince me only of the relatively narrow theoretical scope used by those who have attempted the application.

Since I believe that the fertile idea behind any new or old musical tradition is understandable through application of a kind of scale theory not different from that currently in use in laboratory psychology, I hope to help make possible the rejuvenation of many a tradition by this means. For instance, in most avant-garde music today, the organization of time by means of pitch, metrics, and periodic form is in eclipse. If any further vital ideas generating new movements in musical composition are to spring from these traditional nerve centers of musical practice, a radically new functioning of them is imperative. It is this particular problem to which I am at present addressing myself.

If the older side of the generation gap is in error to believe that things will right themselves if only they can be enabled to continue as usual, the younger side is equally rash to invite a clean break with the past. One of the most difficult problems for music to surmount, once the crisis of which I spoke earlier is hard upon us, will be how to find the new relevance of traditional modes of musical organization. Needless to say pitch—not only as melody, but as harmony and as tonality—flourishes in such neo-folk idioms as rock; but its organizing power is vastly less sophisticated than that of concert music. If we are not to descend as in this case to lesser levels of organization in all our art, we must find ways to make pertinent and interesting radically new approaches to these now almost "outmoded" dimensions of music.

The wide separation between "easy-to-get" survivals of musical tradition and rarified extremes of experimentation is already seeking rapprochement. We find this trend not only in the use in rock music of electronic and other "advanced" techniques, but also in the tendency of much avant-garde music to theater, even to comic theater in the vaudeville tradition. It is as though in the midst of the most recondite scientism, a down-to-earth reminder of music's entertainment function bursts out.

Insofar as any entertainment is of greater human value than "killing time," it *is* art. In what has usually been called art, the emphasis has traditionally been on the "profounder" values of life, expressed symbolically. Art has not always even intended to entertain, but the more it has sought to reach a wider public the more it has used techniques of entertainment. Today, when the role of entertainment media in reaching and beguiling masses of people is so all-pervasive, it behooves artists to assert as strongly as possible their influence to deepen the content as well as the impact of mass-consumed entertainment. It also behooves them to assert the minority rights of exceptional people, for whom much of mass entertainment is boring and trivial. This entails, to some extent, creating occasions for less popular art which are lively and pertinent to life as it is being and as it *can be* lived. Near-exclusive concentration on the art of other times and places is not only stifling but also dangerous, in our present circumstances. We may well lose all grasp of the relevance of art to life through our historicism, thus emasculating the very father of artistic creativity.

Whether an artist is a revolutionary or not (and an artist is well suited to that role), he is by nature a nonconformist. That is so fundamental a trait of artists that to insist that art reaffirm the status quo, as do the Russians, is to attack the basic health of art itself. No matter how assiduously an artist may try to conform to norms and standards, he is temperamentally unsuited to do this. He may not be antisocial or pathological, but he is certain to find ready-made adjustments to convention intolerable. It would be well to study carefully apparent exceptions to this, such as J. S. Bach (reputedly a *bourgeois paterfamilias* in good standing with his religion). There can be found in almost all such cases some important area of life in which the artist diverged profoundly from the standards of his times. If there was in truth no such area in Bach's life, it will prove most interesting to study him as an exception.

I think that this applies to *all* lives, except that lack

of courage or of clarity of direction in a life may mire it down into conformity. A great artist cannot lack courage or clarity of purpose. So he is set against conformity; and a time like the present, which makes large demands for conformity, renders every artist to some degree an outsider.

Art is not the servant of social solidarity. On the contrary, it is frequently the bringer of change and unrest. But neither is it an excuse for any kind of self-indulgent idiosyncrasy. It is nothing less than a vigorous and seriously responsible denial of society's prerogative to dictate norms.

The revolutionary position of all great religious leaders inexorably silts over with centuries of orthodoxy. The founders of all the world's great religions have in all cases exacted shockingly non-conformist demands as conditions of discipleship, in a self-dedication sharply distinct from the institutional and usually oppressive religions which they challenged. To approach *essential* truth from any sector of existential space demands that one put behind himself all other ambitions. Nothing short of such a commitment avails; and it is useless to imagine that it can be made vicariously, by the intercession of a hierophant or by inclusion in an organization.

Art makes something of the same imperious claim upon its devotees. The muse is well known to be a proud and arbitrary mistress, awarding favors where she will, as heedless of pleas as of cajolements. Not only is she said to be untamable, but also, goddess-like, to be jealous and demanding of unstinting loyalty and service, regardless of returns. The artist does not decide to say something and then draw upon his artistry to express it effectively. He struggles to discover what seeks to be said through him, channeling it as skillfully as he can by his craft into an intelligible experience. If nothing seeks expression through him, then that is his misfortune. He can only be ready for the effort in case he finds it possible.

What a far cry this is from the docile little *Gebrauchs-musiker* society sometimes claims it wants. But society is fickle, too, and much more apt to woo the difficult and uncouth artist who defies customs and categories.

It is perhaps commoner today to *abuse* the freedom of being an artist. Once established as a bona-fide artist (and that is no small task) a dishonest man can indulge eccentricities in the name of artistic freedom. Because a pseudo-artist has little to give, his art gradually grows stale, and his egocentric game comes to an end. Because people are aware of this possibility, it is a slow process for a truly innovative artist to gain recognition. Generally he has to have had a very great effect on many exceptional people before a wider public can know him for what he is.

But in all this we are still speaking of a rather limited public, of a very specialized group of people. If we concern ourselves with really great numbers of people, the problem becomes still more perplexing, the rules of the game still less clear.

In general, the wider public has great difficulty in comprehending what art is. They are apt to mistake it for amusement, or for some special kind of status-making, or for propaganda. The artist's problem in trying to reach many of these people is extreme. They are suspicious of his non-conformity, and of his enigmatic social role.

Faced as we are today by social and ecological conditions which imperatively require change, we really choose only what *kind* of change we shall undergo, and this only to the extent that we can wrest control of the situation from relentless processes of development already in motion. People who would cling to a status quo are dangerous dreamers. Not only an artist but every person needs to become a responsible non-conformist. One thing we should emphatically do is to alter habits of the use of art which foster conformist attitudes.

One of the crucial causes of the generation gap is the perception of this crisis by many young people, who can also see clearly how resistant their elders are to such a perception. Their frustration and apprehension at this disastrous blindness lends extreme urgency to their protests and causes.

It is interesting to observe that the character of the Madison Avenue-dubbed "now generation" is not modeled on the scientist or the engineer but on the artist. While technology is admittedly one of the few hopes in an otherwise desperate situation, great numbers of young people turn to the arts and to religion for sustenance. They are, I think, one jump ahead of events. While it is true that the population problem, pollution problems, poverty, and a host of other extremely urgent crises can be solved only by technological virtuosity of the highest order, even with all these matters well under control the best we could hope for would be a world-wide affluent society.

There is more to making the world a beautiful place to live than simply to stop polluting the air and water. And there is more to living a good life than having enough to eat and a decent place to live. The spate of amusement purveyed by mass media offers a poor solution to leisure time needs, since it is largely aimless and irresponsible. With greater awareness of the need for change and with real artistic standards to replace exploitative commercial ones as a basis for the entertainment industry, we could achieve a vast improvement in public attitude on many fronts.

The so-called radical youth, who are by no means all hippies and yippies, want to bring to confrontation the crisis in human relations which reflects the intolerable living conditions of a majority of people. These conditions are not primarily material, although material conditions afford an obvious place to start in trying to effect a change for the better.

It is here that the tie-in with religion becomes most evident. It is clear that the kind of institutionalism which organized religion offers is not at all satisfactory to many young people. Typical adherents of the leading Western religions rely too much on their congregations as bastions of middle-class convention. They are mostly too little concerned with self-transcendence, not nearly willing enough to take the lead in social reform, to put at rest the consciences of many people, especially young people.

Unfortunately a young person is more likely to find a lively awareness of the self-transcendent in life among drug users than among conventionally religious people. If this omission does not actively capitulate him into drug addiction, neither does it recommend conventional religion to him.

With the exception of minority groups like the Quakers, religious groups have not yet become leaders in pressing for constructive social reforms. More and more the young turn to secular leadership in these matters.

The fact that great numbers of the young today are actively religious and yet are not joiners of churches poses a crisis for conventional religion. In effect the youth are saying to the religions: "Shape up." The more contemplative oriental religions are having a wider appeal than commoner Western religions.

In these connections it is a fact that *Sergeant Pepper's Lonely Hearts Club Band* is more pertinent than Bach's *B Minor Mass* or Beethoven's *Ninth Symphony*. John Cage's total admission of environment noise into music is far more meaningful, in a crowded, information-loaded world, than is the cultivation of the analytical listening habits prerequisite to a sophisticated appreciation of classical sonatas or Baroque fugues. The model of behavior learned in aesthetic situations should carry over into everyday life. Most of us have more use today for the ability to concentrate in the midst of distractions, than for the intellectual ability to follow intricate formal patterns. Compositional techniques dealing with great complexity can tell us more about dealing with order and disorder in a complex world than can the relatively simple aesthetic structures of eighteenth century musical forms.

Some years ago I felt impelled to ask myself searchingly, "Why are you an artist? What good is there in being one? Is it simply in order to make a living doing what you enjoy? If a world crisis of sufficiently overwhelming scope should occur, would you consider the profession of art a nonessential occupation?"

It is in seeking answers to these questions that I have been led to the kinds of speculations I am here making. It seems to me the arts can be, perhaps are on the verge of becoming extraordinarily pertinent and valuable human activities. But on the whole, in their functioning as art, they are not so; nor are most of the arts thought by most people to be capable of becoming really essential areas of human activity.

Like most people who are deeply committed to and involved in the arts, I experience some of the isolation and the wish for isolation attendant upon being an artist. The experience of sensitivity is painful; the act of creation is as revealing of private surfaces as of depths of common humanity. It is a rare artist who has no problem with vanity, no "temperament." But being at the same time a teacher, I am continually reminded of society's basic requirement of professionals: that they serve humanity objectively, not out of cupidity or vanity. I therefore turn a critical eye to some artists' self-intoxicated poses; but at the same time I contradistinguish and assert the rightness of artists' nonconformism. When society itself is sick, this may take strange forms. It is above all in this non-conforming relation to society that art is "ahead of its time." Many severe protests now widely voiced by young people were vigorously set forth two or three generations ago by avant-garde artists. The destructiveness of avant-garde art is more an appearance than a reality.

An artist is like a sensitive instrument, tuned to respond promptly and perceptively to cultural conditions. It is time our society awoke to the importance of such instruments. The twentieth century is a great period in the history of art, but twentieth century civilization may well fail to take advantage of this greatness.

Many people believe we are living through a transition in human history at least as great and as fraught with danger as any which has ever occurred. There is, so to speak, an abyss facing us, over which we have somehow to cross. I believe that not only the bridge which will bear our weight but also the bridgehead on the opposite rim of the canyon cannot be built without the contributions of artists.

To translate this metaphor into down-to-earth details would be to contribute materially to the solution of the task it symbolizes. It is first of all the task of artists to make this translation.

This is a position of leadership, and one which

takes a certain amount of daring, most especially since the artist is not a likely man to whom the general public will turn for such guidance. And if the artist is interpreting his mandate to nonconformity as license to repudiate society's needs, he will fail in his leadership.

What is more likely than that failure is a negative response to society's perennial deaf ear to the artist's perceptions. He could then become a nagging Cassandra, saying "I told you so!' after it's too late.

If it is not to be too late, then we must not fail to close the generation gap and in addition to that the cultural lag between the vanguard of humanity's creative geniuses and the present moment, in which alone we can act. Our artists are not letting us down. Let us hope we do not let ourselves down by not hearing what they say.

≈ *Chapter 1* ≈

ORIGINS

AN OVERVIEW OF TONALITY

The *common-practice* period of music history (roughly 1600–1900) witnessed the establishment of a rich and complex musical language. Its basic grammar—tonality—still pervades much of today's popular music. Just a summary of tonal vocabulary and techniques would require far more than the space available here. However, three significant concepts require explanation, since the inexorable challenges to these concepts ultimately led composers to follow "new directions in music."

First, the concept of *key* defines the basic pitch vocabulary of tonality (Forte 1979). Music reduced to source material becomes scales of ordered intervals beginning on different pitches which help define its key. Figure 1.1a shows a simple phrase and a reduction of it forming a major scale. Tonality defines these pitches as diatonic to the key and those foreign to the scale as chromatic to the key. Figure 1.1c shows the standard three forms of the minor scale (natural, melodic, and harmonic, respectively).

Second, *consonance* (stability) and *dissonance* (tension) permeate the relationships of tonal materials (Aldwell and Schachter 1978). Principles of consonance and dissonance can be observed in the overtone series (integer multiples of a fundamental frequency). This infinite series, shown here in Figure 1.2 through eight pitches only, gives prominence to its lower more

a)

b)

c)

Figure 1.1. a) From Wolfgang Amadeus Mozart's (1756–1791) *Theme and Variations: Ah! Vous Dirai-je Maman.* b) A derived C-major scale. c) Three forms of the C-minor scale.

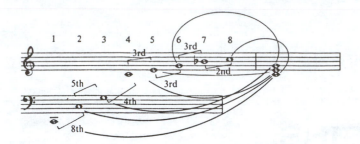

Figure 1.2.   The overtone series on C with primary lower intervals marked and a derived C-major triad.

audible three primary consonant intervals: octaves, fifths, and thirds which create a triad—a three-note chord built in thirds (Backus 1969; Benade 1976; Hall 1980). Most harmonies of tonal music consist of these consonant triads (Roederer 1974). In tonality, pitches outside of triads, often called non-harmonic tones, typically resolve to triads.

Finally, subtle concepts of *hierarchy* pervade most tonal music (Benward 1982). Two primary pitches provide fulcrum and weight. The dominant note or triad falls on the fifth note of the key. It requires resolution to a tonic note or triad of a key which falls on the first note of a key's scale. Figure 1.3a shows these primary chords in tonal hierarchy with examples of other less important secondary chords. This figure also shows a fragment of a work with the three tonal principles at work: key, consonance, and hierarchy (Figure 1.3b).

The interplay of these and other tonal principles provided a refined musical language for composers of the common-practice period. Their music, steeped in rich tonal traditions, parallels that of classic realism in the visual arts. So complex is the syntax of this language that implied relationships often occur even when not explicitly present.

At the turn of the century, many tonal composers faced critical challenges to their highly developed tonal language (Slonimsky 1971). Chromaticism often outweighed diatonicism, non-harmonic tones often overshadowed harmonic tones, and hierarchy had become more implied than a sense of key could withstand (Hartog 1957).

Figure 1.4 demonstrates some of the complex tonal ambivalences of late-nineteenth-century (Romantic period) music. The three principal concepts of tonality are barely perceivable here. While many composers clung to tonal traditions (neo-Romanticists such as Elgar and Rachmaninoff), many composers felt the need to seek new materials and alignments of those materials (Harder 1973; Sternfeld 1973; Thompson 1973; Yates 1967).

Figure 1.3.   a) The primary and secondary chords in C major. b) From Ludwig van Beethoven's (1770–1827) *Sonata Op. 2, No. 3.*

x = non-harmonic tones

Langsam und schmachtend

Figure 1.4. From Richard Wagner's (1813–1883) *Tristan und Isolde* (Prelude).

EXPANDED SCALE RESOURCES

One of the ways composers initially sought new order without tonality involved the exploration of alternative scales (Austin 1966). Traditional church modes, the pre-seventeenth-century antecedents of tonality, returned in new guises. Figure 1.5 shows six somewhat standard modes often used in impressionistic (1894–1915) works, with their Renaissance (sixteenth-century) names. Note that in each mode, the half-step patterns apply to different members of the series, giving a different sounding scale even though the pitch content of each mode remains the same.

Figure 1.6 shows Debussy's use of Aeolian mode on D as the basis for his pitch materials. The first four measures indicate the mode through repeated tonic notes (D in the lowest voice) and a scale-like melodic line. The B♭ creates the characteristic Aeolian half-step between scale degrees 5 and 6 (see Figure 1.5). The C♯, which commonly indicates a tonal leading tone, is conspicuously absent here. Debussy establishes modal integrity so that the variances with D minor can be heard. The B♮ beginning in measure 5 briefly suggests D Dorian mode (half-steps between 2-3 and 6-7; see Figure 1.5). Listeners experienced with tonality can often force modal music into tonal molds. Debussy fights this tendency, however, by avoiding leading tones.

The whole-tone scale was another popular

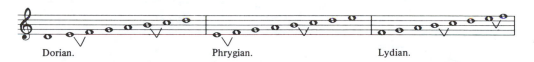

Dorian.   Phrygian.   Lydian.

Mixolydian.   Aeolian.   Locrian.

Figure 1.5. The standard modes.

Triste et lent (♩ = 44)

p expressif et douloureux

Ce rhythme doit avoir la valeur sonore
d'un fond de paysage triste et glacé

m. d.

Figure 1.6. An example of modal composition from Claude Debussy (1862–1918); *Prelude: Des pas sur la neige* (Footsteps in the Snow—1910). A. Durand, Paris.

Figure 1.7. Claude Debussy. Dover Publications, Inc. Permission granted.

resource used by composers early in the twentieth century (Fink and Ricci 1975). This scale divides the octave into six equal whole steps, creating symmetry. Figure 1.8 shows a whole-tone scale beginning on C, and another beginning on D♭. These are the only two actual possibilities, since beginning on D duplicates both the tones and intervals present in the C whole-tone scale. Composers discovered that this lack of potential for modulating to different whole-tone keys created severe drawbacks. As well, the characteristic sound of the whole-tone scale soon wore thin. Figure 1.9 presents an example of the C whole-tone scale in use.

Composers of the early twentieth century adopted folk modes and materials as well as traditional modes

styles can form. Such scales can create a consistency and predictability for listeners as in tonal music.

Pentatonic (five-note) scales derive in part from simplified versions of folk music (Simms 1986). Folk music often encompasses complicated and exotic tunings as well as subtle cultural connotations. Western tradition, however, extracted the simplified scale elements of five notes as shown in Figure 1.12. The music here consists entirely of five notes: B-C♯-E-F♯-G♯. As with whole-tone scales, the lack of half-steps helps to create tonal ambiguity.

Synthetic scales involve the creation of unique scales for the purpose of composition (Slonimsky 1947). Figure 1.13a shows an example of a work by American impressionist Charles Tomlinson Griffes (1884–1920) based on a synthetic scale. Here the scale used does not conform to traditional tonal-modal interval orders. In Figure 1.13b, the first scale based on F derives from these opening notes. The scale of the entire movement appears in Figure 1.13b. With synthetic scales, composers can freely determine their own functional relationships by using the same techniques available to common-practice composers: rep-

Figure 1.8. Two whole-tone scales.

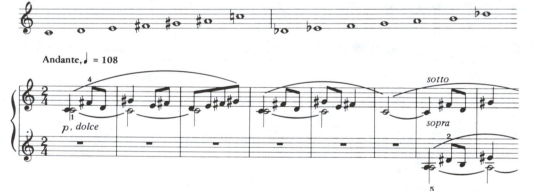

Figure 1.9. From Béla Bartók's (1881–1945) *Mikrokosmos* (1926–37), Vol. 5, No. 136. Whole-tone scale. Boosey and Hawkes, NY.

and whole-tone scales (Kostka 1990). In Figure 1.11a, Debussy uses a Spanish mode in Habañera style. The melody in the lower staff convincingly indicates a D-based scale, clarified and established by repetition of the important intervals of difference between it and traditional tonal scales and modes. The augmented second suggests the harmonic minor on C♯, but the use of the D♮, a half-step above the tonic, negates that possibility (see Figure 1.11b).

Octatonic or 8-note scales have often been used by composers like Igor Stravinsky and Béla Bartók (Salzman 1988). The octatonic scale is formed by alternating whole- and half-steps to create another symmetrical scale. Thus C-D-E♭-F-F♯-G♯-A-B-C forms an octatonic scale. This scale and other synthetic scales can provide templates on which compositions or even

etition and cadence. Unfortunately, real clarity of tonics and dominants, so characteristic of tonal music, can hardly have the same impact since often only one piece (or at best a few pieces) exist in any particularly synthetic scale. Moreover, synthetically derived materials can sometimes be mistaken as chromatic tonality or modality, even when this is not the case.

Figure 1.10. Béla Bartók. Dover Publications, Inc. Permission granted.

a)

b)

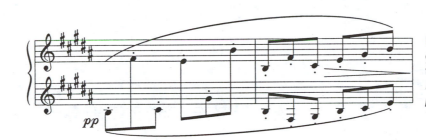

Figure 1.11. a) Use of folk modes in Claude Debussy's *La Soirée dans Grenade* from *Estampes* (1903). A. Durand, Paris. b) Mode derived from *La Soirée dans Grenade*.

Figure 1.12. An example of pentatonic composition from Claude Debussy; *Prelude: Les collines d'Anacapri* (The Hills of Anacapri—1910). A. Durand, Paris.

a)

b)

Figure 1.13. a) Use of synthetic modes in Charles Tomlinson Griffes's *Sonata* (1918). G. Schirmer, NY. b) Two synthetic modes from Griffes's *Sonata*.

EXTENSIONS OF TRIADIC HARMONY

As common-practice music matured, non-harmonic tones increased in number and, while still embellishing their harmonic counterparts, began to pull gently at triadic structure (Dallin 1974; Mellers 1969). As exploration continued, a hierarchy of dissonances surfaced. Some non-harmonic tones seemed more consonant than others. The more consonant non-harmonic tones often extended the thirds of the triads themselves. Figure 1.14 shows a series of triads with added thirds creating continuous seventh chords. Note that where non-harmonic tones resolve into triads, these seventh-chord projections do not. Figure 1.15 shows a series of expanded-by-third triads—seventh and ninth chords—with some tones resolving to triad tones and others not. This ambiguity is

a trademark of turn-of-the-century impressionistic composers. Figure 1.16 shows a dominant thirteenth chord. Note how chord members do not resolve into the triad.

Spacing also can be a critical component. If the thirteenth chord of Figure 1.16 were collapsed to within a single octave, a dissonant chord would occur where seconds rather than thirds would seem to be the basic building blocks (resembling *clusters* as shown in Figure 1.17 and discussed further in chapter 3).

Ninth, eleventh, and thirteenth chords have so many tones present that contrary motion within them can create contrapuntal chaos, with few of the voices distinguishable and voices often colliding with one another. Thus, such chords often appear in parallel motion, referred to as *planing*. Planing involves freezing chords and then moving them as a unit to form melodic lines. Chords become a by-product of such melodies and are heard as moving groups of notes rather than as separate harmonies. Figure 1.18 shows an example of diatonic planing.

Figure 1.19 shows a more substantial use of planing. Here the freezing of the basic pattern remains so fixed that significant chromaticism occurs. The triads of Figure 1.20 combine to create all twelve tones over a pedal point G in the bass. It would be possible to analyze each harmony independently. However, such an analysis would belie the fact that these harmonies result from planing.

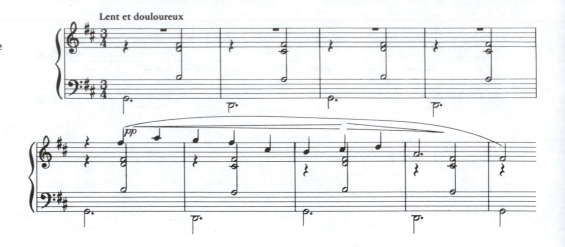

Figure 1.14.   An example of seventh chords used in Eric Satie's (1886–1925) *Trois Gymnopédies No. 1* (1888). G. Schirmer, NY.

Figure 1.15.   An example of seventh and ninth chords in Maurice Ravel's (1875–1937) *Sonatine* (1903).

Figure 1.16.   An example of a dominant thirteenth chord in Claude Debussy's *Prélude à "L'Après-midi d'un Faune"* (1894).

Figure 1.17. Collapsed thirteenth chord and resultant dissonance.

Figure 1.18.   An example of diatonic planing in Claude Debussy's *Feuilles mortes "Dead Leaves"* from his *Préludes, Book II* (1913).

Figure 1.19.   Another example of planing from Claude Debussy's *La Soirée dans Grenade from Estampes* (1903). A. Durand, Paris.

Figure 1.20.   An example of triadic planing from Maurice Ravel's (1875–1937) *Le Tombeau de Couperin* (1917).

Figure 1.21. Maurice Ravel. Dover Publications, Inc. Permission granted.

Composers also sought to create complex harmonies by combining two or more keys simultaneously (Hartog 1957). This *polytonality* produces rich chromatic textures, especially when the keys have few common tones. Figure 1.22a presents an example of polytonality using the keys of C major and F♯ major simultaneously. Note how the resultant scales in Figure 1.22b have only two notes in common: B and F (E♯).

Composers using polytonality often establish strong tonal centers rather than allowing the different keys to intermingle and thus reducing their recognizability. In Figure 1.24, Bartók uses different key signatures, different staves, and particularly different material for each key—B major melodic figuration versus C major harmonic planing—to achieve this separation.

Some composers add the element of collage to polytonal techniques (Machlis 1979; Martin and

sense of seven different key centers. Interestingly, E♮ and G♮ do not appear in this otherwise very chromatic passage. While the result might appear chaotic, because each idea is uniquely orchestrated and identifiable as quotation, the polytonality works effectively. Collage therefore provides a viable technique to establish and clarify polytonality. Charles Ives (1874–1954) used quotation to help further separate keys when creating polytonality in his music.

Composers also sought ways of building chords from intervals other than thirds (Forte 1955; Lester 1989; Miller 1930; Persichetti 1961). In Figure 1.27, the harmony results from stacked fourths (Hindemith 1937). Only the first chord of the second measure (with the word "wonder") defies this analysis. Note how the melody contrasts with the harmony by moving almost exclusively in seconds. The stacked chords make planing almost unavoidable. There is no doubt of the non-tertian nature of these chords since no dissonant tones resolve or hint of triadic organization.

Figure 1.28 presents a more complex interplay of non-tertian harmonies and develops more contrapuntal voice motion. The first chord consists of stacked fourths (B-E-A) with a doubled B in the top voice. The third, fourth, and sixth chords are similarly stacked in

a)

b)

Figure 1.22. a) From Igor Stravinsky's *Petrushka* (1911). b) Scales of C and F♯ major derived from *Petrushka*.

Drossin 1980). This effect combines polytonality with distinctly different ideas. The results often contain polyrhythms, polymeters, and polytextures from the overlapping of diverse musical styles. Figure 1.25 shows this process in use. Figure 1.25 actually has seven different keys—six contrapuntal melodies with chords in a seventh key scattered throughout the resultant texture. Some of the melodies share materials and all modulate freely. This results in a polytonal "feel" rather than a

Figure 1.23. Igor Stravinsky. Dover Publications, Inc. Permission granted. Stravinsky (seen here fourth from the left) appears with the Hindemith Quartet (composer Paul Hindemith is standing).

fourths. Chords five and seven are inversions of fourth chords and need only an octave displacement of one pitch (B below E for chord five, and F♯ between C♯ and B for chord seven) to be seen as similar projections of fourths. Chords two, eight, and nine are ambiguous with either a note missing (e.g., chord two could be seen as stacked fourths if the B were in the bass and an E added just above it) or as triads with added pitches. The final triad seems almost dissonant in

Figure 1.24. From Béla Bartók's *Out of Doors Suite* (1926). Universal Edition.

Figure 1.26. Charles Ives. Dover Publications, Inc. Permission granted.

Figure 1.25. Polytonality involving seven separate keys simultaneously.

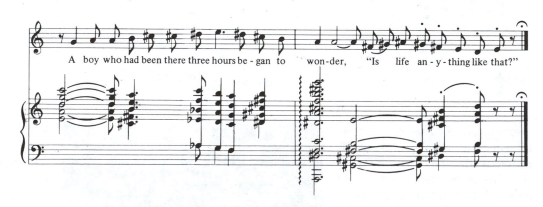

Figure 1.27. An example of chords built with fourths from Charles Ives's *The Cage* (from *114 Songs: 1884–1921*). Published by the composer and later by New Music Edition.

Figure 1.28. Contrapuntal techniques in nontertian harmony from Paul Hindemith's (1895–1963) *Le Cygne* (from *Six Chansons*, 1939). B. Schott's Soehne, Mainz.

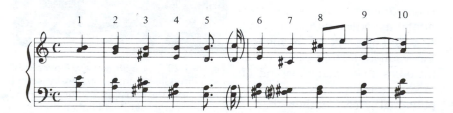

this context. Chromatic pitches here derive from the projections of perfect fourths.

Expanding triads into ninth, eleventh, and thirteenth chords, using more than one key simultaneously in polytonality, and exploring new interval foundations for harmonies all expand the composer's palette of available harmonic materials. Each of these approaches helps to defuse tonality and in so doing provides new directions into diverse harmonic vocabularies (Howat 1983; Myers 1971).

MUSICAL HIERARCHY

As tonal cohesiveness deteriorated, hierarchical structure also slipped away (Lerdahl and Jackendoff 1983; Narmour 1983; Schenker 1933; Schoenberg 1969). Subtle chromatic embellishing chords with complex but expected resolutions grew so distant from basic key concepts that recognition of tonic and dominant became obscured. The simple rhyming phrases of tonality disappeared, often obscuring hierarchy. Ferruccio Busoni wrote eloquently: "Let me take thought, how music may be restored to its primitive, natural essence; let us free it from architectonic, acoustic and esthetic dogmas; let it be pure invention and sentiment, in harmonies, in forms, in tone-colors (for invention and sentiment are not the prerogative of melody alone); let it follow the line of the rainbow and vie with the clouds in breaking sunbeams" (Busoni 1911).

With tonal superstructure gone, composers evolved uniquely personal languages that often appeared in only a few works. Many composers became preoccupied with certain chords. Scriabin's *mystic chord*, as shown in Figure 1.29a for example, is a

kind of fourth chord inclusive of both augmented and diminished forms. Figure 1.29b shows a brief example of how Scriabin uses this chord in his work.

Figure 1.29. a) Alexander Scriabin's *mystic chord*. b) From Alexander Scriabin's *Poème* Op. 69, No. 1 (1913).

This concept, that certain verticalities form the foundation for entire works, can contradict the lyric in music when taken to the extreme. The emphasis turns to vertical subtleties—their texture, timbre, and duration—separating them from melodically-directed tonal music. Figure 1.30 shows how such "events" can be organized logically and musically even though they often seem remote from one another in terms of range and/or separative rests. The texture here remains fluid, yet shaped by the progression of events.

With music freed from tonal expectations, areas other than pitch rose to the forefront as foci for experimentation. Meter relaxed into what some have called *time-suspension*. Figure 1.31 shows two of the many ways

Figure 1.30. An example of musical pointillism from Anton Webern's (1883–1945) *Six Bagatelles* for string quartet (1913).

Figure 1.31. From Arnold Schoenberg's (1874–1951) *Sechs Kleine Klavierstücke* Op. 19 (1911). Used by permission of Belmont Music Publishers, Pacific Palisades, CA 90272.

composers freed music from the restrictions of meter. First, on-beats are avoided—especially downbeats—to diminish their importance. Second, irregular small sub-divisions of the beat blur implied metric accents.

Composers also explored timbre as they continued to expand the repertoire of new music. The percussion sections of orchestras often introduced new instruments. Edgard Varèse's *Amériques* (1922) for orchestra, for example, requires ten percussionists utilizing twenty-one different instruments. This work also expands the resources of the traditional orchestra with normal complements of winds often doubled (e.g., six trumpets, five trombones, etc.). Varèse further requires the hecklephone, contrabass tuba, and contrabass trombone. *Amériques* (1922) and Schoenberg's *Gurrelieder* (1911–13, for 5 soloists, choir, and large orchestra) represent two of many such gargantuan post-Romantic orchestral works.

While some composers clung to tonality, others saw new instruments as a turning point for their musical style. For many, a common musical language had disappeared and each composer was free to pursue their own experimental direction. For some, this meant creating new vocabularies or complete reexaminations of the very nature of sound and the complicated ways in which humans act and interact in its presence.

As we shall see in the following chapters, reactions against tonality and metric constraints as well as inclusive approaches to new sounds led composers toward new goals and new directions in their music.

Vectoral Analysis
Edgard Varèse: *Density 21.5*

(For information on vectoral analysis and procedures see Preface.)

1. Historical Background: Edgard Varèse (1883–1965) was born in Paris of Italian-French parents and studied principally mathematics and science at school until he was eighteen (Varèse 1972). Varèse then entered the Schola Cantorum where he studied composition with Vincent d'Indy, Albert Roussel, and Charles Widor, becoming as well a very close friend and confidant of Ferruccio Busoni. Many of Varèse's early works were destroyed by fire. Varèse came to the United States in 1915, organizing both orchestras and concert societies for new music in New York City. The greater part of his known music was composed during the 1920s and 1930s—notably *Octandre* (1924), *Intégrales* (1925), and *Ionisation* (1931). From that time until the early fifties, Varèse did not compose (Wehmeyer 1977). Varèse then composed *Déserts* (1954) and *Poème électronique* (1958), both involving electronics. Varèse was

clearly influenced by the iconoclastic Ferruccio Busoni and Carlos Salzedo with whom he founded the International Composers' Guild in 1921. His music also shows the marked influence of Stravinsky's early primitive period (Ouellette 1968; Wen-Chung 1967).

2. Overview: *Density 21.5* was completed in 1936 and written for Georges Barrere for the inauguration of his platinum flute (21.5 is the density of platinum). The work was revised in April of 1946 for a *New Music Quarterly* publication in July of that year, and subsequent performances follow this later form. The work is in three main continuous sections with the first and last having similar lyric qualities.

The first note of each of the three sections (shown in Figure 1.33a, b, and c), when taken out of context, becomes the first three notes of the piece (F-E-F♯; as shown in Figure 1.33a). This kind of structure—materials flowing naturally from a single motive—replaces some of the more tonal expectations of key and hierarchy and provides a kind of consistency that helps to give the work a natural sense of flow (Bernard 1987).

3. Orchestration: Many effects available on the flute are explored in this piece including range extremes, dynamics within the various registers, articulations, and so on. Figure 1.33b shows an excerpt employing slapped keys, a percussive effect produced by playing softly and hitting the key simultaneously (+).

4. Basic Techniques: The principal motive of this work appears at the outset of the first phrase: F-E-F♯ (see Figure 1.33a). Note that this motive also implies a concept of statement (F), different statement (E), and return with variation (F♯) which characterizes the work's form. Within the first section, one finds many references to the opening motive. For example, measure 2 continues the first phrase with basic expansion of intervals and extension (four notes instead of three). The second phrase begins the same way as the first, but continues with variations based on inversion (F♯-G-F♮) and repetition (see Figure 1.34). The third phrase retrogrades the extension of the first phrase and intervallically expands the motive to G-B♭-G. Almost every note of the first section evolves from the opening three-note motive. Some reappearances of the motive involve extensive variations, while other appearances represent simple variations (inversions, etc.). However, all of these variations reflect in some way the concept of statement, different statement, return with variation, implicit in the motive of the piece. The synthetic scale used at the beginning and throughout the work is based on the eight-pitch base of the opening eight bars. Varèse also saves important notes—notably D (which does not occur until bar 11) and B (which does not occur until bar 18).

Figure 1.32. Edgard Varèse. BMI Archives. Used by permission.

Figure 1.33. Opening materials of each section of *Density 21.5* © 1946 by Colfranc Music Publishing Corp.

Figure 1.34. The opening eight bars of *Density 21.5* © 1946 by Colfranc Music Publishing Corp.

Figure 1.35. Repetition in *Density 21.5* © 1946 by Colfranc Music Publishing Corp

The second section of *Density 21.5* establishes a contrasting pointillistic theme (see Figure 1.33b). Note the material here: E-C♯-E, clearly a variant of the opening motive. Even the highly contrasting and repetitive climax of the work represents an extended inversion of the opening motive. The third section returns to the opening lyric motivic variations.

Interestingly, 70 out of the first 83 intervals of this work are seconds, primes, or fifths. Whether Varèse intended such a relationship with the title of the work is beside the point, as such extreme interval consistency contributes to the overall tightly integrated structure of the piece.

5. Vertical models: One would not expect to find vertical possibilities in a work for solo flute. However, over time, figure repetition can coalesce and suggest harmonies. In Figure 1.35, two of the prominent intervals (seconds and fourths) are emphasized by repetition. This passage contains tonal ambiguities (nonresolution of tritones) and contrasts these with highly directed dynamics. Note also how the D♮ is saved until it reaches an explosive triple forte.

6. Horizontal models: The expansion of the original motive is prevalent. Figure 1.33a shows how the interval of the second expands to the augmented fourth (as mentioned previously). Note how the passage tends to suspend musical time. Only the opening note occurs on a downbeat with the remainder of the phrase freely sculpted from the available durations of the measures.

7. Style: Varèse's *Density 21.5* is a three-part work drawn from an initial three-note motive of major and minor seconds. The flute's range and available effects are extensively explored as are the concepts of expansion and diminution of intervals, and saving pitches for intense points of arrival. Phrases join freely without marked tonal cadences or resolutions. The musical language, though not tonal, is articulate and consistent. Varèse creates his syntax from a non-tonal vocabulary of materials (Bernard 1987; Schuller 1965).

Readers should compare this vectoral analysis with those of the next three chapters (for their differences) and the last two chapters (for their similarities). The chromaticism of the Webern example in chapter 2 compares favorably except in its serial approach. The melodic line of the Varèse contrasts significantly with Webern's pointillism. The Glass example in chapter 9, however, compares more favorably to Varèse's work in terms of motive repetition and the small amount of material used.

GEORGE ROCHBERG: NO CENTER

I had the pleasure of hearing George Rochberg present the following paper at UCLA in 1969 to a large and enthusiastic audience. It was an exciting time as can be seen in Rochberg's wonderful commentary. The lecture stunned the audience initially because many were expecting a more or less dry lecture on serialism. At the conclusion of the presentation, I wound my way to the stage following a long line of well wishers, my only goal being to ask Rochberg if I could publish his lecture in *The Composer Magazine*. Much to my surprise he agreed immediately and in the weeks that followed he edited it carefully and graciously. As I read it now, it seems as fresh as that day in 1969 when I first heard it.

> The winds of change are blowing. Harder. Stronger. Gusts up to twenty, thirty, forty miles per hour. Gale warnings all up and down the coast. Tornados and hurricanes; maybe. Tidal waves, too. It's getting so you can hardly stay on your own two feet without holding on to something or somebody.
>
> Borman, Lovell, and Anders are in orbit around the moon.
>
> They just brought the men from the Pueblo back to the States.
>
> The Paris talks are getting nowhere. Fast.
>
> Columbia. Berkeley. Martin Luther King. Robert Kennedy. Black. White. Yellow. Brown. Red.

> There's a revolution going on. All over. Students and workers. There's a New Left. There's a New Right. There's also a new President.
>
> Borman, Lovell and Anders are orbiting the moon. They'll be home on Friday. With luck. After that the winds will blow even harder.
>
> Art and Life. Life and Art. They've gotten all mixed up. And no one can really tell the difference any more. It's causing terrific confusion.
>
> Look at the theatre. You can't tell the difference anymore between the actors and the audience. Participatory Theatre: like Participatory Politics (Clean for 'Gene) and Participatory Democracy. Group-grope. Love thy neighbor, all your neighbors. "Talk to me naked."
>
> They want to erase all the old differences, all the old distinctions. Tabula Rasa. The "Now." Feel; don't think. Burn; don't create. Take over the university. No more classes.
>
> The winds of change are blowing. Harder. Stronger. Gale warnings up and down the coast. If I were Black, I'd join the Black Militants, not because they're right but because I couldn't help myself.
>
> Burn, Baby, Burn. Open wide the Doors of Perception. Acid Pot. The Electric Circus is short-circuiting the Central Nervous System. The neurobiologists and biogeneticists are about to invade the C.N.S. R.N.A. D.N.A. Everybody look-alike, sound-alike, act-alike. Don't know why there's no sun up in the sky, Stormy Weather. Let's make special people for special tasks. Let's change the world. Cybernetics, computers, servo-mechanics, loops, input/output, feedback. Brave New World. Soma holiday. Re-entry. Dangers of.
>
> I must create a system of my own or else be enslav'd by another man's.
>
> My business is not to reason and compare.
>
> My business is to Create.
>
> Blake.
>
> Malcolm Lowry said: "Never trust a writer who doesn't burn." Our business is to create, not to reason and compare. We are in the business of Poetry. "Intelligence," said Borges when he was interviewed by Ronald Christ, "has little to do with poetry. Poetry springs from something deeper; it's beyond intelligence."
>
> What's our problem? Syntax? Semantics? The trouble with Varèse's music is Varèse. Every man has his own deserts. What are you doing to fill your existential vacuum?
>
> I'm trying to correlate everything I ever learned with everything I ever experienced. Metaphors. Correspondences. Analogies. Hallucinations of artistic vision. Plurality of sensibilities. Multiplicity. Simultaneity. Eternal Recurrence. Cyclical Return. The Eternal Present Eternally.

Blake's "contraries" appeal more to me than Aristotle's "unities." Unity of Varieties vs. Variety in Unity. In the same interview Borges said something about style which reminded me of Ives's remark about Substance and Manner. He remembered that Bernard Shaw had said "that, as to style, a writer has as much style as his conviction will give him and not more." Then Borges went on to say: "If a writer disbelieves what he is writing, then he can hardly expect his readers to believe it."

Our business is not to reason and compare—but to create—and burn—and make poetry, each in his own way—whatever way that is.

Rilke—war-letter, June 28, 1915: ". . . The whole sad man-made complication of this provoked Fate, that exactly this incurably bad condition of things was necessary to force out evidences of whole-hearted courage, devotion and bigness. While we, the arts, the theatre, called nothing forth in these very same people, brought nothing to rise and flower, were unable to change anyone."

Norman Mailer. *Why Are We In Vietnam.* Four-letter words of the whole sad man-made complication of this provoked Fate. The Language of Despair. The Obscenities of human suffering and Pain.

The saddest confession of all: "We . . . were unable to change anyone." Man only learns, if indeed he learns at all, from living, not from the example of Art. Then why Art?

I'm trying to correlate everything I know with everything I feel. Sense and Sensibility. So is everyone else. Are we making it? Can we make it?

The Art of Combination, "Ars Combinatoria." Borges. Rauschenberg. Robert Lowell. MacLuhan. Ives first and foremost. Gunter Grass/Brecht/Shakespeare and Coriolanus/The Plebian Revolt/The Workers Strike in East Berlin. Velikovsky's "Oedipus and Akhnaton." Myth and History. Fact and Fiction. The Theatre and its Double. Antonin Artaud. Borman, Lovell and Anders. The Moon of the Mind in orbit around the Sun of the Heart.

The art of combination is an attitude, an exploration of deep inner space, mental space.

Are we making it? Can we make it? Beckett talks because he can't stand to hear the silence that surrounds him.

Where do you draw the line? Is there somewhere to draw it?

Right You Are If You Think You Are. Pirandello.

Poetic Vision. Blake.

The Iconography of Imagination. Northrup Frye.

The New Image of Music. George Rochberg.

Some people think if you put Noise and Revolution together you've got Art. Herbert Marcuse says: "So it (art) wants to become an essential part of reality, to change reality."

The saddest confession of all: "We . . . were unable to change anyone." Graffiti. The Obscenities of human suffering. Pain and Frustration.

That's how Dada got started. After the Great War, the War to End All Wars and Make the World Safe for Democracy, oh Woodrow Wilson. Intellectuals and coffee-house aesthetes proclaiming a new Revolution and a new Reality. A new Style of Life. Art vs. Power and money. All they changed was art and made it "Modern."

Reality. Where is it? Outside or inside your head?

The New Left. S.D.S. Underground movies. Superstars. Pornography. Hippies. Futz. Hair. Acid. Pot. The Cop-out. Rock: Folk and acid. Strobe Lights: a fury of electricity. Mixed media. Multi-media. The New Confusion: where does Life End and Art Begin? Outside or inside your head?

The art of combination is not a theory. It is an attitude.

Art wants to "become an essential part of reality. It wants to change reality." The world outside your head is the world of politics and control, tanks and troops, science and technology. The world of power and money. War and Death. You can't change that with art. Then why Art?

In the end art gets pushed back into art, into the studio, into the gallery, museum, concert hall, theatre. In the end art gets pushed back into your head. Poetic vision. Taste. Fire and Algebra. The Iconography of human imagination.

Art is the effort to keep man in the state of permanent Revolution. Until he becomes fully Human.

We are Faust, the Arch-Romantic.

Art is the Creation of a mental realm to which there are no known limits. Keep man in a state of permanent, perpetual Revolution. Until he becomes fully human.

We are Faust, the Arch-Romantic. We want Eternal Youth. And we want it Now.

We keep murdering Innocence over and over again to prove something to ourselves. But no one knows what that is.

New choices open up: Perception rather than Logic. Taste rather than Method. Imagination rather than Ideation. Existence rather than Predetermination.

The very multiplicity of human languages, dialects within languages, regional inflections of dialects proves the impossibility of predetermining anything. Which is the same as predicting anything. After you've thought that one through, think of the plurality of human cultures, past and present, and the infinite varieties of ways man has developed to live, to eat, to sleep, to make love, to bring up his children, to immortalize his spirit. Life transformed into Art.

We are Life. We are Faust. In love with Eternal Recurrence. With the Eternal Present Eternally.

Where are you? You have to decide. Because you can't have it both ways. Life or Art. Politics or Poetry. What do you want? You can't be outside and inside your head both at the same time. Where are you?

Only the first time is a surprise. After that it's either a bore or a pleasure. If it's a bore, who needs it? If it's a pleasure, it might be worth repeating. And who knows: You might become famous. What Price Glory.

Repetition. Children love to repeat things that give them pleasure. The Joys of Innocence.

Only Love makes Repetition possible. After the first time there's no surprise. The repertoire is a form of Love. How does a new piece get into the Repertoire? Any Repertoire?

Why do you want to write music nobody can love? Do you hate yourself? Or do you hate them? But let's get one thing clear: record companies don't create the repertoire.

Obsolescence. Cultural exhaustion. Perceptual weariness. The winds of change blow everything before them from view. Sometimes nothing is left in its path. Where are the Snows of Yesteryear? What is History? And Where?

I used a tune in my Alchemist Music which I thought was by Tylman Susato, a Renaissance composer-printer. A musicologist I know told me recently that Susato got it from someone else, they don't know whom. Does it make any difference? It's a good tune.

Jorge Luis Borges tells the story of Pierre Menard who wanted to write Cervantes' "Don Quixote." Not re-write it. Write it. It was very hard work but he did manage a couple of chapters which, not surprisingly, came out word for word like Cervantes.

I stand in a circle of time, not on a line. 360° of past, present, future. All around me. I can look in any direction I want to. Bella vista.

Time. History. Series of step-wise stages of evolution. Linear view. Cause and effect. The logic of events. Systematization with blinders.

The center piece of my *Music for the Magic Theatre* is a transcription, that is, a completely new version, of a Mozart adagio. I decided to repeat it in my own way because I loved it. People who understand, love it because they know it began with Mozart and ended with me. People who don't understand think it's by Mozart.

Assemblage. Collage. A Complex of Attitudes and ideas. *Dissimilar* attitudes and ideas. Surrounded by a vague aura of association.

Why does a collage or an assemblage need to be created from junk? Why not the opposite?

Tabula Rasa. Wipe the slate clean. Start all over again. Erase memory. Eradicate the Past. Can we?

The Emperor of China who built the great wall ordered all the books burned except those that dealt with agriculture and astronomy. The ancient Chinese were among the world's greatest historiographers. They kept complete records of everything that happened. He, the Emperor who ordered the book burning, wanted to be called the "First-Emperor."

Ray Bradbury wrote a book called *Farenheit 451* in which the principal job of the firemen was to burn old books that would keep alive the memory of past ways and ideas the leaders wanted dead.

In Cromwell's England it was proposed that all the archives then residing in the Tower of London be burned. The idea was to start all over again.

Borges, commenting on Hawthorne's parable "Earth's Holocaust" says: "In other words, the plan to abolish the past had already occurred to men and—paradoxically—is therefore one of the proofs that the past cannot be abolished. The past is indestructible; sooner or later all things will return, including the plan to abolish the past."

Why do you want to write music that no one can remember? Do you hate music?

Art is the alchemical process of transformation which takes place in the furnace of the heart and mind. We transform ourselves into Art. Transcendent use of Life. Use yourself.

Our perspective of history and time has deepened, lengthened, widened. On the way to the moon Borman, Lovell, and Anders saw the Earth. It is a small globe that hangs in Black Space.

Do you reject Evolution? Do you reject History? What are you trying to forget? The Past is indestructible. Sooner or later all things will return. We repeat Beethoven because he's worth repeating. Not to sell more tickets or more records. You've got to keep things straight.

Simultaneous streams of sounding bodies. A vibrating galaxy of suns, moons and planets. Each different, each unique. Coming together, colliding, penetrating, attracting and repelling.

Everything we love belongs to us. That includes the past and the future. We are the present.

Simultaneities of cries of Pain, shouts of Joy, songs and dances of Love and War, Life and Death. All coming together, colliding, penetrating, repelling. Enlarging the inner space, the deep black space of the mind. Tracery of electric circuits in the Central Nervous System. Memory: a micro-system of orbits in the mental realm. Orbits, Elipses, Penetrations of the Moon of the Mind, the Sun of the Heart.

We are in the grip of Evolution. Trials and Errors. Dry runs. Wet runs. Selection. Refinement. Maturation of human consciousness and its powers of perception and conception. Of its ability to master opposites, to hold in fine balance the ferocity of tension of opposites. Simultaneous streams of events, gestures, perceptions. To conceive and develop a sense of the whole pattern. You can't change anyone but yourself.

Linearity: series. One thing at a time. Exploration in depth of single impulse. Single vision. Exclusivity.

Non-linearity: in the round. Time is a ring of fire, a circle, not a line. Movement in any direction. In all directions at once if you can keep your balance. Inclusivity.

The art of combination is not a theory. It is an attitude. New problems for the composer because he needs to depend entirely on his own taste, his own range of musical experience. Sensory order takes precedence over external logic and methodology. He stands unprotected before the winds of change. He stands only on what he has come to love. He is what he loves.

Anonymity. *Anonymous/20th Century.* Leonardo Ricci, architect, city-planner, dreamer. Earth is man's Home. What I mean is: how can anyone presume to give the performer freedom in his name. Are *you* free? Can you give anybody anything but love? If you want to write music no one can remember, why ask the performer to share your non-act of love? Do it anonymously.

Collective behavior. Indian music. Jazz. The Beatles. Free collectivity of performers/composers. Mutual sharing, give and take. Let's keep things straight. You've got to decide what you want.

A collage or assemblage is a composed collectivity of objects or gestures. What has that to do with being "original?" The copyright law was designed for the nineteenth century. To protect the inalienable right of each individual to the property he created. Publishers talk of "properties." Writers are in "stables." How do you pay royalties to the collective unconscious?

Ars Combinatoria. Inclusive vs. Exclusive. "Unity of Varieties" vs. "Variety in Unity." Combination of opposites. Blake's "contraries." Search for new inner balances and outer surfaces. The created illusion of new images. A new collective consciousness.

History is not our master. We can choose. Our real limits are defined by biology and the Central Nervous System. The liberation of the imagination from dogma implies the freedom to move where the ear takes us and to bring together everything which seems good to it. We are not Slaves of History. We can choose and create our own time.

Borman, Lovell, and Anders came home. Magnificent Men.

The winds of change are blowing. Harder. Stronger. Every minute.

I'm trying to stay on my own two feet.

☙ Chapter 2 ☙

ATONALITY AND SERIALISM

ATONALITY AND PITCH CLASS

The term *atonal* was often applied derogatorily to early works of this century (Lester 1989; Brindle 1975). Public acceptance of atonal works was quite mixed, as shown in this review in the *Paris-Midi*, of May 29, 1913:

> ... musical cubism has made its appearance in the fair city of Paris. By singular irony of fate, it was in the venerable hall of the Conservatoire, the temple of all tradition, that this revelation took place ... offering to its habitués the first performance of three piano pieces by Arnold Schoenberg. This composer hails from Vienna, preceded by an intriguing reputation. Every performance of one of his works in Austria and Germany has provoked disorders, police intervention, transportation of the wounded to the hospital and of dead bodies to the morgue. At the sound of the last chord the listeners would come to blows, and music lovers strewn on the floor would be picked up in bunches. So we waited with impatience the first contact of this explosive art with French sensibilities ... But all expectations were deceived. True, there were some uncomfortable smiles, some anguished sighs, some stifled groans, but no scandal erupted. Arnold Schoenberg would not believe it. (Slonimsky 1969, pp. 310–11)

Atonality suggests that pitches do not belong to tonal scales and do not resolve in traditional ways to other pitches. Atonal music often contains pitches which occur in widely disparate octaves. To account for these extensive interval separations, composers often thought of pitches as independent events requiring new terminology. The term *pitch class* refers to pitches without regard to their register. The pitch class C, therefore, refers to all Cs regardless of the octave in which they appear. Pitch classes can also be designated by number—a sometimes useful notation for analysis. The standard for numeric conversion is C = 0,

D♭ = 1, and so on. All members of pitch class C, therefore, belong equally to pitch class 0. This standard is arbitrary but useful. As will be seen, describing music in terms of pitch classes and converting these pitch classes to numbers has many applications, especially for the analysis of atonal music (Babbitt 1961).

SETS, VECTORS, AND SUBSETS

Many composers have used pitch-class sets in their compositions (Beach 1979; Straus 1990). Pitch-class sets are groupings of contiguous pitches (melodic, harmonic, or a combination of both) that can be related to one another regardless of their order or transposition. Since grouping does not necessarily follow the same kind of simple harmonic order of tonal music, grouping pitches into sets often can pose problems with different groupings creating very different interpretations. The following examples have been chosen for their more or less obvious groupings; readers should be aware that not all music groups so naturally.

The most common notation for pitch-class sets uses brackets and commas without spaces (Forte 1973). [1,2,3,4] indicates a pitch-class (pc) set of D♭, D, E♭, E. A set that exactly parallels (left-to-right equals bottom-to-top) the ordering of notes in the music analyzed is called an "ordered" set. Creating an "unordered" set, however, allows us to see similarities between sets that might not otherwise be apparent. For example, the ordered set [4,2,5,6] appears different than the ordered set [6,4,5,2] and yet when the numbers are organized incrementally into unordered sets they equate to the same set [2,4,5,6]. Comparing unordered sets therefore can be very useful, even when, as will be seen shortly, sets approximate rather than equate.

In Figure 2.1, the group of notes F, E♭, F♯, A becomes the set [3,5,6,9] (E♭ = 3, F = 5, F♯ = 6, and A = 9 in ascending order). In order to compare sets logically, they should be transposed so that they begin with 0. Hence, the [3,5,6,9] set transposes to [0,2,3,6] by subtracting the first number in turn from each number of the set. Applying the same basic processes to the second chord in Figure 2.1 produces: F = 5, D = 2, A♭ = 8, E = 4 or [2,4,5,8] in ascending order. This set also reduces to [0,2,3,6] with the first number subtracted from the rest so that the set begins with 0.

a)

Figure 2.1.   Two uses of the same pitch-class set.

Not all sets reduce so easily. Many reduced pc sets require further reduction to reach what analysts call their *prime* form. Prime forms ensure that the set occurs in its smallest configuration of pitch classes (least distance between elements of the set). Reducing some groups to their prime forms requires circular permutation of the set by transferring the leftmost number to the right and adding 12 in turn to each member of the set.

One easy way to find a set's prime form involves using a clock face as shown in Figure 2.2. Circling the pitch classes of a grouping and calculating the smallest distance between outer notes and successive inner notes produces the prime form of a set. Figure 2.3a presents an example grouping and its representation on the clock face (Figure 2.3b). Clearly, the closest all-encompassing outer notes are 2 and 7 moving clockwise. The proximity of 2 to 3, being closer than 5 to 7,

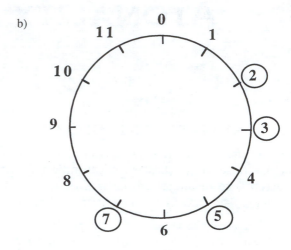

Figure 2.3.   Using the clock face of Figure 2.2 to determine the best order of the notes E♭, F, G, and D.

gives the series as [2,3,5,7] which, when transposed to 0, gives [0,1,3,5] as the prime form.

A pc set can generate an almost unlimited number of different variations (Cope 1997). Yet as numerous and different as such variations may be, they still have their basic pitch-class set in common and hence *sound* similar and *analyze* the same. Figure 2.4 provides an example of the use of a single pc set [0,1,3,5,6,8,10] to generate music. Note that the generated set variances are grouped distinctly and clearly though they appear quite different in pitch content.

Figure 2.5 shows a passage in which three sets are used in a simple palindrome. Here, the first and last groups were generated from the same set [0,1,3,6,8,9], as were the second and fifth groups [0,1,3,5,7,9], and the third and fourth groups [0,1,3,5,6,8]. In this case, the sets are grouped harmonically so that the retrograde can be heard even though the actual pitch content of the groups generated from the same sets differs.

Interval vectors are represented by six-digit lists. A vector presents a count of each interval present in the set (Forte 1989). The first column represents minor seconds (interval class 1), the second column major seconds (interval class 2), the third column minor thirds (interval class 3), and so on, out to the augmented fourth (interval class 6) with the intervals beyond considered inversions of these six (7 = 5; 8 = 4; 9 = 3; 10 = 2;

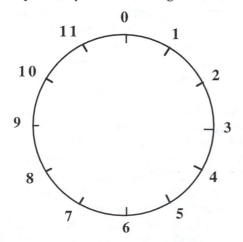

Figure 2.2.   A clock face for determining the best order of a pitch-class set.

11 = 1). Note that all the intervals present must be counted. Figure 2.6 shows a chord whose interval vector equals 111111. It contains one each of the above-named intervals.

In most cases different sets have different vectors. However, in some cases different sets have the same vector called a Z-complement (Forte 1973). Some sets invert to themselves at particular intervals. Figure 2.7 shows an example of this kind of inversion. Here, when the mirror—filled-in notes—of the first chord is reduced it becomes the same set as the first.

Using the concepts of set reduction, Z-complements, and inversion, contemporary composers can use sets in much the same way that classical composers use motives or particular harmonies. Figure 2.8 shows a musical example exploring two Z-complementary sets. The first measure's set vector (111111) equals that of the second measure's set.

Figure 2.9 shows another more contextual example of the use of pitch-class sets. The circled notes here demonstrate the similarities between pc sets. Note

how the set [0,1,4] appears both melodically and harmonically with the latter grouping interweaved between voices and sets. These similarities provide consistency and motivic interrelationships to music that can otherwise seem to wander without coherence. Other sets also appear in this example. Few works are integrated to the extent that all groupings fit the same or even similar sets. Just as tonal music involves many different harmonic functions, music based on pc sets emphasizes one or two sets without using them to the exclusion of other sets.

The use of pitch-class sets is not without its critics, however. Many argue against composer intention while others claim that these relationships, for the most part, remain unheard (Williams 1997; Wittlich 1975). On the other hand, in Berg's *Wozzeck* (1926) relationships of similar pc sets between the themes of each character present serious evidence of composer intention. Various theorists have analyzed Stravinsky's *Rite of Spring* (Forte 1973) to draw links between pitch sets (principally harmonic).

Figure 2.4. Generation of pitch materials from the set [0,1,3,5,6,8,10].

Figure 2.6. Chord having a 111111 interval vector.

Figure 2.5. Sets used in a palindrome.

Figure 2.7. A set that inverts to itself.

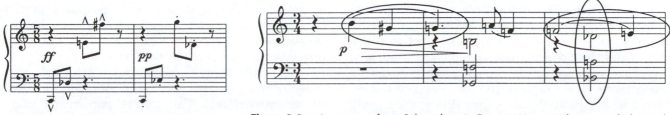

Figure 2.8. The use of Z-complementary sets.

Figure 2.9. An excerpt from Schoenberg's Op. 11, No. 1 with sets circled. Used by permission of Belmont Music Publishers, Pacific Palisades, CA 90272.

Regardless of composer intention, pitch-class sets have caused many mathematically inclined composers to define their work through the use of unordered pitch sets (Bent and Drabkin 1987). The more works analyzed in this manner, the more that seem to be thus composed. For example, George Crumb's *Madrigals* (1969), the beginning of one of which appears abstracted in Figure 2.10, contains many composer-created interrelationships of pitch-class sets. Crumb has grouped pitches in such a way that the [0,1,2,6] set appears as a prime motive of the piece (Figure 2.10a). The groupings sound similar even though they often have few pitch classes in common. Crumb also interlocks subsets of [0,1,2,6]: [0,1,6] and [0,1,5] as shown in Figure 2.10b. This work also makes excellent use of Z-complements and overlapping sets.

a)

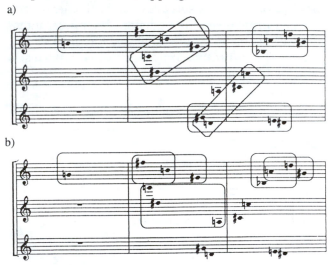

b)

Figure 2.10.   Two analyses of music from George Crumb's *Madrigals*.

To this point we have compared pc sets that reduce to equivalent sets or non-equivalent sets with the same vectors. It can be just as useful, however, to compare similar sets that are not equivalent (Forte 1973; Rahn 1980). One way to do this is to compare subsets. This can be accomplished on a number of levels. First, two sets can have a number of common invariant pitch classes. For example, the sets [4,5,9,10] and [3,4,8,9]—the first two chords in Figure 2.11a—have two invariant pitch classes, the subset [4,9]. This invariant subset is used as a transition between the second and third chords (as a sextuplet). Second, sets may have common pitch classes when reduced to prime forms. For example, [0,1,3,6,9] and [0,1,4,6,9] have four common elements (one different element) and, as shown in Figure 2.11b, can be used developmentally.

a)

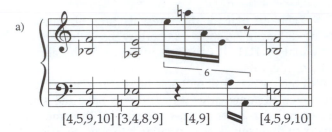

[4,5,9,10] [3,4,8,9]   [4,9]   [4,5,9,10]

b)

Figure 2.11.   a) An invariant subset. b) The use of sets with common pitch classes.

Similar sets with different numbers of elements also can produce interesting results when compared as shown in Figure 2.12. Here, the second set [0,1,5,7] has four members of the first set [0,1,2,5,7]. Obviously, however, the fewer number of elements two or more sets have in common, the less the sets resemble one another and the more of a reach such comparisons become.

Figure 2.12.   Using sets with different numbers of elements.

Figure 2.13.   Using sets with similar but not equivalent vectors.

Vectors also can be compared for similarity to produce sets of different but related interval content. For example, the vectors 223111 and 222121 have four interval counts in common. One pitch has moved causing the third and fifth categories to change one degree in different directions. Figure 2.13 demonstrates how two chords with these vectors can be used in succession to enhance their similarities and, possibly, take advantage of their differences.

Yet another way of comparing pc sets (and consequently using related sets compositionally) involves using ordered sets. This can be particularly useful when analyzing or composing melody or counterpoint. Figure 2.14a shows an example of two sets that are equivalent to [2,3,5,6] or [0,1,3,4]. Note, however, that the melodic order of the notes differs between the examples. This rather trivial passage is followed by a more subtle one in Figure 2.14b. Here, the two ordered sets [3,5,6,2] and [11,10,8,7] reduce to [0,1,3,4] but appear in different pitch classes. However, the difference in order ([2,3,5,6] equivalent to [7,8,10,11]) produces a compelling (retrograde) variation. Another way of viewing these sets involves transposing them to their ordered equivalents as in 3,5,6,2 and 6,5,3,2 (the second group transposed down a perfect fourth). This shows how the reversed middle members of the first set have shifted to the left.

The complement of a pitch-class set consists of all of the pitch classes excluded from that set. Therefore, the complement of [0,1,2,4] is [3,5,6,7,8,9,10,11] or [0,2,3,4,5,6,7,8] when converted to base 0. Supersets that contain all the sets of a contiguous phrase or section of a composition *and* their complements are called Kh-complexes. Supersets that contain all of the sets of a *work* and their complements are called Nexus sets (Forte 1973; Lewin 1987).

Messiaen's music reveals enlightening pc-set relationships between chords that might otherwise appear as disparate. Messiaen (1908–1992) studied at the Paris Conservatoire (1919–1930) with Paul Dukas, Maurice

Figure 2.14.   a) Differing melodic order in equivalent sets. b) Variations in non-reordered sets.

Using equivalent and unequivalent-but-related prime forms of pc sets along with invariant forms, variations in vectors, and ordered sets all contribute to similar sounding and related groups of pitch classes (Forte 1973; Lewin 1987). Composing with such complex but often audibly-similar groups can produce music imbued with a deep level of organization and logic. Combined with intuitive and musical goals, pc-set analysis and composition provide a valuable resource for composers and listeners alike.

Pitch-class sets may belong to larger sets called supersets (Forte 1973, 1985). Finding supersets that contain many or all of the sets of a phrase or composition provides another opportunity to observe what such sets have in common. Supersets that exceed a certain number of elements, however, reveal very little about their subsets. For example, the superset [0,1,2,3,4,5,6,7,8,9,10,11] is the superset for all existing subsets and thus hardly provides much new information about the subsets that reference it. The superset [0,1,3,4,6], however, as a superset of the two subsets [0,1,3] and [0,2,3,5], indicates a meaningful relationship. The subset [0,1,3] here appears as the first three pitch classes of [0,1,3,4,6]. The subset [0,2,3,5] occurs as the last four pitch classes of [0,1,3,4,6] as [1,3,4,6] reduced to base 0. A superset that accounts for all the sets of a contiguous phrase or section of a composition is referred to as a k-set (Forte 1973; Cope 1997).

Emmanuel, and Marcel Dupré (Bell 1984). His major works include *La nativité du Seigneur* (1935), *Les corps glorieux* (1939), *Livre d'orgue* (1951), *Visions de l'amen* (1943), *Vingt regards sur l'enfant Jésus* (1944), the *Catalog des oiseaux* (1956–58, a catalog of bird calls), the *Turangalîla-symphonie* (1948), and the *Chronochromie* (1960). His music is marked by his use of bird calls, interest in rhythmic modes (Messiaen 1950), specialized use of certain scales, religious influences, and intense use of color (Griffiths 1985).

Messiaen composed *Quatuor pour la fin du temps* (quartet for the end of time) in 1941 while imprisoned in a Nazi concentration camp. It was there that the work received its premiere on dilapidated instruments including a piano with several missing keys. *Quatuor pour la fin du temps* consists of eight movements of which the third and fifth are for solo instruments—clarinet and cello respectively. The first movement involves all four instruments in an improvisatory-sounding counterpoint of contrasting ideas. Influenced by bird song, the violin, cello, and clarinet each weave their soloistic lines above a thick-textured homorhythmic piano part. The violin part includes many rests while the cello, once begun, has no rests whatsoever. The dynamics remain very soft for most of the movement.

Before discussing how pc-set analysis reveals important relationships in this quartet, other interesting techniques are worth mentioning. Messiaen utilizes the medieval technique of isorhythm in his first movement. Isorhythm involves separate organization of pitch (called color) and rhythm (called talea) into series of different lengths. When these series are joined, the overlap creates a continuously varying set of combinations. In the piano part of this movement, for example, the rhythm consists of seventeen elements while the pitch sequence consist of twenty-nine elements. By overlaying these series Messiaen creates a smoothly varying bed of chords upon which the other instruments superimpose their bird-like counterpoints. The cello has a similar isorhythmic structure.

The first eight chords (see Figure 2.15), while all different in pitch content, alternate between the [0,1,2,4,7,8,9] and the [0,1,3,5,6,8,10] sets. This consistency of harmonic vocabulary provides a static underpinning for the counterpoint taking place in the other instruments and for the isorhythm occurring in the piano part itself. To the trained ear, the chords, while different in terms of pc content, oscillate back and forth between pc sets subtly previewing the consistent harmonic vocabulary for the entire work.

developed the twelve-tone approach in the years 1917–1923, during which time he composed little music, devoting his energies to performance and development of the new techniques and applications he had discovered. Serialism seemed to him to be the natural conclusion of the complex chromaticism that had been developing in Western European music during the previous sixty years.

Twelve-tone composing first requires the creation of a row, an ordered progression of the twelve different notes of the chromatic scale (Neighbour, Griffiths, and Perle 1980; Spinner 1960). Figure 2.16 shows three different rows by three different serial composers. Note how Schoenberg's row (a) avoids suggesting a tonal center (i.e., successive notes do not exist in the previous note's implied key signature). On the other hand, Berg's row (b) establishes a strong tonal sense with many triadic references—the first seven notes existing in the G melodic minor scale (Berg 1952; Perle 1977). Webern's row (c) develops certain integrated cross-referencing within the row itself (e.g., the second half of the row is intervallically the reverse of the first half).

Figure 2.15. The first ten chords of Messiaen's *Quatuor pour la fin du temps* for clarinet, violin, cello, and piano.

SERIAL TECHNIQUES

As composers explored new territories in the early years of the twentieth century, musical traditions continued to collapse (Perle and Kasemets 1961; Dallin 1974; Griffiths 1981). Audiences groped for tangible indications of commonality. Stravinsky remarked: "Is it any wonder, then, that the hypercritics of today should be dumbfounded by a language in which all of the characteristics of their aesthetic seem to be violated?" (Stravinsky 1936, p. 176) New musical languages appeared not only with each school of thought or composer but within different periods of an individual composer's life (Boretz and Cone 1971; Lang 1960).

One of the more important developments during these early years of the twentieth century was twelve-tone composition, often called serialism. Twelve-tone composition derived from the Germanic musical tradition, and was created by Arnold Schoenberg with the hope of it becoming a common composing language (Machlis 1979; Salzman 1988). Schoenberg

Once a composer has created a row, called the *prime* version, certain variants are produced (Tremblay 1974). The *retrograde* represents the prime version of the row listed backwards; the *inversion* is the prime version of the row listed upside down; and the *retrograde inversion* represents the prime version of the row listed both upside down and backwards. Notice that the variations Schoenberg chose to develop extend the motivic development principles that German composers had used (particularly since Beethoven). Each of these versions appears in Figure 2.19 based on the Schoenberg row of Figure 2.16a. Interval integrity is maintained throughout with each interval reproduced exactly as required by each variant. However, pitches need not remain in the octave shown (pitch class equivalency).

The numbers above each note of the prime version (Figure 2.19) indicate the position of the note in the row. It can also be useful to list interval classes by indicating the number of half-steps separating each row member from the first note or even from one another (not shown). Some composers find these latter approaches more informative than one which simply indicates row order.

The prime form of the row and each variant (P, I, R, RI) occur in twelve transpositions (each beginning on twelve different notes). Figure 2.20 shows the original row beginning on B♭, then A, then A♭, and so on demonstrating the different levels. The Arabic numerals next to the rows here indicate a new beginning interval class referenced to the first pitch of the initial prime form.

Composers often choose to show all the versions of a row at once in a matrix. This box of 144 squares (see Figure 2.21) is created by cross-hatching twelve vertical lines with twelve horizontal lines—actually thirteen if you include the outer layers of the matrix itself. Placing the prime form of the row across the top of the matrix (left to right) and the inversion down the left of the matrix (top to bottom) creates a frame for the interior rows. To complete the matrix, the com-

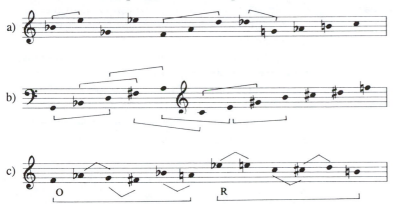

Figure 2.16. Three 12-tone rows from: a) Schoenberg's *Variations for Orchestra* Op. 31; b) Berg's *Violin Concerto*; c) Webern's *Symphonie* Op. 21.

Figure 2.17. Arnold Schoenberg. Dover Publications, Inc. Permission granted.

Figure 2.18. Alban Berg. Dover Publications, Inc. Permission granted.

Figure 2.19. Prime, retrograde, inversion, and inversion-retrograde of row from Schoenberg's *Variations for Orchestra*.

Figure 2.20. Transpositions—beginning on successively lower notes—of row for Schoenberg's *Variations for Orchestra*.

poser fills in (left to right) the transpositions of the original, allowing the notes of the inversion to dictate the beginning notes. The Arabic numerals next to the primes and inversions indicate a new beginning interval class referenced to the first pitch of the initial prime form. Arabic numerals next to the retrogrades and retrograde inversions indicate new beginning interval classes referenced to the first pitch of their own initial prime forms.

Any version of the row now can be quickly read from the completed matrix. For example, primes occur left to right, inversions top to bottom, retrogrades right to left, and retrograde inversions bottom to top. The matrix thus represents an extremely valuable tool for analysis or composition of serial music. Figure 2.22 shows a completed matrix using pitch classes instead of pitch names, again based on the Schoenberg row of Figure 2.16a.

ody and harmony here derive from a single version of the prime form of the row. The numbers here refer to row order and not interval classes.

The second type of twelve-tone composition (here called category B) employs more than one version of the row at a time. Figure 2.23b shows three versions of the Schoenberg row of Figure 2.16a used simultaneously. Unlike category-A composition, maintaining twelve-tone integrity in category-B composition is difficult (e.g., notes frequently are repeated immediately or even simultaneously, often creating non-row-centered sonorities).

Early in the development of twelve-tone theory, Schoenberg and others adopted a variety of techniques that expand the potential of serialism (Basart 1961; Williams 1997). The simplest of these variations is repetition. Since most music includes repetition of notes or chords, such repetitions seem natural in serial composi-

	I_0	I_6	I_8	I_5	I_7	I_{11}	I_4	I_3	I_9	I_{10}	I_1	I_2	
P_0	Bb	E	Gb	Eb	F	A	D	Db	G	Ab	B	C	R_0
P_6	E	Bb	C	A	B	Eb	Ab	G	Db	D	F	F♯	R_6
P_4	D	Ab	Bb	G	A	Db	Gb	F	B	C	Eb	E	R_4
P_7	F	B	Db	Bb	C	E	A	Ab	D	Eb	Gb	G	R_7
P_5	Eb	A	B	Ab	Bb	D	G	Gb	C	Db	E	F	R_5
P_1	B	F	G	E	Gb	Bb	Eb	D	Ab	A	C	Db	R_1
P_8	F♯	C	D	B	Db	F	Bb	A	Eb	E	G	Ab	R_8
P_9	G	Db	Eb	C	D	Gb	B	Bb	E	F	Ab	A	R_9
P_3	C♯	G	A	F♯	Ab	C	F	E	Bb	B	D	D♯	R_3
P_2	C	F♯	G♯	F	G	B	E	Eb	A	Bb	C♯	D	R_2
P_{11}	A	D♯	F	D	E	G♯	C♯	C	F♯	G	Bb	B	R_{11}
P_{10}	G♯	D	E	C♯	D♯	G	C	B	F	F♯	A	Bb	R_{10}
	RI_0	RI_6	RI_8	RI_5	RI_7	RI_{11}	RI_4	RI_3	RI_9	RI_{10}	RI_1	RI_2	

Figure 2.21.   A matrix of the row from Schoenberg's *Variations for Orchestra*.

T	4	6	3	5	9	2	1	7	8	E	0
4	T	0	9	E	3	8	7	1	2	5	6
2	8	T	7	9	1	6	5	E	0	3	4
5	E	1	T	0	4	9	8	2	3	6	7
3	9	E	8	T	2	7	6	0	1	4	5
E	5	7	4	6	T	3	2	8	9	0	1
6	0	2	E	1	5	T	9	3	4	7	8
7	1	3	0	2	6	E	T	4	5	8	9
1	7	9	6	8	0	5	4	T	E	2	3
0	6	8	5	7	E	4	3	9	T	1	2
9	3	5	2	4	8	1	0	6	7	T	E
8	2	4	1	3	7	0	E	5	6	9	T

Figure 2.22.   A pitch class matrix of the row from Schoenberg's *Variations for Orchestra* (T = ten and E = eleven).

Composers typically utilize rows in one of two ways in serial composition (Perle 1962). The first way (here called category A) derives all successive notes from one version of the row at a time. Figure 2.23a shows a category-A created composition using the Schoenberg row of Figure 2.16a. All notes of both mel-

tion. Therefore, immediately repeated notes and chords are not considered deviations from the basic integrity of serialism. Patterns of notes (e.g., two-, three-, and four-note groupings) also may be repeated immediately after they have sounded, making it possible for composers to initiate more individually varied styles.

Overlapping one version of the row with another is also fairly common in serial composition. In this variant, the last note (usually) of one version becomes the first note of the next. Composers also use anticipations of coming material, creating interesting implosions of row content (Brindle 1975). Figure 2.24 shows the first eight notes of a row in the voice part. The ninth through twelfth notes of the row actually appear in the piano part *before* the voice part begins (anticipation). These last four notes are then repeated with variation as accompaniment until they fall in their right places numerically.

Combinatoriality typically involves subsetting. A subset is a group of notes, smaller than twelve, that evenly divides into twelve (e.g., 6, 4, 3, and 2). Terminology includes: hexachord, a group of six notes (two in a twelve-tone row); tetrachord, a group of four notes (three in a twelve-tone row); trichord, a group of three notes (four in a twelve-tone row); and dichord or dyad, a group of two notes (six in a twelve-tone row).

Combinatoriality comprises combining subsets containing mutually exclusive note contents (Boulez 1971). Figure 2.25 should help explain this process.

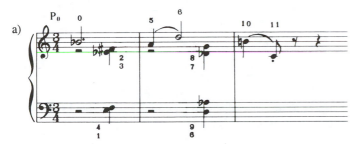

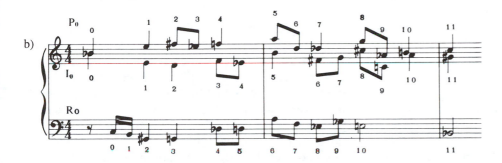

Figure 2.23. a) Category-A composition and b) category-B composition based on the row from Schoenberg's *Variations for Orchestra*.

Figure 2.24. Example of note repetition and anticipation in twelve-tone composition from Schoenberg's *Sommermud*. Used by permission of Belmont Music Publishers, Pacific Palisades, CA 90272.

COMBINATORIALITY

While category-B twelve-tone composition poses problems of harmonic continuity and serial integrity (Lester 1989), composers nonetheless seem interested in the complexities available in contrapuntally using many variants of the row simultaneously. Combinatoriality resolves many of the discontinuities resulting from the use of category B.

Notice that the second hexachord of the prime version of the row (i.e., D, D♭, G, A♭, B, C of P° in that order) equals the pitch content of the first hexachord of the inversion of this row beginning on G (I₉ top to bottom beginning in the ninth square left to right in Figure 2.21). Note, however, that the order of the notes has changed: they now read G, D♭, B, D, C, and A♭ (bottom voice measure 1) instead of D, D♭, G, A♭, B, C

Figure 2.25. Combinatoriality using the prime (top voice) and the inversion (bottom voice) of the row from Schoenberg's *Variations for Orchestra*.

(top voice measure 2). As would be expected, the second hexachord of this inversion (bottom voice in measure 2) has the same note content as the first hexachord of the prime nontransposed version (top voice in measure 1). Such mutual exclusivity between subsets allows composers to combine two complementary subsets to create a new but related row. Combining two such versions in a category-B-type composition also can help create a more continuous twelve-tone (category-A-type) continuity, while at the same time providing the explorations possible in the contrapuntal environment of category-B composition.

INTEGRAL SERIALISM

Pantonality (this, not atonality, was the term used by Schoenberg), or "inclusive of all tonalities," is not important because of chromaticism, but in its extreme composer control over pitch. Serialization of the other parameters, integral serialism, begins with the creation of a row as it does in pitch organization and continues by using basic variants (Jameux 1991; Koblyakov 1990).

Anton Webern's *Variations for Piano*, opus 27 (second movement) employs a dynamic row of nine values as shown in Figure 2.26 (Kolneder 1968; Forte 1998). Webern follows this prime order with a variation of the retrograde (the third trichord—now the first—in original order) as shown in Figure 2.27. Articulations in this work directly relate to individual pitches of the row as shown in Figure 2.28. For example, the second note of every version of the row used in the second variation is staccato, and so on. Careful analysis of rhythm and form (a cyclic mirror canon) shows that these parameters also evolve serially.

Whether any of these machinations are audible is irrelevant. Even tonal composers worked with intricate motivic and chromatic techniques which become evident to the ear only after repeated listening and score study. Some critics of integral serialism argue against what they sense as mathematical and apparently non-musical composing processes. However, if

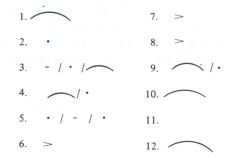

Figure 2.26. Dynamic row from Anton Webern's *Variations for Piano*, Op. 27.

Figure 2.27. Retrograde of the dynamic row from Anton Webern's *Variations for Piano*, Op. 27.

Figure 2.28. Articulation row from Anton Webern's *Variations for Piano*, Op. 27.

used musically, these procedures help create quality music.

The piano work by Milton Babbitt shown in Figure 2.29 demonstrates serialized control of dynamics, rhythm, and pitch. The pitch content of this piece follows combinatorial principles. The basic row is shown in Figure 2.30. Note that this form of the row appears in the lower voice of the first two bars. The first hexachord of the original form of the row beginning on E contains notes that are mutually exclusive of those in the first hexachord of the original beginning on B♭. Therefore, by combining the prime version on E (as in the upper voice) with the original nontransposed version, Babbitt creates combinatoriality. The first measure here contains twelve different notes as does the second measure, thus avoiding inconsistent note repetitions or doublings.

The rhythm of this piece also involves serial principles. The hexachordal subgroupings within each measure have a held note that balances the other notes. In the bass voice, for example, the held note (fifth in the six-note sequence), suggests a five-note grouping followed by a single note. The same is true of the first hexachord of the row in the upper voice (i.e., 5/1). In the second bar, the grouping is distinctly different. Here, the held note (fourth of the subset), divides the hexachord into groups of four and two notes each in both voices. The rhythm clearly follows a 5/1/4/2 pattern. In the upper voice in measure 3, the order 2/4/1/5 appears in the upper voice. This ordering (2/4/1/5) represents the retrograde of the original rhythmic row (see Figure 2.31).

To create an inversion, Babbitt inverts dichordal subsets by reversing their order. Therefore, the inversion of 5/1/4/2 becomes 1/5/2/4 and, in turn, the retrograde inversion becomes 4/2/5/1. Figure 2.29, measures 3 and 4 (bass voice), represents a retrograde inversion of the prime version of the rhythmic row. Serialization of rhythmic principles continues in this manner for the remainder of the piece.

Dynamic serialization, while simpler in this work, is still important to its basic structure. Here, each version of the row links with a dynamic: prime, *mp*; retrograde, *mf*; inversion, *f*; and retrograde inversion, *p*.

In his now-famous article "Who Cares If You Listen," Milton Babbitt speaks of this "high degree of determinacy":

> In the simplest terms, each such "atomic" event is located in a five-dimensional musical space determined by pitch-class, register, dynamic, duration, and timbre. These five components not only together define the single event, but, in the course of a work, the successive values of each component create an individually coherent structure, frequently in parallel with the corresponding structures created by each of the other components. Inability to perceive and remember precisely the values of any of these components results in a dislocation of the event in the work's musical space, an alteration of its relation to all other events in the work, and—thus—a falsification of the composition's total structure. For example, an incorrectly performed or perceived dynamic value results in destruction of the work's dynamic pattern, but also in false identification of other components of the event (of which this dynamic value is a part) with corresponding components of other events, so creating incorrect pitch, registral, timbral, and durational associations. (Babbitt 1958, p. 126–27)

Figure 2.29. Measures 1–8 from Milton Babbitt's *Three Compositions for Piano* (1947). © Copyright 1957 by Boelke-Bomart, Inc.; used by permission.

Figure 2.30. Pitch row from Babbitt's *Three Compositions for Piano.*

P: 5 - 1 - 4 - 2
I: 1 - 5 - 2 - 4
R: 2 - 4 - 1 - 5
IR: 4 - 2 - 5 - 1

Figure 2.31. Rhythm rows from Babbitt's *Three Compositions for Piano.*

Babbitt speaks of the confusion surrounding his article in an interview:

> I gave a lecture at Tanglewood in 1957 about the state of the contemporary composer. The then-editor of *High Fidelity* heard it and asked me to write it down. I had been improvising it and didn't want to write it down, but they had a copy of the tape and asked me if I would take it and put it in some kind of publishable shape. The title of the article as submitted to *High Fidelity* was "The Composer as Specialist." There was no imputation whatsoever of "who cares if you listen," which as far as I am concerned conveys very little of the letter of the article, and nothing of the spirit. Obviously the point was that I cared a great deal who listened, but above all how they listened. I was concerned about the fact that people were not listening. But theirs of course, was a much more provocative title, and journalists are concerned to provoke, and do. It wasn't "who cares if you listen." It was this: If you're not going to take our activities in as serious and dignified a manner as we take them, then of course we don't want you to listen. (Cagne and Caras 1982, p. 37)

Oliver Messiaen was one of the first in Europe to use rigid rhythmic control (augmentation, diminution by one half, one third, one fourth, etc., of the prime). His *Quatre études de rhythme* (especially number 2, *Mode de valeur et d'intensités*), published in 1949, was one of the first works to include integral serialization of all elements. Though based more on modal than twelve-tone principles, Messiaen serialized 36 pitches, 24 durations, 7 dynamics, and 12 articulations.

Messiaen's influence on the younger composers of France, combined with twelve-tone theory, enabled Pierre Boulez to arrange twelve different durations, twelve articulations, and twelve dynamics in row forms. This serialization is particularly noticeable in Boulez's *Structures* (1952) and his *Second Piano Sonata* (1948). Figure 2.32 shows the series for *Structures*.

Bernd Alois Zimmermann's *Perspectives* for two pianos (1956) uses serialization of pitch, texture, rhythm, dynamics, attacks, and pedaling representing somewhat of a landmark in its degree of systematic composer control. The third movement of Ruth Crawford's (1901–53) innovative *String Quartet* (1931) includes systematic control over pitch, duration, dynamics, and rhythm. This third movement, a double canon, uses only dynamics to create a canon in the viola and cello and a second canon in the two violins. The resulting dovetailing of dynamics (one voice in crescendo and the other in diminuendo) foreshadows timbre modulation—shaded dynamics creating timbre movement from one instrument to another (see chapter 4).

The increased precision that techniques such as serialism requires of both performer and audience prompted Charles Ives, in the *Postface* to his *114 Songs* (1922), to remark: "Some of the songs in this book, particularly among the later ones, cannot be sung, and if they could, perhaps might prefer, if they had to say, to remain as they are; that is, 'in the leaf'—and that they will remain in this peaceful state is more than presumable." (Boatwright 1961, p. 131)

Pierre Boulez, in an interview with the author, refers to the problems of academic serialism:

> Yes, academic, and in the strong sense of the word. It does not matter whether the academic

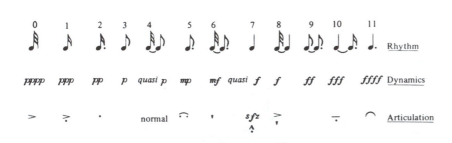

Figure 2.32. Serialization in Boulez's *Structures*.

Figure 2.33. Pierre Boulez.

is after Schumann, after Bach, after Wagner, or after a new serial type; the academic is something which I cannot accept at any time. The main problem, to my mind, is to find a purely musical way of thinking and not something which is parascientific. (Cope and Wilson 1969, p. 79–80)

By the late 1940s, the demarcation between more and less control had been clearly drawn and defined. Interestingly, highly serialized music often sounds like indeterminate music (discussed in chapter 5).

VECTORAL ANALYSIS
ANTON VON WEBERN: *SYMPHONIE*, OP. 21

(For information on vectoral analysis and procedures see Preface.)

1. Historical background: Anton von Webern was born in Vienna in 1883 and died in Mittersill in 1945 near Salzburg, where he had moved to avoid the Allied bombings (Anderson 1976; Rossi 1969; Salzman 1988). He studied with Guido Adler at the University of Vienna and received a doctorate in musicology in 1906. Webern conducted in the provincial theaters and the Vienna Workers Symphony Concerts. He remained in Germany during the Second World War working as a proofreader for a Viennese publisher, even though performances of his music were banned by the Third Reich. He died as a result of gunshot wounds accidentally inflicted by an American occupation troop stationed in Mittersill.

2. Overview: This work is in two short slow movements. The first movement is a two-part (each repeated) binary form with the second section a large canonic development of the first section. The second movement is a theme with seven variations.

3. Orchestration Techniques: The *Symphonie* is scored for nine solo instruments: clarinet, bass clarinet, two horns, harp, two violins, viola, and cello. The major difference between this and Webern's previous work (Op. 20) is *klangfarbenmelodien* (timbre pointillism). Note that in the opening of the work, Webern uses very few notes without range, rest, or timbre separations (e.g., horn and harp and pizzicati cello, etc.; see Figure 2.35).

4. Basic Techniques: The row of this work appears in Figure 2.36. This row reads intervalically the same in both directions (a palindrome), which makes the prime identical with its retrograde (transposed) and the inversion identical with the retrograde inversion (transposed). Therefore only twenty-four forms of the row actually exist, not the usual forty-eight.

Webern's *Symphonie* begins with a double canon in contrary inverted motion in four parts (Forte 1998). Horn 2 begins the prime form of the row on A with imitation of the prime form on C♯ beginning in mea-

Figure 2.34.   Anton Webern.

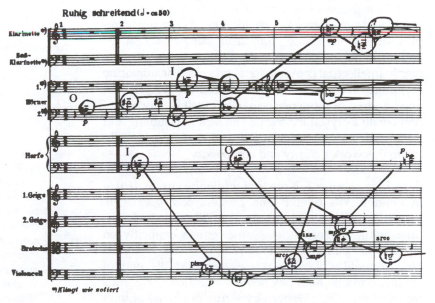

Figure 2.35.   The first seven bars of Anton Webern's *Symphonie*, Op. 21, first movement showing the beginning of the double canon.

Figure 2.36.   Palindrome row from Webern's *Symphonie*, Op. 21.

sure 4 in the harp. The harp also initiates the inversion on F in measure 2, which is imitated by the first horn in inversion beginning on A in measure 3.

Note how the opening section rotates around A (see Figure 2.37). The thirteen notes here (Eb is doubled) all sound register frozen in category-B composition. All twelve notes do not appear until the twenty-third note of the piece (Eb) appears in the harp.

Figure 2.37.   Rotation around A in the opening section of Webern's *Symphonie*, Op. 21.

5. Vertical Models: Harmony does not play a significant role in this work. Notes occurring simultaneously are based on minor seconds and concomitant projections (e.g., the ninth and seventh), augmented fourths, or major sixths.

6. Horizontal Models: Melodic techniques result from the complex canonic treatment and the variants based on *klangfarbenmelodien*. The leaping lines and rests often contradict standard melodic interpretation. The opening four bars in the second horn provide the model for the work in terms of melodic vocabulary.

7. Style: Webern's *Symphonie* (Op. 21) is a very complex serial work whose pointillism, *klangfarbenmelodien*, and canonic interweaving of row versions reflect a highly intellectual compositional process. The miniature ensemble (in contrast to the late Romantic orchestras of one hundred or more performers) as well as short duration create a crystalline focus. The lack of doubling and the serialization of articulations and dynamics contribute to this work's clarity and complexity.

Compare this work with the analysis of Penderecki in chapter 3. Note that while the chromaticism in Penderecki's twelve-tone clusters compares well, the latter work has dramatic gestures and thick textures while Webern's *Symphonie* centers explicitly on single-note pointillism. The Webern work analyzed here resembles the Xenakis example at the end of chapter 8 in that both pay serious attention to rigorous forms of serialism; Webern by virtue of his use of integral serialism and Xenakis through automation based on stochastic (random) principles. Interestingly, the two seemingly opposed concepts of serialism and indeterminacy have many ties.

DAVID COPE AND GALEN WILSON: AN INTERVIEW WITH PIERRE BOULEZ; FEBRUARY, 1969

Galen Wilson and I fought with agents and front offices for two months to interview Pierre Boulez, then conductor of the Los Angeles Philharmonic Orchestra. By the time we succeeded in arriving at his hotel room on a dark and rainy winter afternoon, we both expected an aloof and probably impenetrable host. However, Boulez was, as you can read here, wonderfully open and approachable. Together, the three of us hunkered down in a claustrophobic tenth-floor room on this dreary day and discussed a wonderfully humanized world of new music from a decidedly European perspective during a time of strained relations between our two continents.

Wilson: In an article in *Contemporary Composers on Contemporary Music* Milton Babbitt suggests that the composer is a specialist, that there are levels of music appreciation, and we recognize now that some people are not at the level of the contemporary composer. We no longer have to worry about the crowd, the common man. We have our own audience, which may consist of other composers and close friends, very much like the medical researcher who works in his laboratory for his own little crowd. Do you agree with this outlook?

Boulez: No, I don't agree with that, because the invention of music had nothing to do with the invention of science or medicine. Medicine is a specialty to be shared by only a few, because most do not have that special knowledge. Science is one thing and expression is another. They can have links, of course, but they are not of the same nature.

I think that since the beginning you can very often find extrovert and introvert works in the same composer. If you take Beethoven, for example, the last quartets will never be as popular as the Ninth Symphony. The Ninth Symphony is consciously extrovert; on the contrary, the last quartets tend to be like a diary of himself searching ideas. I think in the life of a composer there are always these two tendencies, not for an audience of specialists, but for himself. He tends to glorify his own thoughts and put them in a kind of musical research. After he grasps something, maybe he wants to enlarge the possibilities and not feel so constricted by the technical medium and compose a work which is more extrovert, more towards pure expression.

There is always for me a mirroring between the two things, the technical more than the scientific: to confuse science and music is really very bad for science. First, science is so far in advance of music in the process of thinking, and on a different track. It is impossible to have them on the same track; it would be a pseudo-track, something which is not real, pure idealism. Science as its purpose has its own kind of imagination. Scientists have an extremely sharp and amazing imagination, but this is not at all the same type of imagination of men who express themselves through music or painting. Therefore I think to make scientific purpose the same as musical purpose is to parody science and not do it justice.

To make science practical and then apply it to music (applied science) is not, I find, necessary for me at all. I myself studied science when I was younger and find now that musical imagination is on a completely different wavelength. I like scientific vocabulary, but that is the wrong type of security. Musical imagination does not have this type of security that people like to have from science; they have the "impression." Many composers feel that if they apply certain scientific vocabulary (there are very many fakes; however, Babbitt's knowledge is reliable), a certain scientific environment to their music and writings, they achieve security. They think they are safe; they no longer have to work in the insecurity of musical invention.

I want that uncertainty. I find it necessary to discover my own way of imagination. One must find his own way and not rely on some analogies. It is much more difficult to find something which is not shaped after this or after that which gives a kind of security, but you must invent. I have not found aesthetics in computers yet; these aesthetics cannot be reduced to any scientific formula. Aesthetics in any form of expression escape any kind of definition. One must not be blind to this. One cannot keep away from aesthetics through some kind of scientific blanket.

Wilson: Living in America, one of our only sources about structure and composition technique has been in *Die Reihe*, and what we read in *Die Reihe* is analysis.

Boulez: But you can see my name only twice in *Die Reihe*, and only one article. I disagree with this pseudoscientific information and I was away from it after the very first days, as I don't like this type of caricature.

Wilson: Would you care to comment on Ligeti's analysis of your *Structures*? It seems so mathematical.

Boulez: This work was a kind of automatic rela-

tionship to be tried just to see how far one can go with the automation of language. They did not analyze the other two pieces because these were beyond their possibilities and were not based on the same principles. One must not isolate these pieces. This was just a border of a system for me.

Cope: Why do contemporary composers dislike each other so much? Is it ideas or personalities? One particular comment I would like your reaction to is this quote from Morton Feldman in an interview with Robert Ashley: "There is only a total insecurity because people don't know who they want to be. This is not only true of the young people. This is true of Boulez. This is true of Stockhausen. You can see this in the way they have approached American 'chance' music. They began by finding rationalizations for how they could incorporate chance and still keep their precious integrity." (Schwartz and Childs 1967, p. 365)

Boulez: I have no reaction except that this is certainly a part of this American nationalism of which we were speaking earlier. American composers, of this type especially, are very bitter about Stockhausen and me because we are in both places, Europe and America. They are not the same way. I have done my best to perform American works in Europe, and I am not responsible if there is no response here. I cannot think that Mr. Feldman is a very first class American composer; he has to do it by himself. You don't gain in personality by attacking other personalities. You must give your personality first. Just saying the others are nothing does not make you something; in fact, it brings you still further down.

Wilson: Feldman refers to "chance" here. Do you feel that you conceive of "chance" in the same way that, say, John Cage conceives of it?

Boulez: No, not at all. I find that so highly unproductive, because "chance" is not an aesthetic category. "Chance" can bring something interesting only one time in a million, and that is not interesting to me at all. Most of the time you do not get that one time which would be interesting and, if you do get it, you get it in the midst of a hundred thousand possibilities which are not interesting.

Wilson: Going to a "chance" concert, then, you feel would be like going to a baseball game, gambling for excitement?

Boulez: Yes, but even a baseball game has rules. Card games, which have much more chance, I suppose, still have rules. Can you imagine a card game with absolutely no rules?

Cope: Like Mallarme saying, "A throw of the dice will not abolish chance," which you have been quoted as quoting, you are saying that, while nothing can be totally chance, nothing can be totally without chance.

Boulez: Exactly. With the combination of the two, you must integrate, and it is much more difficult to compose in this way, integrating on a high level, than in more traditional ways. Composing by chance is not composing at all. Composing, even from the etymological, means to put things together. I am interested as to what chance sounds occur on the street, but I will never take them as a musical composition. There is a big difference between unorganized sounds and those placed within complete organization.

Cope: Many composers today seem to feel that they are being left behind, with so many new concepts and techniques. Do you feel that there is "progress" in music?

Boulez: No. That is like fashion, and composition has nothing to do with fashion. They make styles for the winter season, the spring season, etc., and these tricks are dried up in one year. Then it is finished. You cannot think of music in these very coarse and fashionable terms. Even the term "old-fashioned" fails here. I don't care whether I'm "in" or "out" or "old" or "new," and I have no sense or care for fashion.

Wilson: The young composer is in search of an audience. He sees one group getting an audience and possibly he goes where the audience is.

Cope: Many times, due to university requirements for students, young composers are faced with a "forced" audience, required attendance. Which is worse?

Boulez: These are college games, and no longer composition.

Cope: You once said: "It is not deviltry but only the most ordinary common sense which makes me say that, since the discovery made by the Viennese, all composition other than twelve-tone is useless." Would you explain this?

Boulez: Yes. If you want to go through historical processes, you must go through a process, and if you do not go through the process of the Viennese composers, you have absolutely nothing to say. These tricks we were referring to before, this pure junk, most of the time has absolutely no dialectic, no rhetoric, and no vocabulary. These composers have no experi-

ence in what articulate vocabulary is. They reject it because they are unable to use it. If you do not go through the mental processes which existed then, I cannot see your necessity of composing. Even with more advanced media, I don't see the necessity of composing. If you want to use noises with instruments, or electronic sounds, it's nothing new, first of all, and nothing modern, second, as long as there is really no dialectic which organizes it with a type of dimension which is not just a pure accumulation of things.

Cope: You do not feel, then, that twelve-tone composition is a fashion?

Boulez: No. Twelve-tone is not a fashion. One cannot stay on the twelve-tone construction, but it is not just a fashion. That is why I find so many analyses of twelve-tone music a waste of time. It's like old ladies who make lace. But I have found that if you have not gone through this experience of twelve-tone writing, and tried to enlarge upon it and go forward, you can fall into these traps of "chance" and the parascientific. These latter are mythologies, ways of escaping the real center, the real way of searching the problems. We have a story about a fox who is looking at grapes and, being unable to reach them, he says they are sour. It is the same with these composers of fashion music. They also say they are free. What is freedom? It does not interest me at all.

Cope: What American composers that are living today do you feel represent an honest approach in your terms?

Boulez: In the older generation, Elliott Carter. I find also that Milton Babbitt has an honest approach, but too esoteric in my opinion. Imagination is another question; you can be honest but not imaginative. The point, I think, is to have in reserve a technical background and at the same time to invent something. Inventing without the background is not the same. It reminds me of what one says of some of the underdeveloped countries in Asia that went from the donkey to the jet age: "They come in in jet planes and leave by donkey." They want to have very modern ideas, but have not the background to apply them The invention is spoiled, really, because they do not have the background to exploit it. The two sides are necessary, and if you do not have the right balance between them, then you are nothing. If you have only one mirror, you can see yourself only once, but if you have two mirrors, you can see yourself an infinity of times.

Chapter 3

TEXTURALISM

PRINCIPLES

Cluster chords (often called sound-mass), in contrast to serialism, minimize the importance and order of individual notes while maximizing the importance of texture, rhythm, dynamics, and/or timbre (Dallin 1974; Marquis 1964; Persichetti 1961). Using cluster chords challenges the differentiation between sound and noise—a derogatory term applied to sounds perceived to be antithetical to music.

Mainstream composers have used cluster chords in a variety of ways (Erickson 1975; Goldstein 1974). Gustav Mahler, for example, used panchromatic chords (inclusive of all twelve tones) in the first movement of his *Tenth Symphony* (1910) and Béla Bartók employed clusters in his 1926 *Piano Sonata*. However, Igor Stravinsky used sound-mass most challengingly in his *Le Sacre du Printemps* (1912), where a repetitive string mass of sound is charged with difficult-to-predict harsh accents. The rhythm of the accents drives the *Danse des Adolescentes*, significantly reducing the importance of individual pitches. Figure 3.1 shows the F♭ (enharmonically E) ninth chord of the *Danse* and the resultant increased importance of rhythm (accents).

Henry Cowell's *The Tides of Manaunaun* (1911) and Charles Ives's *Majority* (piano and voice, 1921), present some of the first uses of what some might consider traditional noise as an acceptable musical element (Boatwright 1962; Burkholder 1985; Cowell 1930; Rudhyar 1986). Cowell's *The Hero Sun* (1922) includes a right forearm cluster on the piano's black keys (see Figure 3.2; note that the sharp above indicates black keys while a natural indicates white keys). This use of clusters as both a melodic and percussive device contrasts the open consonances of the left-hand harmonies. Cowell's notations for clusters differ from piece to piece, but the basics appear with explanation in Figure 3.3, taken from the performance notes to his *What's This* (1922). These works, along with Cowell's innovative works such as *The Banshee* (discussed in chapter 4) impressed a large number of composers (Béla Bartók in particular) and culminated in his authorship of *New Musical Resources* (Cowell 1930). Figure 3.4 reveals some of the depth with which Cowell studied both the musical properties and notation of clusters (Higgins 1986; Weisgall 1959). About this example he wrote: "Clusters that do in a certain sense move are, however, quite possible, and it is interesting to consider the vari-

Figure 3.1. From Igor Stravinsky's *Le Sacre du Printemps* "Danse des Adolescentes." Piano reduction of the string parts.

Figure 3.2. Page 3 from Henry Cowell's *The Hero Sun*. Copyright © 1922 (renewed) by Associated Music Publishers, Inc. (BMI). International copyright secured. All rights reserved. Reprinted by permission.

Figure 3.3. Explanation of symbols in Henry Cowell's *What's This*. Copyright © 1922 (renewed) by Associated Music Publishers, Inc. (BMI). International copyright secured. All rights reserved. Reprinted by permission.

Figure 3.4. From Henry Cowell's *New Musical Resources* (1930), p. 128. © Copyright Alfred A. Knopf, Inc. All rights reserved. By permission.

Figure 3.5. Henry Cowell. BMI Archives. Used by permission.

ous ways in which such movement can be introduced." (Cowell 1930, p. 126) Cowell notates both additive and subtractive clusters (subtractive in Figure 3.4), and thus predates similar uses by Penderecki (see Kagel 1959).

John Becker (1886–1961), a regrettably unnoticed innovator of the 1920s and 1930s, included large clusters in most of his works (Riegger 1959). Becker's *Symphonia Brevis* (*Symphony No. 3*, which first appeared in Cowell's *New Music* in January of 1930) derives large clusters from long sustained chords built of seconds using instruments of similar color. Often Becker's clusters integrate entire sections of the orchestra as single percussion-like timbres by means of articulation (short, very loud, and with heavy accents). Figure 3.6 shows the final five bars of the opening section from *Symphonia Brevis*. As the rich contrapuntal fabric unfolds, the music becomes pantonal with the F♯ rooted chord spread over five octaves.

Edgard Varèse uses brass, organ, and Ondes Martenot in his *Equatorial* (1934) to achieve clusters (Cowell 1930). In reference to this work, Robert Erickson writes: "These highly individual sound-blocks are images, ikons, in their own right. They exist as entities in the same way as a melody can be felt to be an entity." (Erickson 1969, p. 144) Many consider Varèse's music an extension of Stravinsky's primitive period (i.e., period extending to the mid-1920s when Stravinsky's so-called neoclassic period began). The massive dissonances of Varèse's *Hyperprism* (1923) and *Octandre* (1924) also have important incidences of clusters.

In *Octandre*, Varèse creates mirror-type clusters as shown in Figure 3.7a and b. In Figure 3.7a, Varèse balances the stacked chromatic pitches with a B♮, a minor third from each end of the cluster. In Figure 3.7b, Varèse separates two small groupings of chromatic half-steps by major thirds. Each of these clusters (bars 15 and 20 respectively) includes octave transpositions and inverted orchestration (e.g., flute over an octave below the clarinet) to create harsh dynamic textures.

Wallingford Riegger's *Music for Brass Choir* (1949) was one of the first large ensemble works to use extended closed clusters. This work opens with ten trombones a half-step apart encompassing the range of a diminished seventh. The final panchromatic chord—ten trumpets, eight horns, ten trombones, two tubas, and percussion—has subtle dynamic shadings with the final four bars marked *lento e pianissimo*.

CLUSTER TECHNIQUES

Apart from the aforementioned Becker work, clusters appear in orchestral works like *Metastasis* (1955) by Iannis Xenakis, and *Threnody for the Victims of* *Hiroshima* (1960) by Krzysztof Penderecki. Probably one of the best-known orchestral works of the past forty years, *Threnody* utilizes a wide variety of string techniques (fifty-two string parts), surprisingly few of which are actually new. More immediately recognizable are the solid bands of sound which widen and contract by means of glissandi. These clusters, some involving quarter tones, create bands of sound often resolved by movement to a single pitch. Many of these clusters contain such heavy overtone influence that, even though only the area of a fifth may actually be covered, one gets the aural impression that all audible sounds are occurring simultaneously. Figure 3.8 shows the final 54 seconds of *Threnody*. Even though the notation is proportional (see Appendix III), the visual cluster bands resemble those suggested by Cowell in his *New Musical Resources* thirty years earlier (refer to Figure 3.4).

Luigi Nono's three choral works *Il canto sospeso* (1956), *La terra e la campagna* (1957), and *Cori di Didone* (1958) are based almost entirely on twelve-tone aggregate choral clusters. These clusters create massive textures within which the voices move as fish through water.

Iannis Xenakis utilizes clusters that result from his use of stochastic processes (see chapter 8 for more detailed discussion). Most of Xenakis's works incorporate incredibly dense sound mass resulting from large numbers of individual instruments of like timbres (pizzicato or glissando clusters, for example). Most of Xenakis's works make elegant use of sound-mass both in terms of rhythm and pitch. Xenakis has had considerable impact in Europe and many have attributed Penderecki's and the Polish School's use of clusters to Xenakis's influence. In a 1955 article, "The Crisis of Serial Music," Xenakis remarks:

> Linear polyphony destroys itself by its very complexity; what one hears is in reality nothing but a mass of notes in various registers. The enormous complexity prevents the audience from following the intertwining of the lines and has as its macrocosmic effect an irrational and fortuitous dispersion of sounds over the whole extent of the sonic spectrum. There is consequently a contradiction between the polyphonic linear system and the heard result, which is surface or mass. (Xenakis 1955, p. 23)

Henryk Górecki's (b. 1933, Poland) *Scontri* for orchestra (1960), includes graphically notated blocks and bands of tones—large black boxes overlapping entire sections of the score. In *Sonant* (1960), Mauricio Kagel calls for speaking and whispering from the ensemble at various pitch levels ad libitum resulting

Figure 3.6.   Page 3 of John Becker's *Symphonia Brevis* (Symphony No. 3). Copyright © 1972 by C. F. Peters Corporation. By permission.

Figure 3.7. From Edgard Varèse's *Octandre* (1924).

in sound-mass. The consequence of such experimentation is not only new notations, but direct applications of partially indeterminate procedures: though clusters are inevitable, exact duplication of the numerous highly variable factors involved causes unpredictable results (Kagel 1959; Persichetti 1961).

Improvisation ajoutée (1962) by Mauricio Kagel, for a four-manual organ and two or three adjunct performers, includes block clusters of sound, performed with hands, forearms, feet, and rapid multichanges in registration with, as the composer states, ". . . improvi-

sation arising through the statistical nature of timbre transformations."

The *Trois Poèmes d'Henri Michaux*, for mixed chorus and orchestra (1963) by Witold Lutosławski, includes cluster chords resulting from extensive use of approximate pitch notation. The rhythmic clusters in the second part ("Le grand combat") involve extremely complex composite rhythms. Stockhausen's *Mixtur* (1964) uses huge cluster effects spatially, as five groups surround the audience. Motivic imitation occurs, yet each performer's independent choice of pitch and timing creates extremely complex sound masses.

Penderecki's *Passion According to St. Luke* (1965) combines simple melodies into dense twelve-tone textures. A continuous thread of contrapuntal material contributes to the cluster effects. Half-sung, half-spo-

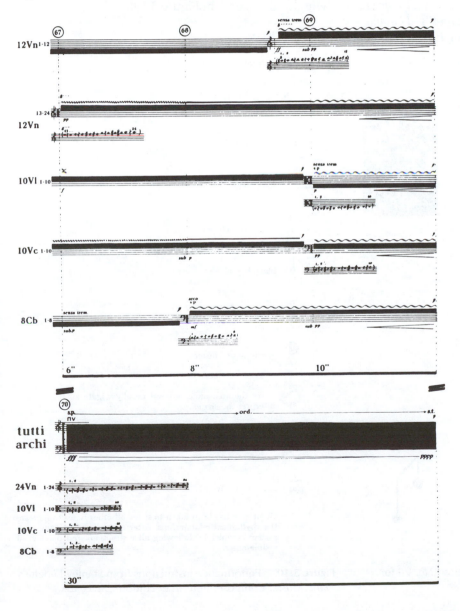

Figure 3.8. From Krzysztof Penderecki's *Threnody for the Victims of Hiroshima* (1960). The notes for each cluster band appear in traditional form beneath them in this proportional notation. Copyright © 1961 Deshon Music, Inc. & PWM Editions. All rights reserved. The two systems here are 24″ and 30″ in duration respectively.

ken backgrounds to crowd scenes produce equally massive clusters that owe their intensity to the text setting as well as to the resulting dissonance.

Pauline Oliveros uses sound-mass in her *Sound Patterns* (1961). Voices, whispers, tongue clicks, lip pops, and improvised pitches within areas of high, middle, and low registers result in thick clusters of sound. The music often resembles the choral effects in Penderecki's *Passion*, yet utilizes timbre more than pitch to achieve the clusters.

György Ligeti's *Atmosphères* (1961) uses a full complement of winds, strings, and percussion, orchestrated to create unique clusters with combination and resultant tones (Christiansen 1973). In *Lux Aeterna* (1966) and *Requiem* (1965, for soprano, mezzo-soprano, two mixed choirs, and orchestra), Ligeti calls for effects in which instruments and individual voices become timbrally unrecognizable. Ligeti's *Lontano* (1967) for orchestra often requires over fifty separate

instrumental voices creating evolving sonic textures. Ligeti's music, unlike Penderecki's, is traditionally notated. While seeming to lack recognizable melodic direction, *Lontano* creates an enormous dynamic and timbral impact.

"The important tones, the ones that are most plainly heard, are those of the outer edges of a given cluster." (Cowell 1933, p. 122) Theodore Lucas, in *Aberrations No. VII* for piano (Figure 3.9), uses a system of cluster notation (white and black keys) denoting duration by visual horizontal length. Graphic music need only show approximate pitch and relative motion (notice here that the two sets of clusters remain static). Stanley Lunetta includes various cluster effects in his *Piano Music*. Notice the interpretative possibilities for the performer (especially with the indication "wiggle all fingers" in Figure 3.10).

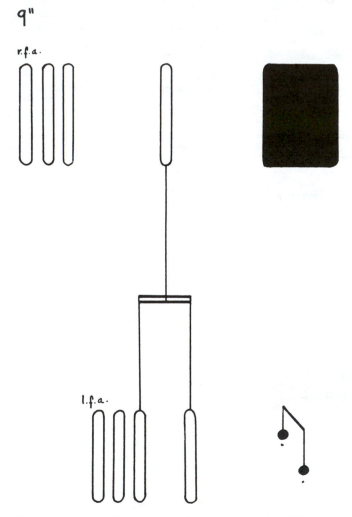

Figure 3.9. From Theodore Lucas's *Aberrations No. VII* for piano. Copyright 1969 by the composer.

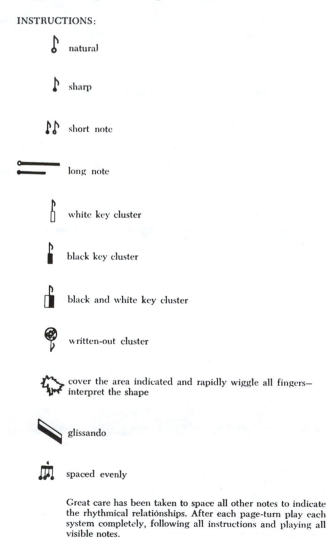

Figure 3.10. Performance instructions from Stanley Lunetta's *Piano Music*. Composer Performer Edition, Davis, CA.

Karel Husa's *Apotheosis of This Earth* for concert band (1971, see Figure 3.11) demonstrates another means of achieving clusters: rhythmic densities producing vibrating "columns" of sound. This approach allows for continuous development of motivic and melodic fragments.

North/White by R. Murray Schafer was, in the words of the composer, "inspired by the rape of the Canadian North . . . carried out by the nation's government in conspiracy with business and industry." The title derives from "white light" which contains all visual frequencies. The piece uses almost all possible audible frequencies producible by a symphony orchestra. *North/White* begins and ends on single notes that enclose tapering clusters producing a kind of crab canon, with the first three sections presented in retrograde order in the second half of the work.

A number of composers, most notably Brian Ferneyhough, have created rich-textured new music often referred to as the New Complexity. Reminiscent of the multi-layered textures of Ives but without the obvious use of quotes, New Complexity compositions often challenge performers and audiences alike with their extreme rhythms, registers, and thick textures.

RHYTHMIC DEVELOPMENTS

Some composers have felt that rhythm has become strangled by common-practice notation, especially by barlines and beat-related constraints (Creston 1964; Erickson 1963; Kramer 1988). Ligeti comments about freeing rhythm in his preface for *Lontano* (1967): "The bar lines serve only as a means of synchronization; bar lines and beats never mean an accentuation, the music must flow smoothly . . ." (Ligeti 1969, p. 2) The score to *Lontano* contains double- and triple-dotted notes, entrances on inner positions of triplets, quintuplets, septuplets, and so on as shown in Figure 3.12. These rhythms diffuse meter and give the music a sense of freedom not normally found in metered music.

Boulez speaks to this point in his book *Boulez on Music Today*:

> The rational use of the opposition between multiplication and division of the [beat] unit will, moreover, give rise to striking contrasts due to the broader span of values brought into play . . . interaction of these various methods of organization can be extremely fertile, and will create an inexhaustible variety of objects—in the same way as in the field of pitch. (Boulez 1971, p. 58)

Other composers have turned to proportional notation to avoid the accent implications of metric notation. Notes in a section of proportional notation marked 30 seconds are performed as they reach the eye—as if the visual left-to-right motion takes 30 seconds. No accents, other than those specifically marked, occur in such notation. Unfortunately, the inexactness of this proportional approach to notation disturbs some composers in that results often differ markedly from one performance to another (see Appendix III for more on proportional notation).

Olivier Messiaen, in his *The Technique of My Musical Language*, develops complex rhythmic formulations such as non-retrogradable rhythms (rhythmic palindromes) and notes with dots or rests added to complicate otherwise simple rhythmic patterns (Messiaen 1950). Messiaen's work has had considerable influence on composers throughout Europe, most notably Pierre Boulez.

Elliott Carter seeks these same goals, but from quite a different perspective. In his *Flawed Words and Stubborn Sounds* Carter speaks of his approach: "The result in my own music was, first of all, the way of evolving rhythms and continuities now called 'metric modulation,' which I worked out in the composition of my *Cello Sonata* of 1948." Later in this same book he writes of new music in general: ". . . what is needed is never just a string of interesting passages, but works whose central interest is constituted by the way everything that happens in them happens as and when it does in relation to everything else" (Edwards 1971, p. 91–2).

Metric modulation, though not an entirely new concept, follows highly complex procedures in Carter's compositions (Carter 1955, 1977; Edwards 1971). In his *Double Concerto* (1961) for harpsichord and piano with two chamber orchestras, the meter and the tempo often change at bar lines as shown in Figure 3.13. These changes, combined with a rich variety of complex rhythmic development within measures, results in highly structured yet free-sounding rhythms. Though some critics express doubt whether such modulations can be performed accurately, sincere attempts to follow these instructions likely achieve the desired effects.

Many composers strike a middle ground between proportional notation and meter utilizing both techniques within a single work, as Ligeti does in his *Aventures*. Electroacoustic music also presents potential for complex rhythmic structures (Babbitt 1962). I discusses this in my article for *Electronic Music: A Listener's Guide* by Elliott Schwartz:

> The major advantage to working with electronic equipment and sounds which seem undiminished by overdone "exploration" is rhythmic freedom. No other ensemble of instruments is equally capable of fractioning time into control-

Figure 3.11.   From Karel Husa's *The Apotheosis of This Earth*. © Copyright 1971 by Associated Music Publishers, Inc.

lable particles as the components of a well-equipped electronic music studio. While some listeners feel that the opportunity to free rhythm from any immediately recognizable meters removes some inalienable musical basic, it must be pointed out that to a large degree meter was introduced only to keep performers together in ensembles; while necessary, it was certainly not particularly musical in itself. The disposition of time is much more controllable in the electronic studio. (Schwartz 1972, p. 214)

Figure 3.12.   Typical rhythmic entrances from György Ligeti's *Lontano* (1967).

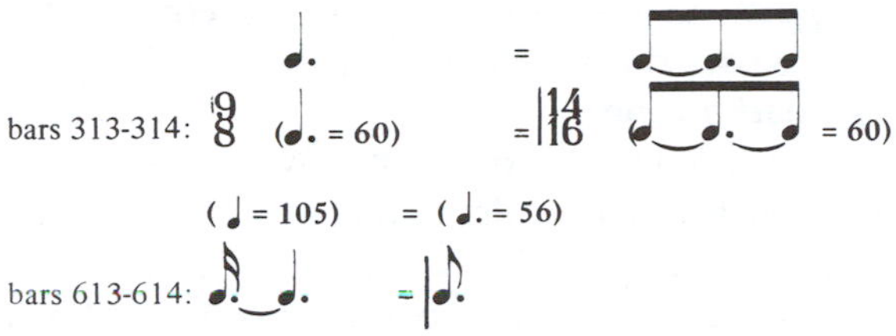

Figure 3.13.   Metric modulations from Elliott Carter's *Double Concerto* (1961).

Figure 3.14.   Elliott Carter. BMI Archives. Used by permission.

VECTORAL ANALYSIS
KRZYSZTOF PENDERECKI:
CAPRICCIO FOR VIOLIN AND ORCHESTRA

(For information on vectoral analysis and procedures, see Preface.)

1. Historical Background: Krzysztof Penderecki (c is pronounced as if it were an s) was born in Debica, Poland, in 1933. He studied at the Music Academy in Cracow, where he eventually taught (Schwinger 1994; Vinton 1974). Influences on his style include Iannis Xenakis and Luigi Nono:

> In 1957, Luigi Nono came to Poland, to visit. He brought some scores with him, and he gave me some. I remember the *Five Pieces* of Webern. I was already writing my own music at that time (1957 or 1958). He gave me some of his music also. I think it was *Il Canto di Spezzo, Varianti* for violin and orchestra, *Cori di de Doni*, the piece for chorus, then *Improvisation sur Mallarmé*, by Boulez. All this was very new for me, and I tried to incorporate these techniques in a very short time. This was in 1958, until the middle of 1959. And then I decided to go my way. (Felder and Schneider 1977, p. 12)

Most of Penderecki's early works require large forces for performance, and range from short experiments in sound (especially *Threnody*, 1960; *Polymorphia*, 1961; and *De Natura Sonoris,* 1967 for string orchestras) to large dramatic opera/oratorios (notably *The Passion According to St. Luke*, 1965, and *The Devils of Loudon*, 1969). The thread of intense drama linked with subtle religious mysticism weaves through his musical style. Recently he has turned to a more neo-Romantic style (Robinson 1983).

2. Overview: *The Capriccio for Violin and Orchestra* (completed in 1967) is a concise concerto-type work in an abbreviated rondo-variations form consisting of variations alternating with returns to the opening material. After the brief opening timpani roll, a cluster chord occurs softly in the winds. Out of this texture grow individual crescendi contrapuntally increasing in number. This process serves as a conceptual model for the remainder of the work, with variations deriving momentum from many sources including timbral, dynamic, rhythmic, and textural variation, rather than the more typical variations of pitch that one usually associates with this form.

3. Orchestration Techniques: Penderecki splits the orchestra into sections of instruments of like timbres including a large percussion battery (five players needed for performance) that creates incisive clusters of sound (e.g., vibraphone, bells, triangles, chimes, harp, and piano used simultaneously). Effects include playing on the other side of the bridge and bowing for noise (strings) with pizzicato (plucking) inside the piano. Double- and triple-tongued repeated notes in the winds give rhythmic drive to stacked clusters.

4. Basic Techniques: *Capriccio* is a free serial work (i.e., eleven-note rows) that develops new rows rather than adhering to a single series. Interval content evolves from minor seconds (chromatic clusters) and resulting octave displacements (major sevenths, minor ninths). Major seconds and various thirds become more important as the work progresses. Intervals expand throughout, creating more complex harmonies.

Figure 3.15.   Krzysztof Penderecki.

5. Vertical Models: Figure 3.16 demonstrates the kind of vertical clustering that Penderecki uses. Notation defines pitch content with duration determined by the length of the thick black lines (Felder and Schneider 1977). Penderecki speaks of his notation:

> I had to write in shorthand—something for me to remember, because my style of composing at that time was just to draw a piece first and then look for pitch . . . I just wanted to write music that would have an impact, a density, powerful expression, a different expression . . . I think this notation was for me, in the beginning, like shorthand, really, coming from drawing the piece. I used to see the whole piece in front of me—*Threnody* is very easy to draw. First you have just the high note, then you have this repeating section, then you have this cluster going, coming— different directions from the one note, twelve, and back—using different shapes. Then there is a louder section; then there's another section, then there is the section which is strictly written in 12-tone technique. Then it goes back to the

same cluster technique again, and the end of the piece is a big cluster, which you can draw like a square and write behind it fortissimo. . . . I didn't want to write in bars, because this music doesn't work if you put it in bars. (Felder and Schneider 1977, p. 13)

In the example of Figure 3.16, the harmonium (a reed-type organ) and piano (using wire brushes inside) cover their approximate visual areas in the time allowed (2/4, with the quarter note approximately set to M.M. 76, though no tempo is given in the score). The resultant textures vary, but nonetheless extend the chromatic clusters. In the opening sections, Penderecki centers on minor second stacked clusters. He then expands this to major second clusters (wholetone). These eventually widen to octave-displaced minor second clusters. A third type of vertical structure appears in the upper right-hand corner of this page. This sound mass moves contrapuntally by alternating quarter tones.

6. Horizontal Models: As with the textures explored in this work, Penderecki concentrates horizontally on the interval of a second. Over eighty percent of the intervals in the opening solo violin line are half or whole steps. Even thirds are often spelled as augmented seconds. These melodic lines become more angular by octave displacement creating sevenths and ninths. Penderecki paces the vertical and horizontal development so that one feels each proceeding at a similar rate of speed.

Penderecki comments on his use of the violin in this piece:

> Sometimes when writing a group of notes in a very fast tempo, like in *Capriccio* for example, I know it is impossible to play all of them. But I did it because then I had achieved a tension in the sound. If I would have written only four or five notes, he would just do it, you know, so you would lose all the tension I have in the piece. I know this exactly. Performers ask me all the time: "Please, this is impossible." I reply that it is absolutely possible—"You will do it." Maybe the player will miss two or three of them, but there is a tension there. (Felder and Schneider 1977, p. 14)

7. Style: Penderecki's *Capriccio for Violin and Orchestra* is a tightly woven, freely chromatic work based on the exploration of seconds both melodically and harmonically. These interval explorations slowly expand over a rondo template. The dramatic context within which the work proceeds depends on large orchestral forces (especially a large percussion section), contrapuntal interweaving of dynamics and

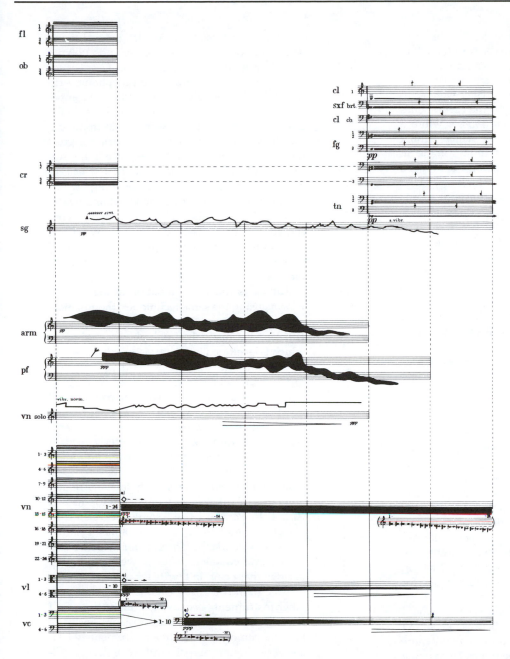

Figure 3.16. Page 29 from Krzysztof Penderecki's *Capriccio for Violin and Orchestra.* Copyright © by Moeck Verlag. Used with permission. All rights reserved.

rhythm, and various effects including microtones. In contrast to the *Symphonie* of Webern (analyzed in chapter 2), Penderecki has created a dramatic style fused with clusters, rhythmic development, and microtonal inflections.

Compare this work to the vectoral analyses of chapter 4 and chapter 10 for similarity in terms of reliance on dramatic elements and explorations in orchestration. The lack of lyricism in Penderecki's writing here contrasts with the Varèse work of chapter 1. The clusters in *Capriccio* resemble those of the Oliveros work in chapter 6.

David Felder and Mark Schneider: An Interview with Krzysztof Penderecki

The following interview took place in Cincinnati's Music Hall, March 31, 1977, following a rehearsal for a forthcoming concert of the composer's music.

Felder: You've experienced an extensive compositional career. Would you trace the development of your style as it exists now, through the various changes and evolutions that you've undergone.

Penderecki: I think the first period of my development, I would say, would be from the first compositions written in my style, *Anaklasis* and *Threnody*. I finished the two pieces in the fall of 1959 and the spring of 1960. As a student I wrote many, many pieces, but they were in a style like Bartók, a little like Stravinsky. They were actually not lessons, though maybe the earliest ones were. Afterwards, in 1957 or 1958, I wrote a piece called *Psalms of David*, in which I think there are some elements you will find in the *St. Luke Passion* later, as in the second a cappella piece. The a cappella sound in *Psalms of David* and *St. Luke* is really the same—I used the same technique. Anyway, I used orthodox twelve-tone technique in the a cappella sections. I used the same technique in the *St. Luke Passion*.

Then I wrote a work for two string orchestras which is influenced more by post-Webern style—*Emanations*. That also contains elements of my later style.

The third piece I wrote is the *Strophes* for soprano, which was influenced by Boulez and maybe Luigi Nono. So the first pieces I wrote, really, are *Anaklasis* and *Threnody*; and that was the beginning of my music. It was something new for me at that time. Afterwards I wrote *Dimensions of Time and Silence*, in which I used the same techniques for chorus that I had used previously with strings. So it was the first piece, really, that used all types of sound that the chorus can produce. The date was 1960. Then, the *First String Quartet*, then *Polymorphia*, which is a very important piece for me, I think. Then, *Flourescences* and *Canon*. I think I wrote the *Canon* before 1961. That's all. I think that in those pieces I tried to explore all possibilities—not only to find my own style because, of course, that was the foremost thought I had in mind, but also to try to find new techniques, for chorus, strings and all instruments.

I think after I finished *Flourescences*, I would say that the first period ends, because I couldn't go and explore anymore. I didn't see any more possibility for developing the things I was doing at that time. So, in 1962, I backtracked a little and wrote *Stabat Mater*. I didn't know which way to go at that time, and I wasn't sure that what I was doing was really right. Maybe I had gone too far and there was no way back. So, I studied counterpoint—specifically, the Netherlands School counterpoint of the sixteenth century. *Stabat Mater* is written using some of the same techniques as Ockeghem and Obrecht also incorporating, of course, some twelve-tone elements. As a matter of fact, I used an advanced polyphonic technique in that piece, so the *Stabat Mater* is the beginning of the second period, I would say.

The second period lasted until 1973, because that is when I finished the *Symphony*. During that time, I just used my own language. I found some new possibilities in Netherlands polyphony. As a matter of fact, in the *St. Luke Passion* you will find both complicated polyphonic writing and also my experience with diverse compositional materials. Also, I should add that in the late 1950s I spent four years in the electronic studio. It helped me develop my hearing a great deal. Without having had experience in the studio, I would never have written *Threnody*, because the studio was something which opened my mind and ears for something new—unlimited possibilities as far as sound is concerned. During the second period in my music I used mostly what I had discovered before. I wrote six pieces like the *Passion*. The second big piece was *Utrenja*.

Utrenja is like a continuation of the *St. Luke Passion*, using the same techniques, though more advanced, perhaps. Something happened after *Utrenja*, because the polyphonic technique which I developed in *Utrenja* is so extreme—and so difficult. The same thing that had happened to me after *Flourescences* happened once again. After I finished *Utrenja*, what more could I do? I don't like to repeat myself. Of course, I could have written many, many pieces in the same style, but I didn't want to. So after *Utrenja*, I wrote some pieces that I think were important for me; for example, *De Natura Sonoris 2*, in which I used some new techniques. Another piece that I think was very important for me was *Partita*. In *Partita*, I used some rock elements, like electric guitars. As a matter of fact, I started by writing a piano concerto, for which I had been commissioned. After a week or two, I decided that I couldn't write for piano because it doesn't sound, really. I cannot use piano with other instruments because it's out-of-tune. So I never really wrote the piece for piano—instead I found a combination of five instruments which are very similar: harpsichord, two electric guitars, harp, and double bass. I used this group of instruments as soloists, as in a concerto grosso.

After that, I wrote a symphony, which is important for me because it is the first large piece I wrote for orchestra. I think the third period begins with the *Awakening of Jacob* and the *Magnificat*, and maybe *Ecloga*. In 1972 and 1973 there are some changes in my thinking, in my music, which I developed after *Ecloga* and *Magnificat*.

Felder: Specifically what changes would you be talking about?

Penderecki: First of all, I've returned to using the normal sound of an orchestra which I missed for so many years while trying to develop new playing techniques for all the instruments. I am no longer using a great deal of percussion, nor am I using special effects. I think I've written enough pieces which utilize all that. I don't think I need it now. Also I think that pitch is becoming more important now. Pitch is an element that I didn't care too much about in my early music (excepting, of course, the *St. Luke Passion*). In some of my pieces, pitch is not very important—what is important is the relation between clusters, between registers, between groups of instruments. The best example of this would be the *Symphony*, using groups of instruments, in this case brass and woodwinds. A similar idea is used in *Partita*. I used only groups of instruments, specifically the group of five soloists against all the string instruments, and then against woodwinds, and then percussion, and then brass, and then combined, and so forth. I don't really use this technique anymore.

As far as orchestration is concerned, I think I use more or less traditional orchestration, I would say. Also, I've employed harmony more than I had previously as in *The Awakening of Jacob*. Before, my music was more polyphonic. I was more interested in setting line, more involved with the horizontal than the vertical. In *Utrenja*, each line is very important—if you pick out the fortieth or thirty-seventh voice, the line is very interesting, and it has a logic. Now, I care more about intervals, as in the *Magnificat*, where the minor third is a very important interval. I start with D, and then the choir starts with F, and all this is combined. In the fugue, the first subject is a combination of seven voices using only minor thirds. The first voice uses only C-A, and the second, F-A♭, and so forth. So I have fourteen different pitches, but the listener will remember the interval. Also, I am repeating things more, which is new for me. You will recognize the same chord in *The Awakening of Jacob* both in the beginning and at the end. I used the same idea—it is also a minor third. I also repeat the harmony more. I am building form by repetition, which is the old way, nothing new.

Felder: You've discussed three stylistic divisions or groupings. Would you consider the first period to be one in which you were trying to expand your vocabulary in different directions, through the use of texture and various other parameters, and then, perhaps, the second period to be one in which you were more concerned with dramatic implications?

Penderecki: Yes, because in the second period I was just using the language I had discovered, using my own compositional language. During the first period I was always concerned about finding something new and being different— finding a different music. I was obsessed that my music must be completely different from any I had ever heard. It was! You know, in 1959, in 1960, with *Threnody,* a completely new style occurred. Maybe there was no path for me to follow after that, because I thought I had done everything.

Felder: Would you consider the third period to be a kind of synthesis of what you tried to accomplish in the first two periods?

Penderecki: It's too early to say yet, I think it began in 1974, and I am still looking. I've completed a violin concerto recently, using a technique similar to that of *The Awakening of Jacob*. Other works include the *Symphony* and the opera for Chicago. It's a very hard piece, because it's a very lyrical opera. The subject is lyric. It's not dramatic at all, except at some moments, but it's very sophisticated and lyric. It has a very beautiful text between Adam and Eve, and Satan and God. The music is very lyric and I couldn't just use the same technique writing the piece. I couldn't do it right using the language from *Utrenja*, or even *Magnificat*. Remember, *Magnificat* is more dramatic. Therefore I had to find something new, maybe something a little like the techniques used in *The Awakening of Jacob*.

Schneider: Something a little more specific—you mentioned earlier the influence of Boulez on some or your music. Could you elaborate?

Penderecki: In my study. It was before I really started to compose what I consider my music.

Schneider: Do you still use any 12-tone or serial techniques? Of course this isn't a very recent example, but in the *St. Luke Passion* you used three rows. . .

Penderecki: Oh, yes, sure. I did use some serial techniques. For example, I used some in *Psalms of David, St. Luke Passion*, and, not as strictly, my instrumental music. On the other hand, the middle section of *Threnody* is written very strictly. *Canon* is not only 12-tone, but also dynamics are controlled—everything is very strictly written. But I don't use these techniques anymore.

Felder: How did you arrive at your notational system? It's a very unique system, and, of course, it's been extremely influential.

Penderecki: I discovered this system for the music I wanted to write. This system was very simple. As a matter of fact, the technique in

Threnody was very easy after I discovered it, you know. It looks fairly easy—just a few clusters going down and up, and different densities, and so on. I think the technique is very clear, and also, it's similar to writing in shorthand. I think I remember writing the piece—you know, thinking about the cluster between C and G, and how the cluster will come between F and C (or something like that). I had to write in shorthand— something for me to remember, because my style of composing at that time was just to draw a piece first and then look for pitch; even more than now I think I was interested in pitch. I just wanted to write music that would have an impact, a density, powerful expression, a different expression. At that time I still played violin, so I tried to find some effects, some new possibilities: playing behind the bridge, on the double bass—playing on the tailpiece, or directly on the bridge, and so on. I tried to use an instrument as an entire body with which I could make music. So, this way I found out what works. For example, striking the strings with the hand—of course, it's a much better effect if you use it with cello or double bass, which are larger instruments. So I experimented a while using this whole process, and then I wrote a piece.

I think this notation was for me, in the beginning, like shorthand, really, coming from drawing the piece. I used to see the whole piece in front of me—*Threnody* is very easy to draw. First you have just the high note, then you have this repeating section, then you have this cluster going, coming—different directions from the one note, twelve, and back—using different shapes. Then there is a louder section; then there's another section, then there is the section which is strictly written in 12-tone technique. Then it goes back to the same cluster technique again, and the end of the piece is a big cluster, which you can draw like a square and write behind it fortississimo. Then, to remember, just write "between G and the two octave lower G", and then divide it for instruments. So, it was shorthand. And then I discovered that it works. I didn't need to write a big score—fifty-two different voices. Also, I discovered new symbols for behind the bridge, for highest pitch. I had to do that, because these didn't exist! It was necessary to do it. I didn't want to write in bars, because this music doesn't work if you put it in bars.

Schneider: Do you consider your notational system where it stands now as indeterminate, to a degree; or, if it is indeterminate, for what purpose?

Penderecki: I think what I said was that this notation was discovered for the music I wrote,

and now, even now, writing different music, sometimes I discover something which helps me notate my ideas. But I think this kind of notation is only for this kind of music. You cannot use the same kind of notation and compose in neo-classical, neo-Bartók, or neo-something idioms. It works only for this music, I think. So it is not a universal notation for everything.

Schneider: Are you worried about how another conductor might interpret some of the notational symbols? For example, in many pieces there are no exact timings marked out for the proportional notation.

Penderecki: Yes, sometimes. Usually I put 'circa' 12" or 24", like in *Threnody* and other pieces. You don't have it in the *St. Luke Passion*, because I think the music has something like its own pulse and tempo. If not, it doesn't really work. It doesn't help if you put in bar lines and write metronome equals 72. I didn't want to write very clear tempos. The idea behind writing the *St. Luke Passion* is similar to Gregorian chant, really. There is no measure at all; just at the beginning. You know, it was very hard for me to find this kind of notation. I couldn't put it in bars. Sometimes, of course, a conductor who doesn't feel this music will do it differently. Of course it can happen. But today you can have tape, or recordings. I think these help a lot.

Felder: In some of your music you ask almost the impossible of certain performers. I can think of one specific example—the part of Phillippe in *Devils of Loudon* has that astronomically high C and, of course, that immediately limits the number of performers who can accomplish it. What purpose does this serve?

Penderecki: If you had asked a musician to play or try something which seems to be impossible—first of all, he tries and sometimes it happens—he can do it. Sometimes when writing a group of notes together in a very fast tempo, like in *Capriccio* for example, I know it is impossible to play all of them. But I did it because then I had achieved a tension in the sound. If I would have written only four or five notes, he would just do it, you know, so you would lose all the tension I have in the piece. I know this exactly. Performers ask me all the time: "Please, this is impossible." I reply that it is absolutely possible—"You will do it." Maybe the player will miss two or three of them, but there is a tension there. I used to do it, for example, using the human voice, writing very, very high for sopranos. You have something which you would never have otherwise—a kind of tension—

because two or three sopranos can sing it, maybe. The others try. Of course, some of them cry a little bit.

Felder: Do you think it's the responsibility of the composer to expand the vocabulary with new works?

Penderecki: Tchaikovsky wrote a violin concerto and the performers at that time said: "It's impossible, it's an unplayable piece, it's too difficult." Now, the student in the conservatory can play it. The technique of the instrument has developed so much. In *Magnificat*, I employ very high D trumpets, really E and E♭. It's very high,

almost impossible, but they tried and they did it. Some didn't, of course. But I like this kind of sound which is produced—being impossible.

Felder: Will you return to usage of the bar as an organizational device?

Penderecki: Oh, sometimes, if necessary. In *The Awakening of Jacob* there are many, many bars. On occasion I write bars *senza misura* freely. I don't really like to put my music in bars, but sometimes it's necessary. I think the composer has to have experience with the orchestra, it's very important.

Chapter 4

TIMBRALISM AND TUNING

TRADITIONAL INSTRUMENT EXPLORATION

The desire for new and different sounds, an important driving force behind experimental music, continued to provoke controversy (Clough 1961; Read 1953, 1976; Rossi and Choate 1969). John Cage refers to such controversies in his 1937 lecture, "The Future of Music: Credo." "Whereas, in the past, the point of disagreement has been between dissonance and consonance, it will be, in the immediate future, between noise and so-called musical sounds" (Cage 1961, p. 4). Interestingly, few actual new sounds have developed that have not coexisted with music since its beginning. The fact that these sounds are now considered musical, however, often creates a division between composers and audiences (Cogan and Escot 1981; Cowell 1933; Garland 1982).

As early as 1912, a group of Italian composers, called Futurists, composed music for machine guns, steam whistles, sirens, and other noisemakers (Payton 1976). Deriving their name from Marinetti's 1909 term *futurismo* (referring to extreme radicalism in all the arts), the Futurists were among the first composers to include noise as an inherent part of their music, not merely as a side effect. Francesco Pratella's theoretical "Musica Futurista" (reprinted in Nicolas Slonimsky's *Music Since 1900*) describes the "music" of steamboats, automobiles, battleships, railways, shipyards, and airplanes. Luigi Russolo (1885–1947), the most noted Futurist composer, constructed many of his own "noise instruments." Though his music and most of the other music of this movement did not achieve popular success and approval in his time, it laid a foundation for experimentation by other composers. Varèse, for example, used sirens and anvils in his *Ionisation*. Mossolov, in his more imitative *Symphony of Machines–Steel Foundry* (1928), includes the rattling of a metal sheet throughout. The Futurist movement in France (*bruitisme*) embraced noise as a viable musical source.

George Antheil's *Ballet mécanique* (1924), probably the most infamous of noise pieces, was largely influenced by this French movement (Pound 1968). The first Carnegie Hall performance of *Ballet mécanique* (April 10, 1927) brought about a violent audience reaction reminiscent of the first performance of Stravinsky's *Le Sacre du Printemps*. Antheil established a paradigm for the avant-garde to come as expressed in "An Introduction to George Antheil" by Charles Amirkhanian:

> Here is a man who once drew a pistol during a piano recital to silence a restive audience; a man who, in 1923, composed a piece of music calling for the sound of an airplane motor; a man who was mistakenly reported by the news media to have been eaten alive by lions in the Sahara Desert; and a man who collaborated with Hedy Lamarr in the invention and patenting of a World War II torpedo. (Amirkhanian 1973, p. 176)

Interestingly, Ezra Pound remarks that Antheil was possibly the first American-born musician to be taken seriously in Europe. This might explain John Cage's later successes there. The *Treatise on Harmony* by Antheil (a 25-page book) details the need for a reappraisal of rhythmic ideas equal to those of melody

Figure 4.1. George Antheil arriving in New York City for the U.S. premiere performance of his *Ballet méchanique* (1927).

Figure 4.2.   Bertram Turetzky.

and harmony: "A sound of any pitch, or combination of such sounds, may be followed by a sound of any other pitch or any combination of such sounds, providing the time interval between them is properly gauged; and this is true for any series of sounds, chords or arpeggios" (Pound 1968, p. 10).

In few other periods of music history have performers played such an important role in the development of new sound resources and instrumental techniques as in the past eighty years. Bruno Bartolozzi, in his now famous book *New Sounds for Woodwind*, classifies the contemporary performer's role in new music as well as the role of instruments:

> Their continued existence in the world of creative composition therefore depends to a very large extent on just what they have to offer the composer, just how much they can rouse his interest and provoke his fantasy. Some composers already show an obvious lack of interest in conventional instruments and have no hesitation in using the most unusual means in an effort to find new sonorities. . . . (Bartolozzi 1967, p. i)

No traditional instrument has escaped the imagination of the composer's creativity. Some performers, however, steadfastly maintain that anything but traditional performance on their instrument violates inherent intention. One must wonder why plucking (*pizzicato*) and muting (*con sordino*), two often-used traditional effects, also do not violate this inherent intention. Certainly, however, short of physical damage to the instrument itself, even the most traditional performer must admit that traditional performance techniques themselves evolved from such experimentation. Donald Erb sums it up well:

> Music is made by a performer. It comes from him rather than from his instrument, the instrument being merely a vehicle. Therefore it seems logical that any sound a performer can make may be used in a musical composition. (Turetzky 1969b, p. 169)

Strings

Four major categories of new string techniques currently exist (Verkoeyen 1970):

(1) percussive effects such as knocking, rapping, tapping, or slapping the strings or body of the instrument—especially in the works of Meyer Kupferman, Eugene Kurtz, and Sydney Hodkinson (Turetzky 1969a, 1969b, and 1974);

(2) singing, speaking, or humming while playing—particularly apparent in the works of Russell Peck, Jacob Druckman, Charles Whittenberg, and Richard Felciano;

(3) unusual bowings inclusive of circular bowing, bowing on or across the bridge, bowing between the bridge and tailpiece, bowing directly on the tailpiece, and undertones (subharmonics) created by bowing with great pressure on a harmonic node—used extensively in the works of Krzysztof Penderecki, Karlheinz Stockhausen, Mauricio Kagel, and George Crumb, among others;

(4) combinations and extensions of traditional techniques (e.g., harmonics, glissandi, fingering without bowing, pizzicati, etc.)—especially notable in the works of Krzysztof Penderecki, György Ligeti, Donald Erb, and Mauricio Kagel (Sallis 1996).

In Figure 4.3, Krzysztof Penderecki requires performers to play between the bridge and tailpiece ($\curlywedge$ and $\mathvarpi$), highest note pizzicato ($\uparrow$), and irregular tremolo ($\mathcal{Z}$) in his *Threnody for the Victims of Hiroshima* (for explanation of the proportional notation used here, see Appendix III).

Notable performers of innovative works for strings include Paul Zukofsky and Max Pollikov (violin), Walter Trampler (viola), Siegfried Palm (cello), and Bertram Turetzky, Barry Green, and Alvin Brehm (contrabass). String groups particularly dedicated to new music and techniques include the Fine Arts Quartet, the Kronos Quartet, and the Composers' Quartet, among others.

Winds

Although differences exist between the ways in which innovative techniques apply to brass and woodwinds and to individual instruments—particularly between the various single-reed, double-reed, and non-reed instruments of the woodwind section—these instru-

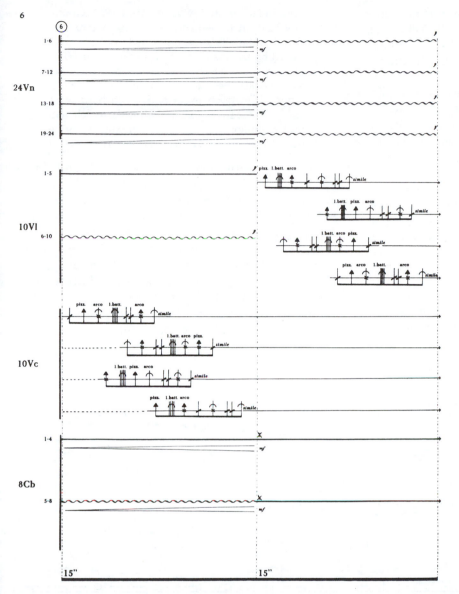

Figure 4.3. From Krzysztof Penderecki's *Threnody for the Victims of Hiroshima* (1960). Copyright © 1961 Deshon Music, Inc. & PWM Editions. All rights reserved.

ment groupings are combined here due to their basic similarities (Bartolozzi 1967; Howell 1974; Livingston and McCarty 1971). Similar effects fall within six major categories:

(1) Multiphonics—the creation of more than one pitch simultaneously on a monophonic instrument. Multiphonics are created by two basic methods: singing along with playing and/or forcing the strong overtone content of a given fundamental to become audible by altering embouchure, fingerings, overblowing, or dynamics. Figure 4.4 shows Toru Takamitsu's use and notation of open and closed holes for fingering in his *Voice* (1971) for solo flute. Multiphonics can also be found in works by Donald Erb, Roger Reynolds, Russell Peck, and Jacob Druckman, among others;

(2) Color fingerings involve pitch and timbre fluctuations by changing the available fingerings on the instrument for the same note (Rehfeldt 1977). Color fingerings are particularly notable in the works of George Crumb;

(3) Jazz effects include a large variety of traditionally avoided sounds such as rips, fall offs, bends, and so on (Rehfeldt 1977)—particularly in the brass works of William Sydeman, Phil Winsor, Donald Erb, and David Cope;

(4) Percussion effects, such as rapping, tapping, fingering without blowing, fingernails on the bell tremolo, and hand-pops (the palm of the hand slapping the open bore of the mouthpiece)—notably in the works of Aurelio de la Vega, Iannis Xenakis, and many others (Rehfeldt 1977);

(5) Use of mouthpiece alone or instrument without mouthpiece, both performable with actual or approximate pitch—occurring in works by Donald Erb, Krzysztof Penderecki, and György Ligeti, among others (Cummings 1974, 1984);

(6) Extension of traditional techniques such as glissandi, harmonics, speed rates of vibrato, pedal tones, flutter tongue, circular breathing, and many others—found in works by composers listed under 1–5 as well as Luciano Berio, Lukas Foss, and Gunther Schuller.

Figure 4.5 shows a particularly good example of a work for solo instrument exploring techniques such as those just described. Donald Scavarda's *Matrix* for solo clarinet (1962) contains a wide variety of new wind techniques including multiphonics (one of the first such uses), smears, breath noise, overtone clusters, use of inverted mouthpiece, and undertones. Scavarda speaks to this point:

> It was in trying to find sounds that were most natural to the clarinet that I discovered what are

now called multiphonics in April 1962. Gradually I began to realize the exciting potential of the simultaneity of sounds that could be produced by the instrument. It was necessary first, however, to discard old habits and attitudes about what the clarinet should sound like. It required an open mind and much hard work and patience to explore and mine these rich, natural complex sounds and eventually to bring them to the surface. (Scavarda 1962, p.1)

Notable performers of woodwind and brass works of the avant-garde include: Aurèle Nicolet, Pierluigi Mencarelli, Savarino Gazzeloni, and Harvey Sollberger—flute; Joseph Celli, Lawrence Singer, and Heinz Holliger—oboe; Phillip Rehfeldt, Detalmo Corneti, and William O. Smith—clarinet; William Scribner and Sergio Penazzi—bassoon; Ken Dorn and James Houlik—saxophone; Gerard Schwarz, Robert Levy, and Marice Stith—trumpet; James Fulkerson, Stuart Dempster, and Vinko Globokar—trombone; and Barton Cummings and Roger Bobo—tuba.

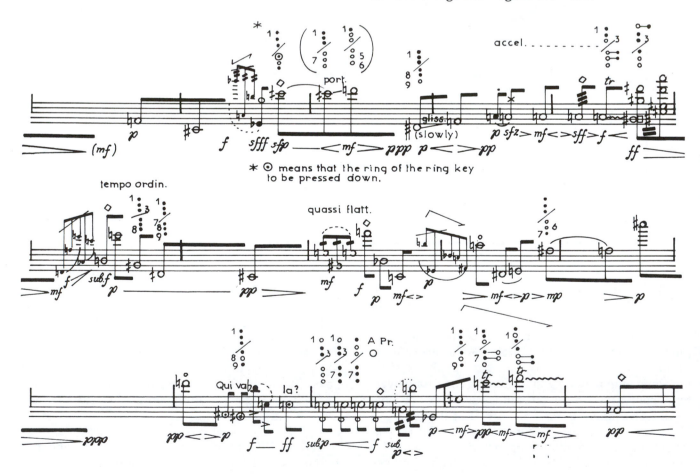

Figure 4.4. Each small vertical line equals 4.5″ in Toru Takemitsu's *Voice*. Beamed notes are slurred. Special fingerings above some notes indicate particular timbres or multiphonics (last two chords of the first system). © 1971 Editions Salabert. With kind permission of Editions Salabert. All rights reserved.

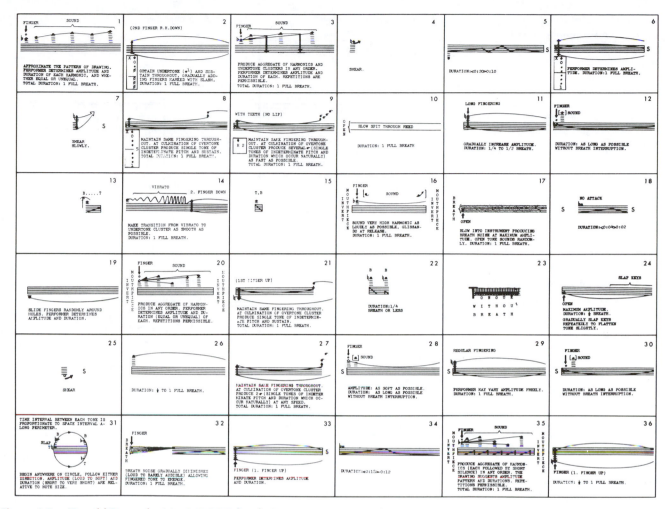

Figure 4.5. Donald Scavarda, *Matrix* (1962) for clarinet.

Percussion

The percussion section includes almost any instrument, whether string (e.g., piano), wind (e.g., slide whistle), or other classification (Brindle 1970; Finkenbeinger and Meyer 1987; Reed and Leach 1969; Varèse 1967). Surprisingly, considering the *noises* many percussion instruments emit, most mainstream composers who use them still refuse to consider the musical potentiality of other less noisy instruments, such as the brake drum, which often appears in pitched collections of different sizes.

Early experimenters in percussion music include John Cage, Edgard Varèse, Carlos Chavez, and especially John Becker, whose *Abongo* (1933) marks one of the first serious efforts in percussion music. Percussion sections since the late nineteenth century have also required new approaches to notation, necessitated by the fact that performers must read as many as six instrumental parts simultaneously, and five-line staves are often impractical (see Figure 4.6). Compos-

ers using more traditional percussion instruments such as timpani, snare drum, xylophone, and so on have developed a variety of unusual techniques including experimenting with various sizes and types of mallets (metal, wood, cloth, glass).

The increasing need for explicit performance directions indicating type of mallet, the action of the mallet, and its exact placement on instruments often requires new notations as well. Figure 4.7a shows the movement of a mallet across a timpani head within a certain period of time. Figure 4.7b demonstrates the exact direction and striking surface on crash cymbals. Figure 4.7c shows the sweep action of wire brushes on a bass drum. Since significantly varying timbres as well as intensity can result from mallet direction and placement on percussion instruments, flexible notations become inevitable and often graphic (see Appendix III).

Notable avant-garde composers using percussion experimentally include Larry Austin, Karlheinz Stockhausen, Frederic Rzewski, Harry Partch, Edward

Figure 4.6. An example of traditional (left) and contemporary (right) percussion notation.

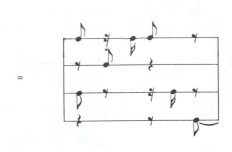

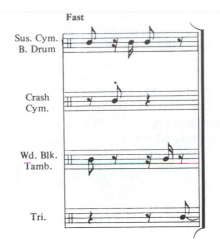

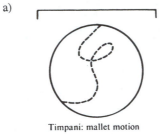

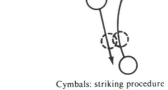

Figure 4.7. Avant-garde percussion notations.

a)

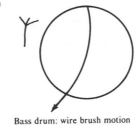

Timpani: mallet motion

b)

Cymbals: striking procedure

c)

Bass drum: wire brush motion

Figure 4.8. Blackearth Percussion Group.

Figure 4.9. William Kraft. Photo by A. A. Friedman.

Miller, Mario Bertoncini, Peter Garland, William Kraft, and many others. Percussionists performing experimental music include Max Neuhaus, Christoph Caskel, Willy Winant, and William Kraft. Often, percussionists tend to be composers as well. William Kraft, for example, is both a percussionist and a gifted and well-known composer.

Voice

The voice, both in solo and choral situations, has in recent years become a focal point of innovation realized both in terms of dramatic use of text and as an independent instrument (Pooler and Pierce 1973). The ability of the voice to act as a percussive string and wind instrument gives it nearly all of the timbre potential of standard orchestral instruments. Only the physical limitations of individual performers pose obstacles to the composer's imagination.

Most vocal experimentation has taken place in three basic areas:

(1) Effects such as panting, whistling, sucking, kissing, hissing, clucking, laughing, talking, whispering, and so on appear in the works of Hans Werner Henze, Krzysztof Penderecki, György Ligeti, Karlheinz Stockhausen, Mauricio Kagel, Pauline Oliveros, Folke Rabe, Richard Felciano, Luciano Berio, and David Cope;

(2) Multiphonics—especially notable in the *Versuch über Schweine* (1969) by Hans Werner Henze;

(3) Muting in the forms of humming, hands over mouth, and slowly opening and closing the mouth—notable in works by Donald Erb and Robert Morris.

Figure 4.10, the *Aventures* of György Ligeti, shows breathing in and out in measures 1–6 indicated by the symbols ▶ = inhale and ◀ = exhale as well as muting

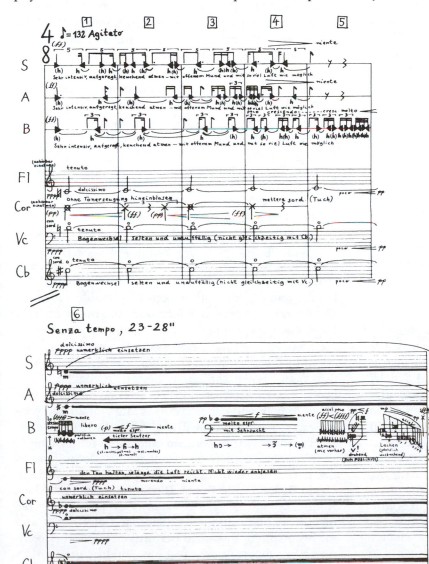

Figure 4.10. From György Ligeti's *Aventures*. Copyright © 1964 by Henry Litoff Verlag. Reprinted by permission of C. F. Peters Corporation.

with a closed mouth *m* in the second system. This work is notable for its lack of text, replaced by a 112-letter alphabet, and alternating metric and proportional notations, shown clearly here between braces one and two. Hans Werner Henze's *Versuch über Schweine* for voice and orchestra is equally impressive in its use of dramatic vocal gymnastics.

Singers known for their performance of new music include Roy Hart, Catherine Rowe, Jan DeGaetani, Bethany Beardslee, Elaine Bonazzi, Joan La Barbara, Neva Pilgrim, Paul Sperry, and the late Cathy Berberian. The New Music Choral Ensemble (NMCE), founded by its director Kenneth Gaburo in 1966, reigned as one of the world's foremost choral ensembles dedicated to the performance of new music.

David Hykes, founder and developer of the Harmonic Choir (1975), practices the art of Harmonic Chant, the singing of more than one note simultaneously by one singer. While Tibetan Buddhist monks and Mongolian throat (*hoomi*) singers have produced music in this manner for centuries, Western singers only have begun using this approach in the past few decades. By performing and recording only in highly resonant spaces such as large churches and abbeys, including New York City's Cathedral of St. John, the Harmonic Choir uses certain singing techniques to produce high harmonics simultaneously with fundamentals. With his colleague Timothy Hill, Hykes has developed five types of Harmonic Chant. These include drones based on subharmonic pitches (higher fundamental), fundamentals as drones over which singers produce melodies based on the overtone series, and contrapuntal harmonic movements of both fundamentals and derived melodies from various related harmonic series.

Keyboard

The early experiments and compositions for piano by Henry Cowell (e.g., *The Banshee* [1925], which involves plucking and stroking the strings inside the instrument), John Cage (e.g., *Bacchanale* [1938] and *Sonatas and Interludes* [1946–48] for prepared piano), and Christian Wolff (whose *For Prepared Piano* appeared in *New Music Quarterly* in April, 1951) aroused great interest. The prepared piano (a technique first explored by John Cage in the mid-1930s) involves the placement of objects such as nuts, bolts, and nails on, around, and between the strings, converting the piano into an instrument sounding like the *gamelan* of Southeast Asia (Bunger 1981). Figure 4.11 shows a number of typical preparations. Resulting timbres change depending on the location of preparations in regard to string length (e.g., placing the object at harmonic

nodes creates a very different sound than placing it between these nodes); the striking techniques used (i.e., initiating the sound via the keyboard creates a sound distinctly different from striking the preparation directly); and the elasticity and density of the material used for preparation. Most preparations will not damage instruments if proper precautions are used—see Figure 4.12, which shows the use of a screwdriver covered with masking tape to insert preparations, thus avoiding any harm to the strings.

Aside from preparation, the following new techniques for piano are currently being explored:

(1) Muting by placing one hand on the string inside the piano between the pin and the dampers and playing the notes on the keyboard with the other hand—usually notated with a + above the note, this technique appears particularly in the works of George Crumb and David Cope;

(2) Harmonics produced by touching a node of the string inside the piano with one hand and striking the corresponding key with the other—used in works by George Crumb, Larry Barnes, and many others;

(3) Bowing the strings with bows created from fishing line. These bows are threaded around and between the strings and then drawn back and forth as one would on a string instrument. Bowing appears particularly in the works of Curtis Curtis-Smith;

(4) Stroking, rapping, tapping, striking, or plucking the strings directly for a variety of different timbres—primarily in the works of Henry Cowell, George Crumb, David Cope, Donald Erb, and others;

(5) Using other parts of the instrument by knocking, tapping, rapping, and so on, particularly on the wood of the lid and body, the metal of the internal crossbars and soundboard, and so on with mallets, hands, and various other objects—notable in works like *Knocking Piece* by Ben Johnston, and music by John Cage, George Crumb, Donald Erb, and many others.

Stephen Scott has developed a bowed piano, influenced by Curtis-Smith's invention, using sets of miniature piano bows similar in design to regular violin bows. Constructed of popsicle sticks with horsehair glued to both ends, these bows create vibrant and continuous sounds. Unlike Curtis-Smith's design, however, Scott's bows also can perform quite rapid pitch changes.

Pianists who actively use these new techniques in the performance of new avant-garde works include David Tudor, David Burge, Richard Bunger, and Aloys Kontarsky. "Blue" Gene Tyranny is known for his inventive compositions for piano and electronics and for his inspired, theatrical performances of other composers' keyboard works (e.g., as "Buddy, the world's greatest piano player" in Robert Ashley's *Perfect Lives*).

David Tudor, William Albright, and Martha Folts have been active in the performance of new music for the organ, as has Antoinette Vischer on the harpsichord. At present these experiments have been more theatrical (organ) and formal (harpsichord) than real in terms of sonic exploration (Steinberg 1961). Works by Mauricio Kagel, Gordon Mumma, Christian Wolff, and William Albright for organ and György Ligeti for harpsichord contain examples of these new techniques.

Conlon Nancarrow (b. 1912) has created unique music for the player piano. His *Studies for Player Piano* utilize punched piano rolls inserted in two Marshall and Wendell player pianos, both with modified hammers; one set covered with leather and the other with steel straps. Nancarrow's complex works vary from jazz-influenced shorter studies (especially his early music) to mathematically proportioned canons. Nancarrow speaks about his work and its relation to traditional instruments in an interview:

> I'm so tied up now with the player piano. I'd have to start thinking again: "Does the hand reach there?" "Can it go here?" The whole thing.

> No, no. You know, when I do these things for player piano, I just write music; and the notes go here, there, wherever. I don't have to think about anything else. I used to, when I was writing for instruments. It's a real luxury not to have to think about all that. (Cagne and Caras 1982, p. 285)

Harp

Carlos Salzedo (1885–1961) developed a wide range of effects for harp, as well as highly original notations and names for these techniques ("gushing aeolian chords," etc.). Salzedo himself composed works utilizing the effects he created. Most of Salzedo's innovations have become standard for the harpist. Other composers utilizing these effects include Luciano Berio and George Crumb, in particular (see also Salzedo 1921, 1929, and 1961).

Ensembles

The previously discussed effects also have been used in combination or in conjunction with extracurricular performer activity, from finger-snapping and music-stand-tapping to the use of costumes, theatrical stag-

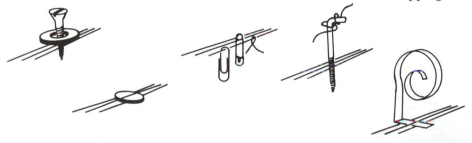

Figure 4.11.   Examples of piano preparations from Richard Bunger's *The Well-Prepared Piano*. Second edition. Litoral Arts Press, 35 Firefly Lane, Sebastopol, CA (1981).

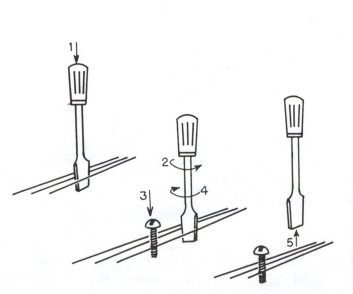

Figure 4.12.   From Richard Bunger's *The Well-Prepared Piano*. Second edition. Litoral Arts Press, 35 Firefly Lane, Sebastopol, CA (1981).

Figure 4.13.   Conlon Nancarrow. Photo by Gordon Mumma.

ing, and use of lighting effects (Anhalt 1984). Often composers use whispers, speaking, and shouting (as in the Crumb example in Figure 4.14) along with the inclusion of ancillary instruments such as triangles hung from music stands, maracas, and a variety of other percussion instruments.

George Crumb's *Songs, Drones, and Refrains of Death* (1969) for baritone, electric guitar, electric contrabass, electric piano, harpsichord, and two percussionists, combines many of the effects discussed here as shown in Figure 4.14. This duet for electric guitar and electric contrabass consists of seven events. Each performer sings or whispers while playing harmonics, glissandi, tremolo, metal rod, and so on. Crumb's *Black Angels* (1970) for amplified string quartet uses both contact and acoustic microphones for balance and for the unique timbre alteration that electronics add to live performances.

Iannis Xenakis, long interested in the creation of new techniques, proves convincingly in *Metastasis* (1953–54) that sixty-one traditional instruments can compete successfully with electronic sound sources. Roman Haubenstock-Ramati, in his *Interpolation* (1958), utilizes an unmanipulated prerecorded tape made by the performer. This enables a single instrumentalist to

achieve ensemble effects using only one instrument as source. His 1961 *Liaisons* for vibraphone includes provisions for a performer-prepared tape begun six to ten seconds after the performance begins. The tape thus serves not as an electronic device, but as a tool to elicit combinations of instrumental tones and effects.

David Cope's *Margins* (1972) for cello, trumpet, percussion, and two pianos emphasizes the marginal aspects of each instrument. The composer explores equally the contrast and developmental possibilities of articulation and timbre. The tempo remains very slow throughout with the beat dividing into multifold groupings of often very quick and pointillistic imitations. Elsa Justel (b. 1944 in Mar del Plata, Argentina), in her work *Fy Mor* (1991), uses only the sounds of kitchen utensils and vocal sounds for unique effects.

Heinz Holliger's *Atembogen* contains many orchestral effects, most of which involve subtle nuances or shadings of breath or bow technique. Examples for winds include exhaling, inhaling, using voice, embouchure without tone, and whistle-tone. For strings, Holliger requires bow with over and under pressure, bowing the tailpiece, and *col legno*. *Atembogen* forms a series of large dramatic gestures based on a through-composed form. For example,

Figure 4.14. From George Crumb's *Songs, Drones, and Refrains of Death*. Copyright © 1968 by C.F. Peters Corporation. Used by permission.

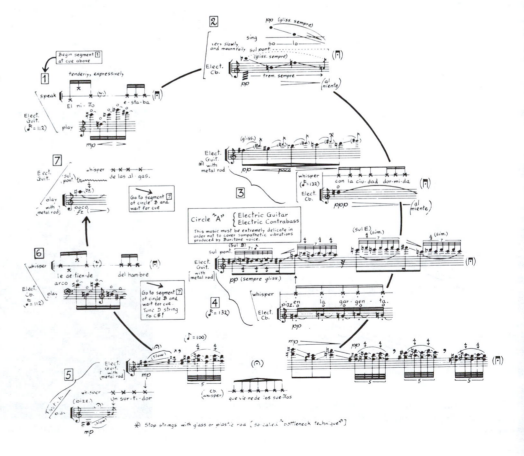

Atembogen's opening four seconds consists of bowing and blowing without producing sound. The work ends similarly with the orchestra slowly releasing bows and breaths from their instruments (Becker 1950; Pooler and Pierce 1973).

Ensembles devoted to performance of contemporary music have contributed significantly to the development of instrument exploration. Such groups commission, perform, and record new music and include the Contemporary Chamber Ensemble, Aeolian Chamber Players, Die Reihe Ensemble, Philadelphia Composers Forum, Kronos String Quartet, Cologne New Music Ensemble, MW 2 Ensemble, the Melos Ensemble, and the ISKRA ensemble, to name but a few. A large number of university-affiliated new music ensembles, consisting of faculty as well as students, also contribute to the growing repertoire of avant-garde music.

Since its 1992 debut at Carnegie Hall with a tribute to John Cage, the Orchestra of the S.E.M. Ensemble has become recognized as one of the foremost large scale ensembles dedicated to new music. Conducted by Petr Kotik, this ensemble has toured Europe performing works by composers such as John Cage, Morton Feldman, Christian Wolff, Alvin Lucier, Earle Brown, Edgard Varèse, Pauline Oliveros, and Maria de Alvear, among others.

Zeitgeist, a chamber ensemble committed to performing contemporary music and founded in 1977, has explored a wide variety of musical idioms, developing close ties with such avant-garde composers as John Cage, Terry Riley, La Monte Young, Frederic Rzewski, and Harold Budd, and pays special attention to nurturing younger composers. Zeitgeist has attempted to reforge links between contemporary composers and their audience—links that, in America at least, had been fractured by the academism of the postwar decades. Zeitgeist's distinctive instrumentation creates an extraordinary range of timbres and textures. Zeitgeist consists of artistic co-directors Heather Barringer and Jay Johnson (percussion), Thomas Linker (keyboards), Robert Samarotto (woodwinds), and executive co-director Lawrence Fuchsberg.

The First Avenue Ensemble, formed in 1982, is dedicated to expanding their art through improvisation, theater, extended instrument techniques, performance art, and the integration of advanced technologies with acoustic instruments. First Avenue has evolved a diverse sonic world characterized by the interplay of tonal, timbral, and textural elements and consists of William Kannar (double bass, computer), C. Bryan Rulon (synthesizers), and Matt Sullivan (oboe, English horn, and wind controller).

The Machine for Making Sense is a cooperative venture between five Australian sound artists. The "machine's" synthesis of the academic and indeterminate has achieved acclaim in Europe, the USA, and Australia as one of the most original groups devoted to contemporary performance. Machine for Making Sense explores distinctions between language, sound, and music, as well as code, sign, and meaning. Members of the ensemble include Jim Denley, saxophone and voice; Chris Mann, voice and text; Rik Rue, digital and analog samples and tape manipulation; Amanda Stewart, voice and text; and Stevie Wishart, violin, live electronics, hurdy-gurdy, and voice.

New Instruments

Transformations of traditional instruments represent only a part of the new sound sources for composers. Harry Partch, unlike Cage and Cowell, created new instruments rather than altering existing ones (though his first such instrument was an adapted viola). Partch's division of the octave into forty-three instead of twelve tones brought the need to create instruments capable of realizing his theoretical concepts (see his *Genesis of A New Music*, 1977). Except for his use of voice, almost all of his works employ original instruments (see Figure 4.16). Partch's *U.S. Highball: Account of Hobo Trip* (1943) and *Account of the Normandy Invasion by an American Glider Pilot* (1945, both early works) reflect his fascination with instruments (Johnston 1974; Partch 1968, 1977; Smith 1982). In *Revelation in the Courthouse Square* (1961), the visual—theatrical—elements become an integral (in his words: corporeal) part of the work. *And on the Seventh Day Petals Fell in Petaluma*, a 1964 work comprising studies in the form of twenty-three duets for *Delusion of the Fury* (1967), explores the harmonic and melodic possibilities of microtones based on his microtonal theories (his word for major is *Otonality*, for minor *Utonality*).

Many recent compositions have extended instrumental possibili-

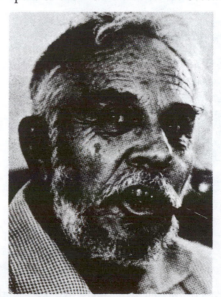

Figure 4.15.   Harry Partch.

Figure 4.16.   Various Partch instruments: a) Gourd Tree (1964) and Cone Tree (1965); b) Zymo-Xyl (1963); c) Mazda Marimba (1963); d) Chromelodeon I (1945–49); e) Bass Marimba (1951); f) Diamond Marimba (1946); g) Boo (1955–57); h) Surrogate Kithara (1953).

ties to anything that can be beaten, blown, or bowed, with each work demanding a new instrument for realization—even a jet engine, for example. Few of these instruments have achieved standardization, as their intrinsic theatrical value lies in their having a direct link to one work or composer.

Yoshima Wada has created a number of successful new wind instruments (see Figures 4.17 and 4.18) that, due to their large size, produce low sounds of soft dynamics often needing amplification. The KIVA Ensemble of the University of California at San Diego explores new instrumental resources (see Figure 4.19), often coupled with electronic amplification or modification. Arthur Frick has created a wide variety of new instruments (see Figure 4.20), many of which are mobile and often have comic effect.

Figure 4.17. Instrument by Yoshima Wada. Photo by Seiji Kakizaki.

Figure 4.18. Instruments by Yoshima Wada. Photo by Seiji Kakizaki.

Figure 4.19. KIVA performance instruments. Photo by Solomon (UCSD).

Figure 4.20. Instrument by Arthur Frick.

George Gonzalez and Peter Richards have built a *Wave Organ* on the bay in San Francisco that amplifies the sound of ocean waves entering into and retreating from large cement pipes. The audience places their ears near to one of several orifices through which both sound and air propagate. Different wave and weather conditions affect the types and dynamics of the sounds produced.

Robert Rutman creates giant instruments, often out of industrial scrap metals. His *steel cello*, for example, consists of a large sheet of steel twisted into a "C" shape with a single string strung from top to bottom. His *bow chimes* have a similar shape but are held in place by a bar.

New instruments require performers with open minds and virtuosity (Hopkin 1996). One could hardly expect as practiced and polished a performance on a new instrument as from an experienced violinist after intense study of a Beethoven concerto. One of two alternatives seems likely: a simple but fully notated score or a more freely improvised score whereby per-

formers substitute their own creativity for familiarity with the instrument. Douglas Leedy chooses the latter in *Usable Music I* (1968) for very small instruments with holes. This work depends almost exclusively on the use of graphic symbols to indicate performance instructions such as "blow" or "draw." This graphic representation requires less attention to exact rhythms and pitches. Robert Moran, in *Titus* (1968), has the score projected on an automobile, pictorially showing the performers' areas and amounts of activity (see Figure 4.21). Each of from five to fifteen performers, using contact microphones, files, hammers, and the like, move around and within the car, visually guided by the score.

Such works require increasing need for performer creativity (Banek and Scoville 1980). Once composers have granted shared responsibilities, it is not difficult to understand the motivation behind graphic or less exact notational systems. New instruments and techniques have evolved simultaneously with unique sounds, creating new and significant composer-performer relationships.

Figure 4.21. Score of Robert Moran's *Titus*. Permission granted by *Source: Music of the Avant Garde*. Composer Performer Edition, Davis, CA.

Other composers and artists involved in creating new musical instruments include Laurie Anderson (electronic tape-bow on violins); Christopher Charles Banta (large marimbas); Bob Bates (mechanical instruments and music machines); Harry Bertoia (sound sculptures); Jim Burton (sound installations); Ivor Darreg (large numbers of microtonal string, wind, and electronic instruments similar in scope to those of Harry Partch); Paul De Marinis (electronic modules); Richard Dunlap (nonconventional instruments for improvisation and theater presentation); Stephen Scott (large sound sculptures); Bruce Fier (architectural sound designs); Cris Forster (notably Chrysalis); Ron George (original percussion instruments and ensembles); Jonathan Glasier (notably his Harmonic Canon); Stephen Goodman (automatic music instruments); Jim Gordon (percussion synthesizers); Jim Hobart (percussion and steel-stringed instruments); Alzek Misheff (hot-air balloons containing portable electronic instruments); Max Neuhaus (sound installations); Jim Pomeroy (music boxes); Susan Rawcliffe (wind instruments); Tom Recchion (folk instruments from found objects); Prent Rodgers (electroacoustical instruments); Stephen von Huene (self-performing sound sculptures); Robert Wilhite (environments); and Richard Waters (notably the metal "waterphone"). More often than not, these composers/instrument builders also perform their instruments (Baschet and Baschet 1987; Boulanger 1986).

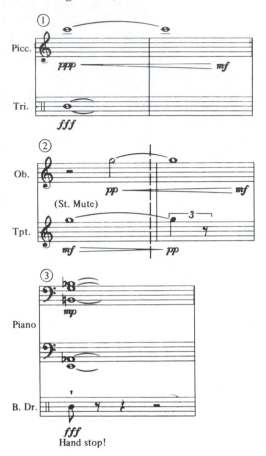

Figure 4.22.   Timbre modulations.

TIMBRE AND SPATIAL MODULATION

With an increasing awareness of the subtle timbres available from various instruments—muting, dynamics, attacks, and decays—comes the realization that many timbres overlap between those instruments. Figure 4.22 shows three such overlaps with new timbres resulting from the combinations. In the first example, a triangle initially masks a piccolo. The piccolo's slow crescendo then gradually modulates from the sound of the triangle. In the second example, a trumpet with straight mute slowly decays as the like-timbred oboe crescendos and so takes over. The effect is indicated by the intersecting vertical dotted line. At the beginning, only the trumpet is heard. At the vertical line, a subtle combination of the two instruments begins. Finally one hears only the oboe. Terms like *obet* or *trumboe* emphasize the significance of the truly "new" sound created by the modulation (Cope 1977). In the third example, a

bass drum masks the piano attack completely. However, as the piano rings out of the bass drum a unique effect occurs: the piano chord slowly decays after the hand-stopped percussion attack disappears.

Works effectively employing timbre modulation include *Sinfonia* (1968) by Luciano Berio, *Lontano* (1967) by György Ligeti, *Ancient Voices of Children* (1970) by George Crumb, and *Apotheosis of This Earth* (1971) by Karel Husa.

Physical spacing and placement of instruments can play important roles in creating antiphonal and directional timbre modulations (Brant 1967; Forsyth 1985; Junger and Feit 1986; Schwartz 1970). Gabrieli's eight- and twelve-part canzonas in the sixteenth century; Mozart's *Don Giovanni* in the eighteenth century; Berlioz's *Requiem* in the nineteenth century; and Berg's *Wozzeck*, Mahler's *Das Klagende Lied*, and Ives's *Symphony 4* in the twentieth century provide historical examples. Henry Brant's experiments with vertical, horizontal, and circular instrumental arrangements have created unique spatial music. In his "Space as an Essential Aspect of Musical Composition," Brant describes many of his experiments in performer arrangements for optimum directional, acoustical, and balance effectiveness (Childs and Schwartz 1967, pp. 223–42). The spatial composing technique of one of his works (*Voyage Four*, 1964) involves percussion and brass on stage, violins on one side balcony, violas and cellos on the other balcony, basses on floor level at the rear of the auditorium, with various woodwind instruments and a few string instruments on the two rear balconies. Three conductors combine to direct the performers, which include tuba, timpani, and chimes in the audience. Brant contends that, if composers realistically understand performance, each composed work should contain specific instructions for performer placement.

Brant discusses his views regarding spatial performance in an interview:

> The competition, from both living and dead composers, is too great for a solo piece; it's also too great for an ensemble that doesn't use spatial separation. What would I write? A string quartet? Besides, I think that particular combination is lopsided. For thirty years I've been trying to devise a rational string quartet; it should be one violin, one viola, one instrument that doesn't exist—a tenor violin, which I'm trying to develop—and cello. (Cagne and Caras 1982, p. 61)

Brant's *An American Requiem* utilizes spatial location of six widely separated instrumental groups and four separated single players including an optional voice. The principal ensemble, a group of sixteen woodwinds, performs on stage in a semicircle with their backs to the audience. The conductor faces the group at center stage. The horn, trumpet, and trombone sections stand in various locations in the hall along with the fifth section consisting of various bells including "pipe-chimes," the construction of which is described by the composer in the performance notes to the work. Two tubas join the brass in homorhythmic unison with single parts for pipe organ, voice, church bells (recorded on tape if necessary), and timpani.

An American Requiem consists of three sections. The first opens with the formative material of the work, a nine-note half-step cluster bordered on each side by whole steps. Each note of this cluster is homorhythmically paralleled by eight other instruments forming a mirror. This integration of melody and harmony continues throughout the work. Contrasting this dissonant music, the winds have a static triad characteristic of both the first and third sections. The quasi-pitched pipe-chimes add a surrealistic touch to the multi-leveled music. The second section develops the polyphony of the first section with contrasting flutters in the brass, trills in the percussion, and a carillon in hemiola with the rest of the ensemble. The third section returns to the triadic variations of the initial expository material.

Spatial modulation involves moving sounds from one point to another. For example, a large number of violins surrounding an audience could produce spatial modulation by having one violin play and then slowly share the same pitch with each violin in turn until the initially-playing violin's turn to play again. Works by Henry Brant, Donald Erb (*Fanfare for Brass Ensemble and Percussion*, 1971), and Cliff Crego (*Implosions*, 1971) employ this technique.

Many composers also use *combination tones* (Backus 1969; Slawson 1985; Winckel 1967). Figure 4.23 shows

that when two tones, one fixed and the other gliding, occur simultaneously, combination tones result. Differential (difference frequency between two pitches) and summational (sum frequency of two pitches) are the two basic types of combination tones. In Figure 4.23, the D signifies the primary difference tone and the thickness of line represents the acoustical impression of roughness (loudness). Composers such as Ligeti (e.g., *Lontano*) have attempted to create and control combination tones in their music. Variations in performance or acoustics can cause distortion or unsuccessful production, however. The Center for New Music and Audio Technologies (CNMAT) at the University of California at Berkeley investigates psychoacoustics including combination tones. Since performance affects the hearing process, with timbre (especially) and time influencing perception, a knowledge of psychoacoustics seems especially important. Figure 4.24 shows these psycho-

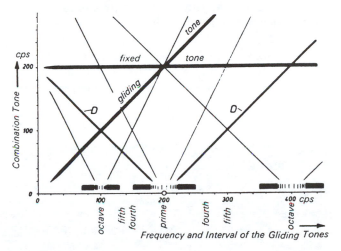

Figure 4.23. Combination tones.

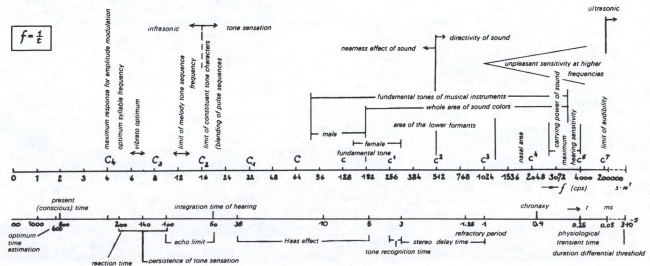

Figure 4.24. Psychoacoustical characteristics in terms of time and frequency. Permission granted by Dover Publications.

acoustical characteristics in time and frequency scale in rough limits of effectiveness.

Elliott Schwartz's *Elevator Music* (1967) accesses the acoustical, directional, and movement possibilities of a multi-story building (von Bekesy 1970; Schwartz 1970). Twelve floors of a building become the stationary stages for twenty-four performers while the audience rides elevators up and down through the constantly changing sonic environment. The small spaces around the elevators leak sound between the floors, providing an interesting aural overlay. The conductor, also the elevator operator, stops at certain floors and opens the elevator doors, while the performers on all floors continue to play regardless of the position of the elevator. The elevator occasionally stops at certain empty floors, as explicitly outlined in the score (Schwartz 1970). Recording of this work, and many of Brant's works, becomes virtually impossible, as space, movement, direction, and theater escape any possible accurate reproduction.

IRCAM (Institut de Recherche et Coordination Acoustique/Musique) in Paris continues to research ways in which sound propagates in physical spaces (Robson 1987). Figure 4.25 shows a diagram of the IRCAM installation, while Figure 4.26 presents a closer view of the Espace de Projection, a performance hall with variable acoustics. Figure 4.27 shows Pierre Boulez (director of the Center) and Gerard Buquet (tubist) in the space with variable shutters and flaps controllable by computers. The Center also houses computer and electronic music facilities.

NON-WESTERN INFLUENCES

For centuries, composers of mainstream Western European traditions have borrowed both stylistic flavors and actual folk materials from music of world cultures (Reck 1977). The list of works and composers includes Franz Liszt (*Hungarian Rhapsodies*), Georges Bizet (*Carmen*, 1875), Edouard Lalo (*Symphonie Espagnole*, 1874), Mikhail Glinka (*Spanish Overtures*) and Rimsky-Korsakov (*Capriccio on Spanish Themes*, 1887), to name just a few. Notable mainstream composers of this century include Claude Debussy (see chapter 1), Maurice Ravel (*Bolero*, 1928), Igor Stravinsky (use of Russian folk materials), Carlos Chavez (*Sinfonia india*, 1936), Heiter Villa-Lobos (*Bachianas Brasileiras*, 1930–45), and Silvestre Revueltas (*Cuauhnahuac*).

Colin McPhee (1901–64) studied the music and instruments of Bali, particularly Balinese gamelans, in the early 1930s. His style changed as a result, and such works as *Tabuh-Tabuhan* (1936) show considerable influence of the *gamelan gong kebyar* (a 20–25 member

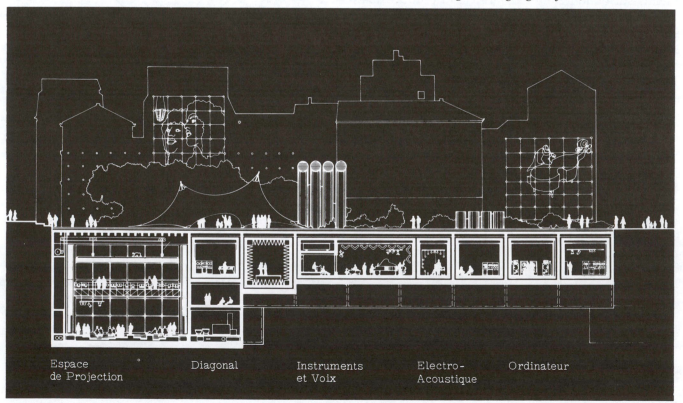

Espace   Diagonal   Instruments   Electro-   Ordinateur
de Projection   et Voix   Acoustique

Figure 4.25.   IRCAM.

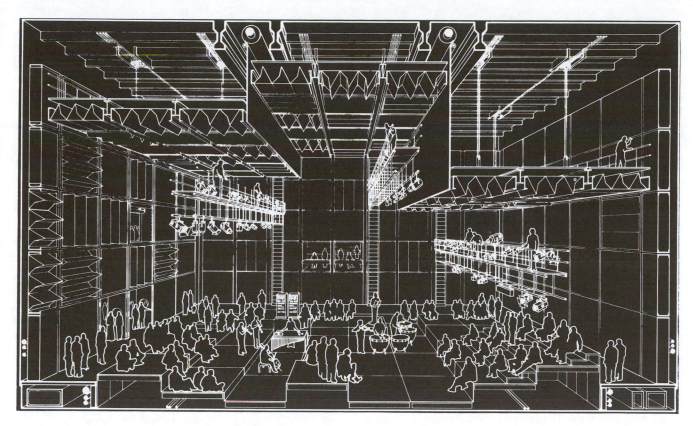

Figure 4.26. IRCAM *Espace de Projection*.

Figure 4.27. Pierre Boulez with Gerard Buquet in the *Espace de Projection*.

ensemble developed from the older *gamelan gong*). Alan Hovhaness (b. 1911) stylistically suggests the music of India and Armenia in his style rather than using quotation or folk instruments (see *Avak, The Healer*, 1946, and *Khaldis*, 1951). The works of Chou Wen-Chung (b. Chefoo, China, 1923), particularly *Soliloquy of a Bhiksuni*, and Oliver Messiaen (1908–1991), with the use of Indian talas (repeating rhythmic patterns), have been influenced by non-Western music.

A few contemporary composers use non-Western instruments in the ensembles performing their music. Lou Harrison (b. 1917), for example, has composed a variety of works utilizing gamelan-type instruments suggesting the kempul, bonang, saron, and gender of the Javanese gamelan as well as American folklike homemade ensembles of gamelan-like instruments (Lieberman and Miller 1998; Yates 1959). Harrison's *Pacifika Rondo* (1963), for a chamber orchestra of Western and Asian instruments, and *Concerto in Slendro* (1961) for violin, celesta, and percussion orchestra, have strong gamelan influence.

Harry Partch's instruments (discussed earlier) show influences of Hindu, African, and folk-American sources. John Cage's prepared piano works of the 1930s and 1940s (particularly the *Sonatas and Interludes* of 1948) also show influences of the gamelan style.

Quotation and stylistic integration of non-Western traditional music are evident in the works of David Cope (b. 1941). His works include Navajo Indian quotation and influence, particularly *Arena* (1974), *Rituals* (1976), and *The Way* (1981), a part of the score to the former appearing in chapter 7. Ruth Lomon's *Five Ceremonial Masks* for piano (1980) also shows Navajo influence. David Ward-Steinman's *Rituals for Dancers*

Figure 4.28. Lou Harrison at USC during 1978. Photo by Betty Freeman.

and Musicians (1936) and *The Tale of Issoumbochi*, Ravi Shankar's (b. 1920) *Concerto for Sitar and Orchestra*, David Fanshawe's (b. 1942) *African Sanctus*, Roy Travis's (b. 1922) *Switched-On Ashanti for Flutes, African Instruments, and Tape* (1933), and *African Sonata for Piano* (1966) represent actual style assimilations.

The styles of some composers depend on and developed from non-Western sources (Chou 1974). Terry Riley's (b. 1935) *In C* (1964), for example, derives from the *jor* section of an Indian raga (from the Sanskrit root *ranja*, "to color, to tinge"), most notably the slow process of variation by textural overlay. Similarly, the works of Steve Reich (b. 1936), especially *Drumming* (1971) and *Four Organs* (1970), show Eastern influence, as does *Einstein on the Beach* by Philip Glass (b. 1937).

The ritual elements of some non-Western music have influenced a number of avant-garde composers, including Pauline Oliveros (b. 1932), Jon Gibson (b. 1940), and Alvin Lucier (b. 1931). Each of these composers has developed works built on ritual-like elements often taken from Indian, Zen, or Asian concepts. Lucier's *Queen of the South* (1972) takes its title from the mystical personality in alchemy known as *Sapientia Dei* (connected with the south wind). This work bears strong resemblance to certain ritual Navajo sand painting techniques:

> The performers sing into microphones or produce sound with oscillators. By means of electromagnetic transducers, large steel plates which are suspended horizontally near the floor are made to vibrate with these sounds. The vibrational patterns are made visible by sand and other granular materials which the performers sprinkle onto these plates. As they change the pitches of their sounds the granular images on the plates shift from one pattern to another. The performers, each with their own plate, are located throughout the performance space—ideally it is a gallery rather than a traditional proscenium theatre. The spectators move freely around these sonically and visually vibrating islands and choose their own degree of involvement with the ritual. (Mumma 1974)

MICROTONES AND TUNING SYSTEMS

The overtone series, first discussed in chapter 1, provides a logical source for creating tuning systems (Backus 1969). Unfortunately, as Pythagoras discovered in the fourth century B.C., this series is infinite and thus provides an infinite number of possibilities. Equal temperament was created to resolve such issues. Pianos currently use a form of equal tempera-

Figure 4.29. Lou Harrison with William Colvig showing a number of instruments built by either or both of these builder/composers. Photo by Betty Freeman.

ment. Unfortunately, equal temperament does not produce pure intervals as relates to their first occurrence in the overtone series. For this reason, composers have devised a number of useful methods for working around these problems.

Microtones result from intonational variations. Orchestral performers play with a wide variety of tunings. Tuning systems, on the other hand, project a limited number of divisions of the octave. Mozart, for example, worked and taught with a 17-note scale, identifying his scale notes through spelling (e.g., C♯ and D♭ were quite differently tuned, the first being higher).

The overtone series (see Figure 2.1) can help to understand tuning in general. The frequency (vibrations per second) of a pitch in this series can be determined by the quotient of any two given notes when the frequency of one of the notes is known. For example, if the frequency of a low C is 100 cycles per second, then the frequency of the C above this fundamental is 200 cycles per second (or 2/1 * 100). The G a fifth above this second note then becomes 3/2 of 200 or 300 cycles per second. To calculate the frequency of a pitch below a known frequency requires that the ratio be inverted. For example, if the third note of the series is 300 then the second note becomes 2/3 of 300 or 200.

Designating the frequency of a pitch as n, the formulae for the octave, fifth, and third become 2n, 3/2n, and 5/4n respectively. Larger intervals then are computed by multiplying their respective fractions. For example, the twelfth (interval between the first and third partials) is calculated as 3/2 * 2/1 (i.e., the ratio for the fifth times the ratio for the octave). Hence, the twelfth is 6/2 * 100 or 300. While this is more simply produced by the previous method, this newer math enables us to calculate other complex intervals. For example, the interval of the major seventh could be calculated as a combination of the 3/2 ratio of a fifth and the 5/4 ratio of the major third. Multiplying these fractions gives us 15/8, or precisely the ratio provided by the partials of C, two octaves above the fundamental, and B, a major seventh above that.

The ratios for a C major scale can be translated to whole numbers representing frequency by beginning on 24 since all of the denominators of these ratios divide evenly into that number. Each of these frequencies results from multiplying the ratio above times the integer 24 (i.e., 9/8 * 24 = 27). The ratios below the frequencies here represent the intervals between the various scale degrees. This tuning produces pure triads on the first (tonic), fourth (subdominant), and fifth (dominant) scale degrees since 24/30/36, 32/40/48, and 36/45/54 all have the ratio of 4:5:6. Tuning systems based on the overtone series are called *just*. Just tuning systems usually calculate intervals based on the three elementary intervals—the octave, the fifth, and the third.

As can be readily seen, however, a number of anomalies exist in this approach. First, all of the perfect fifths in the last example can be reduced to 3/2 except one: D-A (40/27). This creates a so-called "dissonant fifth" compared to the others. Also, the scale has two different ratios for the major second as found by reducing their ratios: 9/8 (C-D, F-G, and A-B) and 10/9 (D-E and G-A). This difference is called the *syntonic* comma. Modulation to keys other than C is impossible as the interval ratios become very different in new keys respective to the new scale degrees. For example, G major has the ratios of its first three notes (G-A-B) reversed from those of C major. Projecting this process to account for chromaticism produces a nearly infinite number of possibilities.

Equal temperament attempts to account for these anomalies by dividing the octave into twelve equal parts. This produces vague approximations of just-intoned intervals. Many believe that the differences between just and equal temperaments are inaudible. Others find the differences between the two important and fundamental. Calculating equal-tempered intervals follows the formula of $i^{12} = 2$ where i equals the interval of a minor second (i.e., 12 minor seconds in the octave [2]). This equation is more properly shown as $i = \sqrt[12]{2}$ or 1.05946. To find the interval of a minor second above C = 24 involves multiplying 24 * 1.05946 or 24.42704. To find the D above this equates to 24 * 1.05946 * 1.05946 or 26.938931798, and so on.

Another way of measuring distances between equal-tempered half-steps involves a unit of measurement called the *cent*. A cent is 1/100th of an equal-tempered half-step. Each half-step therefore equals 100 cents and an octave encompasses 1200 cents. Cents are useful for comparing tuning systems and their various intervals. For example, the equal-tempered major third (400 cents) is 14 cents higher than the just major third (5/4 or 386 cents). The equal-tempered fifth, however, at 700 cents, is just 2 cents flatter than the just perfect fifth (702). For the basic intervals of the equal and just tuning systems, interval ratios are converted into cents following the formula c = 1200/log 2 * log i. Cents are also helpful in that they present a useful way to discuss and evolve other approaches to tuning.

Tuning based on microtonal divisions dates from the time of the Greeks (enharmonic genus) and interest in them revived in the Renaissance with Nicolo Vicentino and his *archicembalo* and *archiorgano*. Gerhardus Mercator's (sixteenth century) fifty-three tones per octave scale represents another particularly notable example. Alois Hába (1893–1972) constructed a quarter-tone piano in the early 1920s and employed a sixth-tone system in the late 1930s. Charles Ives (1874–1954) experimented with microtones in his *Three Quarter Tone Pieces* (1918?) for two pianos tuned a quarter tone apart. Harry Partch (1901–74), in the process of working with microtones (an acoustical division of the octave into 43 tones), developed new instruments nec-

essary for the realization of his experiments. He worked more in isolation than Hába, but has received much attention in the past few years. Composers such as Teo Macero, Calvin Hamilton, and Donald Lybbert have continued similar experimentation.

Quarter tones were used sparsely by Bartók (especially in his *Violin Concerto*, 1938) and Milhaud in the late 1930s and 1940s. The use of twenty-four or more divisions of the octave requires significant revision of the performance techniques on traditional instruments, creation of new or revised systems of notation, and increasingly complex harmonic and melodic vocabularies (Balzano 1980, 1986; Partch 1973).

Julian Carrillo in *The Thirteenth Sound* divides the octave into ninety-five different pitches, numbering each pitch at the end of the stem where one ordinarily would find a note head (Carrillo 1972, p. 64). Harry Partch's forty-three-note approach seems much freer. Many of Partch's instruments have a virtually infinite variety of tunings (Partch 1973). Most of these approaches, however, seem doomed to either extremely limited usage or complete neglect (Boatwright 1965). Theorists and composers who continue to search for new systems often fail to realize that the devising of any such system produces little better than the system in current use. Flexibility of tuning and intonation produce the most valuable results. Composers such as Ben Johnston, Lou Harrison, James Tenney, Kenneth Gaburo, and many others have composed sections, movements, or works to multiple sets of intonations.

Ben Johnston's *Fourth String Quartet* uses a varying number of proportional octave divisions from five to twenty-two, thus creating a flexible set of intonations. Johnston has written extensively on microtonal music and in writing about his *Fourth String Quartet* he sums up its complexity in a few concise words:

> Over the whole of the historical period of instrumental music, Western music has based itself upon an acoustical lie. In our time this lie—that the normal musical ear hears twelve equal intervals within the span of an octave—has led to the impoverishment of pitch usage in our music. In our frustration at the complex means it takes to wrest yet a few more permutations from a closed system, we have attempted the abandonment of all systems, forgetting that we need never have closed our system. (Johnston 1974)

Johnston further describes his version of tuning history in his "How to Cook an Albatross": "In our laziness, when we changed over to the twelve-tone system, we just took the pitches of the previous music as though we were moving into a furnished apartment and had no time to even take the pictures off the wall. What excuse?" (Johnston 1970, p. 65).

The potential of microtones is limited only by the ability of composers to hear musical ideas, the notation to express these ideas (see Appendix III), and performers to accurately perform the results (Orga 1968).

In Javanese music, the *gamelan* uses many instruments with varied tuning systems. The *gambang* (xylophone), *gender*, *saron*, *demoeng*, and *bonang* (set of gongs) use either the *slendro* or the *pelog* tuning system. The slendro consists of wide intervals and the pelog of narrower steps. The slendro resembles a pentatonic scale consisting of five nearly equal intervals of 240 cents. In contrast, pelog tuning consists of two conjunct tetrachords each of which is divided (approximately) into a half-step and a major third, similar to ancient Greek tunings. The two thirds are filled in by two additional tones creating a septatonic scale. These two tuning systems provide the basis for numerous variants that help give gamelan music its unique musical flavor.

Many Pacific Rim composers have imitated such tuning systems and approaches to music. Lou Harrison, for example, has created what he terms the American Gamelan, where his own versions of instruments of Southeast Asian music substitute in gamelans for which he composes. Such gamelans have produced a number of serious protagonists and composers including Jody Diamond, Vincent McDermott, Daniel Schmidt, Jarrad Powell, Jim Madara, Daniel Goode, David Demnitz, Jeff Morris, Shin Nakamura, and Laura Liben.

VECTORAL ANALYSIS
PETER MAXWELL DAVIES:
EIGHT SONGS FOR A MAD KING

(For information on vectoral analysis and procedures see Preface.)

1. Historical Background: Peter Maxwell Davies was born in Manchester, England in 1934 and studied in England at the Royal College of Music and in America at Princeton University with Roger Sessions (Griffith 1982). He co-founded the Fires of London (avantgarde chamber ensemble; formerly the Pierrot Players). Davies's music often includes quotations, new techniques on traditional instruments, and a kind of stylistic heterophony (Pruslin 1979). His better known works include *Miss Donnithorne's Maggot* (1974), *Vesalii Icones* (1970), and *Dark Angels* (1974), all for chamber ensembles of various makeup.

In an interview with Paul Griffiths, Davies remarks:

> You can be thinking of something entirely different, and then you tune into a process that's going on somewhere. It might be a thematic idea, or a purely structural idea, with its main pivots: a big time span, with departure points and arrival points, but you don't know what's between them. I suspect that before you write down anything on paper, you've probably got, with a big work like a symphony, some small ideas and a big design. Then you start thinking through things in terms of the ideas going into the design, and then you start sketching. I'm not a perfectionist in the way that Boulez and Stockhausen are. Once a piece is done it's part of the past . . . (Griffiths 1985)

2. Overview: *Eight Songs for a Mad King* was first performed on April 22, 1969, in London by Roy Hart (voice) and the Pierrot Players conducted by the composer. The eight songs are based on texts created by Randolph Stow suggested by a miniature mechanical organ playing eight tunes, once the property of King George III.

> One imagined the King, in his purple flannel dressing-gown and ermine night-cap, struggling to teach birds to make the music which he could so rarely torture out of his flute and harpsichord. Or trying to sing with them, in that ravaged voice, made almost inhuman by day-long soliloquies, which once murdered Handel for Fanny Burney's entertainment. There were echoes of the story of the Emperor's nightingale. But this Emperor was mad; and at times he knew it, and wept. (Davies 1969)

Each of the eight songs has a separate title with texts in Old English. The notation is metriportional; that is, at times the composer notates meter and at other times the bar-line disappears producing a freer, time-proportionate-to-space notation.

The forms of each of the movements develop intrinsically from the text and do not follow simple AB or ABA models. Humorous and exaggerated gestures appear profusely throughout the songs. At times these gestures become so blatant as to create caricatures.

3. Orchestration Techniques: The instrumentation for *Eight Songs* includes flute (doubling piccolo), clarinet, piano (doubling harpsichord and dulcimer), violin, cello, and a single percussionist who plays twenty-five different instruments including crow call, steel bars, toy bird calls, foot cymbals, railway whistle, Christmas-type jingle bells, chains, and small ratchet. The large number of instrumental effects throughout the score includes multiphonics for voice, clarinet, and flute; tremolo, especially in the voice; use of inside-piano techniques; and vocal effects (breath only, glissandi, screams, harmonics, wide vibrato, etc.). Figure

4.31 shows a number of these effects and the notation the composer uses in his autograph score. This example demonstrates proportional notation, multiphonics, and vertical lines that Davies uses to maintain simultaneous attacks.

Aside from unusual techniques and instruments, Davies also incorporates extreme ranges in all instru-ments, especially in the voice. In Figure 4.31, for example, the voice part covers 3 1/2 octaves (the range eventually covers over five octaves).

Eight Songs for a Mad King also calls for four of the performers (flute, clarinet, violin, and cello) to be placed in large cages on stage, adding a theatrical element to performances. Figure 4.32 shows a photograph of the author's own performance of this work (note the cellist in a large rope cage behind the "king").

Davies comments on the instrumental aspects of the piece:

> The flute, clarinet, violin, and cello, as well as having their usual accompanimental functions in this work, also represent on one level, the bullfinches the King was trying to teach to sing . . . In some ways, I regard the work as a collection of musical objects borrowed from many sources, functioning as musical "stage props" around which the reciter's part weaves, lighting them from extraordinary angles, and throwing grotesque and distorted shadows from them, giving the musical objects an unexpected and sometimes sinister significance . . . The climax of the work is the end of No. 7, where the King snatches the violin through the bars of the player's cage and breaks it. This is not just the killing of a bullfinch—it is a giving-in to insan-

Figure 4.30. Peter Maxwell Davies. Photo by Keith McMillan. Permission by Boosey & Hawkes, Ltd., London.

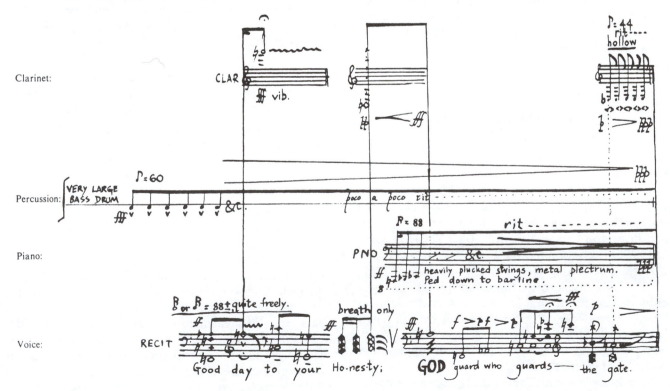

Figure 4.31. Bottom system of page 2 of Peter Maxwell Davies's *Eight Songs for a Mad King*. Examples of instrument exploration. Permission granted by Boosey & Hawkes, Ltd., London.

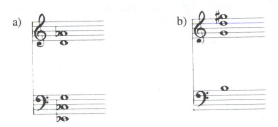

Figure 4.33. Two vertical models from *Eight Songs for a Mad King.*

Figure 4.32.   David Cope performing *Eight Songs for a Mad King* by Peter Maxwell Davies.

ity, and a ritual murder by the King of a part of himself, after which, at the beginning of 8, he can announce his own death. (Davies 1969)

4. Basic Techniques: Davies hybridizes various new techniques in a dramatic and contrasting set of songs. Neotonal—almost impressionistic at times—chromatic techniques contrast a full-blown tonality created by association with one or more of the many quotes present in the work, particularly from Handel's *Messiah*. Often the pitches chosen cloud the harsh timbres. Davies's inconsistencies are integral to his style in this work.

5. Vertical Models: Aside from the quotes and the various noise sections where pitch has little consequence, the harmonies seem based on a highly chromatic set of interval explorations not unlike triadically based sonorities, particularly in the fifth and third songs. Figure 4.33a shows a chord derived primarily from fifths (perfect, augmented, diminished), while Figure 4.33b forms a triad (G major) with an added minor ninth.

6. Horizontal Models: As seen in Figure 4.31, the vocal melody is characterized by wide leaps and elements of harsh dramatic multiphonics. Most of the nonquoted material irrevocably owes its shape to the text and text meaning.

7. Style: In *Eight Songs for a Mad King,* Davies has created a dynamic and dramatic work fashioned around a mad king whose love/hate relationship with birds abounds. Characteristically, Davies creates a "mad" style replete with quotations, bird imitations, new instrumental techniques, flexible notations, extreme dynamic and timbral contrasts, chromatic yet somewhat triadically based harmonic systems, and word-painting. This results in a tight fabric of associative songs highly steeped in new instrumental techniques.

This work compares favorably with the dramatic effect of Penderecki's *Capriccio* in the vectoral analysis of chapter 3 and to some degree with the Glass opera *Einstein on the Beach* presented in chapter 9. The quotation and free chromatic content argue directly with the works in chapters 2 and 8 where the music depends on rigorously prescribed rules of compositional structure.

TOM EVERETT: AN INTERVIEW WITH HENRY BRANT

Tom Everett produced a number of interviews for *The Composer Magazine* as well as a series called "Questions and Answers" where he would pose questions and mail them to various composers. These composers had no idea how other composers responded to the same set of questions and thus the results, when interlaced together, often were quite striking. Note how Brant's comments relate to Pederecki's views in the last chapter's interview.

Everett: What is your reaction to the fact that Polish composer Krzysztof Penderecki was commissioned to write an opera for the American Bicentennial?

Brant: I can imagine two possibilities. One of them is that our U.S. view of musical creation is so highly democratic, that we make no distinction between American and foreign composers, but choose the one who's most gifted whether he's American or not, a citizen or not, a visitor or not. Another possibility, which I fear may be the actual one, is that there's still an American tendency to look with some contempt on our domestic products in concert music and opera and to assume that a native-born American trained here is automatically inferior to a top flight European. I'm afraid that may be the more serious possibility although I do hope not. What do you think?

Everett: Possibly they feel there is not an American composer that would bring in publicity or world-wide acceptance of a new work.

Brant: Well, in that case the assumption seems to be that an opera by a European is superior to one by an American in terms of the publicity it can generate. Suppose that the situation were reversed, with the Polish government considering an opera to commemorate the twentieth Anniversary of the New Polish Revolution; does it seem likely that their democratic principles would extend so far as to find that a gifted American possesses musical powers so superlative as to outweigh the talents of the best Polish composers?

Everett: Have you written in the opera medium?

Brant: Yes, I've written one. I expect to begin work on another in the very near future. My "first" opera, *Grand Universal Circus*, is an effort to introduce into opera the space ideas that I use in my concert music, which means not only different kinds of music heard simultaneously from specific different places in the theatre, but also highly contrasted dramatic situations similarly spaced out. One advantage of this is that plot can be dispensed with to some extent, and replaced by the simultaneous contrasted or contradictory subject-matter. I would not attempt this spatial montage method if story-line or logical dramatic sequence were present, but I'm much less interested in story-line than in a kind of theatre ritual. I'm sure that the spatial montage procedures will be carried much further in my next opera.

Everett: When you write a large work does it help you to know what hall it is going to be performed in? Wouldn't that affect what you can do and how you conceive the piece?

Brant: Yes, always. I begin by checking out the first hall where the projected new work is going to be performed.

Everett: Then do you adapt a work for another setting?

Brant: It has to be workable in almost any hall, and without major alterations in my basic spatial plan for the location of the performers. In my initial plans I always think of possible adaptions of the spatial arrangements and it's been very rare that any hall has been spatially unadaptable to my music. Avery Fisher Hall in New York, for example, would be a very difficult place for any spatial piece of mine because the throw from back to front is so vast that sounds proceeding from different parts of the hall reach the audience at different times. My *Voyage 4* was written for Woolsey Hall at Yale University and requires deep balconies running the entire length of the side walls plus a large rear balcony. This layout does not exist every-

where, which limits the performances of this piece. Some of the fine old halls and churches in Boston, with their deep continuous balconies, would be ideally suited to my space music.

Everett: Are you interested in having your works published, made available in print?

Brant: Some are.

Everett: I'm just thinking of the problem you would have if you're constantly reworking or revising a work to the situation; publishers would be reluctant to put it in a final print.

Brant: All my musical material is fully notated and in final form. That isn't to be changed. It's only the location of the performing forces and the separation between them where adaptions must be made, and occasionally in dynamics. If for instance, something for a few instruments with low dynamic markings is played in a vast space it would be only realistic in performing it to use higher dynamic levels. That's occasionally necessary, but as a rule not. There are very few occasions where I've had to do it.

Everett: Many of your pieces are concerned with spatial location, and so forth, of the players and music comes from many directions. How did you develop this sense; was it through trial and error? Did you study acoustics and do you experiment with every piece you write? Just how did you become interested in this and find certain solutions to problems you had?

Brant: About 1950, I was writing a kind of music that was polyphonically as complex as I could make it. I wanted to have a lot going on, with much simultaneous and highly contrasted material, and it seemed that I couldn't pile on much more without producing a confused amalgam, impossible to keep track of in its details, where separate linear constituents would collide over the same octave and get in each other's way. I didn't know how to make such polyphonic complexity intelligible and was unwilling to accept a less dense polyphony as a solution.

About this time, when I was teaching at Juilliard, I heard for the first time some Gabrieli canzonas with the choirs properly spaced at the back and front of the hall, and then I performed Ives' *Unanswered Question*, spacing the three elements as far apart as possible. Shortly afterward in Paris, I heard the Berlioz *Requiem* at the Invalides with the spacings that he intended. All these experiences together pointed to a clear solution for my dense polyphony—namely, a controlled use of spatial resources. I didn't write the first multi-spatial piece, it was composed in 1952 by a former student of mine, Teo Macero. He heard the same spatial music that I had and he suggested to me a piece for five jazz groups, all spaced widely apart in the hall, to include improvisation as well as written material. It's a remarkable piece and quite neglected. He composed this work, *Areas*, in early 1952, before I wrote my first spatial piece *Antiphony I* later the same year. In *Antiphony I* I worked out the main spatial procedures which have guided my subsequent work, and the acoustical assumptions underlying *Antiphony I* have since been confirmed by repeated experiment. The first is that the wider the distance between the performing groups, the less influence they have on each other, especially in terms of harmony. This should be obvious, something any musician can try for himself, but what musicians find workable by trial and error under practical conditions later proves to be scientifically accountable in acoustical terms. Such discoveries can also be codified in theoretical form, and that is the usual history of all musical discoveries. First, musicians try them and find out practically how they work, then acousticians account for this workability in scientific terms and theorists codify procedures.

What I'm doing spatially is now in the stage of practical trial to find out what works easily and unmistakably; if it doesn't work I'm not interested in the theory, the acoustics or anything else. My assumptions are simple and obvious, perhaps so much so that many musicians would consider them too infantile to bother with. For example, if you want two instruments to sound in the closest possible relationship, you must place the two performers as close together as possible. They can then play more exactly in rhythm together if that's your intention, and more exactly in tune, and more closely in harmonic relationship. If you want them unrelated in these respects, then separate them as much as possible. The separation device led to a surprising conclusion, many times verified, which is that the influence that the separated constituents have over each other is so much canceled out that the result, for practical purposes, is as though each were playing in a different octave range. You can write, then, highly contrasted textures freely over the same octave and they will appear to "pass" each other without harmonic collision, just as though they were written in different octave registers. This means that the amount of polyphonic or heterophonic material you can crowd into the seven octaves that are available to us is immensely more if the participating constituents are physically widely separated than if all were situated in the same location, such as the stage area. This phenomenon is out of the speculation stage; anyone may try it and will be sure to get a similar result.

Another spatial device originates, I believe, in Ives' *Unanswered Question*. He assigns not only particular tone quality, but also a specific, highly contrasted kind of music, to each particular location in the hall, permitting no change in the character of the music proceeding from any given location. This procedure is the opposite of Renaissance antiphony, where groups were likewise stationed in different locations, but all stated the same or similar material, usually one group at a time, and sometimes two or more simultaneously. Each group by itself usually presents four-, five- or six-part polyphony. The combining of two groups will thus result in eight or more polyphonic parts, and twelve or more when three groups combine. When the groups are widely separated, as they should be, the time-lag which exists in many halls and churches makes it almost impossible to get exact rhythmic coordination between two, three or four separated groups, and the result is frequently an unintended montage of diatonic near-polytonality.

In this connection, Leopold Stokowski told me that some years ago he obtained permission, after much difficulty, to perform Gabrieli's canzonas at St. Mark's Church in Venice (the church where Gabrieli worked), and that immediately the most complicated passages for the separated groups in combination became acoustically perfectly easy and clear, the ensembles coordinating perfectly without any special effort. I find this a convincing indication that these Gabrieli canzonas must have been specially written for the specific spaces of St. Mark's Church. It would accordingly have been entirely practical for Gabrieli to have written his twelve-part polyphony for combined separated groups if they could thus be so easily and clearly coordinated. But nowadays one finds very few places where this is possible. This problem was brilliantly solved by Ives, with his conception of separated groups, each in itself rhythmically controlled, but so planned as to dispense with overall rhythmic coordination. In 1950, when I began work along these lines, if you were to write for two groups that didn't keep together rhythmically, it was looked upon as a rather bold and dangerous idea. (This was before the word "aleatoric" was known.) But aleatoric is not the right term here, because there is scarcely any element of chance involved and no improvisation at all. It is simply that a certain amount of leeway, within well-defined limits, is permitted in the rhythmic relationships between the separated groups. Thus, time-lag present in many halls can become an advantage, if several simultaneous tempos are set up, each accurate in itself, but uncoordinated in the aggregate. Rhythmic relationships, of course, can be controlled in lots of other ways, but the first thing is to give up the idea of absolute all-over rhythmic coordination between all the separated groups.

Some of my contemporaries take the spatial dimension into account, but consider its use optional, and prescribe only minimal distances between the groups. Some supply directions to separate the groups "if convenient." That to me is like saying "play C if convenient, if not, play C♯ or some other pitch." If the separation is really necessary for musical reasons, then it is mandatory and it must be emphatic, with maximum distances prescribed. Separations between soloists or small groups placed at opposite sides of the stage are not emphatically perceived (aurally) by the audience unless the stage is very wide, at least 60 feet across, and then only if there are no other performers in the middle of the stage between the separated groups on each side. But for real spatial impact on the audience, the distances between groups must be maximal, as for instance between the stage and the back of the hall. Maximum vertical separations, as between the ceiling area and the floor level of the lowest seats, are likewise emphatic in their spatial impact, and should be used to enhance spatial effect whenever available.

In the matter of vertical spacing one of my favorite questions is this: you have written a duet for piccolo and bass tuba, the lines entirely unrelated, and requiring no rhythmic coordination. You are to position one instrument in the ceiling and the other in the basement. What is your choice? To me it's obvious that the piccolo goes in the ceiling where it will appear to be even higher in pitch than its actual notes, and the tuba in the basement will seem even lower-pitched than it actually is. But often the first reaction of colleagues, before making the experiment, has been, "wouldn't it be interesting to place the piccolo low and the tuba high?" For me that would be comparable to whatever interest might result from playing a wind instrument standing on your head or singing in that position, but I find this sort of speculation a mere interesting caprice. It's not the kind of thing that I'm looking for, which is a norm for everyday practice; like the length and attack of a note. In other words, I am seeking new but normal and natural procedures.

Everett: Do you find that often musicians are reluctant to go through the physical movement that your music requires? Are they reluctant to actually move to another part of the auditorium,

or that they have been rehearsing the piece without the proper spatial dimensions?

Brant: Occasionally what happens is that conductors make the mistake of doing the first reading with all the groups rehearsing at once and sometimes they go so far as to say "Let's have it together on the stage just so we can get an idea of how the thing goes, and then spread out." That's absolutely disastrous because music which is written with specifically planned spatial arrangements becomes total chaos when played from a single location. The most efficient, time-and-energy-saving procedure is to rehearse each group first in a separate room, then combine them in the hall in exactly the locations to which they will be assigned at the concert. As far as the individual musicians are concerned, they are sometimes initially disconcerted by the distances between groups, since in accordance with their traditional training they strain to hear all the parts. Once they understand that precision in their individual efforts is as important as in any music, and that the spaces between groups actually increases the distinctness in the projection of what they are playing, the musicians are most often quick to assist and cooperate in the spatial procedures prescribed.

Everett: That's right. But the reasoning is sound from a conductor's standpoint, to possibly want to rehearse that way. It shows they don't have a true understanding of the music. For ensemble purposes, that sounds reasonable to pull everyone together so that you don't have the problem of these spatial effects.

Brant: The way my pieces are written, any group can be easily rehearsed by itself because it doesn't depend on the other ones at all either for musical completeness or for coordination. Seldom more than an hour is necessary for the rehearsal of any one group. At that point, everything will generally go without difficulty when all are assembled in their proper locations in the large hall, usually with no more than one or two run-throughs with perhaps a few stops now and then. In large halls a P.A. system is a practical aid at the full rehearsals, so that the conductor can communicate easily with distant musicians or sub-conductors. Sometimes performers ask me whether accurate intonation and precise rhythm are important, or whether approximate playing will sound just as well in spatial music. When assured that fine detail makes just as much difference in spatial music as in any other kind, because in spatial setups distance and position will more intensely identify what is coming from each direction, musicians are nearly always ready to do their best.

Chapter 5

INDETERMINACY

IMPROVISATION

Baroque figured bass and the classical concerto cadenza represent two examples of improvisation in traditional music. The figured bass typically provides only bass notes and short-hand numbers for intervals occurring above the bass. The figured bass allows performers the creative possibility of improvising and developing rhythmic and melodic fragments and motives. Performances, therefore, are predictable only within certain limits. Cadenzas, up to the late eighteenth century, were rarely written out in detail, giving performers the opportunity to improvise in a manner best suited to their own particular talents. Donald Erb refers to the latter in remarks about his own *Concerto for Percussion and Orchestra* (1966):

> The work is cast in the traditional concerto format of three movements. The solo part is in the eighteenth and nineteenth century virtuoso tradition. The cadenzas in the second and, especially, the third movements harken back to the eighteenth century tradition of having the performer improvise much or all of the cadenza. A variation on this idea was used in the first movement, where instead of having the soloist improvise a cadenza I had the entire orchestra, other than the soloist, improvise it. (Erb 1966, p. 1)

It seems logical for composers, rather than refusing to admit the improvisational aspects of music, to use improvisation to their advantage.

Allan Bryant states that improvisation is "Similar to free jazz, oriental and African music, things which are impossible to write out" (Bryant 1968, p. 26) and "Free, wild music and ideas that wouldn't come about with single composers working alone" (Bryant 1968, p. 24). Foss adds: "Cardew is right to worry about ethics of improvisation. It needs it. Improvisation: one plays what one already knows" (Foss 1968, p. 17).

Contemporary improvisation has its roots in jazz with such artists as Miles Davis (e.g., *Bitch's Brew*), the Modern Jazz Quartet, John Coltrane, Albert Ayler, Denny Zeitlin, Pharoah Sanders, Coleman Hawkins, Django Rheinhardt, Lenny Tristano, Ornette Coleman, Don Cherry, Eric Dolphy, Freddie Hubbard, Scott LaFaro, Charlie Haden, Billy Higgins, and Ed Blackwell (Logon 1975; Schuller 1968). Cecil Taylor (first with Steve Lacy and Buell Neidlinger, later with Bill Barron and Ted Curson) was also an important pioneer. Taylor's keyboard skills and intense energy produced imaginative improvisations. More recently George Lewis, Anthony Braxton, Sun Ra, and the Art Ensemble of Chicago have created richly improvised performances and albums.

A number of contemporary composers associated with improvisation have been actively involved in jazz, particularly third-stream composers such as Gunther Schuller. Much contemporary improvisation in the avant-garde, however, originated from the performers' inability to accurately realize the complexities of recent music. Composers, perhaps out of frustration, perhaps because the result was the same or better, chose to allow certain freedom in performance. Luciano Berio, for example, in his *Tempi Concertati*, requires the percussionist to hit every available instrument as fast as possible. Exact notation of this passage would be impractical or even impossible. Performances of such passages are generally predictable and effective without a single notated pitch or rhythm.

Some composers disagree that improvisation and indeterminacy share common roots. Speaking to this point William Hellermann defines the distinction:

> It seems to me that there is a fundamental difference between aleatoric and improvisational music. Improvisation is concerned with the realization in real time of defined artistic goals. Aleatory, by its very nature, does not recognize the existence of goals. Both differ from the traditional "classic music" by leaving open to the

performer the choice of the specific materials to be used in the piece. They are often lumped together for this reason and, also, because they are both thought to be "free." Actually, freedom is not really the issue. Improvisation, at its highest, seeks meaning through spontaneity. Aleatory declares meaning to be spontaneity. Both of these are very restrictive states. I find that in my own works, I am increasingly concerned with improvisation, and never with anything I would call aleatory. (Hellermann 1971, p. 82)

The reasons that most composers use improvisation include:

(1) Performing from notation often produces relatively predictable results. Improvisation, on the other hand, often creates unique performances.

(2) Improvisation often produces rhythms and patterns that would otherwise paralyze performers if completely notated. As an example, the subtle and refined improvisatory character of syncopations before and after the beat in jazz makes exact notation a near impossibility. Even if these syncopations were notable, they would not retain the same kind of musical freshness that they do when improvised.

(3) Many contemporary composers feel that improvisation exists in all music to one degree or another and allowing explicit improvisatory freedom creates rewards that far exceed risks.

Groups since the 1960s dedicated to improvisation include the New Music Ensemble (Austin, Lunetta, Mizelle, Woodbury, Alexander, and Johnson); Sonic Arts Group (Mumma, Ashley, Behrman, and Lucier); the Musica Elettronica Viva (Allan Bryant, Alvin Curran, Jon Phetteplace, Carol Plantamura, Frederic Rzewski, Richard Teitelbaum, and Ivan Vandor); and the University of Illinois Chamber Players, directed by Jack McKenzie. Whatever the means of producing sound (electronic or instrumental), the music performed results from the interaction of the performers, most of whom are composers. Lukas Foss remarks: "I thought I had invented a new kind of improvisation. I now know that I was merely the first not to sign my name" (Foss 1968, p. 17). The 1957 U.C.L.A.-based Improvisation Chamber Ensemble under the direction of Foss consisted of piano, clarinet, cello, and percussion (Foss 1963, 1964). The Improvisation Chamber Ensemble performed primarily from jazz-like charts indicating only the initial ideas needed to create a work. Many rehearsals yielded polished results in performances which, while varying somewhat, were more formal than free improvisation. This group also performed improvised interludes between the movements of Foss's *Time Cycle* (1960) for soprano and

Figure 5.1. Lukas Foss.

orchestra. Foss enjoys equal reputations as a composer, conductor, pianist, educator, and spokesman for his art. As Music Director of the Brooklyn Philharmonic, the Buffalo Philharmonic, and the Milwaukee Symphony, Foss has been an effective champion of living composers.

Foss's compositions of the last twenty-five years prove that a love for the past can be reconciled with innovation. The essential feature in his music is the tension, so typical of the twentieth century, between tradition and new modes of musical expression. This tension is most explicit in such works as *Baroque Variations* for orchestra (1967), which deconstructs works by Handel, Scarlatti, and Bach. The work has received frequent international performances and has had a strong influence on younger composers. On the other hand, traditionalism is not absent in such experimental works as *Echoi* (1961–63), which, along with Foss's *Paradigm* and *Solo Observed*, is considered one of the major contemporary works for chamber ensemble.

Etudes for Organ by Lukas Foss requires four different improvisational techniques, one for each movement. In the first movement, the performer varies an exactly-notated single-line melody by freely repeating note groups. In the second movement, performers may choose the order, rhythm, octave, and/or number of notes desired from groups of notes. Forearm clusters dominate the third movement, with spontaneous choice of rhythm and white or black key clusters. The form of this movement falls into four sections: ABA-Coda. The fourth movement includes performer choice of a four-part "religious or patriotic" hymn around which two secondary performers play four-note clusters at either end of the keyboard. These auxiliary performers interfere, *poco a poco*, with the hymn performance. Foss has used pitches (in I, II, and IV), rhythms (in I), timbre (in III), and dynamics (in II, III, and IV), each in a somewhat traditional manner, while freeing other aspects of composition and performance for improvisation.

Cornelius Cardew of AMM, which also included Lou Gare, Eddie Prevost, and Keith Rowe, adds: "The past always seems intentional, but at the time it appears to be accidental" (Cardew 1968, p. 18). The MW 2 Ensemble of Poland uses traditional instruments with two dancers and an actor, tapes, projection, and scenery (see Figure 5.2) in improvisation. Performer interaction therefore involves theatrical as well as musical improvisation (Brinkman 1979).

Figure 5.2.   MW 2 Ensemble of Poland.

Morton Feldman expressed his ideas as to how music exists as time, not of, in, or about time:

> . . . This was not how to make an object . . . but how this object exists as Time. Time regained, as Proust referred to his work. Time as an Image, as Aristotle suggested. This is the area that the visual arts later began to explore. This is the area which music, deluded that it was counting out the seconds, has neglected.
>
> I once had a conversation with Karlheinz Stockhausen, where he . . . began beating on the table and said: "A sound exists either here—or here—or here." He was convinced that he was demonstrating reality to me. That the beat, and the possible placement of sounds in relation to it, was the only thing the composer could realistically hold on to. The fact that he had reduced it to so much a square foot made him think Time

was something he could handle and even parcel out, pretty much as he pleased.

> Frankly, this approach to Time bores me. I am not a clockmaker. I am interested in getting Time in its unstructured existence. That is, I am interested in how this wild beast lives in the jungle—not in the zoo. I am interested in how Time exists before we put our paws on it—our minds, our imaginations, into it. One would think that music more than any other art would be exploratory about Time. But is it? Timing—not Time—has been passed off as the real thing in music. (Feldman 1969, p. 75)

William Duckworth's *Walden Variations* (see Figure 5.3) demonstrates improvisational graphic notation. The page shown (the third and final in the score) represents a free improvisation. The events and movements to and from events are ambiguous and can be freely interpreted. Dancers, readers, slides, movies, and/or lights may be employed in keeping within the general spirit of the piece as performers understand it. Completed in 1971, *Walden Variations* represents a nonstructured improvisation-based work with open instrumentation.

In the above-discussed works, the composer still claims credit for one or more of the compositional aspects of the resultant work. Giuseppi Chiari's *Quel Che Volete* brings to mind Morton Feldman's statement: "Down with the Masterpiece; up with art . . ." (Feldman 1967, p. 43). This piece consists entirely of verbal instructions ranging from indications suggesting materials not be played in a virtuosic manner to exchanging instruments among performers. However vague the score may appear, close reading reveals composer intention: "you must try and play in a traditional manner," "play as if playing was a gift," and "We must never overdo." Likewise, in *Sonant*, Mauricio Kagel uses verbal descriptions of the framework within which performers should improvise. These often intricate instructions may more appropriately produce desired results than traditional notation.

Luciano Berio's *Circles* (1960) for female voice, harp, and two percussionists includes a variety of "improvisation boxes." Figure 5.4 shows the two percussion parts (top and bottom groups of staves) with the voice in the middle. The improvisation boxes should not be confused with the small boxes that graphically represent the mallets required: i.e., the first small box in the two top lines from the left. The percussion parts here would be either impossible or highly constrained if written out. Berio notates pitches and instrumentation in specific detail. Rhythm is left to the performer. Often Berio stacks

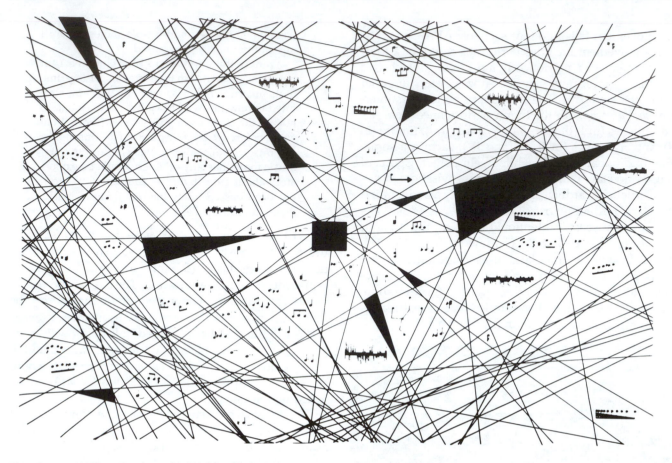

Figure 5.3.   William Duckworth's *Walden Variations*.

Figure 5.4.   From Luciano Berio's *Circles*. © Copyright 1961 by Universal Edition.

notes vertically in such a way that performers can proceed in any order desired. Occasionally pitches are proportionally distributed within boxes to indicate their approximate rhythmic placement or to introduce new groupings of notes. Dynamics, on the other hand, often appear as limits (i.e., *mf~pp*) with smooth crescendi and diminuendi indicated by dovetailing notations. This score contains no performance directions except the placement of instruments. Berio, it seems, feels that his notations are obvious. With the boxes occurring in only one or two parts at a time, Berio maintains control over the direction and flow of the work, allowing the improvisations to give life to each successive performance.

Robert Erickson's *Ricercar à 5* (1966) for five trombones uses many improvisational techniques. This work may be performed with five trombonists or one trombonist and four prerecorded trombones on tape. The score varies from exact notation to control of only one or two elements—most often dynamics and pitch. The interplay between parts requires sensitive and interpretative performance. The work was written for trombonist Stuart Dempster who speaks of these points in an interview.

> Question (Frank McCarty): So you began to compile a body of new sounds and techniques through research, practice, and mimicry. I assume you incorporated some of these in the improvisational music that was popular among the San Francisco composers of that era.

Answer (Stu Dempster): Yes, those pieces gave me the first opportunity to couple my "funny sounds" with other "funny sounds" made by tapes and by other musical instruments such as Pauline's (Oliveros) accordion and Mort's (Subotnick) clarinet. I also became interested in working with composers. I did a demo for Berio in the early 1960s and asked him for a piece, never thinking he'd really do it. Later (1966), when I was working with Bob Erickson on a commission, I decided to resurrect the Berio idea. I wrote him a letter . . . and learned he was already right in the middle of the piece. The *Sequenza* (also involving improvisation techniques) was written in a way for two of us, myself and (Vinko) Globokar, who had played sketches of what became the B section. But as Berio and I worked together on the final version it became more and more my piece since he saw in me—in my performance—more and more the character of Grock, the famous European clown, about whom the piece is actually written. In the meantime, Erickson and I were spending many a Tuesday morning developing a vocabulary of sounds and sound-mixes which resulted in his composition of the *Ricercar à 5* . . . (McCarty 1974, p. 33–4)

The score to Phil Winsor's *Orgel* includes a sheet of twelve basic improvisatory boxes for organ and organ recorded on tape. The verbal indications above each box (see Figure 5.5) plus the timing and directions in the score (not shown) help to create this free improvisation.

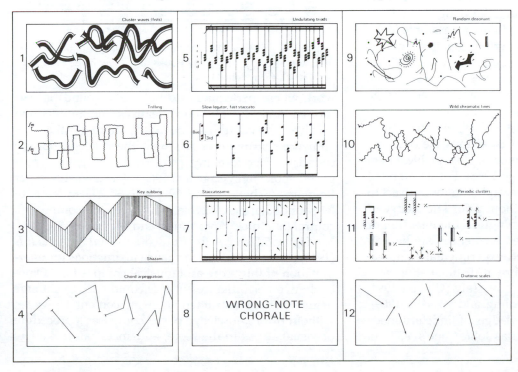

Figure 5.5. From Phil Winsor's *ORGEL I* (page X). Copyright © 1975 by Pembroke Music Co., Inc. International Copyright secured. 62 Cooper Square, NY 10003. Copying or reproducing this publication in while or in part violates the Federal Copyright Law. All rights reserved including public performance for profit.

In the last few years, improvisational techniques have helped produce a renaissance of new performance situations. Whether as a result of, or a reaction to, the restrictions of traditional notation, the creative collaborations between composers and performers help to enrich the continuum and significance of new music.

INDETERMINACY

William Hayes's *The Art of Composing Music by a Method Entirely New, Suited to the Meanest Capacity* (1751) describes a technique of composition using notes indeterminately spattered onto staff paper by running a finger over a stiff brush dipped in ink. Mozart used dice-throwing to create music (*Musical Dice Game*, K. 294d). Other indeterminate techniques have been attempted, even as early as the eleventh and twelfth centuries, but none with the vigor and philosophical implications of the composers of indeterminacy since the middle of the twentieth century.

Beginning in the early 1950s, John Cage developed an affinity for chance techniques using the *I Ching*. Christian Wolff had brought the English translation of this important book to Cage's attention at that time, Wolff's father Kurt Wolff being founder of the publishing house, Pantheon Press, that published it. The *I Ching*, the first written book of wisdom, philosophy, and oracle (attributed to Fu Hsi, 2953–2838 B.C.) indicates action as a result of six tosses of three coins (originally, the tossing of yarrow sticks). The example in Figure 5.6 shows all combinations of ▬ and ▬ ▬ with six tosses (heads giving ▬ and tails giving ▬ ▬). Having asked the question, "Should I use an example of the *I Ching* in this book?" and performing the required tosses, I received the following answer as a result: "Kun (indicates that in the case which it presupposes) there will be great progress and success, and the advantage will come from being correct and firm. (But) any movement in advance should not be (lightly) undertaken."

Experimental music, that is, actions the outcome of which are not foreseen, is more a philosophical than an audible phenomenon (Cage 1966). Form, intended or not, is inherent in all music, and therefore subject to analysis. It is impossible, without prior knowledge of the composer or work, to distinguish the intention or nonintention of the composer. Audiences can be presented with highly organized experimental compositions of the same general genre, instrumentation, and techniques, without reacting adversely (Corbett 1994; Higgins 1964; Kayn 1966; Young and Zazeela 1969). However, when prior knowledge of indeterminacy exists, or when a work such as John Cage's 4'33" (a

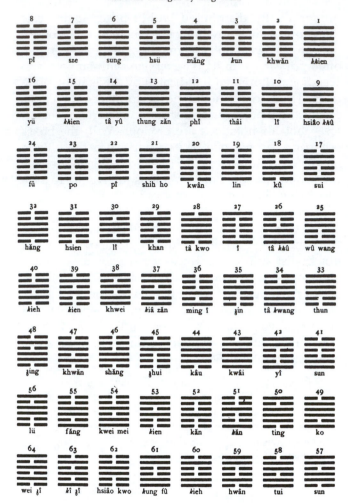

Figure 5.6.   The Hexagrams from the *I Ching*. Permission for reprint granted by University Books, Inc. New Hyde Park, NY, NY 11040. Copyright 1964.

work where performers do not make sound) is performed and the audience realizes the unintention involved, reactions can be much more hostile. The audience's struggle occurs with the concept, not the sounds. "Therefore my purpose is to remove purpose," spoke John Cage in a 1962 interview with Roger Reynolds (Schwartz and Childs 1967). The idea is to let sounds happen, to free them from the composer's control (Shattuck 1968; Young and Mac Low 1963).

Figure 5.7 shows the full score to Paul Ignace's *It Is* (1946). There are no performance instructions for interpretation of this score as a musical composition. Obviously two performances of *It Is* could vary to extreme degrees in both instrumentation and content. However, without prior knowledge of the composer's procedure or visual access to the score, audiences can make few

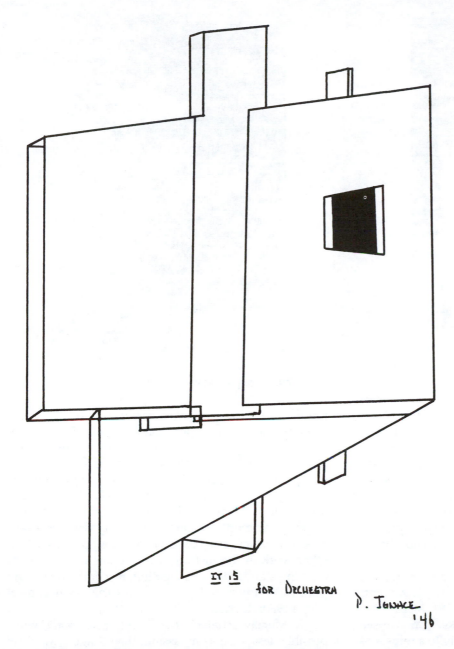

Figure 5.7.   Paul Ignace: *It Is.*

decisions concerning determinacy or indeterminacy. Earle Brown's *December 1952* is similar in nature, but more visually musical in that its short vertical and horizontal lines of varying thicknesses more easily convert to rhythmic, dynamic, and pitch realization.

Hindemith refers to chance as "one of the ugliest modern musical diseases" (Schwartz and Childs 1967, p. 89). However, most critics deal with the forms and individuals involved rather than the *concept* of indeterminacy (Copland 1968; O'Grady 1981; Satie 1977). As Cage has said, "If one is making an object and then proceeds in an indeterminate fashion, to let happen what will, outside of one's control, then one is simply being careless about the making of that object"

(Schwartz and Childs 1967, p. 341). However, if one is making an indeterminate object then proceeding *determinately* seems just as reckless.

Some critics point out that indeterminacy is not actually possible and hence argue against the rationale for attempting to approach it. Cage refers to his disappointment and the compromises that arise from the knowledge that he hasn't really done it, but merely has been ". . . going along in that general direction" (Schwartz and Childs 1967).

The terminology of indeterminacy involves certain basic American/European divisions (Childs 1969; Xenakis 1971; Yates 1967). The European term *aleatoric*, derived by Boulez from *alea*, French for risk, and origi-

Figure 5.8. John Cage. Photo by Dorothy Norman.

Figure 5.9. Morton Feldman. BMI Archives. Used by permission.

nally from the Latin word meaning dice, employs chance techniques within a controlled framework, more related to improvisation than indeterminacy (Boulez 1964). Morton Feldman has remarked, "This is true of Boulez. This is true of Stockhausen. You can see this in the way they have approached American 'chance' music. They began by finding rationalizations for how they could incorporate chance and still keep their precious integrity" (Schwartz and Childs 1967, p. 365). Boulez has expanded on the basic differences between aleatoric and chance techniques (see interview in chapter 2).

The division between American and European indeterminacy grew deeper during the 1960s and 1970s (Gagne and Caras 1982; Landy 1991; MacKenzie 1971; Sutherland 1994). Boulez remarks: "Do you see what we are getting back to? Constantly to a refusal of choice. The first conception was purely mechanistic, automatic, fetishistic; the second is still fetishistic but one is freed from choice not by numbers but by the interpreter" (Boulez 1964, p. 42). England's David Bedford and Brian Tilbury, however, championed the American cause of indeterminacy, mirroring much the same discoveries and excitement engendered by Cage and Feldman in the early fifties (Sutherland 1994).

COMPOSER INDETERMINACY

Many works are indeterminate with respect to composition but determinate with respect to performance (Cage 1966, 1973, 1979a, 1979b). Typically this music is predictable before performance but composed using of some type of chance operation (Behrman 1964). Often such works appear in traditional notation and almost always imply determinate performance. In his *Music of Changes* (1951), Cage followed the *I Ching* to indeterminately create twenty-six large charts indicating aspects of composition (durations, tempos, dynamics). It took nine months to create *Music of Changes*, every aspect of which was based on coin tosses. Possibly no other work in the history of music has required such exacting standards in its creation, its composer having purposely attempted to withdraw his own control (Cope 1980; Reynolds 1965, 1968, 1976).

R. Murray Schafer's *The Tuning of the World*, while possibly less all-encompassing than Cage's *Music of Changes*, is modeled after the proportions of what Schafer terms the world's "soundscape" (Schafer 1977). His work involves the recording of post-industrial soundscapes and the design of soundscapes. His process of listening, called *ear cleaning*, has significant consequence in his view: ". . . take a sheet of paper and give it a sound . . . By giving the paper a voice we have exposed its sound-soul. Every object on the earth has a sound-soul."

Magic squares (and cubes) have also been used as raw material for formal compositional techniques. These matrices of numbers add, subtract, divide, and/or multiply to the same number regardless of the direction taken. Figure 5.10 shows a simple magic square and one possible interpretation in music. Note that the addition of every line, including the two diagonal lines, equals 15, and no line contains more than one each of the numbers used.

Many wonder why such formalisms could not be achieved by using more musical and less mathematical means. Writings by and about Xenakis often contribute, for example, to confusion about this and other indeterminate techniques (Olson and Herbert 1961). The following discussion between Lukas Foss and Iannis Xenakis may provide some clarification:

> Foss: Iannis, all the music of yours that I know is built on mathematical premise, mostly probability. Is there any aspect to chance that is not mathematical, that is, not probability theory?
>
> Xenakis: All my music is not based on mathematics—there are parts of it which use mathematics. As to chance, it is not like dice or tossing a coin, this is ignorance, as if there were impossibility of predicting. What does chance mean to you?
>
> Foss: Anything I cannot control. (Cage, Foss, and Xenakis 1970, p. 40)

Dick Higgins's *Thousand Symphonies* involved the machine-gunning of one thousand pages of blank orchestral manuscript. Performances, though necessarily constituting some performer interpretation of the resultant holes, are basically determinate. "My machine-gunning of scores actually represents the concretization of a fantasy I had of setting the police (or armies) to composing music with their most familiar instruments—guns, machine guns. In fact . . . we actually organized an orchestral performance of the gunshot notations according to a system I worked out, and it sounded quite lovely" (letter to the author).

Mauricio Kagel's *1898* (1973), for eleven to seventeen instrumentalists and twenty to twenty-five children's voices, is freely orchestrated so that even nonpitched instruments can participate. The performance instructions provide further insight:

> The purpose of these tape recordings, among others, is to demonstrate that what is needed is not "reliable" musical education but the very opposite: an unorthodox system of changeable, ambivalent invitations to express oneself acoustically—rather than "musically." (Kagel 1979, p. 89)

This is later followed by:

> What is the difference between proper and artificial laughter? One can almost be certain that the responses to the ambiguities inherent in this unambiguous question will produce complex aural situations. (Kagel 1979, p. 89)

PERFORMER INDETERMINACY

Music that is determinate with respect to composition but indeterminate with respect to performance often appears as musical mobiles (Gagne and Caras 1982). The performance process resembles mobiles in art, where the shape, color, and design of each part are fixed, with the order and angle constantly changing.

Karlheinz Stockhausen's *Klavierstück XI, No. 7* (1957), printed on a long roll (37 by 21 inches), opens onto a special wooden stand supplied with the score. This work contains nineteen fragments, which may be played in any order. Performer instructions require glancing at the score and then playing whichever fragment may catch the eye.

> At the end of the first group, he reads the tempo, dynamic and attack indications that follow, and looks at random to any other group, which he then plays in accordance with the latter indications. "Looking at random to any other group" implies that the performer will never link up expressly chosen groups or intentionally leave out others. Each group can be joined to any of the other 18: each can thus be played at any of the six tempi and dynamic levels and with any of the six types of attack. (Stockhausen 1957)

1	4	2	3	5
2	3	5	1	4
5	1	4	2	3
4	2	3	5	1
3	5	1	4	2

Pitch: (Using 0–11 ordination—beginning on C)
    Line 1—Lines 2 and 1—Lines 2, 1, and 3—etc.
    (Reducing numbers over 11 by 12—e.g.
    C♯ E D D♯ F D♯ G G E A G♯ G♯ B etc.)
Rhythm: 1 = ♪ 2 = ♩ 3 = ♩. 4 = 𝅗𝅥 5 = 𝅝
Timbre: 1 = horn 2 = flute 3 = piano 4 = violin 5 = cello

Figure 5.10. A magic square and possible musical interpretation.

The work concludes when a fragment occurs for a third time. Thus, performances may involve anywhere from three (the first one randomly observed three times in succession) to thirty-eight factorial (that is 38!—or 38 times 37 times 36 times 35 totaling over 3.5 million) fragments. Figure 5.11 shows the score from measures 27 to 32 of Stockhausen's *Stop* (1965). This "Pariser Version" (there is another version for full orchestra) requires eighteen performers in six groups of like timbres. This "recipe" work has determinate form (note the durations at the top of each measure) yet lacks determinate directions for performance ("noises," for example, has vague meanings). Stockhausen has a sense of the outcome in terms of form, contrast, balance, and direction—note the occasional exactly notated overlapping events—but little sense of rhythm, entrance order, and pitch. This type of work, though very different from the mobile structure of his *Klavierstück XI, No. 7*, still reflects music that is relatively determinate with respect to composition but indeterminate with respect to performance.

Henri Pousseur's piano solo *Caracteres* (1961) includes cutout windows and randomly placed score pages so that the order of the fragments cannot be predicted. Henry Cowell's *Mosaic Quartet* (1934) provides blocks of music from which performers construct performances.

Referring to his *Available Forms I and II* (1961–62), Earle Brown writes: "The title of the work refers to the availability of many possible forms which these composed elements may assume, spontaneously directed by the conductors in the process of performing the work. The individual musical events are rehearsed but the performances are not" (Brown 1964). In Brown's *Available Forms I* for orchestra, the score is projected at the back of the stage for the performers to read (Brown 1967). The conductor then indicates a number, which represents one of the large numerals indicated in the score. The performers read and improvise within the context of the information given in the indicated block.

In *Indeterminacy*, Cage describes Bach's *Art of the Fugue* as an example of composition which is indeterminate with respect to its performance, based on the lack of directions in regard to timbre, dynamics, sequence of notes, and durations, making available a wide range of possible realizations (Cage 1966, p. 35).

Barney Child's *Nonet* includes an *event machine* (a numbered acetate overlay and two rotating color-coded discs), which provides the order, timing, and selection of events. In Morton Feldman's *Intersection 3*, the duration, number, and timbre of sounds are determined by the composer while the dynamics and range (high, middle, and low) remain indeterminate during performance (Feldman 1966, 1969, 1985; DeLio 1996).

John Cage's *Atlas Eclipticalis* (see Figure 5.12) includes the use of contact microphones placed in various locations on the instruments. Though somewhat

Figure 5.11. From Karlheinz Stockhausen's *Stop.* © Copyright Universal Edition. All rights reserved.

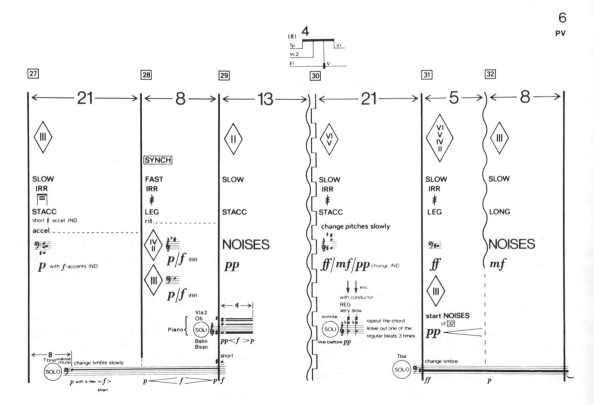

graphic in notation, this work provides pitches and directions of movement. As seen in Figure 5.13, the notation of *34′45.776″ for a Pianist* (1954) has graphic and explicit elements.

Iannis Xenakis defines music without in-performance conflict as *autonomous* (inclusive of most music to the present day) and the music of games (inclusive of music with conflict between groups or individuals during performance) as *heteronomous* (Xenakis 1971). Xenakis's *Duel* (1958–59) comprises materials like that of mobiles: a set of six events, each precisely written. Unlike mobiles, however, Xenakis's strategic games

use tactics determining which events permit interruption, with choice of events decided by performers.

Strategie (1962), for two forty-four-member orchestras, employs Xenakis's *strategie musicale*, the application of the mathematical theory of games to music. Xenakis uses seven basic sounds whose structure follows a stochastic base calculated with an IBM 70690 computer. Four hundred possible combinations exist between the two orchestras seated on opposite sides of the stage. An electric scoreboard set at the back of the stage lists the points gained and lost according to the composer's rules. "At the end of a certain number of

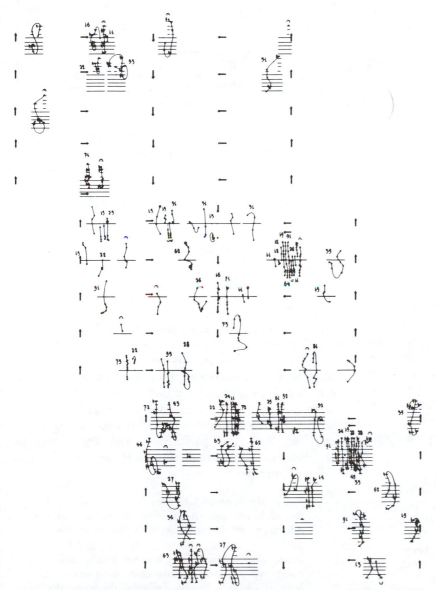

Atlas Eclipticalis, French Horn 5, Percussion 4, Cello 7, **pages 245, 309, and 157**

Figure 5.12. From John Cage's *Atlas Eclipticalis*. French Horn 5, Percussion 4, Cello 7, pages 157, 245, and 309. Copyright © 1962 by Henmar Press, Inc. Reprinted by permission of C. F. Peters Corporation.

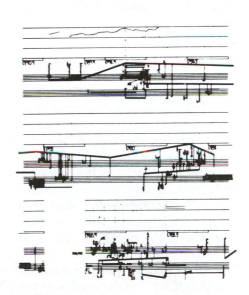

Figure 5.13. From John Cage's *34′ 46.776″ for a Pianist*. Copyright © 1954 by Henmar Press, Inc. Reprinted by permission of C. F. Peters Corporation.

exchanges or minutes, as agreed upon by the conductors, one of the two is declared a winner and is awarded a prize" (Xenakis 1971, p. 122).

Roman Haubenstock-Ramati's *Mobile for Shakespeare* for voice, piano, celeste, vibraphone, and three percussionists represents a good example of mobile indeterminacy (see Figure 5.14). Each box in the mobile gives a fairly straightforward, mostly traditionally-notated fragment. Haubenstock-Ramati has composed every note here. Performances will differ significantly, however, depending on the different routes taken between boxes.

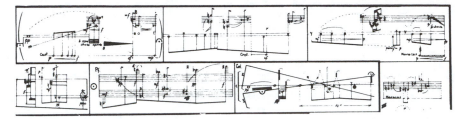

Figure 5.14. From Roman Haubenstock-Ramati's *Mobile for Shakespeare.* © Copyright by Universal Edition. 1968. Used by permission.

COMPOSER AND PERFORMER INDETERMINACY

Music can be indeterminate with respect to both composition and performance (Cage 1967, 1969, 1976). Christian Wolff's *Duo II for Pianists* (1958), for example, involves no score and all materials are indeterminate, except for the use of pianos indicated by the title. *Duo II* has no designated beginning or ending, these being determined entirely by the performance situation. Nam June Paik's *In Homage to John Cage* (1959) is likewise indeterminate in respect to both composition and performance. In its first performance Paik leaped offstage to Cage's seat, removed Cage's jacket and, as Calvin Tomkins puts it: "slashed his (Cage's) shirt with a wickedly long pair of scissors, cut off his necktie at the knot, poured a bottle of shampoo over his head, and then rushed out of the room" (Tomkins 1965). Paik later telephoned members of the audience to inform them that the work was completed.

Cage has also explored *contingency*-type indeterminacy:

> I have been writing pieces that I call "music of contingency," in which there is a rupture between cause and effect, so that the causes that are introduced don't necessarily produce effects. That's what contingency is. One piece, *Inlets*, uses conch shells, for example; if instead of blowing a conch shell, you fill it with water and tip it, it will sometimes gurgle and sometimes not. You have no control over it. Even if you try very hard to control it, it gurgles when it wishes to . . . when it's ready to. Sometimes if you rehearse with it and think that you've got it down pat,

you'll discover as I do, I'm sure, that it foxes you and gurgles when it chooses. (Cope 1980)

John Mizelle's *Radial Energy I* (see Figure 5.15) allows extensive freedom in choice of sound sources, number of participants, location of performance, and interpretation. In the explanation accompanying the score, Mizelle describes in detail the periods of silence between performances before the first opportunity for the piece to be concluded: one hundred fifty years. Other complete performances may last over 382 years, depending on initial performance time, with duration of the performances (between the periods of silence) computed by addition, squaring, cubing, and so on of the initial performance duration. Likewise the area of performance could be expanded, as the composer states, "to other planets, galaxies, etc. When all of time and space are transformed into sound, the piece (and the universe) ends."

Barney Childs's *The Roachville Project*, a sound sculpture for four to ten performers, verbally describes a situation in which performers and audience create an instrument out of available materials and improvise during and after its construction. Emphasis in *The Roachville Project* moves toward situation, theater, and full participation (see Figure 5.16).

Sylvano Bussotti's *Five Piano Pieces for David Tudor* (1959), a graphic score, was performed in Los Angeles three times in one concert, by three different performers. More conservative members of the audience, obviously appalled by the lack of recognizable similarities between performances, reacted antagonistically to both the performers and the work. In reference to these performances Halsey Stevens has pointed out that:

> . . . if Mr. Bussotti had wandered into the hall and didn't know what was going on, he would not have had the remotest idea that those three performances, or any one of them, might have been his own piece. They were so totally different in every respect that the only thing he could lay claim to was having designed the score, not to having composed the piece. Aleatoric music, it seems to me, as it is frequently pursued, is an amusing parlor game . . . (Cope 1973, p. 30)

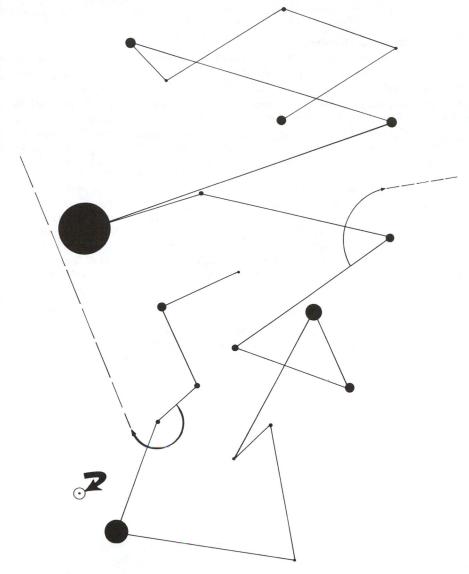

Figure 5.15. From John Mizelle's *Radial Energy I*. Permission granted by *Source: Music of the Avant Garde*. Composer Performer Edition, Davis, CA.

Had these performances been recorded and subsequently transferred into traditional notation for performer interpretation, the resultant works could have avoided the controversy. Had the piece then been performed three times, repetition would have replaced the creativity inherent in the original work (Layton 1964).

Figures 5.17 to 5.21 show the variety of notations John Cage has used, and a general cross section of types of his works. *Concert for Piano and Orchestra* (Figure 5.17, *Solo for Piano*) was written for and first performed at the 1958 Cage *Retrospective Concert* in New York City's Town Hall, with the composer conducting. The staging included a large battery of electronic equipment with Cage slowly bringing his hands together over his head in clocklike fashion. This gesture controlled the duration of this work of otherwise indeterminate notes and rhythms.

Cage's *26'1.1499" for a String Player* (1955, see Figure 5.18) has been realized by Harold Budd for Bertram Turetzky's Nonesuch recording. Both *Variations I* (1958, see Figure 5.19) and *Fontana Mix* (1958, see Figure 5.20) graphically plot areas and physical locations for performance. The score to *Fontana Mix* indicates the contact areas on the instruments and their striking points. Since Cage has not restricted instrumentation, it is not possible to predict the outcome of a performance. Moreover, since the score results from randomly overlaying various translucent sheets, the score itself looks different in each performance. Once created, however, performers should conform to the score in very determined ways so that improvisation or reliance on past experience does not occur.

Variations IV (1963) requires performers to lay score transparencies over a map of the performance

The Roachville Project

4 to 10 performers, minimum duration 30 minutes.

Provide a great deal of material, most of which should be capable of sound production, either immediately (wires, pipes, blocks, tubes, containers, bits and pieces of musical instruments, junk, etc.) or potentially (material which when assembled or altered or worked with can be made; maybe, to produce sound in some fashion).

The piece begins with the arrival of the performers at the material. They begin to assemble the material, as they please, any way they wish, into a "musical instrument" of sorts. The complete construction is to be a unit—that is, separate people may work for a while on separate sub-units, but these must eventually be built into the complete construction. All that is necessary for assembling, finally, is ingenuity: the means of assembly (nails, staples, glue, string, sticky tape, leather straps, bailing wire, rivets, etc.) are up to the performers. Performers may converse together concerning problems of assembly and sound potential, but this must be done very quietly, and other conversation is to be avoided; performers may test parts they are working on for sound as they are assembling (i.e. test string tension by plucking, test resonances by tapping, etc.) but this must also be done very quietly. At a stipulated time, or when all agree that the instrument is completed, the performers improvise music on it, for any length of time. The composition is finished with the completion, at a pre-arranged time or by agreement among the performers, of this "piece-within-a-piece." All material provided need not, or perhaps will not, be used. If passing members of the audience wish to become performers they may, as long as the total working number of participants never exceeds 10.

Deep Springs
April 1967

*Roachville and White Mountain City were "settlements just over the White Mountain summit from Owens Valley. . . . A writer visiting there in 1864 tells all that we know of those would-be mining centers. The 'city' from which he wrote was on Wyman Creek, on the Deep Spring slope; its rival, Roachville, was on Cottonwood Creek, and was named by its proprietor, William Roach. . . ."

W. A. Chalfant, The Story of Inyo

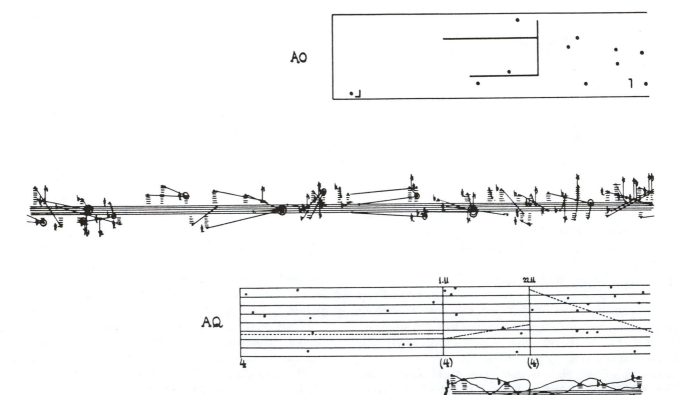

Figure 5.17. From John Cage's *Solo for Piano (Concert for Piano and Orchestra).* Copyright © 1958 by Henmar Press, Inc. Reprinted by permission of C. F. Peters Corporation.

area that then determines the source and direction of sounds. A recording made in a Los Angeles art gallery includes Cage performing electronic equipment along with the candid conversations of the audience. Cage created a final realization of this work by selecting, evaluating, splicing, and manipulating the resultant tapes. *Theatre Piece* (1960, Figure 5.21) uses number charts to graphically represent actions.

Paintings (1965) by Louis Andriessen (Figure 5.22), for recorder and piano, has a graphic score. Even with the instructions, one cannot predict the results in performance. William Bland's *Speed* (1968) for organ (see Figure 5.23) uses traditional left-to-right reading, up/down pitch representation, and block-cluster chord notation, encouraging indeterminate performance.

Other composers employ varying degrees of graphic notations to achieve equally varied results (Sumner 1986; Young and MacLow 1963). Anestis Logothetis's scores appear at first glance as works of visual art. If one reads the instructions for his works carefully, however, clues appear that indicate aspects of composer intention (e.g., *Clusters, Odyssee*, 1963, or *Ichnologia*, 1964). Robert Moran often utilizes graphic notations, but unlike Logothetis, gives clear indication of instrumentation and possible interpretation of visual symbols (see *Four Visions*, 1963, in Karkoschka's *Notation in New Music*, or *Bombardments No. 2*, 1964). Boguslaw Schaffer has pointed out the advantages of graphic music, at least for its usefulness to mainstream musicians. In Schaffer's 1963 *Violin Concerto*, the

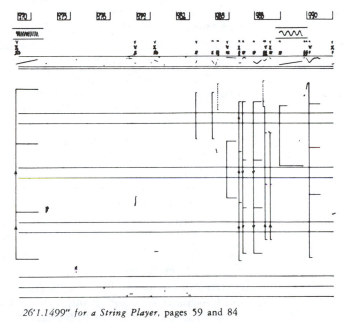

Figure 5.18. From John Cage's *26' 1.1499"* *for a String Player.* Copyright © 1955 by Henmar Press, Inc. Reprinted by permission of C. F. Peters Corporation.

26'1.1499" for a String Player, pages 59 and 84

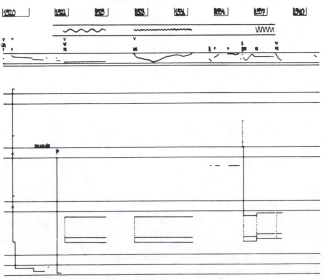

Figure 5.19. From John Cage's *Variations I*. Copyright © 1958 by Henmar Press, Inc. Reprinted by permission of C. F. Peters Corporation.

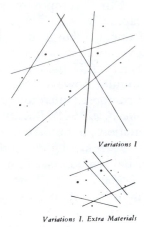

Variations I

Variations I. Extra Materials

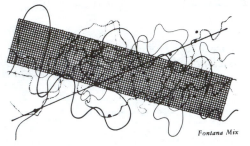

Fontana Mix

Figure 5.20. From John Cage's *Fontana Mix*. Copyright © 1958 by Henmar Press, Inc. Reprinted by permission of C. F. Peters Corporation.

Figure 5.21. From John Cage's *Theatre Piece Part VI* (one of eighteen unnumbered pages). Copyright © 1960 by Henmar Press, Inc. Reprinted by permission of C. F. Peters Corporation.

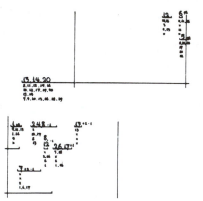

Figure 5.22. Flute part of Louis Andriessen's *Paintings*. Copyright © by Herman Moeck Verlag. Used with permission. All rights reserved.

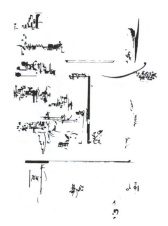

cadenza, consisting primarily of thick black waves of twisting lines, is transcribed into one possible traditionally notated version. The result, based on a rather literal translation, derives time in terms of left-to-right proportionality, pitch in terms of up-and-down relativity, and flow in terms of visual motion. This traditional version is incredibly complex, nearly unplayable, and, to some, totally foreign to the work as a whole. The plasticity of the graphic notation allows for creation of music as complex as the traditionally notated version, yet without the studied end result.

Figure 5.24 shows a portion of the score to Roman Haubenstock-Ramati's *Jeux 2* (1968) for two percussionists. Though mobile in structure, the graphic nature of the fragments themselves makes determinacy on the part of the composer or performer an impossibility. Note the difference here between *Jeux 2* and *Mobile for Shakespeare* (1959, Figure 5.14), the latter having composer control over the fragments, thus indicating performer indeterminacy. Possibly Europe's most experimental protagonist of the varieties of indeterminacy, Haubenstock-Ramati continues to explore the areas founded by John Cage, Earle Brown, and Barney Childs.

Figure 5.25 shows Robert Moran's *Sketch for a Tragic One-Act Opera*. The graphic nature of the score (even though instrumentation is traditional as shown in the left margin) contributes to composer-performer indeterminacy. This graphic sketch defines texture and dynamics more than pitches or rhythms. Other composers involved with indeterminate techniques include Folke Rabe, Bo Nilsson, Cornelius Cardew (Cardew later disowned this style to compose *political-reformation* music), Roland Kayn, Allan Bryant, Joseph Byrd, Richard Maxfield, Philip Corner, Douglas Leedy, Robert Ashley, and James Fulkerson (Brecht 1991).

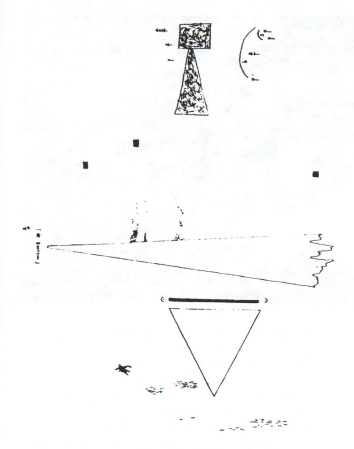

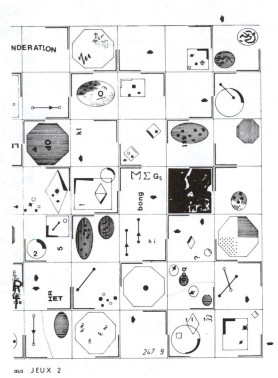

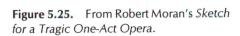

Figure 5.23. From William Bland's *Speed* for solo organ.

Figure 5.25. From Robert Moran's *Sketch for a Tragic One-Act Opera.*

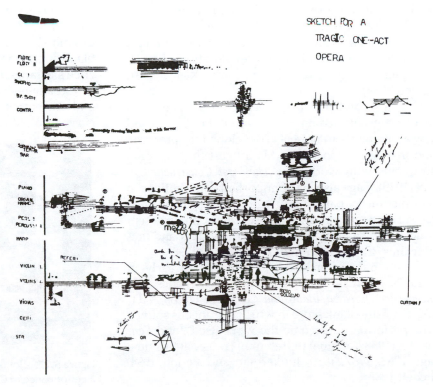

Figure 5.26. John Cage (standing at left) conducting a recording session of a percussion work by Lou Harrison (white shirt, far right) around 1940. Accidental superimposition of two photos created the music and bass drum in the upper center.

VECTORAL ANALYSIS
JOHN CAGE: *CARTRIDGE MUSIC*

(For information on vectoral analysis and procedures, see Preface.)

1. Historical Background: John Cage (1912–1992) studied with Henry Cowell and Arnold Schoenberg (Kostelanetz 1969, 1970, 1991, 1996). Cage's music in the 1930s developed chromatically with tone-row fragments and rhythmic rows. His *Sonata for Clarinet* (1933) provides a good example of his music at the time. This work contains no effects whatsoever, but rather develops a kind of free twelve-tone process showing definite rows but little exploration of serial techniques (Cage 1962; Metzger and Riehn 1981; Pritchett 1988).

Cage's second period developed in the late 1930s when he concentrated on diverse timbral resources and a new aesthetic about noise. He developed the prepared piano in 1938 and increased his interest in percussion instruments with works like *The First Construction in Metal* (1939). Cage also made important contributions to electronic music, particularly with the *Imaginary Landscape* series begun in 1939. These works all represent characteristic Cage explorations into new sonic and timbral realms (Cage 1962; Revill 1992; Shultis 1998).

Cage's indeterminate period developed early in the 1950s when he became interested in chance. His *Concerto for Prepared Piano and Orchestra* (1951), *4'33"* (1952, a mostly blank score in which extraneous sounds to the performance become the work itself), and *Fontana Mix* (1958; for tape) represent his music at this time (Cage 1962, 1967, 1980; Junkerman and Perloff 1994; Pritchett 1988).

Throughout his career, Cage actively referenced his work to the other arts. He collaborated with choreographer Merce Cunningham, artist Robert Rauschenberg, and sculptor Jasper Johns. Cage's concept of, and search for, what he terms the "possibility of saying nothing" have influenced numerous other composers, artists, and writers. Few critics doubt that twentieth-century music would have evolved as it did without Cage's contributions (Bosseur 1993; Boulez 1990; Duckworth and Fleming 1989; Paik 1978).

2. Overview: *Cartridge Music* was completed in 1960. The score consists of four transparent sheets described as follows: sheet one: nineteen 1/8-inch black dots arranged randomly; sheet two: ten 1/4-inch circles arranged randomly; sheet three: a single two-inch-diameter circle numbered as a clock in five-second increments (0 to 60); sheet four: a very long curved dotted line with a circle.

Figure 5.27. John Cage and David Cope during preparation of a performance of *Cartridge Music*. Photo by Carol Foote (1980).

The score to *Cartridge Music* also contains twenty numbered nontransparent sheets having various inscribed shapes, the number of which corresponds to the number of the sheet. Each performer makes a personal score from these materials. First, each performer chooses a nontransparent sheet with its number corresponding to the number of cartridges available to that performer (cartridge here referring to a contact microphone or record player needle cartridge). The performer then places the transparent sheets randomly over the numbered nontransparent sheet with the last curved dotted line arranged so that the circle at the end of the dotted line contains a point outside of a shape and so that the dotted line intersects at least one point within one of the shapes. Figure 5.28 shows how the score might look—only one of a nearly limitless number of possibilities. Note that the dotted line (ending at the upper left) terminates in a filled circle and that it intersects a point inside one of the shapes (i.e., intersects a point inside the large shape, lower right-hand side of the score). The performer then reads the dotted line from one end to the other (either direction is acceptable), making note of intersections with lines, circles, and dots. Each of these intersections correlates with specific actions given in the performance notes as in "intersection of the dotted line with a point within a shape indicates a sound produced in any manner on the object inserted in the cartridge corresponding to that shape."

Figure 5.28. From John Cage's *Cartridge Music*. Copyright © 1960 by Henmar Press, Inc. Reprinted by permission of C. F. Peters Corporation.

Timing of *Cartridge Music* is gauged by a stopwatch, represented by the circle located near the center of Figure 5.28. This arrangement then regulates one moment (the performer's choice) of the work, with total duration being fully at the discretion of the performers. The actions during that minute take place only over periods created by intersections of the dotted line with the time circle. In this case, since the circle has not been intersected, no specific times are given.

Performers should prepare each minute of the scheduled performance prior to the first rehearsal following these instructions. Exact schedules of actions are then made with clear indications of what procedures are necessary and their exact timing. Each part must be prepared separately from any other performer's part. Performers freely choose the instruments on which contact microphones are placed. "All events, ordinarily thought to be undesirable, such as feed-back, humming, howling, etc. are to be accepted in this situation." Cage comments on *Cartridge Music* in an interview:

Cope: Did you in the process of recording the piece listen to what you were doing?

Cage: We did, so to speak, what we had to do. You are usually a bit too busy to listen. And the idea is that the players confound one another. That's one of the ideas of the piece. So that if you do listen to what you're doing, you're apt to get the wrong attitude toward the piece. What you have to develop is an indifference to whether your work is effective or ineffective; let happen what will. In my mind it arises from the experience that is so frequent in American life, of traffic congestion, and how to take it with what I call a sober and quiet mind, how to remain susceptible to divine influences. (Cope 1980)

3. Orchestration: In a 1980 performance, I used the insides of a piano, connecting and performing the contact microphones directly on the strings and the sounding board. Other performers chose bass drum and tam-tam. Springs, wind-up toys, and a variety of other smaller instruments were also employed with effective results. Cage remarks further:

I can't recognize *Cartridge Music* from one performance to the next. Somewhere I tell that story of going into a house . . . and the hostess to be nice had put *Cartridge Music* on in another room . . . I turned to her and asked, "What is that music?" And she said, "You can't be serious." I said, "It's very interesting; what is it?" And then she told me. I was pleased that I couldn't recognize it . . . I don't hear it, you see. I performed it . . . with David Tudor, and we made a recording when Earle Brown was in charge of Time Records. Earle asked David and me if . . . we wanted to hear the end result. Neither one of us wanted to hear it. (Cope 1980)

4. Basic Techniques: *Cartridge Music* is an experiment the actions for which the final result cannot be foreseen. Cage has no way to predict the sounds of a performance. While performers make the score as a first step, they rehearse carefully as the second step.

Cope: In a performance of *Cartridge Music*, does it cross your mind that this is a good performance, a bad performance, or enjoyable . . . ?

Cage: If I think that way then I won't hear very well. The only time that I think that things are good or bad is when some other intentions than are proper to the piece take over. That happens so frequently with orchestral music, where the players don't do what they're supposed to do. Then I don't think that it's good or bad, but has moved out of the realm of music into the world of society and becomes a theatrical situation that was not intended at all. (Cope 1980)

5, 6. Vertical and Horizontal Models: Since any possible timbres can occur in this piece, no model can exist.

7. Style: *Cartridge Music* represents Cage's mature approach to indeterminacy. He has carefully divorced himself from creative control over the elements of this work. Cage's indeterminate approach to composition resembles the stochastic concepts espoused by Iannis Xenakis in chapter 8. In both cases, rigorous formalisms result in unpredictable outcomes. The Oliveros vectoral analysis in chapter 6 reveals similar attributes with indeterminacy left to a particular performance situation. Each of these examples relates in interesting ways to the serial concepts found in chapter 2, but does not relate well with the music found in chapters 1, 3, 9, and 10.

DAVID COPE: AN INTERVIEW WITH JOHN CAGE

John Cage gracefully granted me an audience at the home of his dear friend Norman O. Brown (also a major figure in the twentieth century and known affectionately as "Nobby") in Santa Cruz in 1980. I had no idea at the time what an interview with Cage meant. I came with a few prepared questions but quickly abandoned them and any preconceptions I had about the interview. Cage talked for most of four hours without a break. I did not have to edit his comments for he spoke literately, comprehensively, and with more lucidity than anyone I have ever known, then or since. At the end of our interview it was I who was exhausted and Cage, age 66 at the time, who was energized. The following represents but a brief excerpt from our hours together.

Cope: After studying a good deal of your music and writing, I find a number of correlations (possible) between the ways in which you describe your listening processes and the methods of composition you employ. How much did and does your approach to listening affect your approaches to composition?

Cage: My composition arises out of asking questions. I am reminded of a story early on about a class with Schoenberg. He had us go to the black-board to solve a particular problem in counterpoint (though it was a class in harmony). He said: "When you have a solution, turn around and let me see it." I did that. He then said: "Now another solution, please." I gave another and another until finally, having made seven or eight, I reflected a moment and then said with some certainty: "There aren't any more solutions." He said: "O.K. What is the principle underlying all of the solutions?" I couldn't answer his question; but I had always worshipped the man, and at that point I did even more. He ascended, so to speak. I spent the rest of my life, until recently, hearing him ask that question over and over. And then it occurred to me through the direction that my work has taken, which is renunciation of choices and the substitution of asking questions, that the principle underlying all of the solutions that I had given him was the question that he had asked, because they certainly didn't come from any other point. He would have accepted that answer, I think. The answers have the question in common. Therefore the question underlies the answers. I'm sure that he would have found my answer interesting; though he was very brilliant—he may have been thinking of something else.

Cope: The concept of *zero* is an important one to understanding both what you say and what you compose. The reference is made in the questions and answers section of this issue of *Composer*: "I always want to start from zero and make, if I can, a discovery." It is, very honestly, very difficult for me to imagine starting with zero, no less beginning there in my own compositions. What techniques does one acquire to achieve this; even more important, how do you renew that zero after a new discovery is made?

Cage: It's exactly the problem that I face all the time and it's very difficult, because we have a memory. There's no doubt of it. And we're not stupid. We would be stupid if we didn't have memory. And yet it's that memory that one has to become free of, at the same time that you have to take advantage of it. It's very paradoxical. Right now, I am refreshed and brought, so to speak, to zero, I think, through my work with Joyce.

I don't know how he actually worked. I know more than I used to know. Writers like Louis Mink and Adeline Glashine have helped. One of these mentions that you can't understand Joyce unless you have an unabridged dictionary and the eleventh edition of the *Encyclopedia Britannica*. And if you have both you can then see doors open on passages in *Finnegan's Wake*, which are more or less lifted from one or the other. He used these reference texts in a way that facilitated and stimulated his work.

In my way, I do the same thing in my most recent work. The passage about water in the next to the last chapter of *Ulysses*, which was Joyce's favorite chapter, was no doubt taken out of the encyclopedia just as I took some recent work relating to charcoal out of the encyclopedia. I added to it, of course—and I'm sure he did, too—but the skeleton was there for the having, so to speak. The dictionary is a gold mine and so is the encyclopedia. Joyce had that very great one, which I used to have as a child, but unfortunately no longer have. It was put in a garage in Southern California and mildewed, otherwise I would try to get hold of it. Now it's very hard to find that edition.

I had the notion when I was asked to write for the Walker Art Institute in the series on "The Meanings of Modernism," to write a text against the 'march of understanding,' and to make clear the virtues of remaining ignorant in the face of art. Mink says that it is no longer possible to take this naive attitude, that enough is known about *Finnegan's Wake* to make it imperative to know more and ultimately to destroy it. I work at . . . keeping it mysterious. Instead of understanding it, I would like, if I can, to help keep the work of Joyce mysterious.

Satie has avoided problems of being understood through seeming to people to be too simple to bother to analyze, I think—so that people leave his work alive without analyzing it. But I didn't do that. I analyzed it and I still find it beautiful. I think it was because he had, as I've had, a rhythmic (empty time) structure rather than a structure connected with the surface result (the notes). I'm arguing on the other side of the fence from Steve Reich and from critics in general, many of whom say that my work is trivial since it can't really be analyzed in the conventional sense. What can be analyzed in my work or criticized are the questions that I ask. But most of the critics don't trouble to find out what those questions are. And that would make the difference between one composition made with chance operations and another. That is, the principle underlying the results of those chance operations is the questions . . . the things which should be criticized, if one wants to criticize, are the questions that are asked.

I had the experience, in writing *Apartment House 1776*, of wanting to do something with early American music that would let it keep its flavor at the same time that it would lose what was so obnoxious to me: its harmonic tonality. My first questions were superficial and so resulted in superficial variations on the origi-

nals. Not having, as most musicians do, an ear for music, I don't hear music when I write it; I only hear it when it's played. If I heard it when I was writing it, I would write what I've already heard; whereas since I can't hear it while I'm writing it, I'm able to write something that I've never heard before. The result was that I was working so fast, and against a deadline in the case of *Apartment House 1776*, that my first questions were simply questions about subtraction from the original Billings. Namely, seeing that a situation had four notes, I would ask, "Are they all four present, or only three, or two, or one?" And unfortunately, the first time I did it, I did it with respect to a piece that was interesting in itself, so that when I subtracted from it, it remained interesting. When I played it, it was new and beautiful. And so, not being able to hear them, I then did that with respect to the forty-three other pieces, and it took me a long time. When I got to a piano and tried them out, they were miserable. No good at all. Not worth the paper they were written on. It was because the question was superficial. I hadn't found what was at the basis of my trouble with tonal music. I hadn't rid the music of the theory. The cadences all remained recognizable.

Then I thought I should include silence. I did that (asking, "Are four present, or three, or two, or one, or none?") and again wrote a beautiful piece. I again wrote all forty-four pieces and again they were not good. So I came back to the problem and saw that I had to go deeper into it. Finally I took—my question was for each line—which tones of fourteen tones in one of the voices were active, and I would get through chance operations an answer like this: number one, seven, eleven, and fourteen. That would mean that the active one was first a sound, then silence. The first sound I would write from Billings, put it down and extend it all the way up to the seventh tone; and at the seventh tone, a silence would begin that would last to the eleventh tone. I would then write the eleventh tone, and it would last to the fourteenth, and at the fourteenth, a silence. Therefore the cadences and everything disappeared; but the flavor remained. You can recognize it as eighteenth century music; but it's suddenly brilliant in a new way. It is because each sound vibrates from itself, not from a theory. The theory is no longer in power. The cadences which were the function of the theory, to make syntax and all, all of that is gone, so that you get the most marvelous overlappings.

Cope: In relating *Finnegan's Wake* to, say, *A Lecture on Nothing*, when you actually marked off the seconds, etc. (sometimes, for example, placing a very few words for ten seconds and at other times a great many for the same duration), rhythm seems to play a very important part in the performance process.

Cage: Yes. The same would be true of *Empty Words* if I read that now. I had a very strange experience. When I finished the first part of *Empty Words*, I read that when people asked me to give a lecture. When I finished the second part, I read it instead of the first, the third instead of the second, and so on. And then it became necessary to read all four for a projected *Tomato* recording which hasn't been published yet. I had, through reading excessively the third and fourth parts, forgotten how to read the first and second. Fortunately I had written the introductions, the head notes, which are printed in *Empty Words*, and so I studied those carefully. They told me how to do it. I had written out very clearly the directions. But most people don't read those head notes, so they don't know how to read it. For instance, Jackson MacLow complains that he likes *Empty Words* when I read it but he doesn't himself enjoy reading it. If he would read how to read it, he would enjoy it. What you do is take the stanzas in the first and second parts and you count them in relation to a total length of time, which is 2 1/2 hours, and you find out what the time length of each stanza is by division. Then ones that have few words in them have silences or opportunities for space, whereas the ones that have many words have to be read very quickly. You then have a rhythmic situation that is absolutely fascinating. If you pay attention, as I say in the introduction, to each single letter, and not to the groups in their ordinary sound, it becomes most interesting. It gets more musical, the more you pay attention to the time and to the sounds.

Cope: I often state, and believe to be true, that there is no piece of music written in the past thirty years that has not felt the influence in some measure of John Cage. I know of few composers who do not pay full respect to you regarding their own work. How do you react to this?

Cage: I try to be totally ignorant of that. That's the only way I know of to solve it. I don't think it's accurate, though. I think that when a person does something he does it originally, even if he's thinking of something he calls an influence. I really think that each person does his own work.

Cope: I guess the kind of influence I am referring to is that of, for example, Lutosławski, who,

when I saw him a few years ago, claimed that his music was radically changed after he heard your *Concert for Piano and Orchestra.*

Cage: That's a very good example. He does say that he made certain changes in his work after hearing mine. What he did, of course, was original to him and that's exactly what I'm saying, so I don't feel any problem there at all and I enjoy his work when I hear it, and I enjoy it as *his* rather than as *mine*. I think that's what is good about my influence, if there is one, that there are more possibilities open to people than there were when I was young.

When I was young you had either to follow Stravinsky or Schoenberg. There was no alternative. There was nothing else to do. You could perhaps have felt that you could follow Bartók, or you could have translated that Bartók into Cowell or Ives; but we didn't think that way then. We thought Schoenberg or Stravinsky; and the schools certainly felt that way. I think, for example, that folk music was thought of only in the way that Stravinsky thought of it. Now, of course, there are 1001 things to do, and I think that that's partly a result of a kind of step that not only I took, but others took.

Cope: Are you familiar with some of the work that was done about eight years ago with wiring plants with electrodes and tying these through synthesizers?

Cage: Yes; I've done that.

Cope: What were the results?

Cage: It was most interesting, and I have a project (unfortunately it hasn't taken place yet) to amplify a city park for children. It was to be done at Ivrea near Turino where the Olivetti company is. There is a marvelous hill in the center of the city that is high and has a beautiful view of the Alps, and is isolated enough from the traffic sounds so that you hear the sounds of the plants. The project fell through, but I was invited to do the same kind of project in Rome and also in Zagreb; but I haven't accepted it until I accept the place. I was spoiled by that marvelous situation in Ivrea where the silence—when you weren't playing the plants—was very audible and beautiful; you could hear it as if you were in a concert hall. In other words, I wanted the silence of the mountain to be heard by the children after they had heard the sounds that they themselves had made by playing the plants. We were going to have a programmed arrangement so that every now and then the plants were going to become unplayable, and the children would be obliged to hear the silence. Otherwise the children would have been making noises continually.

Did you hear the music with cactus (*Child of Tree*)? That was what that came out of. For a dance of Merce Cunningham's I used cacti. I made the sounds on cacti and a few other plant materials. That led to the idea of amplifying a park, and that's led to the idea that I've found quite fascinating: a piece of music performed by animals, and butterflies, which sounds fantastic now but is almost within reach, I think, of our technology.

It was a question where someone would come to me and say that they wanted to study. People still do that. I receive letters that say that so and so has come to the conclusion that he must study with me, and would I accept this situation. I mostly refuse. Now and then circumstances arise or a letter is such that I break my rule. I then don't teach, but I let the person come as an apprentice. The trouble with that is that when I find out who the person is, I become interested in him or her and I end by teaching a little bit, perhaps.

I have worked recently with a film maker, for example. He wasn't really studying music, rather film making. Therefore he was perfectly willing to help me in my music work because it didn't disturb his film making any more than it disturbed my music making. And he was discovering from something that wasn't teaching, really. He is currently making films with elaborate uses of chance operations, and applying it to every aspect of film making. The results are quite marvelous. One sees films like one has never seen. Robert Rayher is his name.

In 1969 at the University of California at Davis, I taught a course. In the beginning I stated that we didn't know what we were studying. I had also said when they asked me to come and teach, that I would only teach if everyone in the class got an "A." They agreed to that and it became acknowledged that that was happening, so it was a very large class. Assuming that we didn't know what we were studying, we subjected the entire university library, which included books that you could get from Berkeley, to chance operations, so that each person was reading his book instead of everybody reading the same book. This was pointed out through chance operations. If the book a student was to read wasn't in, the student read the book preceding or following, according to chance operations, in the catalog. If the book he found was too big, he then subjected the book itself, or the parts of it, to chance operations, so that he knew which part to read. The result was that everyone studied and knew different information and was interesting to everyone else in the class. Rather than being in competition with one another, we all became givers of gifts. It was a very happy, pleasant and productive class, and productive of all kinds of things. There were some people who were cooking and other people who were making films, writing music, and so on.

Cope: Some of your critics have mentioned to me that one major factor in being alienated from your thoughts and music is that of a sense of avoiding skills, or avoiding a practiced or virtuoso approach. Their notion of 'skill' and 'virtuoso' is based on deciding something is good and working to intensify that narrowly as a goal until it is spectacular. Do you agree with the criticism (or even believe it to be a criticism), or are such critics simply missing the point of your ideas?

Cage: That's a mistake on their part. Most of my music is written for virtuosos. The orchestra music is not written for virtuosos because orchestral musicians are not virtuosos. But the *Music of Changes* was written for David Tudor, and he is a virtuoso pianist. The *Etudes Australes* were written for Grete Sultan, and are probably the most difficult piano pieces ever written, demanding skills that include even how to sit at the piano. I receive over and over again letters from virtuoso pianists who find these pieces fascinating, most recently from Roger Woodward. He says that he's fascinated by them. I've heard different pianists play them and I'm delighted to see that the pieces will have a long life; again, in opposition to the general critical thought that my music will evaporate into thin air the day I die—which I don't think is true. If it did, I think there is enough of it around that it would germinate again, that it would come back. But I'm not concerned, really.

The pieces that I'm writing now for Paul Zukofsky he says are the most difficult violin pieces that have ever been written. He objects to that difficulty and he can't work at them for more than about five minutes at a time. He has to stop and rest. Too difficult. On the other hand, he has explained to me, since I don't play the violin, that the history of violin literature has been one of increased difficulty as time goes on, so that it's only reasonable that these pieces should be more difficult than previous pieces for the violin.

We've worked on these closely now for three years. Now we're revising them, because through questioning me more closely, Zukofsky discovered that he had taught me about the difference of the strings and the practicality of using them; had given me, so to speak, a little bit of knowledge and, instead of letting the chance operations play utterly, I had modified them by what I thought was appropriate, violinistic. So now we are revising them and going back and letting the chance operations play utterly, and only modifying them when, from Zukofsky's point of view, it's literally impossible. The result is that it is a give and take between practicality and chance operations.

And it is this kind of use of chance operations that takes place in choreography, because when we leave architecture or the dance—things that depend on gravity and physicality—and move to something that, as Kierkegaard says, is free from physical problems, then we get into the area of great freedom that we think is characteristic of music. But if you then come back to music, not through its theory, but through the playing of an instrument, and the attendant virtuosity, then it becomes like dancing or architecture; whether or not the person can do it is the question.

Zukofsky is courageous; he is willing to do the impossible, which is what Schoenberg demanded in the *Violin Concerto*. And Zukofsky is willing at the same time that he is complaining. I keep track of his answers to my questions: of what is possible when you have your finger on such and such a string, and this finger on such and such another string, what you can do with the third finger. And we are going to publish the results. I have quite a card index; it includes all the questions regarding three fingers and what you can do with the fourth. He regrets that he published that article about all the possible harmonics. Some composers using it have written music that doesn't make sense, he says. I'm working partly with that article but also, again, getting Zukofsky to edit it, or to revise it where necessary. So that these pieces are being made as a choreography on the violinist, which is the opposite of what a reasonable composer would do. Stockhausen, for instance, said to me once, "If you were writing a song, would you write music or write for the singer?" I said unhesitatingly that I would write for the singer. And he said, "That's the difference between us; I would write music." But then he wrote a song for Cathy Berberian and she couldn't sing it, because he asked her to whistle. She can do everything but she can't whistle. It had to be changed.

Cope: It would seem to me that even on another level there is skill necessary in developing the right questions; how and when to ask these questions in the compositional process?

Cage: I have enormous amounts of energy; I still do. And so I've never made composing easy for myself. Many people discount chance operations altogether as a simple way to make music. But it isn't. It's very time-consuming and very tedious; I've developed it to a high point.

Cope: In *Music of Changes* you spent at least nine months . . .

Cage: Yes, and these etudes (*Freeman Etudes* for violin) have taken three years; I'm nowhere near the end of them, and some of them will be literally impossible to play. It's just hopeless to think that they would be played, so we've decided to include them in the series but to synthesize them.

Cope: Was there any thought to do as Ives mentioned, to have them "remain in the leaf," as in *114 Songs*, where it is suggested that they should not be performed at all?

Cage: I am going to write them anyway, knowing that they can't be done, because nowadays we can synthesize them. In Ives's case it was just due to his point in time, I think. He would have wanted them performed now, if he were working now. He would be foolish not to. In other words, it would be "un-Nancarrowish." What's needed in this case is a 'player violin.'

Or violin four hands! At the same time that I've been writing the *Violin Etudes*, I have been writing pieces that I call "music of contingency," in which there is a rupture between cause and effect, so that the causes that are introduced don't necessarily produce effects.

Cope: Is the fact that recent pieces have taken so long to compose related simply to larger forces and longer pieces or to a deeper relationship with the fact that intricate chance operations take immense amounts of time to work out?

Cage: In the early '40's I wrote *The Book of Music* for two pianos, which is an extensive piece, and which took me a long time. That, I think, was the first piece that took a great deal of time for me. I had in mind to write a long piece that would last the whole evening. It didn't have a title but it turned into those pieces called *She is Asleep*. The part of the evening up to the intermission was to be the female principle, and the part after intermission was to be the male principle. That division is the division of *The Book of Music*, too; in two parts. I wanted to do it then with prepared piano, singers, and with chamber music that would make an evening. I only started the first part and then dropped the project. Then the next big work that came was the *Music of Changes*, and then those time length pieces. Things got longer and longer . . . *Atlas*, and so on . . . endless.

My plan, when I finish the violin pieces, is to write for another virtuoso. I'm fascinated nowadays by the virtuosos, not as a musical solution only, but as an example to society of the possibility of accomplishing the impossible, because our society in general now has serious problems. If they aren't solved, we are in, as Fuller puts it, "danger of oblivion." The example of the virtuoso seems to me more and more necessary to a society that thinks that nothing can be done. Most people don't lift a finger to help society because they think it is hopeless. That's why I insist upon this virtuoso situation and carrying it to impossible lengths now. Grete Sultan's devotion to the *Etudes Australes* is fantastic. She can now play, I think, the first twenty-four all the way through, and they are incredibly difficult, and she has had, as I have, bad arthritis. But at my advice she is on the macrobiotic diet and, like me, has shown incredible improvement. Her ability now is amazing. It's extraordinary. She plays beautifully.

Chapter 6

EXPERIMENTALISM

FUNDAMENTALS

Experimentalism represents, for the purposes of this text, a redefining of the boundaries of music (Austin 1969; Landy 1994; Shattuck 1968). "Art as life" or "art as everything" both qualify. The influence of artists such as Marcel Duchamp, Man Ray, Robert Rauschenberg, Wassily Kandinsky, and many others has been profound. Mainstream composers like Schoenberg, who was himself an expressionist painter of repute, and Stravinsky were influenced by expressionistic painters like Picasso. In the avant-garde, cross-relationships, particularly between composers and artists such as Erik Satie (Man Ray), John Cage (Robert Rauschenberg), and Earle Brown (Alexander Calder), abound (Higgins 1966).

The music of Erik Satie, particularly in works like *Vexations* (1893?, a 24-hour marathon work for piano), appear among the first to clearly demonstrate experimental tendencies (Painter 1992). The *Musical Sculpture* (undated) by Marcel Duchamp is also noteworthy as an example of concept art. Duchamp's early work *The Bride Stripped Bare by Her Bachelors, Even* is especially provocative. His *Erratum Musical* (1913) substitutes numbers for notes. Petr Kotik has made two current realizations, one for two pianos, the other for five instruments. The dada artists and later the antiart, concept art, and minimal art movements have all preceded parallel activities in music (Motherwell 1951).

Paul Nougé, active in the surrealistic movement, points out in his *Music Is Dangerous* (1929) that most known uses of music—relaxation, forgetting, and pleasure—are but subtle facades for music's emotional dangers, drawing proofs from ancient modal theories wherein each mode provoked distinct emotions (phrygian: excitement; lydian: calming; etc.). Nougé's *iatric* music attempts to establish music's profound remedial capabilities. Most important, however, Nougé proposes that audiences are not safe from musical effects:

"Our answer is that the concept of spectator, which seems to play so important a role in certain minds, is one of the grossest imaginable." (Nougé 1973) Nougé's writings have not had direct influence over recent experimentalism. However, such expressions as ". . . how we may defend ourselves against music . . . Evidently, the easiest way is to refuse once and for all to have anything to do with it . . ." describe the results many experimental works have had on audiences.

Robert Rauschenberg has substantially affected a number of composers, possibly more than any artist aside from Jackson Pollock and Marcel Duchamp. His *Erased de Kooning Drawing* is exactly that: a de Kooning drawing, one he obtained directly from the artist himself, erased as completely as possible using a special selection of erasers collected by Rauschenberg. The act of decomposing the work of art becomes, in this instance, the act of creation of a nearly blank sheet of paper, showing only slight depressions in the paper where the original drawing once existed. If any act can be considered plausible art, then Rauschenberg's erasure presents a work as viably artistic as the original drawing.

Rauschenberg's *Black Painting* of 1952 demonstrates both the conceptual nature of his work and the complexity of shading provided the right lighting. This painting is entirely black. Rauschenberg has focused on the reflective nature of the paint and viewers see as much as they wish to in the monochromatic canvas. Paul Ignace indicates some of the rationale behind his motivations in creating experimental music in a letter to the author.

> When I was first asked to compose a piece for orchestra I had no idea what they wanted, except an experience of some kind. I wrote and asked for a complete list of the other works included in concerts of the series, and when I discovered that the concert preceding the night of my premiere included Berlioz's *Symphonie*

Fantastique, I made up my mind. I insisted that my work be unrehearsed (there wouldn't have been much anyway, as those things go) and that I would bring score and parts the night of the concert. Imagine the shock when the conductor and players opened their music to find the work that they had performed the night before . . . but they performed it, much to the anger and horror of the audience and reviewers. They were angry, of course, not at the sounds but at my plagiarism (legal, according to copyright laws) but few realized they listened to the sounds in an entirely new way—something very good, very creative, in my way of thinking. No, I did not receive money for my endeavor! (The work, by the way, was titled *Symphonie Fantastique No. 2.*) (letter to the author)

Yehuda Yannay's *Houdini's Ninth* (1970) represents experimental theater quite representative of this genre. Bernard Jacobson characterizes one performance in this excerpt from *Stereo Review*:

A man cycled onto the stage, put a record of the (Beethoven) Choral Symphony finale on a phonograph, and proceeded to mix some kind of culinary concoction onto the surface of the actual disc, with bizarre effects on the sound. This was interwoven with an episode involving a double-bass player in a sort of straitjacket, and dominating the proceedings was a projection of an incredibly stupid poem published in *Dwight's Journal of Music*, Boston, on December 17, 1870. It was in honor of Beethoven's centenary, and took a very encouraging view of his affliction of deafness: "A price how small," it cheerily informed him, "for privilege how great, / When thy locked sense groped upward and there / The shining ladder reaching through the air." (Jacobson 1970)

Encouraged by the words of social philosophers Marshall McLuhan and R. Buckminster Fuller, and his own studies with Eastern philosopher Suzuki, John Cage developed a personal philosophy expressed in his sweeping statement, "Everything we do is music." His works encompass most of the experimental concepts of the past sixty years: electronic, improvisatory, indeterminate, exploratory, and experimental (Born 1974; Cage 1969, 1973; Kostelanetz 1968, 1970). From Cage's work in the 1930s, when he originated the prepared piano, to his extension of multimedia happenings, he remained the remarkable enigma (Kostelanetz 1967, 1980). Cage's ideas and works amuse, startle, antagonize, and somehow also encourage the worlds of music, dance, and art. If change be the mark of greatness, then John Cage has surely reached this pinnacle. Nothing in music will surely be the same after him (Cage 1957, 1982; Duckworth 1995).

Aside from Cage, no other composer has achieved the shock value of, and relevance to, experimentalism, except perhaps La Monte Young. In particular, his *Composition 1960 #3*, the duration of which is announced and the audience told to do whatever they wish for the remainder of the composition, and *Composition 1960 #6*, where the performers stare and react exactly as if they were the audience, represent excellent examples of experimental music.

Critics of these and other experimentalists address themselves to the pointless philosophies implied (Byron 1975). To these, I. A. MacKenzie has replied:

Art is imitation, repetition, memory, or rejection of life. Nothing is created by man, just recreated: a storeroom to collect the bits and pieces of the whole he feels worthy of saving, to be brought to life again whenever the need occurs, but never as good as the original. Art exists only as a refuge against new experience, un-recreated experience with reality: second-hand living. The terms "musician," "painter," "writer," merely break these limitations down further for easier construction, assimilation, and comfort. I am none of these. I am not an artist. I do not imitate, or need of developing a memory with art, for a thousand million possibilities of the present confront me, and I don't want that number diminished by one. I am a mapmaker, a suggester of possible routes for those interested in experiences with what has already been created—everything. I am similar to the "artist" in that I do not create, dissimilar with him in that I do not pretend to. Untouched by style, convenience, or tradition, the elements I observe (not manipulate) I discovered, but only for myself and my discovery has style, convenience just as yours. I do nothing that anyone else could not do easily and do not pretend to. I only give directions when someone wishes them and would be happy to stop anytime . . . Everything exists: why should I mechanically alter one thing into another, one thought into another? All exists, it is much more to find the original. (Cope 1970, p. 2)

New experiments are necessary, important, and contribute to the arts. Cage speaks of this in *A Year from Monday*: "Art's in process of coming into its own: life." and "We used to have the artist up on a pedestal. Now he's no more extraordinary than we are." (Cage 1967, p. 6) Tristan Tzara adds: "Art is not the most precious manifestation of life. Art has not the celestial and universal value that people like to attribute to it. Life is far more interesting." (Motherwell 1951, p. 248) These views extend our definitions of music to include danger music, conceptualism, biomusic, and soundscapes (Byron 1975; Palmer 1981; Partch 1973; Prévost 1995; Schafer 1974).

DANGER MUSIC

The history of danger music includes Paul Nougé's *Music Is Dangerous* (Nougé 1973). As Nougé points out, while we may use music for relaxation, forgetting, or pleasure it . . . "probably entails serious consequences" (Nougé 1973). This book describes many accounts of unfortunate encounters with the dangers of music:

> Sometimes we find peculiar stories in a newspaper. A few weeks ago, a young American went home after coming out of a performance of Tannhauser, and killed himself; not without having first written a note in which he explained that where Tannhauser had weakened, he, yes he, would set a better example of courage and grandeur. (Nougé 1973)

More recent danger music involves more direct conflict with performers or spectators (Johnson 1980). For example, the score to Nam June Paik's *Danger Music for Dick Higgins* reads: "Creep into the Vagina of a Living Whale" (Cage 1969). Figure 6.1 shows Paik during a 1962 Fluxus performance.

The visual arts have had direct influence on danger music. The artist Ayo, for example, has created a number of finger boxes each containing an unknown object. Viewers experience the art by placing their fingers into these small creations, some of which contain felt, fur, and similar benign objects. Some of the boxes, however, contain razor blades, broken glass, and pocketknives.

Figure 6.1.   Nam June Paik during a 1962 *Fluxus* performance.

Though blood has spilled during danger music performances, violence seldom occurs as a direct consequence of composer intention (Higgins 1966). Accidents often are welcomed, however. Such was the case with two happenings in 1962. The first involved a somewhat bloodied Robert Whitman at Bennington College. The second saw a woman spectator/performer at an Al Hansen happening fall from a window down a number of stories and eventually through a glass roof.

Robert Ashley's *Wolfman* (1964) exemplifies danger music. This work includes prerecorded tape with a voice screaming through a microphone creating feedback turned to extremely loud levels, easily reaching decibel counts above danger points. The recording of this work, with instructions "to be played at the highest possible volume level," constitutes direct danger to those listening in a small room.

Figure 6.2.   Robert Ashley.

Phil Corner's adaptation of his own prelude from *4 Suits* creates interesting danger music:

> I threw out a rifle and then slowly picked it up and pointed it at the audience (no one bolted for the doors, by the way) . . . counterpointed by a woman who slowly picked up a bouquet of roses—there was a countdown . . . at the end of which she threw the flowers into the audience, all over, with great love and joy, while I silently let fall the rifle and slunk offstage. Yet this was apparently not the right message for some, as I was accosted afterwards by one of the Up Against The Wall Motherfucker crowd, and yelled at: "Next time a real rifle!" (letter to the author)

Corner's *One antipersonnel-type CBU bomb will be thrown into the audience* represents another example of danger music. Corner speaks of this work:

> I tried to push the concert situation to a point where those present would have to feel the immediacy of the situation—their situation, since this had to be something in which those present shared a complicity. Failure! Could I have been that naive? For the audience reaction is not predictable. I discovered that right then and there. For that reason the thing was not even ever done. The defenses against identify-

ing with the victims, with putting ourselves in their places, is too strong. Guilt is covered up by a selfish fear. A self-serving, even dishonest one, I might add. I felt it then and still do. The idea that that would really be acted on, that a real terrorist act would be announced so and carried out in this way seems to me incredible. Finally though, the "performance" would have been to announce the cancellation of the performance. (letter to the author)

Daniel Lentz comments in the Coda of his *Skeletons Don't Say Peek*:

I too am sad. In fact, I am very sad. Men are still fighting wars and playing music. Some are guerrilla wars, and some are guerrilla compositions. But they are, nevertheless, war and music. They are fought with weapons and instruments. There is so little difference. One type is used for the defense of an army or nation; the other, for the defense of a vestigial culture. Do we need the protection of generals and composers? Do we need their incredibly scary anti-ballistic-missile systems and synthesizers? Shouldn't we attempt their destruction, before they destroy us? From whom are they protecting us? From the Russians? The Princetonians? What, in the late-middle twentieth century does weaponry have to do with music? Can we eliminate one without first eliminating the other? Won't the metaphor be too powerful until it is taken away? Has there ever been an instrument built which wasn't used? Couldn't the players you saw in action tonight just as well have been aggressive soldiers of war? Did you watch closely their gestures? Is there a real difference between them and the Special Forces? Are they not identical mentalities? They are out to kill us and you sit there waiting. Are you all crazy? Can't you see, nor hear? But wait . . . don't blame the players. We are only cogs in the great hierarchy. We follow directions. The artistic generals tell us what to do and when to do it and the manner in which it is to be done. They are not even spe-

cific. Aren't they kind, as they destroy us? We are like you: just poor citizens caught up in the immense musical-industrial complex. Sure, if you threaten us or our friends, we will play for you. We have no recourse but to protect our "raison d'etre." (Budd 1969)

Prior to this final announcement, all the instruments have been taken from the performers, placed in front of the piano, and saluted. The act of not playing, the drama of confronting the audience, contradicts traditional performance concepts.

While at the University of California, Santa Barbara, Lentz formed the conceptual music California Time Machine ensemble. The CTM performed extensively on the West Coast and toured Europe in 1969 and 1970. In 1973 Lentz founded and directed the San Andreas Fault ensemble of eight singers and players (with Lentz conducting). Its repertoire consisted of pieces specially composed for it by Budd, Eister, Stock, Strange, Lentz, and others. In 1982 Lentz founded the Daniel Lentz Group. His works include *After Images: 1980*, *Apologetica: I Cantori* (1998), and *Missa Umbrarum* (1991).

In Lentz's *Anti Bass Music* (see Figure 6.3) a number of notations relate the concert situation to the battlefield. This work, supplied with four optional endings that may be performed in multiples, includes a reading of a list of American composers not killed in Vietnam, and the use of twenty-five to one hundred laughing machines (Lentz 1972; MacLow 1970).

CONCEPTUALISM

Minimal and concept music are so closely related that separation becomes difficult (Johnson 1980; Moore 1970; Nyman 1974). Works such as Robert Rauschenberg's *White Paintings* (canvases covered as evenly as possible with white paint) parallel conceptual music such as John Cage's classic *4'33"*. This latter work received its first performance in August 1952, at Woodstock, New York by pianist David Tudor. Using

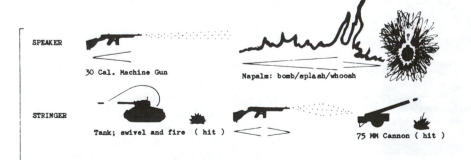

Figure 6.3. From Daniel Lentz's *Anti Bass Music*, page 11.

a stopwatch, Tudor covered the piano keyboard at the beginning of each movement, playing nothing, but timing the movements marked by Cage in the otherwise blank score (movements of one minute, forty seconds; two minutes, twenty-three seconds; and thirty seconds respectively). Unfortunately, the brilliance of Tudor's dramatic performance had the adverse effect of limiting this work to piano (the score reads "for any instrument or combination of instruments"). Virtually any sound or combination of sounds with a total duration of four minutes and thirty-three seconds will successfully realize the score, from thinking-in-a-bathtub to silence by a symphony orchestra. Cage has clarified the concept behind such works:

> . . . where it is realized that sounds occur whether intended or not, one turns in the direction of those he does not intend. The turning is psychological and seems at first to be a giving up of everything that belongs to humanity—for a musician, the giving up of music. This psychological turning leads to the world of nature, where, gradually or suddenly, one sees that humanity and nature, not separate, are in this world together; that nothing was lost when everything was given away. In fact, everything is gained. (Cage 1961, p. 8)

Rauschenberg's *White Paintings* link further with *4'33"* in that the *White Paintings* involve the shadows of spectators, variance of lights, reflections, and so on which turn the seemingly blank canvas into a counterpoint of visual activity. In *4'33"*, the coughs, laughter, and other audible movements of the audience as well as extraneous sounds become, in fact, the work. In both cases the creator has produced a conceptual work of art (Gaburo 1975; Johnson 1974; Knowles 1976).

La Monte Young's concept music includes *Composition 1960 #7*, which contains only the notes B and F# with the instructions: to be held for a "long time." *Composition 1960 #10* requests that the performer "draw a straight line and follow it." In 1960, at Berkeley, Young presented a composition that consisted of turning loose a jar full of butterflies on an unsuspecting audience. Other compositions of 1960 include his famous line piece:

> My *Composition 1960 No. 9* consists of a straight line drawn on a piece of paper. It is to be performed and comes with no instructions. The night I met Jackson MacLow we went down to my apartment and he read some of his poems for us. Later when he was going home, he said he'd write out directions to get to his place so we could come and visit him sometime. He happened to pick up "Composition No. 9" and said,

"Can I write it here?" I said, "No, wait, that's a piece. Don't write on that." He said, "Whadaya mean a piece? That's just a line." (Young and Zazeela 1969)

Karlheinz Stockhausen's *Mikrophonie 1* (1964) uses only one sound source, a large tam-tam upon which performers manipulate the various verbal instructions of the score, "scraping, trumpeting," and so on.

Eric Andersen's *Opus 48* ("Which turns anonymous when the instruction is carried out") is sent through the mail on a piece of cardboard that states in total: "Place the chosen tautology." Tom Johnson, in his book *Imaginary Music*, includes a number of unplayable concept pieces (Johnson 1974). His *Celestial Music for Imaginary Trumpets*, shown in Figure 6.4, cannot be performed but only conceptualized or imagined. Robert Moran's *Composition for Piano with Pianist* states: "A pianist comes onto the stage and goes directly to the concert grand piano. He climbs into the piano, and sits on the strings. The piano plays him" (Moran 1973, p. 44).

Accidents (1967) by Larry Austin contains instructions for the pianist to perform the music without creating actual sounds. The required speed of performance makes *accidents* unavoidable. As if repenting, performers must return to each gesture in which an accident occurred (i.e., a sound made) and repeat it until error-free (silence).

The German-originated but often New York-based movement Fluxus (which included Paik, Young, Dick Higgins, Eric Andersen, Thomas Schmidt, Jackson MacLow, and George Brecht) led the conceptual art/ music movement for a number of years, finally becoming a publisher of art objects. Empty objects provided the objectives in the experiments of these composers, poets, and artists. Often their works do not contain hints of intended action or what materials to use (Osterreich 1977; Zimmerman 1976). Figure 6.5 shows George Maciunas's view of the Fluxus art movement. The references to "Spikes (sic) Jones" and Duchamp suggest the levity that many members of the group felt about their projects. Figures 6.6 and 6.7 provide photo documentation of some of the members of Fluxus. Other individuals involved (but not shown here) included Jonas Mekas, Bob Watts, Ben Patterson, and Joe Jones.

Text sound music is based on the *textljud kompositioner* of two Swedish composers, Lars-Gunnar Bodin and Bengt-Emil Johnson in 1966. Termed sound poetry, speech music, and even lexical music, its origins extend back to the Futurists (in Italy) just after the turn of the century. Works in this genre expand to include reading and speaking as music by using ono-

Figure 6.4.
From Tom
Johnson's
*Celestial Music
for Imaginary
Trumpets.* ©
Copyright 1974
by Tom
Johnson. All
rights reserved.
Used by per-
mission. From
*Imaginary
Music* by Tom
Johnson, Two
Eighteen Press,
NY.

ART	FLUXUS ART-AMUSEMENT

To justify artist's professional, parasitic and elite status in society, he must demonstrate
  artist's indispensability and exclusiveness, he must demonstrate
  the dependability of audience upon him, he must demonstrate
  that no one but the artist can do art.
	To establish artist's nonprofessional status in society, he must demonstrate
	  artist's dispensability and inclusiveness, he must demonstrate
	  the selfsufficiency of the audience, he must demonstrate
	  that anything can be art and anyone can do it.

Therefore, art must appear to be complex, pretentious, profound, serious, intellectual, inspired, skillfull, significant, theatrical, it must appear to be valuable as commodity so as to provide the artist with an income.
 	
To raise its value (artist's income and patrons profit), art is made to appear rare, limited in quantity and therefore obtainable and accessible only to the social elite and institutions.
	Therefore, art-amusement must be simple, amusing, unpretentious, concerned with insignificances, require no skill or countless rehearsals, have no commodity or institutional value.
	The value of art-amusement must be lowered by marking it unlimited, massproduced, obtainable by all and eventually produced by all.
	Fluxus art-amusement is the rear-guard without any pretention or urge to participate in the competition of „one-upmanship" with the avant-garde. It strives for the monostructural and nontheatrical qualities of simple natural event, a game or a gag. It is the fusion of Spikes Jones, Vaudeville, gag, children's games and Duchamp.
	
	George Maciunas
	
	from: Happening & Fluxus
	   Materials put together by H. Sohm
	   Kölnischer Kunstverein 1970

Figure 6.5.   *Fluxus* by George Maciunas from *Happening and Fluxus.* Materials assembled by H. Sohm, Kölnischer Kunstverein, 1970.

Figure 6.6.   Mieko Shiomi and
Alison Knowles during a performance of *Disappearing Music for
Face (smile-no smile)* at the Washington Square Gallery on October
30, 1964.

Figure 6.7.   Fluxus members (left to
right): Emmett Williams, Robert Filliou,
George Brecht, Eric Andersen, Thomas
Schmit, Robin Page, and Ben Vautier at
the exhibition of *Happening and Fluxus*
at the Kölnischer Kunstverein. Photo by
Ad Petersen.

matopoeia and other intricate textural processes to produce rhythmic and contrapuntal sound structures. Often these works incorporate long repetitions of text in solo or ensemble situations, with changing and developing emphasis, accents, and meaning. Frequently these works also use electronic processes to alter timbres.

Composers of conceptual music/art early in this century include Hugo Ball, Tristan Tzara, and Kurt Schwitters in the 1920s, Marcel Duchamp in the 1930s and 1940s, and John Cage in the 1950s and 1960s. Composers currently interested in the genre include John Giorno, Aram Saroyan, Brion Gysin, Beth Anderson, Robert Ashley, Anthony Gnazzo, Tim Bell, Stephen Ruppenthal, and Charles Amirkhanian. Amirkhanian has produced a large number of text-sound works, including *Seatbelt Seatbelt* (1973), *Mugic* (1973), *Mahogany Ballpark* (1976), and *Dutiful Ducks* (1977).

BIOMUSIC

Biomusic, music typically created by natural biological means rather than by conscious attempts at composition, has produced many interesting revelations in recent years. For example, a number of composers have become interested in "brain-wave" music performance (Henahan 1970; Moore 1970). Human brains and, for that matter, those of other advanced animals, operate using of electric current. Amplifying such energy produces enough current to serve as control voltages on synthesizers utilizing normal electronic music gear such as oscillators and filters (see chapter 7). Stockhausen notes:

> . . . I attended a concert in which David Tudor, together with a composer at Davis, California, where I taught for six months, were performing a piece with "brain waves." The performance, in the beginning, seemed to be very magic-like, a table lifting society, and it seemed to promise quite a lot because of the way they were watching and looking at each other. The speakers' cardboard membranes were pushing the air, and these pulsations—a kind of colored low noise— were produced by the performer's brain waves. It's the same effect as if air were being pumped into a tire. So what? There's a certain periodicity which becomes more or less irregular, maybe interesting for doctors. (Cott 1973, p. 43)

Composer David Rosenboom has developed procedures far more sophisticated than those described by Stockhausen (Rosenboom 1976). Rosenboom has been widely acclaimed as a pioneer in American experimental music since the 1960s. He is a composer,

performer, conductor, interdisciplinary artist, author, and educator. He incorporates performance art, computer music systems, interactive multimedia, compositional algorithms, and the structure of the brain and nervous system.

Sounds of the humpback whale also have been used as biomusic:

> Quite apart from any esthetic judgment one might make about them, the sounds produced by Humpback whales can properly be called songs because they occur in complete sequences that are repeated . . . Humpback whale songs are far longer than bird songs. The shortest Humpback song recorded lasts six minutes and the longest is more than thirty minutes. (*Songs of the Humpback Whale* 1968)

Not only have recordings and tapes of the *songs* of the humpback whale become popular in and of themselves, but these songs have equally impressed composers. George Crumb's *Voice of the Whale* (*Vox Balaenae*, 1971) ". . . was inspired by the singing of the humpback whale, a tape recording of which I had heard two or three years previously" (Crumb 1971). Likewise, composers like Allen Strange and Priscilla McLean have completed works influenced by this highly developed water mammal.

Yehuda Yannay's *Bugpiece* involves yet another life form as biomusic. This work uses live notation in the form of:

> . . . one beetle, one centipede, and five or six ants. These insects were in a real sense the "composers" and conductors, even if Yannay did set up the parameters as to how the chance operations would work. All the lights in the auditorium were turned off, the overhead projector was turned on so the audience and performers (with their backs to the audience) could see the bugs running around in a plastic box set on the projector. Different areas of the "playing field" represented varieties of loud and soft. Green, yellow, and blue gels represented high and low pitches. The ants did most of the running, even one was maimed. The beetle stayed around the sides, but did make one mad dash across the field. To spark things up, the centipede was a late entry, and he chased the beetle. (Barnes 1972)

Plant-created music is described vividly in an article from *Rolling Stone*:

> It could be said they were singing, but that is too anthropomorphic a way to describe the sounds the plants were emitting: strange electronic garglings, ethereal chirpings and shriekings to a mysterious nonlinear rhythm that reveals the

secret life-pulse of the vegetable kingdom. Then something very strange happened. A spectator gently held a knife to one of the stalks and addressed the plant. "Hey you! Perk up or you get it." The words plunged the room into sudden silence. The plants stopped singing. Coleuses may be pretty but they certainly aren't dumb. Somehow the threatened plant conveyed a warning of danger to its pot-mates, and they responded by entering a sort of suspended animation . . . discovery of an early-warning system among plants is just one of the revelations that have come to three electronic music specialists at Sounds Reasonable, Inc., a recording studio in Washington, D.C. There, Ed Barnett, Norman Lederman, and Gary Burge have been experimenting with ways to create music from the silent vibes of plants. So far their efforts have yielded a single, called "Stereofernic Orchidstra" . . . the record is a studio mix of four plants, an Indian azalea, a philodendron, a Boston fern and an amaryllis, recorded at the National Botanical Gardens. The first side features the raw plant "voices" tuned to different pitches on an oscillator. It sounds like a demonic, atonal violin section in electrofrenzy. On the second side the plants control the changes on an ARP music synthesizer. The result is more musical, but no less bizarre. (Wiggins 1975, p. 12)

John Cage speaks of his work in related areas:

I've had for a long time the desire to hear the mushroom itself, and that could be done with very fine technology, because they are dropping spores and those spores are hitting surfaces. There certainly is sound taking place. . . . It leads, of course, to the thought about hearing anything in the world since we know that everything is in a state of vibration, so that not only mushrooms, but also chairs and tables, for instance, could be heard . . . (Cope 1980)

Remarkably, while representing some of the oldest forms of organized sound on earth, biomusic still engenders a wide variety of emotions from its spectators (Huff 1972).

SOUNDSCAPES

Pauline Oliveros's *Sonic Meditations* uses natural sounds quite apart from biomusic (Oliveros 1973).

V: Take a walk at night. Walk so silently that the bottoms of your feet become ears.
    and
XVII:
    Ear Ly
    (For Kenneth Gaburo's NMCE)

1. Enhance or paraphrase the auditory environment so perfectly that a listener cannot distinguish between the real sounds of the environment and the performed sounds.

2. Become performers by not performing.

Other composers, such as I. A. MacKenzie, design works without any direct reference to sound other than that inherent in the environment (see Figures 6.8 and 6.9). MacKenzie's wind sound sculptures (1930s) involve wind, water, or fire and need neither performer nor audience (see Figure 6.10). The wish, before he died, of having these sculptures placed where no one would be able to hear them bears close resemblance to the self-destructing sculptures of Jean Tinguely.

The following excerpts from an interview with MacKenzie in 1968, just three months before his death, represent his portrayal of the concert stage as the archvillain of true creativity.

MacKenzie: Basically, I was curious about the fundamental concept of whether I, or mankind for that matter, was really important in the functioning of music . . . I still followed traditional notation . . . but demanded less and less skill for the performer since it was not to be had anyway . . . my preoccupation seemed to be with creating instruments which played themselves . . . Musicians and composers . . . seem to delight in creating codes and systems that will separate them more from the common man and, I'm afraid, their audiences . . .

Cope: Was publication possible?

MacKenzie: Out of the question. By 1927 my music had become so involved in new instruments of my own invention, the publisher would have had to publish the instrument with the music. By 1930, I abandoned the written music completely anyway, believing that I should be more interested in sound than codes . . .

Cope: . . . What was your . . . reaction [to universities]?

MacKenzie: My reaction was harsh . . . The teachers were very dull; more interested in talking about sound than in sound; mostly more interested in themselves. Many times I would hear visiting composers lecture on their works . . . only to find that the lecturer was just flesh and blood, not a god . . . I found quickly that for me, at least, the university and its intellect and pomposity was creatively bankrupt: it offered nothing but security . . . and the same old traditional claptrap . . . As long as people continue to raise gods, not people, the situation won't change. As long as so-called great performers are regarded

ATR E EWH   IC H AL O NEF AL   LS...

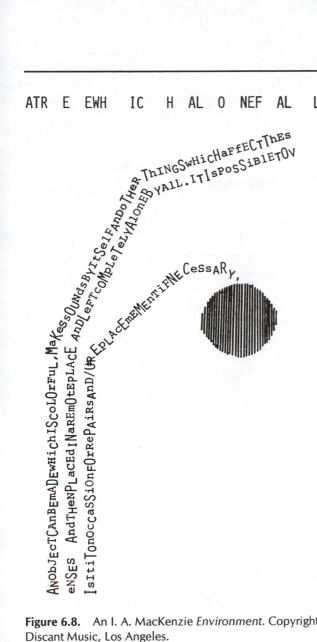

Figure 6.8. An I. A. MacKenzie *Environment*. Copyright by Discant Music, Los Angeles.

FEWeR LoVEs THaN tIME ALLoWS....

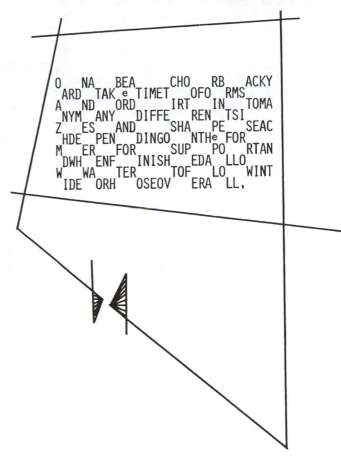

Figure 6.9. An I. A. MacKenzie *Environment*. Copyright by Discant Music, Los Angeles.

as towering musical figures, instead of rather grotesque finger gymnasts, the situation won't change. The university has contributed to this as well, creating a caste system . . .

Cope: . . . you say that around 1930 you began just creating instruments.

MacKenzie: Yes. But, more important, instruments without human performers. By 1934, early spring, I had created my first wind-sound sculpture . . . an elaboration of the old Chinese wind chimes . . . in fact, that's where I got the idea . . . I used to listen to storms approach through their sound and somehow felt I was "tuning in" on nature (nature being something I have always felt to be more impressive and profound than man or myself, to be exact) . . .

Cope: What do you consider yourself?

MacKenzie I don't. Categorizing, defining and

such limit creativity . . . Whether one thing is a work of art, and another not, is unimportant. This is cataloguing, not problem-solving. Problems are: God, beauty, nature; creating with or without them, or to them or from them. Creating is solving; cataloguing is avoiding . . . I don't dislike systems or codes any more than money; but, as before, if these are used by someone to catalogue their own or someone else's work, they have become destructive rather than helpful . . . I create what I like, in hopes that God, nature, and people (in that order) may like some or all of them . . .

. . . My sketches are, I suppose, my musical notation. However . . . when I create the work, I let it go its own way, and I sort of follow along. Problems of balance and so forth are worked out as I go along; intonation is achieved through experimentation until I have what I want . . . I am in complete control of pitch, timbre, and . . .

Figure 6.10. From *The Composer*, Vol. 1, No. 1 (June 1969). Copyright by The Composer, 1969.

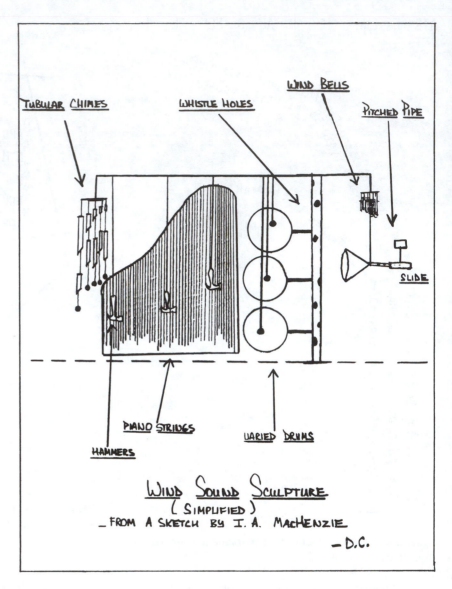

length . . . I hope the sculpture will last forever, though forever is a long time (I think).

Cope: How do you regard the partially controlled aspects?

MacKenzie: With joy. Certainly rhythm is partially controlled . . . and the same with harmony and melody, which are the least controlled.

Cope: Does it disturb you when, leaving the instrument alone, it is performing without human audience?

MacKenzie: Human audience? That's up to humans. It's never without an audience . . . I have been moving toward something, not away from something. I have never maintained that I am right or even important; I am just doing what I think I can do best . . . I have learned two very important things about sound: (1) it exists,

period. No more, no less. There is no good or bad except in individual terms . . . and (2) music (sound) communicates nothing. If I were to define (not categorize) Art, I would have to say it is that which communicates nothing. Rather, it incites or creates something new in each of us (I can say "Hello" and you can reply "Hello." This is communication, bad as it is, but it is not Art. Art's beauty and importance is that it does not communicate!) . . . Sounds hold an interest for me; I don't give a damn how one produces them . . . One last thing: if one should consider the nightingale and its music and inspect closely the battery of technique in use, he might reconsider his own bloated self-view: certainly music is sound (the existence of the former term owes to social implications only) and man, or even his life, has contributed little enough to expand its vocabulary. (Cope 1969, pp. 35–42)

Other sculptors and artists have worked in similar areas (Fontana 1987; Grayson 1977a, 1977b). The German sculptor Hans Haacke, for example, a member of Atelier 17 in Paris and a founder (along with Pene, Mack, and Vecker) of Group Zero (a group dedicated to breaking ties with the past of non-objective art), creates wind and water sculptures, as did Harry Bertoia. Japanese environmental artist Shinoda produces elaborate metal sculptures with sound as a by-product. Composer Jon Hassell also has explored acoustical environments and large-scale outdoor sound-sculpture events (especially *Nadam*, a "sound-space" work). His *Landmusic Series* (1969–72), like Oliveros's *Sonic Meditations*, incorporates texts as scores: "Underground thunder spreading across an open field." Another work in the series calls for compact battery-powered speaker, microphone, and amplifier combinations to be planted in trees to produce subtle sound amplifications of "wind, leaves, birds, and squirrels who come near . . . " (Johnson 1974, p. 14). Terry Allen's three lead-covered eucalyptus trees (1986) installed in San Diego are equipped with especially designed loudspeakers that gently call to passersby with Navajo chants, Aztec poems, and Thai bands. These specially-designed trees are inconspicuously hidden in a forest of eucalyptus on the campus of the University of California, San Diego.

Alvin Lucier pioneered many areas of music composition and performance, including the notation of performers' physical gestures, the use of brain waves in live performance, the generation of visual imagery by sound in vibrating media, and the evocation of room acoustics for musical purposes. His recent works include a series of sound installations and works for solo instruments, chamber ensembles, and orchestra in which, by means of close tunings with pure tones, sound waves are caused to spin through space. His works include *Panorama* (1997), *Clocker* (1994), *Music on a Long Thin Wire* (1992), *Crossings* (1990), and *Still and Moving Lines of Silence in Families of Hyperbolas* (1985).

Alvin Curran's music ranges from rarefied string quartets and blaring ship horn concerts to Holocaust memorial installations; from MIDI grands to computerized rams' horns. The sounds of places and things, real and imagined, are Curran's alphabet. He co-founded the radical collective Musica Elettronica Viva with Frederic Rzewski and Richard Teitelbaum in 1966. In the 1970s, Curran created a series of solo performances. These included *Songs and Views of the Magnetic Garden, Light Flowers/Dark Flowers,* and *Canti Illuminati* for natural sounds, voice, keyboards, and found objects in a lyrical post-minimalist style. In the 1980s, Curran produced large-scale environmental works on lakes and rivers and in ports, quarries, caverns, and public buildings: *Maritime Rites, Waterworks, Monumenti, Tufo Muto, Notes From Underground* (in collaboration with the artist Melissa Gould). Using radios as geographical music instruments Curran created concerts with musicians spread all over Europe in *1985—A Piece for Peace* and in his Holocaust commemoration *Crystal Psalms* in 1988.

The World Soundscape Project explores sonic environments. Based in Canada near Vancouver and directed by R. Murray Schafer, this project attempts to bring together research on the scientific, sociological, and aesthetic aspects of the environment and has produced five significant documents to date:

1. *The Book of Noise*;
2. *Okeanos* (a ninety-minute quadraphonic tape composition by Bruce Davis, Brian Fawcett, and R. Murray Schafer, dealing with the symbolism of the ocean);
3. *The Music of the Environment* (an article on the concept of the World Soundscape; the first treatment of the acoustic environment as a macrocultural composition);
4. *A Survey of Community Noise By-Laws in Canada*;
5. *The Vancouver Soundscape* (a combination two-record set and booklet detailing a sonic study of the city of Vancouver and its environs, and concluding with two very significant chapters dealing in turn with "Noise Pollution Problems" and "Toward Acoustic Design"). (Schafer 1973)

The recordings of the World Soundscape Project include sounds of surf and suburban baseball games. Most remarkable are the extremes of everyday sounds pinpointed in this collection; sounds which ". . . too often people ignore (or think they ignore)" (Schafer 1973). The focus of these experiments are revealed in an open letter called *a brief introduction*:

> Acoustics as a design study has been limited to closed environments: concert halls, soundproof rooms and the like. It is time that acoustic design be applied to the environment as a great macrocultural composition, of which man and nature are the composers/performers. To disguise an acoustic ambiance with background music or masking noise, to block it out with ear muffs, cocoon-like sound-proof rooms or automobiles is not, in our view, a satisfactory solution to the problem of noise nor is it a creative approach to acoustic design. (Schafer 1973)

After hearing "Moozak at the Oakridge Shopping Mall," and "A Ventilator at Eaton's Department Store," one can hardly escape the intimacy and beauty of "Full Surf . . . on a Gusty March Afternoon," or

"Children's Voices, Recorded on the Playground of Seymour School . . . "

Annea Lockwood (b. 1939 in Christchurch, New Zealand) studied composition at the Royal College of Music, London, with various composers at the Darmstadt Ferienkurs für Neue Musik (1961–62), and completed her studies with Gottfried Michael Koenig in Cologne and Bilthoven, Holland. During the 1960s Lockwood collaborated extensively with choreographers, sound poets, and visual artists, and created a number of works that she herself performed such as *The Glass Concert*. In this work a variety of complex sound textures are drawn from industrial glass shards, tubes, and so on. In synchronous homage to Christian Barnard's first heart transplants, Lockwood created the *Piano Transplants* (1969–72) in which old, defunct pianos were variously burned, 'drowned' in a shallow pond in Texas, and partially buried in an English garden.

Lockwood later turned her attention to installations and performance works focused on environmental sounds, taped life-stories, and low-tech devices such as her *Sound Ball, World Rhythms* (1975), *Conversations with the Ancestors* (1975), *A Sound Map of the Hudson River* (1980), *Delta Run* (1982), and the surreal performance piece based on the *Sound Ball, Three Short Stories* and *Apotheosis* (1985). In the mid 1980s, she turned to acoustic instruments and voices in works ranging from *The Angle of Repose* (for baritone Thomas Buckner with flute and Thai khaen), to ensemble pieces such as *Thousand Year Dreaming* (1991). Recent works include *Shapeshifter* (1996), *Tongues of Fire, Tongues of Silk* (1997), *Ear-Walking Woman* (1996) for prepared piano, and *Duende* (1997).

David Dunn (b. 1953 in San Diego) was assistant to the American composer Harry Partch from 1970 to 1974 and remained active as a performer in the Harry Partch Ensemble for over a decade. Dunn has worked in a variety of audio media including traditional and experimental music, installations for public exhibitions, video and film soundtracks, radio broadcasts, and bioacoustics. His compositions and wildlife sound recordings have appeared in hundreds of international forums, concerts, broadcasts, and exhibitions. Dunn's *Tabula Angelorum Bonorum 49* is a suite of pieces for computer-processed voices based on the mystical investigations of the Renaissance mathematician/astrologer John Dee in collaboration with psychic medium Edward Kelly. His *Chaos & the Emergent Mind of the Pond* is an audio collage of digital field recordings of the sounds generated by microscopic aquatic insects, recorded in freshwater ponds in North America and Africa.

Though quite a few years must pass before the trials of many of the experimental concepts and works included here find their real value, their vitality and originality cannot be overlooked, regardless of their inherent threats to traditional definitions of music (Corner 1982; Davis and Gold 1986).

MULTIMEDIA, MIXED MEDIA, AND INTERMEDIA

Media forms are both the rational extension of ballet and opera and the result of the need for visual activity in connection with electroacoustic music. Many multimedia works also grew out of experiments with indeterminate forms such as happenings.

Alexander Scriabin's *Prometheus—The Poem of Fire* (1910) is one of the first examples of extended media composition with origins not directly related to opera or ballet. The scoring calls for large orchestra, chorus, piano, organ, and *clavier à lumières*, an instrument with a keyboard-controlled lighting console. The *clavier à lumières* part appears in traditional musical notation with each key associated with a color. Scriabin directly ascribed tonal regions with colors (e.g., F minor as blue, the color of reason; F major, the blood red of hell; D major, the sunny key; etc.). With *Prometheus*, Scriabin envisioned far more than a superfluous light show. His concepts embodied a deeply philosophical and religious symbolism with beams and clouds of light moving throughout the hall. The chorus, draped in white robes, vocalize on vowel sounds. Unfortunately, *Prometheus*, completed in early 1910, premiered in 1911 without the *clavier à lumières*—without any lighting, in fact. The work waited until March 20, 1915, just five weeks before the composer's death, to receive any lighting complement at all. Even then, only weak color projections moved on a small screen, falling considerably short of the composer's intentions.

Prometheus has had a revival in the past few years, with numerous attempts at fulfilling Scriabin's wishes. Unfortunately, most of the results seem diluted by the lack of real musical translation of sound into light. Schoenberg's *Die Glückliche Hand* (Op. 18, 1910–13) also requires lighting, which proved technologically unfeasible during Schoenberg's lifetime. The Dadaists and those artists who worked in the Bauhaus were also among the first to demonstrate interest in using various media.

Aside from early commercial performances that employed perfumes—*The Song of Solomon* was performed in Paris in 1891 with sound, light, and perfumes, for example—and Scriabin's aforementioned *Poem of Fire* that was not effectively realized, Erik Satie's *Relâche* (1924) was one of the first landmarks of media forms. René Clair's film, also a landmark in cinematography for 1924, the understated Satie music, the ballet, and the surrealistic scenery all combined to create an extraordinary interplay of often contradictory images.

Theatrical elements in new music also hold close historical ties with ballet. While many mainstream composers (notably William Schuman and Aaron Copland) have created ballets for dance groups (especially for Martha Graham), it was John Cage and the Merce Cunningham dance group who combined the forms, with each profiting from its juxtaposition with the other (Hansen 1968; Higgins 1964; Nyman 1974). The special relationship between Cage and Cunningham will be discussed in more detail under Multimedia.

Richard Maxfield writes, "I view as irrelevant the repetitious sawing on strings and baton-wielding spectacle we focus our eyes upon during a conventional concert. Much more sensible either no visual counterpart or one more imaginatively selected such as lighting, cinema, choreography, fireworks, trees . . . " (Young and MacLow 1963).

The aesthetics of media forms remain targets at which many an active as well as passive participant seem to take special aim. Two composers, Robert Ceely and Paul Goldstaub, sum up the points of view quite succinctly:

> Ceely: . . . it [multimedia] is most interesting in that it usually fails.

> Goldstaub: The first time I conducted [Toshiro] Mayazumi's *Metamusic* (certainly a multimedia work of classic stature) it brought home the simple truth that people have overlooked for centuries: concert going is partially a visual and social experience, as well as musical. If composers can use this to enrich the quality of the experience of their music, everyone gains. (Everett 1972, pp. 20–21)

The term multimedia often is used synonymously with intermedia and mixed media. The terms theatre pieces, merged medium, environmental works, happenings, and so on all add to the confusion. To avoid this conflict of terminology, I will use the following three major categories of media forms (Gibb 1973, pp. 23–25):

(1) Multimedia is a loose structure in which the various media do not depend on each other for meaning. Happenings represent excellent examples of multimedia in that each element can stand on its own merits.

(2) Mixed media tends toward equalization of elements, though any hierarchical order is possible. Environments fit this media form in that, though the elements depend on one another, they are mixed, but not truly integrated.

(3) Intermedia has all elements in balance and integrated to the fullest degree. Merged-medium fits this category well in that all elements are equal and integrated (Gibb 1973, pp. 23–25).

A number of forms fall within these three main categories and some in more than one category:

Multimedia
(loosely knit composite forms)
happenings
collage
theatre pieces
ballet
light-show

Mixed media
(more integrated, with varying degrees of importance of elements)
opera
film and TV
kinetic theatre

Intermedia
(very integrated, each element depending on the others for the work to hold together)
merged-medium
environments
films
meditations

Two important factors must be considered carefully in categorizing media forms:

(1) Composers have been very flexible in their usage of the above terms. Indeed, use of certain terminologies may not fit the above definitions. The author's work *Deadliest Angel Revision* (1971), for example, is billed as multimedia when in fact it classifies more accurately as intermedia. Therefore one cannot always accurately judge a composition by its nomer (Salzman 1974; Young and Zazeela 1969).

(2) None of the above classifications implies a quality judgment. Each category represents only a starting point from which one can then relate the forms consistently.

Multimedia

The summer of 1952 marked some of the first multimedia happenings when John Cage, David Tudor, Robert Rauschenberg, and Merce Cunningham teamed to play records, read lectures from stepladders, dance, use projections, and display white paintings at Black Mountain College (Becker and Vostell 1965; Cage 1967, 1973; Cunningham 1969; Fetterman 1996; Kaprow 1966). The concept involved a random sequence of non-random activities. That is, the order and combinations of activities were indeterminate, but the dance, projections, and paintings in themselves were not (Duckworth and Fleming 1996; Hansen 1968; Nyman 1974). The resultant events allowed each art form to retain its identity but contribute to the whole as each performer reacted to another's performance (Pellegrino 1983; Zahler 1987).

April 17, 1958 saw the introduction of *Poème électronique* by Edgard Varèse in collaboration with architect Le Corbusier at the Brussels World's Fair (see chapter 7). *Poème électronique* was performed within a pavilion shaped externally like a three-peaked circus tent and internally like a cow's stomach. The composition, 480 seconds in length, was accompanied by projected images of paintings, narrative, and montages. Neither Varèse nor Le Corbusier made an attempt to correlate the visual images and sounds, though occasional simultaneity of rhythm or spatial relationships occurred. The intense organization of each artist's approach to his own material, however, was so apparent that correlation seemed almost inappropriate. The performance, attended by nearly three million people, remains as one of the most culturally significant representations of multimedia in history.

In the late 1950s and early 1960s, composers, artists, filmmakers, and architects joined together for the ONCE festival of contemporary music in Ann Arbor, Michigan (Cage 1961; Mumma 1967). The Space Theatre of Milton Cohen, the Cooperative Studio for Electronic Music of Robert Ashley and Gordon Mumma, and the Ann Arbor Film Festival of George Manupeli contributed to this event. Mumma's *Music from the Venezia Space Theatre* (1964), composed for Cohen's Space Theatre, was " . . . an hour long program of light projection, film, sculpture, modern dance and electronic music, and (first) performed by an ensemble of the ONCE group. The projected images of the Space Theatre, which evolved continuously between the realistic and the abstract, were as diverse as the sound sources, and moved through the entire space surrounding the audience" (program notes on Lovely Music 1091).

Multimedia, as an offshoot of the American experimental school, also has developed along lines more indeterminate than structured (Kostelanetz 1968, 1970; Kirby 1965). Roger Reynolds's *Ping* (1968), based on a text by Samuel Beckett, represents an excellent example of a somewhat improvisatory work that explores theatrical possibilities. Three performers playing flute, piano, harmonium, bowed cymbal, and bowed tam-tam, augmented by a twenty-five minute tape, are amplified using contact microphones. A twenty-two minute film and one hundred and sixty slides of Beckett's story (projected alternately to the left and right) add visual material. Effects in and around the performance area result from matrixed mirrors projecting secondary images, blurs, and colors. The score, which includes durations, pitches, and dynamics, allows improvisation from all performers, including the projectionists. For example, the projectionists may, within certain limits, alter images using filters and prisms. Reynolds's *The Emperor of Ice Cream* (1962) includes projections of the score (both graphic and traditional in notation) for the performers—eight singers, piano, percussion, and bass. Each projection, or score page, represents twenty seconds of time, and the position, movement, and choreography of each performer is indicated by dotted lines. Theatrical effects result from instructions in the score, some as performance cues, others spoken, with performers also acting and dancing.

Morton Subotnick's *Ritual Electronic Chamber Music* involves four performers at game boards controlling the channel or amplitude of the electronic tape or one of four projections (Subotnick 1968). Each performer's selection sets up choices for other players. In the center, a *High Priestess* moves while lights play on her body. The work may be performed without an audience or in a very small chamber.

"Relevant action is theatrical (music [imaginary separation of hearing from the other senses] does not exist) . . . " (Cage 1961, p. 15). So speaks John Cage of, among other things, an audience's ability to see and hear sounds outside the performance itself. Feelings, smells, and even tastes, he believes, have been unfairly neglected by most composers. More often than not, Cage's approach to multimedia is philosophical: accept *all* sounds, sights, and other sensory experiences that occur in and around a performance situation equally, regardless of their origin. *Water Walk*, for example, first performed over Milan television in 1958

Figure 6.11.   Morton Subotnick.

by Cage, who was a quiz show contestant, includes banging a rubber fish inside a piano on the strings while Cage waters a vase of roses and a pressure cooker spurts steam.

Peter Maxwell Davies's *Eight Songs for a Mad King* (see vectoral analysis, chapter 4) requires the flute, clarinet, violin, and cello players to sit in cages " . . . representing, on one level, the bullfinches the King (George III) was trying to teach to sing . . . the percussion player . . . the King's brutal keeper, who plays him off stage at the end, beating a bass drum with a cat-o'-nine-tails" (liner notes on Nonesuch 71285). While the use of cages contributes to the drama, the intensity of this highly acclaimed work is still caught aurally in recordings.

Boguslaw Schäffer's *Audiences No. 1–5* (1964, see Figure 6.12) involves projections, drama, and music. His happenings include *Non-stop* (1960) for piano (with a duration varying from six to four hundred and eighty hours) and *Incident* (1966) lasting four hours.

The score to George Crumb's *Voice of the Whale* (*Vox Balaenae*) composed in 1971 instructs performers to wear black half masks or visors and the stage to be bathed in deep blue light. The music for this work clearly retains its identity without the visual complement.

Multimedia also finds a place in rock idioms, often with extraordinary results. The Velvet Underground, for example, toured America as a part of Andy Warhol's multimedia show *The Exploding Plastic Inevitable* in the mid-1960s. Pink Floyd's 1980 performance of *The Wall*, an extensive light show, has proven very influential. The group played in front of and behind a huge wall (seventy feet high) that was both constructed and destroyed during performances. Multidi-rectional speakers, along with complicated lighting and projections, contributed to this ambitious multimedia event. Led Zeppelin's laser shows and Funkadelic have since developed extensive media productions. Visual theatrics seemed almost a requisite for rock performances in the 1980s. Kiss, Ted Nugent, Black Sabbath, Alice Cooper, and Ozzy Osbourne all have contributed to a diverse popular multimedia culture.

One particularly good example of multimedia composition is Donald Erb's *Souvenir* (1970) for dancers, instrumental ensemble, electronic tape, projections, and props. *Souvenir* is an 82-minute work of intense sonic and visual activity. The scoring includes 12–20 wind and percussion players who surround the audience in the dark. These performers are accompanied by electronic tape consisting of a slightly out-of-tune perfect fifth (B-F♯) that acts as a drone. The performers begin during the second minute, signaled by the conductor who flashes a light cue at the end of each minute during the performance. All performers play *pianissimo* using either long tones within a minor second of either of the tape pitches or short pointillistic effects. These sounds slowly grow throughout the work until reaching *fortissimo* at around seven and one-half minutes. The parts consist of text and must be memorized since the piece is performed in the dark.

Elements enter according to the following schedule:

minutes:
0–1
1–2: nothing; just tape
2–3: players quietly begin to play
3–4: slide projections begin
4–5: dancers enter
5–6: weather balloons added

Figure 6.12. Boguslaw Schäffer: *Audiences No. 4.*

6–6.2: silly string sprayed

7–8.2: continue (or end) conductor strikes gong, signaling ping-pong balls to be dumped

The performance space is filled with black light that reflects luminescent tape on dancers carrying small sponge rubber balls of various sizes. Projections (optional), chosen to fit with the joyous, positive nature of the work, add to the effect of the black lights. Weather balloons, 8- to 12-foot war surplus balloons, also covered with luminescent paint, bounce into the hall whereupon the audience usually begins to participate. Luminescent silly string is then sprayed into the space, inundating the performers and audience. Finally, about 5,000 ping-pong balls painted with luminescent paint fall into the audience from the ceiling becoming the souvenirs of the performance. Erb sums up the style of *Souvenir*: "One reason that it works (is that) it is an outgoing and happy work; non-neurotic" (personal letter). Audiences first become mesmerized by the visual material and then, with growing anticipation, become actively involved by pushing balloons in the air, dodging silly string, and ultimately throwing ping-pong balls during the near cataclysm of sound and energy that surrounds them.

Allan Kaprow catalogs some of his basic concepts for multimedia in the following ways:

a. The line between art and life should be kept as fluid, and perhaps as indistinct, as possible . . .

b. Therefore, the source of themes, materials, actions, and the relationships between them are to be derived from any place or period except from the arts, their derivatives, and their milieu . . .

c. The performance of a Happening should take place over several widely spaced, sometimes moving and changing locales . . .

d. Time, which follows closely on space consideration, should be variable and discontinuous . . .

e. Happenings should be performed once only . . .

f. It follows that audiences should be eliminated entirely. (Kaprow 1966)

Antonio Russek (b. 1954 in Torreon, Mexico) founded the Independent Center for Musical and Multimedia Research, a meeting place for musicians and artists from many disciplines. He has composed extensively for dance, theater, television, and film and his works have been performed in many countries. Other composers and artists using multimedia techniques include Jean-Jacques Lebel, Wolf Vostell, George Brecht, Kenneth Dewey, and Allan Kaprow.

Mixed Media and Intermedia

When one or more of the arts dominates or integrates with the others, as often happens, the form no longer qualifies as multimedia, but rather as mixed media or intermedia (Kirby 1969; Nyman 1974; Salzman 1974). Daniel Lentz's *Sermon* (1970) for string quartet modified by electronic filters, reverberation, ring modulation, and gate device, involves score projection. Once the score becomes readable to the audience it becomes visually important. Lentz has created an artistic score in color: red = played, blue = sung, green = hummed, yellow = whistled, violet = spoken, brown = whispered, with an orange line surrounding the score page referencing time. This results in greater visual excitement and more meaningful notation for the performers and a good example of mixed media.

Robert Ashley's *Public Opinion Descends Upon the Demonstrators* (1961) uses prerecorded sounds played by a single performer on electronic playback equipment only when a member of the audience acts or reacts by speaking, glancing, looking about, gesturing, looking toward a loudspeaker, or leaving (Ashley 1961). It soon becomes obvious to most audiences that composer, performer, and audience share equal responsibility in creating this engaging work.

Barton McLean's *Identity* series of compositions involves audiences directly in the creation of sounds and ultimately the music. More complete and detailed than Stockhausen's *Musik für ein Haus* or Sigmund Krauze's experiments with environmental music in Poland and Germany, McLean's *Identity* series includes works for specific buildings and situations. One of these (for the Cultural Center in South Bend, Indiana) is, in the composer's words:

. . . a true environmental experience in that the hearer who walks through it reacts to the sounds both passively and actively. This latter aspect, perhaps the most unique in its conception, although allowing for the overall direction and control of the work to remain in the hands of the composer, nevertheless provides to the listener the opportunity to participate in smaller, but highly meaningful choices. Thus, the hearer, in exercising creative choices of his own which shape the smaller details of the work, enters into the actual creative experience. Furthermore, no musical training is necessary for this interaction, since it is set up so that all choices made by the hearer on this smaller structural level are equally valid. On the other hand, for those who have more time and intuitive ability, it is possible to grow with the work and, upon repeated hearings, to exercise intelligent choices on gradually higher and higher planes. (personal communication)

This work (building) is controlled in terms of lighting, speaker activity, and so on by the audience, whose actions trigger a variety of sounds. The placement of photoelectric cells, microphones, and various visual control devices throughout the building produces a self-contained environment.

Figure 6.14 shows the extent to which media technologies have become sophisticated during the past decades. This diagram represents one of the media rooms at the Learning Resources Center at Middle

Figure 6.13.   Donald Erb.

Tennessee State University in Murfreesboro. The figure demonstrates the potential of media in education and communications, as well as in the arts.

Ron Pellegrino has developed laser scanning and projection systems that extend electronic music instrumentation into the realm of light (Pellegrino 1983). Figure 6.15 shows a simple laser scanning system. Sound from a synthesizer, computer, or collection of generators controls a power amplifier that in turn uses galvanometers for the projection of a single laser beam. Figure 6.16 presents three possible laser setups using (in turn) frequency modulation; frequency, amplitude, and ring modulation; and frequency with amplitude modulation.

Paul Ignace's *Feast* (1964) incorporates as many senses as possible within the framework of a mixed-media work. Preferably for two people, *Feast* makes sounds, smells, tastes, touches, and sights available. Ignace does not evoke particular responses, but makes available as many choices as possible. In *Feast*, no action (relevant or not) can be considered unimportant.

Figure 6.17 shows two views of *Pavilion*, completed in 1969 (Klüver, Martin, and Rose 1972). This extraordinary building, the site for many multimedia compositions, offers numerous effects, such as enshrouding the building in fog, mirroring the internal ceiling, and so on. A wide range of stylistically different composers have used the facility for composition and performance.

Mauricio Kagel's *Match* for two cellos and percussion incorporates a dramatic game that unfolded in

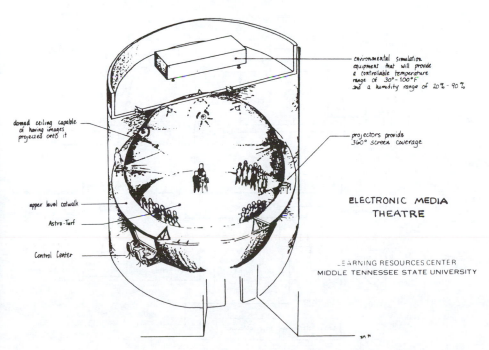

Figure 6.14.   Electronic media theater. Permission granted by the Learning Resources Center, Middle Tennessee State University.

full-blown detail to the composer in a dream (Kagel 1972). Characterized by visual humor—which met with immediate applause at its premiere in Berlin in October of 1965—*Match* produces strikingly serious music that led to what the composer has called a "shaking concert of derision" at the end of the first live performance (Kagel 1968). The intense and dramatic music, when fused with visual humor, results in a complicated collage of varying grades of emotional polarities. Regarding a portion of *Match* the composer has noted:

> During the first rehearsal of these uncertain measures I was told by the interpreters that the passage in question reminded them of the most memorable of the circene scenes: the death leap. Such an appreciation was already known to me;

Figure 6.15. A simple laser scanning system. Copyright by Ron Pellegrino. All rights reserved. Permission granted by the author.

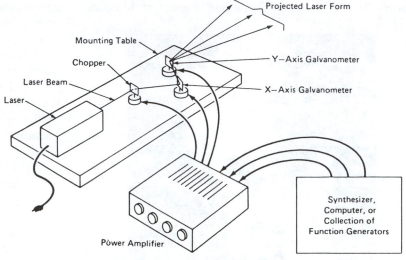

Figure 6.16. Three designs for a laser generator. Copyright by Ron Pellegrino. All rights reserved. Permission granted by the author.

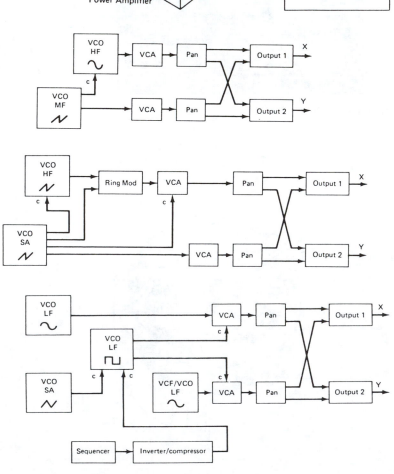

the similarity between this situation with what was dreamed a few weeks previously left no room for doubt: both musicians were suspended in mid-air with their cellos on top of their heads and by means of slow pirouettes they produced very sharp, brilliant sounds. The roll of the drum, that from some point in space resounded over the entire environment, maintained the spectators in pure tension until leading to an aggressive attack on the cymbal. Thus was overcome the first of the mortal leap with good fortune. (Kagel 1968)

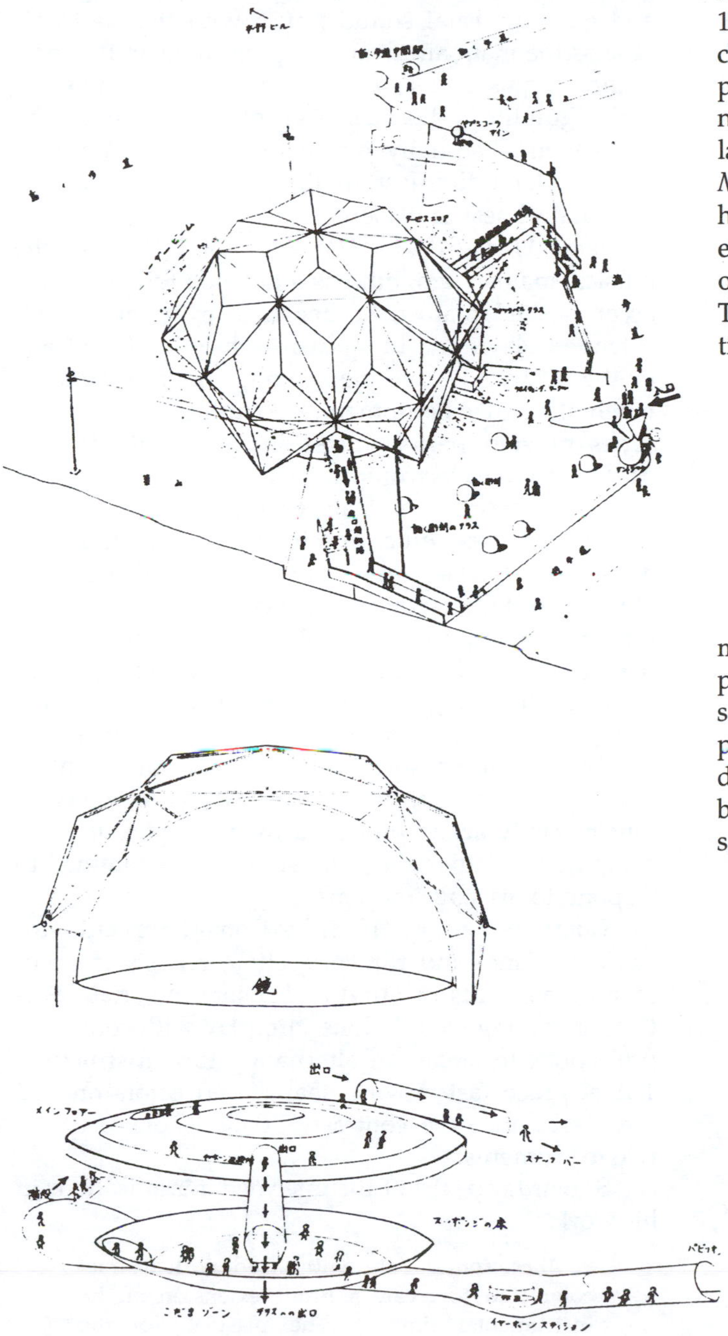

Robert Moran is possibly one of the most prolific and well-known mixed-media composers (Hoffman 1973). His *Hallelujah*, for twenty marching bands, forty church choirs and organs, carillons, rock groups, a gospel group, and the entire city of Bethlehem, Pennsylvania, was first performed in 1971 and represents a landmark in mixed-media performance. His earlier *39 Minutes for 39 Autos* for thirty-nine amplified auto horns, auto lights, Moog Synthesizer, thirty skyscrapers, radio stations, a television station, dancers, and so on was premiered on August 29, 1969 in San Francisco. This work provides further example of large-proportion mixed-media. The composer has remarked:

> In my work, *39 Minutes for 39 Autos*, I attempted to make everyone a musician. One hundred thousand persons participated in the premiere. My *Hallelujah*, commissioned by Lehigh University, used hundreds of musicians . . . in this composition I tried to make every musician a human being. (personal letter)

Moran's works embrace a wide variety of mixed-media explorations. *Divertissement No. 1* (1967) for popcorn, electric frying pan, and any instrumental soloist, for example, requires performers to read popping corn as noteheads on five-lined white-staved dark sunglasses. *Bombardments No. 4* (1968), for trombone and tape, invites the trombonist, wrapped in a sack, to become a visual gargoyle with legs, slide,

Figure 6.17. Schematic drawings of the main building of *Pavilion* in Japan, 1969.

Figure 6.18. Mauricio Kagel.

arms, and body movements all sharing in the vision of a struggling shape.

Composer John Whitney and his painter brother James began their experiments in 1940 with abstract film and infrasonics, a series of pendulums mechanically connected to a wedge-shaped aperture influencing an optical soundtrack that produces sine wave oscillations (Whitney 1965, 1980). Like the soundtrack notations of Norman McLaren (discussed under electroacoustic music), the Whitney experiments provided new sources of media materials. John Whitney speaks to this point:

> It is hoped that the partnership of sound and picture will attract the attention it deserves in artistic circles. The problem that confronts the individual consists of a number of difficulties whose acquaintance he may already have made in the course of his experiences in modern music or painting. Whether the necessary technical apparatus will always be placed at the disposal of the artist is a question that touches on an elementary problem, whose solution lies hidden in the darkness of the future. (Whitney 1960, p. 71)

Salvatore Martirano's *L'sGA* (1968) is a massive and intense mixed-media work overloading the senses with dramatic, visual, and aural messages. *L'sGA*, in the composer's words, is:

> Lincoln's Gettysburg Address for actor, tape, and film, using a helium "bomb" which the actor breathes from at the end of the piece so that his voice goes up a couple of octaves . . . all you need to do is catch a few words now and then to understand what the meaning is. You hear "government" and you hear "people." And thus I would hope that the person watching would create the framework of specific and exact meaning according to how he sees things. Because I'm not forcing him to catch on to a sequence of events in which each one has to be understood for the next one to make sense. It's almost kind of throwing it in all different places and gradually, I would hope, the conception is built up in the audience. (Proceedings 1968, p. 43)

Groups devoted to mixed-media performance include ZAJ (pronounced thack; a Mexican Theater of the Absurd); THE (Harkins and Larson; formed in 1975 at CME in San Diego); and individual performers such as Stuart Dempster (performances of Robert Erickson's *General Speech for Trombone*, 1969, being most notable).

Figure 6.19 shows *Metabiosis V: A Light, Sound and Audience Environment* (1972) by Ronald Pellegrino (Pellegrino 1983). This audience-participation mixed-media work explores its environment using visual and musical cues.

Merrill Ellis's *Mutations* for brass choir, electronic tape, and light projections is a dramatic and integrated intermedia work. *Mutations* begins with a standard concert setting. Suddenly the hall plunges into darkness, the players leave the stage while making vocal and other unusual sounds, and, with the electronic tape as the main aural source, projections in the form of films, lights, and so on flash on the ceiling and walls and engulf the audience in a sea of visual activity. The performers eventually return to the hall to perform again under a dim flashing light. The work concludes in total darkness and silence.

Jerry Hunt (1943–1993) was not known to the musical mainstream, but has a devoted following. An accomplished pianist, he began to experiment with extended playing techniques after meeting John Cage in the 1960s. He designed, built, and programmed much of his own equipment. He was best known for a series of solo performances in 1978 that featured drama and live electronic music.

Hunt's work often featured theatrics based on an interrelated electronic, mechanic, and sound-sight interactive transactional system. A central theme in Hunt's work is shamanism as a cultural precedent for the agents of modern technology. A life-long student of mysticism and the occult, Hunt's theatrics are themselves highly suggestive of ceremonial practice, featuring stylized movement and gestures, incorporating hand-made props such as staffs and rattles, often assembled from found objects. His accompanying music was typically produced by a complex array of computers, synthesizers, and sensors programmed to respond to his stage motions.

Landscape Journey (1963) by Donald Scavarda, for clarinet, piano, and film projection, reflects the contrasting elements of aural and visual materials. Sections involving sound alone interplay with soundless projections to create an alternating formal structure. The abstract, fast-moving shapes and colors on two screens balance the contrast and dependence of the two instruments.

Scavarda speaks of the intermedia implications in his work:

> . . . these sounds (are synthesized) with abstract color film to create a filmic extension of the instrumental timbres. The plasticity of the slowly shifting instrumental timbre is further "pushed" by the use of dramatic silences and contrasts with the rapidly moving film which is gradually introduced as the work evolves . . . Here the film does not have a notational func-

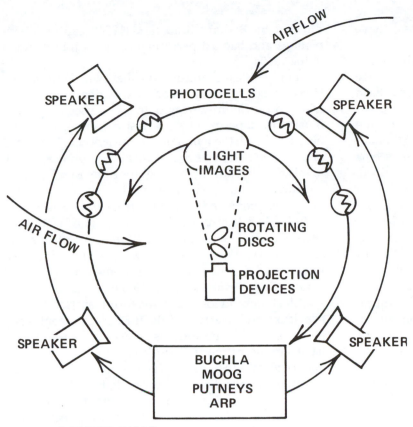

AIRFLOW

SPEAKER   PHOTOCELLS   SPEAKER

LIGHT IMAGES

AIR FLOW

ROTATING DISCS

PROJECTION DEVICES

SPEAKER   SPEAKER

BUCHLA
MOOG
PUTNEYS
ARP

**AIR TURNS DISCS
LIGHT IMAGES**

Figure 6.19. *Metabiosis V: A Light, Sound, and Audience Environment* by Ron Pellegrino. © ASUC, Inc. c/o American Music Center, 210 Broadway, Suite 15-79, NY 10023.

Figure 6.20.   Merrill Ellis (photo by Ron Bray: North Texas State University, Electronic Music Center, Denton, Texas).

tion but rather is an intrinsic part of the structure of the piece. Thus, timbre is perceived visually as well as aurally. The two projectors, placed immediately in back of the piano bench, are "performed" by the pianist, who also operates a rheostat controlling a single lamp (which lights the scores) in an otherwise darkened hall. (personal letter)

In music videos, composers have the opportunity to correlate music with the visual arts, exploring freely—due to the advent of sophisticated digital editing machines—abstract and representational expression (Khatchadourian 1985; Shore 1987; Weidnenaar 1986; Youngblood 1970). Home video machines and computer software now allow for intimate viewing and the ability to freeze frame, fast-forward, and otherwise create personalized versions of videos. In certain styles of music (predominantly rock), music videos have become a staple of the medium, more standard in some ways than the traditional aural-only performance of compact discs and tapes. While slower to develop in the avant-garde, many composers have used this format to their advantage.

Marshall McLuhan discusses video in the context of new music:

The TV extension of our nerves in hirsute pattern possesses the power to evoke a flood of related imagery in clothing, hairdo, walk, and gesture. All this adds up to the compressional implosion—the return to non-specialized forms of clothes and spaces, the seeking of multi-uses for rooms and things and objects in a single word—the iconic. In music, poetry and painting, the tactile implosion means the insistence on qualities that are close to casual speech. Thus Schoenberg and Stravinsky and Carl Orff and Bartók, far from being advanced seekers of esoteric effects, seem now to have brought music very close to the condition of ordinary human speech . . . the great explosion of the Renaissance that split musical instruments off from song and speech and gave them specialist functions is now being played backward in our age of electronic implosion. (McLuhan 1964)

Nam June Paik began studying television and video in the 1960s. His experiments with video feedback and loops as well as other abstract techniques proved seminal to the history of the medium as an art form. More recently, Robert Ashley has used videos as an integral part of the theater he creates. As these pioneers further develop alternatives to the naive and often commercial use of video, other composers have turned to it as well.

Experimentation with music videos has been limited somewhat to five areas: avant-garde jazz, new age music, performance art, minimalism, and rock. Each of these styles seems well suited to the medium. For example, the performance tradition of jazz fits the visual experience of the video format well. Minimalism, with its lack of new musical material, seems heightened by the accompaniment provided by video. It is clear that work will not be limited to these styles in the future. However, for the reasons given above, our attention will be directed to them in particular.

The video by The Art Ensemble of Chicago, called *Live from the Jazz Showcase* (1982 University of Illinois performance—52 minutes), creates a surreal blend of dance, costume, and music. The performers wear masks and body paint and dance while the music fuses American jazz with traditional African music. Directed by William Mahin, this video artfully captures, through long-shots and close-ups, the extraordinary nature of the performance. Likewise, *The New Music* (1985), by Bobby Bradford and John Carter, directed by Peter Bull and Alex Gibney, represents a brief portrait of the performers during an avant-garde performance of an Ornette Coleman-derived free-jazz arrangement using a variety of instrumental exploration techniques. Elvion Jones's *Different Drummer*, directed by Edward Gray (1984), is an explosive documentary of the drummer's life using experimental performance techniques. In contrast, Weather Report's video *The Evolutionary Spiral* (1984), directed by Larry Lachman, strives to "travel from the birth of the universe, through ancient cultures and the high tech world of today, then on to a vision of art in the future . . ." (from the cover of the cassette).

New age videos represent the work of composers on the Windham Hill label, particularly, and include Mark Isham, William Ackerman, George Winston, and Alex De Grassi. *Autumn Portrait*, directed by Stanley Dorfman (1985), presents soft ambient music mirroring the views of autumnal New England that wash across the screen. No apparent correlation occurs from image to sound. However, tempos link to the speed of camera motion. The various works blend into one another with little distinction save their different instrumentation. Brian Eno's *Thursday Afternoon*, directed by himself (1986), creates an extremely slow-moving abstract portrait of Christine Alicino with a backdrop of very soft ambient music.

Composer/performers such as Laurie Anderson use video to provide a melding of their visual-physical actions and their music. Yoko Ono's *Then and Now*,

directed by Barbara Braustark (1984), captures happenings and bag art performances with John Lennon in the 1960s.

Philip Glass's music for the film *Koyaanisqatsi* (1984) stands out as a major contribution to the genre. Directed by Godfrey Reggio, this film uses image and music in a tapestry of slow/fast camera speeds connected through the tempi of the music. There is no need of narrative here. The choral vocals add immeasurably to this film, beautifully photographed by Ron Fricke.

Robert Ashley, who works primarily in new forms of opera, pioneered opera-for-television. His works include *Your Money My Life Goodbye* (1999), *Atalanta (Acts of God)* (1997), *Automatic Writing* (1996), *The Producer Speaks* (1994), *Perfect Lives* (1983), *Yellow Man With Heart With Wings* (1990), and *Music Word Fire And I Would Do It Again (Coo Coo)* (1981).

Most rock videos follow the formulaic traditions of television and warrant little further comment here. However, a few performers, works, and visuals do have significant merit. *The Mothership Connection Live from Houston* (1986) by George Clinton and the Parliament-Funkadelic directed by Archie Ivey, Peter Conn, and Wayne Isham, for example, represents what one reviewer has called the "post-hippie funk-rock traveling circus." This video has an assortment of live performances and shorter video clips, one of which, *Atomic Dog*, is an important music video with computer animation. *Danspak*, directed by Merrill Aldighieri and Joe Tripician (1983), represents rock music from a number of avant-garde underground artists of New York City. The group Devo, visually interesting in live performance, made the natural transition to music videos in their *The Men Who Make Music* (1979), directed by Charles Statler and Gerald Casale and *We're All Devo* (1983), directed by Gerald Casale. *The Men Who Make Music* was, by some accounts, the first rock video ever made. *We're All Devo* is technically professional and conceptually masterful. This video also includes *Worried Man* by Neil Young, a work from his never released *Human Highway*. Pink Floyd's *The Wall*, while it does not do justice to live performances, has classic footage of this amorphous rock opera. *Gimme Shelter* (1981), directed by David Maysles, Albert Maysles, and Charlotte Zwerin, is a video-verité of the 1969 Altamont Speedway concert of the Rolling Stones. The video includes the murder of Meredith Hunter in what must be one of the most horrifying and terrible moments on video. The chaotic camera work only heightens the effect of this nightmarish scene.

VIRTUAL REALITY AND THE INTERNET

Virtual reality (VR) integrates visual images and music without the need for a traditional performance space (Barfield and Furness 1995; Burdea and Coiffet 1994; Schroeder 1996; Woolley 1992). Most VR involves wearing some sort of helmet that surrounds the participant's eyes and ears encasing them in a separate sensual environment. By controlling various joysticks and levers, participants then interact with their perceived reality.

VR typically involves games with various three-dimensional figures who act and react very much the way humans would. Music contributes to VR by complementing or competing with the visual images. Music can range from simple sound effects triggered by VR interactive events to complicated background music accompanying the action. Imaginative composers have extended these possibilities and have created elaborate sonic landscapes in which sound becomes the focal point, rather than the supporter of the visual imagery.

Vincent John Vincent's program *Mandala* represents one approach to using sound in VR. This non-immersive game uses a video camera to record a silhouette of the user that then interacts with the image of a virtual environment displayed on a screen. One of the games played in Mandala involves a drum kit that allows users to play the instruments they see, thereby creating the sounds and music they hear.

Legend Quest represents another type of VR game that uses a head-mounted display and a so-called "flying" joystick. This multi-user fantasy game incorporates music at its beginning and end and uses natural sounds such as laughter, howls, shrieks, and so on as accompaniment to the action that takes place.

Clearly, excellent opportunities exist for sound and music in VR technology. To date, however, most programs remain primarily visual. The future indicates a stronger musical contribution for, just as with motion pictures, very few virtual activities seem complete without the addition of music.

The Internet offers musicians and composers exciting opportunities to participate in extended media. In its simplest use, the Internet provides users a chance to download music files, listen to music while opening and closing web pages, and hear music as part of various types of video (Greenman 1995; Gurley 1996; Hill 1996). More complex uses of the Internet involve VRML (the Virtual Reality Markup Language, a relative of HTML) and elaborate Java-created simulations. As the World Wide Web continues to grow both in number of sites and number of users, the importance of this medium for music will increase.

The sites listed in the bibliography provide many different kinds of experiences related both to VR and the Internet. Visitors may compose using various types of algorithmic programs (see chapter 8), access notation and synthesis programs, and involve themselves in multi-user collaborative projects through various discussion groups and links. As we enter a new millennium, the number of possible uses for the Internet seems limitless and the opportunities for creation boundless (Heim 1993).

VECTORAL ANALYSIS
PAULINE OLIVEROS: *SONIC MEDITATION XIII*

(For information on vectoral analysis and procedures see Preface.)

1. Historical Background: Pauline Oliveros was born in Houston, Texas, on May 30, 1932, and studied composition at the University of Houston with Paul Koepe (Von Gunden 1983). She received her B.A. degree from San Francisco State College studying with Robert Erickson from 1954–60. She co-directed the San Francisco Tape Center with Ramon Sender and Morton Subotnick from 1961 to 1965 and became the first director of the Mills Tape Music Center in 1966. In 1967 Oliveros became Professor of Music at the University of California at San Diego where she taught until 1981 when she retired to become a Consulting Director of the Creative Music Foundation in West Hurley, New York.

Oliveros has influenced American music extensively through improvisation on the accordion, electronic music, teaching, writing, and her performances involving myth, ritual, and meditation. Her recent commissions include *Ghost Dance* in collaboration with Boston-based choreographer Paula Josa Jones and commissioned by Lincoln Center in 1995, music for the Mabou Mines production of *Lear*, and *Contenders* for the Susan Marshall Dance Company. She has performed at the John F. Kennedy Center for the Performing Arts in Washington, D.C., New Music America Festivals, and in countless concert halls and performance spaces worldwide. In 1985 she founded the Pauline Oliveros Foundation, Inc., to support all aspects of the creative process for a worldwide community of artists. The foundation, under her direction (along with Co-Artistic Director and playwright Ione), produced a music theater work, *Njinga the Queen King* (1993), with Oliveros's original music. From her early years as Director of the Tape Music Center at Mills College to her fourteen-year term as Professor of Music at the University of California at San Diego, and from *Sonic Meditations* to *Deep Listen-*

ing, her compositions, performances, and innovations have established her place in music history.

As a professional accordionist Oliveros has added significant literature to that medium including *The Wanderer* (with the 22-piece Springfield Accordion Orchestra) and *Horse Sings from Cloud* (accordion and voice). Her work ranges from *musique concrète* to conceptual pieces (Oliveros 1982). Oliveros has been an outspoken proponent for women's rights in a world of new music primarily dominated by male composers (Oliveros and Cohen 1982).

2. Overview: The work of Pauline Oliveros, especially that of her conceptual period, requires serious analysis and direct involvement for an understanding of its intent and impact. Figure 6.22 shows the entire score to *Sonic Meditation XIII*.

In performance, groups lie on their backs in a feet-first circle. The cycle referred to in the score originates from the ensemble as a whole rather than any individual. Since loud sounds disrupt the otherwise introspective experience, sounds from performers invariably should be as soft as those from the environment of the performance space. Lasting twenty or more minutes, the work ends more as a result of exhaustion than by a planned or composed sequence of events.

3. Orchestration Techniques: In a 1978 performance, the steady hum of the hall's heating system combined with a sixty-cycle hum from the electric lighting system provided the necessary drone. The performers used humming variants in breath-length phrases on pitches matching those of the drone as closely as possible. The resultant ephemeral work was not only fragile, but suspended the ordinary performance tension. When the work seemed complete, the mesmerized audience refrained from applause for several minutes, providing a special magic to the performance.

4. Basic Techniques: This kind of prose format has been used successfully by a number of composers. Clearly, no two performances will sound exactly alike. However, following the instructions precisely produces broad and lengthy vocalized pitches that reinforce the existing sounds in the performance space.

5. Vertical Models: In five different rehearsals for the above-mentioned 1978 performance and with three different sets of personnel, harmonies consisted of one- to four-voice textures with hairpin dynamics.

6. Horizontal Models: In the 1978 performance, a melody emerged from the entrance patterns of the different voices. This melody varied depending on the breath lengths of the individuals in the ensemble. Since so little happens during performance, this melodic direction becomes a very important feature of the work.

7. Style: *Sonic Meditation XIII* is an experimental work notated in English prose. With the instructions followed exactly, subtle music emerges consisting of soft slow modulations of environment-reinforcing drones.

This Oliveros vectoral analysis resembles Cage's *Cartridge Music* presented in the previous chapter. Only general constraints are placed on performers who can, within the guidelines laid out by the score, freely explore a variety of sonic possibilities. Surprisingly favorable comparisons also can be made with the Webern work of chapter 2, if one compares the

Figure 6.21. "Training consciousness is a large order." Composer Pauline Oliveros. Photo Credit: Becky Cohen, Del Mar, CA.

Listen to the environment as a drone. Establish contact mentally with all of the continuous external sounds and include all of your own continuous internal sounds such as blood pressure, heart beat and nervous system. When you feel prepared, or when you are triggered by a random or intermittent sound from the external or internal environment, make any sound you like in one breath, or a cycle of sounds. When a sound or a cycle of sounds is completed re-establish mental connection with the drone, which you first established before making another sound or cycle of like sounds.

Figure 6.22.   Pauline Oliveros: *Sonic Meditation XIII*.

rigor required of performances between the two works. *Sonic Meditation XIII* contrasts the works presented in the vectoral analyses in chapters 1, 3, and 10 in particular.

MORTON FELDMAN: BETWEEN CATEGORIES

My connection with Morton Feldman consisted of a letter to him requesting an article, his contributing the following article, and my requesting his permission to use the article, which he graciously granted. I was as delighted with his contribution then as I am now. I have left Feldman's upper case "P" on "Perspective," upper case "T" on "Time," and upper case "S" on "Space" for obvious reasons.

Oscar Wilde tells us that a painting can be interpreted in two ways—by its subject or by its surface. He goes on to warn us, however, that if we pursue the painting's meaning in its subject, we do so at our peril. Conversely, if we seek the meaning of the painting in its surface—we do this also at our peril. I will not be as ominous as Oscar Wilde, though this problem does exist when we separate one integral part of any work of art from another.

Music, as well as painting, has its subject as well as its surface. It appears to me that the subject of music, from Machaut to Boulez, has always been its construction. Melodies or twelve-tone rows just don't happen. They must be constructed. Rhythms do not appear from nowhere. They must be constructed. To demonstrate any formal idea in music, whether structure or stricture, is a matter of construction, in which the methodology is the controlling metaphor of the composition. But if we want to describe the *surface* of a musical composition we run into some difficulty. This is where analogies from painting might help us. Two painters from the past come to mind—Piero della Francesca and Cézanne. What I would like to do is juxtapose these two men—to describe (at my peril) both their construction and surface, returning for a brief discussion of the surface, or aural plane, in music.

Piero della Francesca is compounded with mysteries. Like Bach, his construction is his genius. We are looking into a world whose spatial relationships have adopted the newly discovered principles of Perspective. But Perspective was an instrument of measurement. Piero ignores this, and gives us eternity. His paintings indeed seem to recede into eternity into some kind of Jungian collective memory of the beginning of the Christian ethos. The surface seems to be just a door we enter to experience the painting as a whole. One might also say—despite all the facts against it—that there is no surface. Perhaps it is because Perspective itself is an illusionistic device, which separates the painter's objects in order to accomplish the synthesis that brings them into relationship with each other. Because this synthesis is illusionistic, we are able to contain both this separation and unity as a simultaneous image. The result is a form of hallucination which della Francesca is. All attempts at utilizing an organizational principle, either in painting or music, has an aspect of hallucination.

Cézanne, on the other hand, does not recede into an arcane time world. The construction of the painting, which might begin as a pictorial idea, disappears, leaving little trace of a unifying organizational principle. Rather than taking us into a world of memory, we are pushed into something more immediate in its insistence on the picture plane. The search for the surface has become the obsessive theme of the painting.

The Abstract Expressionist painters carried Cézanne's surging surface another step forward into what Philip Pavia characterized as "raw space." Rothko discovered further that the surface did not have to be activated by the rhythmic vitality of a Pollock to be kept alive . . . that it could exist as a strange, vast, monolithic sundial, so to speak, with the exterior world reflecting upon it still another meaning—another breathing.

I'm afraid that the time has now come when I will have to tackle the problem of just what is the surface aural plane of music. Is it the contour of intervals which we follow when listening? Can it be the vertical or harmonic proliferation of sound that casts a sheen in our ears? Does some music have it, and other music not? Is it possible to achieve surface in music altogether—or is it a phenomenon related to another medium, painting?

While thinking about all this—I went to the telephone and called my friend Brian O'Doherty. "Brian," I asked, "what is the surface of music I'm always talking to you about? How would you define or describe it?" Naturally, O'Doherty began apologetically. Not being a composer—not knowing that much about music, he was hesitant to answer. After a little coaxing he came up with the following thought: "The composer's surface is an *illusion* into which he puts something real—sound. The painter's surface is something *real* from which he then creates an illusion."

With such excellent results, I had to continue. "Brian—would you now please differentiate," I said, "between a music that has a surface and a music that doesn't." "A music that has a surface *constructs* with time. A music that doesn't have a surface *submits* to time and becomes a rhythmic progression."

"Brian," I continued, "does Beethoven have a surface?" "No" he answered emphatically. "Does any music you know of in Western civilization have a surface?" "Except for your music, I can't think of any." Now you know why I call Brian O'Doherty.

When O'Doherty says that the surface exists when one constructs with Time, he is very close to my meaning—though I feel that the idea is more to let Time be, than to treat it as a compositional element. No—even to construct with Time would not do. Time simply must be left alone.

Music and painting, as far as construction is concerned, parallel each other until the early years of the twentieth century. Thus, Byzantine art, at least in its uncluttered flatness, was not unlike the Gregorian Chant or the Plain Song. The beginning of a more complex and rhythmic organization of material in the early fifteenth century with the music of Machaut was akin to Giotto. Music also introduced "illusionistic" elements during the early Renaissance by way of inaugurating passages of both soft and loud sounds. The miraculous blending or fusing of the registers into a homogeneous entity, as in the choral music of Josquin, could also be said of the painting of that era. What characterized the Baroque was the interdependence of all the parts and its subsequent organization by means of a varied and subtle harmonic palette. With the nineteenth century, Philosophy took over—or to be more precise—the spectre of Hegel's dialectic took over. The "unification of opposites" not only explains Karl Marx, but equally explains the long era that includes both Beethoven and Manet.

In the early years of the twentieth century, we have (thank Heaven!) the last significant organizational idea in both painting and music—Picasso's analytical cubism, and, a decade later, Schoenberg's principle of composing with the twelve tones. (Webern is even more related to Cubism in its formal fragmentation.) But just as Picasso in Cubism was a summing up—an analysis of the history of formal ideas in painting that extended his own future—this tendency also characterized the great names of music at that time. Schoenberg, Webern, Stravinsky are more the history of music than an extension of musical history.

Picasso, who found Cubism in Cézanne, developed from this a system. He failed to see Cézanne's more far reaching contribution. This was not how to make an object, not how this object exists by way *of* Time, *in* Time, or *about*

Time, but how this object exists as Time. Time regained, as Proust referred to his work. Time as an Image, as Aristotle suggested. This is the area which the visual arts later began to explore. This is the area which music, deluded that it was counting out the seconds, has neglected.

I once had a conversation with Karlheinz Stockhausen, where he said to me, "You know Morty—we don't live in Heaven but down here on Earth." He began beating on the table and said: "A sound exists either here—or here—or here." He was convinced that he was demonstrating reality to me. That the beat, and the possible placement of sounds in relation to it, was the only thing the composer could realistically hold on to. The fact that he had reduced it to so much a square foot made him think Time was something he could handle and even parcel out, pretty much as he pleased.

Frankly, this approach to Time bores me. I am not a clockmaker. I am interested in getting Time in its unstructured existence. That is, I am interested in how this wild beast lives in the jungle—not in the zoo. I am interested in how Time exists before we put our paws on it—our minds, our imaginations, into it.

One would think that music more than any other art would be exploratory about Time. But is it? *Timing*—not Time has been passed off as the real thing in music. Beethoven, in such works as the *Hammerklavier* illustrates this perfectly. All the mosaics, all the patch quilt juxtaposition of ideas happen at the *right time*. One feels one is being continually saved. But from what? Boredom perhaps. My guess is that he is saving both himself and ourselves from anxiety.

What if Beethoven went on and on without any element of differentiation? We would then have Time Undisturbed. "Time has turned into Space and there will be no more Time," intones Samuel Beckett. An awesome state that would induce anxiety in any of us. In fact, we cannot even imagine this kind of a Beethoven.

But what does Cézanne do as he finds his way toward the surface of his canvas? In Cézanne's modulations, intelligence and touch have become a physical thing—a thing that can be seen. In the modulations of Beethoven we do not have his touch, only his logic. It is not enough for us that he *wrote* the music. We need him to sit down at the piano and play it for us. With Cézanne there is nothing more to ask. His hand is on the canvas. Only Beethoven's mind is in his music. Time, apparently, can only be seen, not heard. This is why traditionally, we think of surface in terms of painting and not music.

My obsession with surface is the subject of my music. In that sense, my compositions are really not "compositions" at all. One might call them time canvasses in which I more or less prime the canvas with an overall hue of the music. I have learned that the more one composes or constructs—the more one prevents Time Undisturbed from becoming the controlling metaphor of the music.

Both these terms—Space, Time have come to be used in music and the visual arts as well as in mathematics, literature, philosophy and science. But, though music and the visual arts may be dependent on these other fields for their terminology—the research and results involved are very different. For example, when I first invented a music that allowed various choices to the performer, those who were knowledgeable in mathematical theory decried the term "indeterminate" or "random" in relation to these musical ideas. Composers, on the other hand, insisted that what I was doing had nothing to do with music. What then was it? What is it still? I prefer to think of my work as: *between categories*. Between Time and Space. Between painting and music. Between the music's construction, and its surface.

Einstein said somewhere that the more facts he uncovered about the Universe, the more incomprehensible and alien it seemed to become. The medium, whether it be the sounds of a John Cage or the clay of a Giacometti, can be equally incomprehensible. Technique can only structure it. This is the mistake we make. It is this structure, and only this structure, that becomes comprehensible to us. By putting the "wild beast" in a cage, all we preserve is a specimen whose life we can now completely control. So much of what we call art is made in the same way—as one would collect exotic animals for a zoo.

What do we see when looking at Cézanne? Well—we see how Art has survived—we also see how the artist has survived. If our interest lies in discovering how Art has survived, we are on safe ground. If our interest lies in how Cézanne, the artist, survived, then we're in trouble—which is where we should be.

I have a theory. The artist reveals himself in his surface. His escape into History is his construction. Cézanne wanted it both ways. If we ask him, "Are you Cézanne or are you History?" his answer is, "Choose either one at your peril." His ambivalence between being Cézanne and being History has become a symbol of our own dilemma.

Chapter 7

ELECTROACOUSTIC MUSIC

BACKGROUND

Music composed with or altered by electronics has a long and involved history (Appleton and Perera 1974; Chavez 1937; Ernst 1977; Luening 1964; Schwartz 1972). Early experimental instruments include the *Clavecin Electrique* or *Electric Harpsichord* of Delaborde in Paris (1761) and Elisha Gray's *Electroharmonic Piano* in Chicago (1876). Some composers used these instruments to imitate styles and materials of their times. Many other composers, however, attempted to develop a unique aesthetic wherein any sound could act as a resource for composing (Cope 1975a). E. T. A. Hoffman's *The Automaton* in the early nineteenth century and *The Art of Noises* (1913) by the Italian futurist Luigi Russolo evidence these attempts. From 1920 to 1940, composers such as Otto Luening, Norman McLaren, Pierre Schaeffer, Leon Theremin (who in 1923 invented the Theremin), Friederich Trautwein, Paul Hindemith, and Ernst Toch also began to experiment with electronic instruments.

The series of photographs shown in Figures 7.1 to 7.9 represents a brief synopsis of the evolution of electroacoustic music in the twentieth century. The telharmonium, devised by Thaddeus Cahill around the turn of the century (his patent for an electric music machine was filed on February 4, 1896), appeared inauspiciously in 1906 with its installation in Telharmonic Hall in New York City. The largest of Cahill's instruments appears in Figure 7.1. Figure 7.2 shows the telharmonium in performance.

Around 1920, Leo Theremin invented the Theremin. Originally called the *etherophone* and *thereminovox*, performers moved their hands in its vicinity to create pitches and glissandi between pitches caused by heterodyning. Figure 7.3 shows two Theremins in performance.

Joerg Mager created his *Klaviatur-Spaerophon* in 1925. This instrument, using inductance-capacitance principles with audio-frequency generators, avoided the glissando effects of the Theremin. Mager, sup-

Figure 7.1. Thaddeus Cahill's *Telharmonium* in 1906. Located in the basement of Telharmonic Hall, the *Telharmonium* utilized twelve cogged metal wheels that, when contacting a metal brush, created an electric current.

Figure 7.2. Performing the *Telharmonium*.

ported by both the Heinrich Hertz Institute and the German Telegraph-Technical Office, performed mostly classical masterworks. Figure 7.4 shows the instrument builder in performance using the triple-keyboard organ-like manuals.

Concurrently with Mager's creations in Germany, John Hays Hammond, creator of the Hammond organ, began experimenting with electrical sound production in the United States. His first effort, called the *breathing piano*, uses reflective slats within a soundproof case that opens by the use of an extra pedal. While not explicitly electronic, the concept paralleled that of regenerative procedures in radio. Figure 7.5 shows a working model of this *breathing piano*.

By 1929, Edouard Coupleaux and Joseph Givelet had created the automatic synthesizer that they exhibited at the Paris Exposition. Their "Automatically Operating Musical Instrument of the Electric Oscillation Type" (AOMIEOT) utilized oscillators performed

much the way player pianos operate (paper roll). However, both timbre alteration using filters and pitch bending for vibrato could be created with the potentials far exceeding the player piano. The AOMIEOT appears in Figure 7.6.

One year later, Emerick Spielmann created the Superpiano, an instrument that utilizes devices to interrupt light on photoelectric cells that in turn generates alternating currents for pitch. Figure 7.7 and Figure 7.8 provide examples of performance and of the tone wheels built into the machine.

The *ondes martenot* represents one of the most successful pioneering electroacoustic musical instruments prior to present-day digital synthesizers. The *ondes martenot* was created by Maurice Martenot around 1928, but not fully developed until the mid-1930s. Dimitri Levidis's *Symphonic Poem* used this instrument in its premiere. Looking like a clavichord, it follows the same basic principles of the Theremin but with a much

Figure 7.3. Leon Theremin in a performance with his namesake instrument.

Figure 7.4. Joerg Mager performing on the *Klaviatur-Spaerophon* around 1925.

Figure 7.5. Hammond's *breathing piano.*

Figure 7.6. Edouard Coupleaux and Joseph Givelet with their "automatic synthesizer."

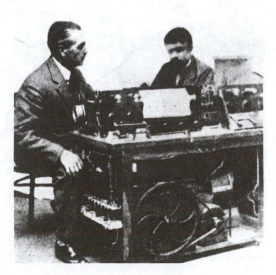

Figure 7.7. The *Superpiano* in performance.

Figure 7.8. The *Superpiano* construction.

more traditional look and touch. The monophonic pitch is controlled by a lateral movement of a finger ring attached to a metal ribbon. Using an intriguing silencing device, performers can hide the glissandi so obvious when performing the Theremin. Figure 7.9 shows a performance model of the *ondes martenot*.

Many composers, including Oliver Messiaen, Darius Milhaud, Arthur Honegger, and Edgard Varèse, effectively used the *ondes martenot* in their works. In 1936, Varèse said, "I am sure that the time will come when the composer, after he has graphically realized his score, will see this score automatically put on a machine that will faithfully transmit the musical content to the listener . . . " (Varèse 1936). A year later, John Cage remarked: "To make music . . . will continue to increase until we reach a music produced through the aid of electrical instruments" (Cage 1966, p. 3).

French composers Pierre Schaeffer and Pierre Henry developed *musique concrète* by recording natural sounds at various speeds and splicing together various

lengths of the tape to create rhythms. These experiments represent the first truly serious analog electroacoustic music. The pioneering work of composers like Percy Grainger (whose *Free Music* of 1935 used four Theremins) also explored electroacoustic resources. Along with Burnett Cross, Grainger later created a free music machine using various oscillators. The works of John Cage, Vladimir Ussachevsky, and Otto Luening brought attention to these new sound sources during the four-year period 1948–52—the years of real discovery and experimentation. The Tapesichordists, as Luening and Ussachevsky were called in a *Time* magazine review of their renowned Museum of Modern Art concert of October 28, 1952, continually improved their working conditions, equipment, and technical knowledge until they were taken seriously in the early 1960s (Prieberg 1960; Russcol 1972).

Milton Babbitt's *Vision and Prayer* (1961) and Karlheinz Stockhausen's *Mikrophonie I* (1965) demonstrate the contrasting aspects of electronic and *musique con-*

Figure 7.9. The *ondes martenot* (1977 construction).

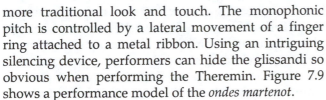

Figure 7.10. Pierre Henry.

crète composition. *Vision and Prayer* consists of pure electroacoustic sounds with the voice part carefully notated by the composer (Babbitt 1964). *Mikrophonie I* involves the recording of two performers playing on one six-foot gong with music created primarily by performing processes such as grating, scraping, and so on (Stockhausen 1972). Two other performers control directional microphones, filters, and volume control.

The nearly unlimited new resources of timbre and rhythm in electroacoustic music produced many incredible claims such as "New Music for an Old World Dr. Thaddeus Cahill's Dynamophone An Extraordinary Electrical Invention for Producing Scientifically Perfect Music" titling a *McClures'* magazine article of July 1906 (Schwartz 1972, p. 241) or Casio's 1981 claim that one can " . . . become an instant musician . . . easily, without the long years of training necessary for mastering a regular instrument."

Synthesizers enabled composers to control most pitches, dynamics, envelopes, durations, and, except for performance acoustics and audience receptivity, the performance itself (Dobson 1992; Griffiths 1979; Schrader 1982; Strange 1982; Trythall 1973).

Igor Stravinsky remarked:

> What about the much publicized "infinity of possibilities" in connection with the new art material of electronically produced sound? With few exceptions "infinite possibilities" has meant collages of organ burbling, rubber suction (indecent, this), machine-gunning, and other—this is curious—representational and associative noises more appropriate to Mr. Disney's musical mimicries. (Stravinsky and Craft 1963, p. 25)

Ernst Krênek almost seems to answer Stravinsky's objection in his article "A Glance over the Shoulders of the Young":

> To the superficial observer, it appears that the phenomena demonstrated so far in electronic music: levels of colour, texture, density, consistency and mass of sound material, are of a considerably lower intellectual level of musical consciousness than the aspirations which were associated with the demanding music of the past. Perhaps this only represents a beginning; history cites us many examples of the way in which creative energy has been expended on the achievement of progress of one dimension while temporarily impoverishing the other dimensions of the subject. (Krênek 1958, p. 16)

Luciano Berio comments:

> When someone hears electronic music it doesn't reverberate to other levels of his experience, as instrumental music has and does. Up to now I feel electronic music has been developing, evolving as a bridge between what we know and what we don't know yet. It is not without reason that the best musical works that have been produced up until now (from the early 1950s to the present) are those that try to make this connection. (Felder 1976, p. 11)

FUNDAMENTAL CONCEPTS

Two basic sound sources exist: electronic and *musique concrète*. There seems to have been, at least in the early fifties, a definite desire by composers to choose between them (Judd 1961; Pellman 1994; Wells and Vogel 1974). However, by 1960, especially with Stockhausen's *Gesang der Jünglinge*, both sources held equal footing.

After choosing materials as shown in the extremely simplified schematic in Figure 7.11, composers manipulate, combine, eliminate, or alter sounds using reverberation, modulations, speed changes, splicing, and so on. Filtering (see Figure 7.12) is a typical form of manipulation used. Another important form of manipulation involves voltage control. When, for example, a composer wishes to warm a sound, tremolo (amplitude modulation—AM—continuously changing dynamics) or vibrato (frequency modulation—FM—continuously changing pitch) can create the desired effect. Controlling the output of one oscillator by the sine wave output of another oscillator at the proper frequency makes this process automatic (Manning 1985; Naumann and Wagner 1986; Pellegrino 1973).

Synchronizing events into a composed order by means of editing, rerecording, mixing, speed alteration, and so on (shown in the last stage of Figure 7.11) readies a work for performance (Judd 1972; Meyer 1964). Classic studios utilize the editing of previously recorded sounds (or short groups of sounds) to create works. While most electroacoustic music involves a certain amount of editing, classic electronic music evolves most timing, order, and so on by editing (Cary 1992; Cope 1975a; Deutsch 1993; Oliveros 1969). This classic approach (used for example in the *Poème électronique*, 1958 by Edgard Varèse—out of necessity, since synthesizers were not yet in use) is still employed by some composers. The introduction of keyboards, sequencers, multitrack recorders, and so on has offered alternatives to many such classical approaches (Bates 1988; Emmerson 1986). While keyboards, sequencers, and so on make real-time performance possible, some feel this leads to less serious efforts rather than to good music. No doubt, classic and standard electroacoustic means can both serve the talented composer well, each having its advantages and drawbacks.

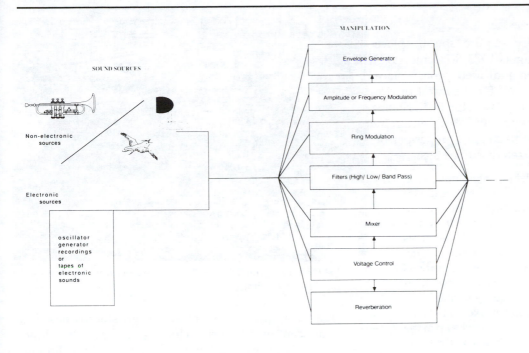

MANIPULATION

SOUND SOURCES

Non-electronic
sources

Electronic
sources

oscillator
generator
recordings
or
tapes of
electronic
sounds

Envelope Generator

Amplitude or Frequency Modulation

Ring Modulation

Filters (High/ Low/ Band Pass)

Mixer

Voltage Control

Reverberation

Figure 7.11. Electronic music diagram.

PLAYBACK

RECORD

SYNCHRONIZATION AND EDITING

Splicer/Edit

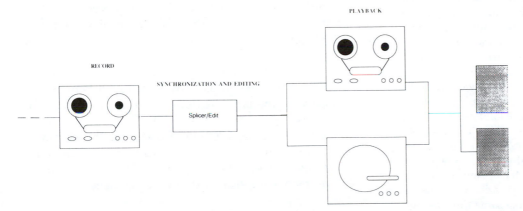

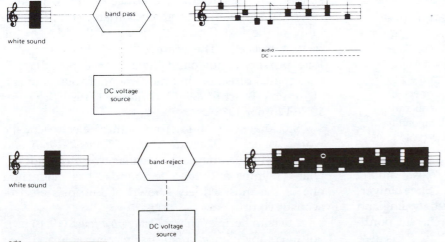

band pass

white sound

DC voltage
source

audio
DC

band-reject

white sound

DC voltage
source

audio
DC

Figure 7.12. Band-pass and band-reject filters from Electronic Music by Allen Strange. © Copyright 1972. Wm. C. Brown Company Publishers, Dubuque, Iowa.

Many compositions also require specific placement of loudspeakers (Douglas 1973; Maconie 1971). Some composers have even indicated proper placement of the tape machine itself for theatrical or dramatic effect. In *Musik für ein Haus* (1968), Karlheinz Stockhausen specifies the locations of all electronic devices in a two-story house to create a proper performance (Cott 1967). Stockhausen discusses this:

> . . . I should like to explain . . . just how loudspeakers are properly placed in an auditorium (a procedure which is becoming better and better known to me and which demands the greatest care in the particular place in question, as well as often up to four hours of time from me and several other collaborators sitting in various parts of the hall). In Madrid, for example, Kontarsky, Fritsch, Gehlhaar, Alings, Boje, and I took several hours to set the loudspeakers up. Some of them were even lying on their backs up in the balcony, and others were on stands on the stage, and we had put pieces of wood under the front edge of each speaker so that they were pointed up at the ceiling and the sound was only reflected into the house at an angle at a greater distance. We set up two loudspeakers contrary to the usual way with their diaphragm sides at an acute angle directly toward the wooden walls in order to prevent hiss and to enable the people sitting right in front of these loudspeakers—at a distance of about 5–7 meters (16 ½ to 23 feet)—to hear the loudspeakers standing on the opposite side, as well as those which were diagonally opposite. In principle we try to send the sound of the loudspeakers, particularly when instrumentalists are playing at the same time, as high as possible into the house and to achieve a smooth acoustic match, especially in four-track reproduction. (Stockhausen 1969, p. 65–66)

Pierre Boulez offers the following observations:

> I think that you cannot do good work in this area until you have teams working together. You must have composer and technician alike. Four things, really: composer, technician, good equipment, and a company or factory with money to back the operation, as well as performers in some cases, and as long as these elements cannot work together you will have small laboratories without any outstanding results. (Wilson and Cope 1969, p. 84–85)

Highly sophisticated studios do exist, among them the Institute of Sonology at Utrecht State University in Holland, the EMS studio in Putney, England (see Figure 7.13), the Institut de Recherche et Coordination Acoustique/Musique (IRCAM) in Paris (see

Figure 7.13.   The SYNTHI 100 of the Electronic Music Studios (London) Limited.

chapter 4), and a host of advanced studios based at American universities, including the Columbia-Princeton Laboratory, studios at the University of Illinois, North Texas State University, the University of California at San Diego, the University of California at Berkeley (CNMAT), Stanford University (CCRMA), and many others (Berio 1956; Holmes 1985).

Milton Babbitt's *Ensembles for Synthesizer* (1961–63) concentrates on compact rhythmic textures and formal aspects of the tape medium avoiding obvious timbral displays (Davies 1964, 1968). Charles Wuorinen's *Time's Encomium* (1968–69), realized on the RCA Mark II Synthesizer at the Columbia-Princeton Center, evidences instrumental style in both its serial roots and extremely complicated rhythmic passages.

EXAMPLES

One of the most popular early tape pieces, Stockhausen's *Gesang der Jünglinge* (1955–56), combines singing with electronically produced sounds. *Musique concrète* manipulation produces variable comprehensibility of the text (Daniel 3, "Song of the Men in the Fiery Furnace"). The score calls for five groups of loudspeakers to surround the audience. Stockhausen uses spatial direction and movement of sounds to create drama (Boschi 1989; Maconie 1971, 1990; Schaeffer 1952; Wörner 1973).

Stockhausen's numerous other electroacoustic works, especially *Kontakte* (1960), *Telemusik* (1966), and *Hymnen* (1969)—the latter a collage of electronically altered hymns and *concrète* sounds—has made him one of the most widely known of Europe's electroacoustic composers.

Luciano Berio's *Thema: Omaggio à Joyce* (1958) uses voice (completely *concrète*) first recognizably and then transformed into a fantastic array of sounds by means of splicing and tape speed variation. Berio's *Visage* (1961) is a classic example of electroacoustic music, an imaginative and strikingly dramatic work originally composed as a radio program. Cathy Berberian speaks only the word *parole* (Italian for *words*), but

Figure 7.14. Karlheinz Stockhausen. Copyright Werner Scholz.

Figure 7.16. Charles Wuorinen.

through intense crying, whispering, laughing, and so on evokes an emotional gamut almost without peer (Cross 1967; Ellis 1968).

John Cage was among the first Americans to employ electroacoustic techniques. His *Imaginary Landscape No. 5* (1951–52) uses a score for preparing a recording. All of Cage's works must be studied in light of his indeterminate concepts of musical technique (see chapter 5) and as such should be considered a cooperative effort between himself and performers.

Vladimir Ussachevsky's early works (from 1951 to 1954), including *Sonic Contours*, *Transposition*, *Reverberation*, and *Composition*, represent experiments, principally based on the sounds of piano and flute. His *A Piece for Tape Recorder* (1955) is less of an experiment, yet obvious enough in construction to serve as an educational or introductory tool for electroacoustic music. His long-time association with Otto Luening and Milton Babbitt has produced, especially at the Columbia-Princeton Electronic Music Center, a large number of works, particularly tape in combination with live performance. Ussachevsky's *Of Wood and Brass* (1965) uses tape loops of

Figure 7.15. Milton Babbitt.

varying lengths on which pre-recorded *concrète* sounds of wood and brass are fed through a ring modulator. This and others of Ussachevsky's later works represent highly sophisticated examples of electroacoustic music—quite individualistic and advanced in comparison with his early work (Ussachevsky 1960).

The RCA Mark II Synthesizer, located at the Columbia-Princeton Center since 1959, has served as the source of a large number of important compositions by Babbitt, Ussachevsky, and Luening—especially the first totally synthesized extended work, *Composition for Synthesizer* (1961) by Milton Babbitt (Babbitt 1964; Luening 1964, 1981).

Experiments in 1940 by Norman McLaren with film soundtracks created a unique and less expensive approach to electroacoustic notation. By cutting notches in film, and by scratching and painting on the soundtrack portion of film, McLaren produced a wide variety of electroacoustic sounds. Lejaren Hiller, who with Leonard Isaacson wrote *Experimental Music* (1959), describes situations in which composers, with pens filled with magnetic dyes, could compose on unmagnetized tape without the aid of any elec-

Figure 7.17. Vladimir Ussachevsky. BMI Archives. Used by permission.

tronic equipment, excepting a tape recorder for experimentation and synchronization.

Mario Davidovsky's *Study No. II* (1966) for tape involves extremely quick-moving electroacoustic sounds each placed in order by splicing (classic electronic music). The straightforward ABA form and the use of only sine and square waves mark another unusual feature of this work. Davidovsky ignores many of the possibilities of electroacoustic sound production.

Morton Subotnick, an innovator in electroacoustic music, composes works involving instruments and other media including interactive computer music systems. Most of his music requires computers or live electronic processing. The work that brought Subotnick celebrity was *Silver Apples of the Moon*. Written in 1967 using the Buchla modular synthesizer (an electroacoustic instrument built by Donald Buchla utilizing suggestions from Subotnick and Ramon Sender), *Silver Apples of the Moon* contains synthesized tone colors striking for its day, and a control over pitch that many other contemporary electroacoustic composers of the time had relinquished. Subotnick also creates a rich counterpoint in marked contrast to the simple surfaces of much electroacoustic music. Subotnick wrote *Silver Apples of the Moon* in two parts to correspond to the two sides of a long playing record, marking the first time an original large-scale composition had been created specifically for the disc medium—a conscious acknowledgment that the home stereo system constituted a legitimate form of performance. The exciting, exotic timbres and the dance-inspiring rhythms caught the ear of the public. The recording of *Silver Apples of the Moon* was a bestseller, an extremely unusual occurrence for any contemporary concert music at the time.

Subotnick followed *Silver Apples of the Moon* with several more important compositions for LP realized on the Buchla synthesizer: *The Wild Bull*, *Touch*, *Sidewinder*, and *Four Butterflies*. Each of these pieces is marked by sophisticated timbres, contrapuntal textures, and dance sections. In 1975, fulfilling another record company commission, Subotnick composed *Until Spring*, a work for solo synthesizer. In this work, Subotnick made changes in settings in real time that were stored as control voltages on a separate tape, enabling him to duplicate his performance controls and to subsequently modify them if he felt the desire to do so. While the use of control voltages was nothing new, it suggested to Subotnick a means of exacting control over real-time electronic processing equipment.

The next step in Subotnick's use of control voltages was the development of the "ghost" box. This fairly simple electronic device consists of a pitch and

Figure 7.18.   Mario Davidovsky.

envelope follower, amplifier, frequency shifter, and ring modulator. The performers' sound signal is sent into the ghost box and then processed by control voltages stored on tape. As the tape does not produce sound, Subotnick refers to its sound modification as a "ghost score."

The first piece involving an electroacoustic ghost score was *Two Life Histories* (1977). The bulk of Subotnick's output for the next six years was devoted to compositions involving performers and ghost scores. Some of the more notable works in the series include *Liquid Strata* (piano), *Parallel Lines* (piccolo accompanied by nine players), *The Wild Beasts* (trombone and piano), *Axolotl* (solo cello), *The Last Dream of the Beast* (solo voice), and *The Fluttering of Wings* (string quartet).

As a performer, David Tudor represents a touchstone for some of the most radical musical activity of the twentieth century. The praise accorded him by the composers whose music he has performed attests to Tudor's unique ability not only to meet the requirements of fully notated scores, but also to accomplish more than anyone had imagined in music in which some degree of indeterminacy was a compositional principle. As a composer, Tudor employs custom-built modular electronic devices, many of his own manufacture. He chooses specific electronic components, transducers, and their interconnections that define both composition and performance. His sound materials unfold through large gestures in time and space, and many of his compositions are associated with collaborative visual forces: light systems, dance, television, theater, film, or four-color laser projections. His works include *Three Works for Live Electronics* (1996), *Neural Synthesis* Nos. 6–9 (1995), and *Pulsers* (1984).

A number of rock groups have employed electroacoustic sound materials in their music (Dockstader

1968). The Beatles (especially in *Sgt. Pepper's Lonely Hearts Club Band*), the Jimi Hendrix Experience, and The United States of America used electronically produced or altered sound. For the most part, however, these uses represent experiments, exploiting such sounds for shock or text emphasis rather than actual musical development. By the late 1980s, however, rock and pop groups used synthesizers and various effects modules as standard instruments in their ensembles. Notable among these groups are The Grateful Dead (*Dark Star*), Soft Machine (*Joy of a Toy*), Mothers of Invention (*Penguin in Bondage*), Todd Rundgren (*Born to Synthesize*), King Crimson (*Pictures of a City*), Yes (*Close to the Edge*), Weather Report (*Nubian Sundance*), Tangerine Dream (*Rubycon*), and Frank Zappa (*Roxy and Elsewhere*, *Lumpy Gravy*, and *Uncle Meat*). The Who's Pete Townshend employed feedback effectively in *My Generation*, a work that was quite influential in the creation of punk rock. Devo (described by Rolling Stone as "a group of Captain Beefheart-influenced dadaists") included massive electronic instrumentation. As rock enters the second millennium, it is difficult to find a single group not electroacoustically connected in some way.

Walter Carlos (now Wendy Carlos), on the other hand, developed electroacoustic orchestrations of works by Bach (e.g., *Switched-on Bach* and *The Well Tempered Synthesizer*) that represent an interesting application of the Moog instrument. These works demonstrate levels of speed and accuracy far beyond human capability. Isao Tomita's realizations of Stravinsky's *Firebird*, Holst's *The Planets*, and Mussorgsky's *Pictures at an Exhibition* demonstrate the synthesizer's ability both to imitate acoustic timbres and to orchestrate quasi-real sounds in novel and striking ways.

Electroacoustic music also has flourished in Latin America with composers working in a variety of private and institutional studios. Important composers represented on recordings include Joaquin Orellana (b. Guatemala, 1939; particularly *Humanofonía I*, 1971); Oscar Bazán (b. Argentina, 1936; particularly *Parca*, 1974); Jacqueline Nova, (b. Belgium, 1936, d. Colombia, 1975; especially *Creación de la Tierra*, 1972); Graciela Paraskevaidís (b. Buenos Aires, 1940; especially *Huauqui*, 1975); and Coriún Aharonián (b. Montevideo, 1940; particularly *Homenaje a la Flecha Clavada en el Pecho de Don Juan Diáz de Solís*, 1975).

The obvious loss to the audience of visual activity during performance of recorded works has inspired a number of offshoots: combination of live performers with tape; live electroacoustic music; and tape used in conjunction with projections and/or theatrical events (Leitner 1978; Nyman 1974). In fact, as discussed in the last chapter, the need for visual activity in electroacoustic music performances played a large role in the development of multimedia.

John Cage was the first to employ entirely live electroacoustic techniques in his *Imaginary Landscape No. 4* (1949, first performed in 1951) in which twelve radios are performed by two individuals each (twenty-four performers in all). His *Imaginary Landscape No. 1* (1939) uses commercial recordings in combination with more conventional percussion instruments.

Works for live performer(s) and tape have been popular over the past few decades. Henri Pousseur (b. 1929), for example, in *Rimes pour Différentes Sources Sonores* (1959), treats the orchestra and tape antiphonally, contrasting the available materials of each. The speakers are placed on stage in such a way as to visually accentuate the contrast. Otto Luening (b. 1900) and Vladimir Ussachevsky, who worked together on *Rhapsodic Variations for Tape Recorder and Orchestra* (1954), were among the first Americans to realize and experiment with live and prerecorded sound sources. Bruno Maderna (in *Musica su Due Dimensioni*) began studies in this area in 1952 at the NW German Radio in Cologne. These early examples extended the contrast possibilities of live and recorded sources.

Figure 7.19.   Otto Luening.

Collages (Symphony No. 3) by Roberto Gerhard (1960) represents one of the most dynamic works written for tape and orchestra. This large seven-section work employs a *concrète*/electronic tape not unlike that used by Varèse in *Dèserts* contrasting a dramatically pointillistic orchestral score.

Kenneth Gaburo's 1962 work *Antiphony III (Pearl-white Moments)* combines sixteen soloists in four groups performing live with taped electronic sounds and incorporates antiphonal interplay between the two sources. *Antiphony III's* tape part includes both electroacoustic sounds and sounds more imitative of the live performers, expanding the echo effects otherwise restricted in live performances.

Donald Erb, in *In No Strange Land* (1968) for trombone, double bass, and tape, includes more complementary possibilities of electronic and instrumental sounds. His use of imitative techniques involves instruments with neoelectronic sound effects, thus minimizing the musical disparities between electroacoustic and instrumental materials. In *Reconnaissance* (1967) Erb uses a Moog synthesizer performed live with viola, piano, bass, and percussion, achieving both the visual complement of live performance and the available sonic resources of electronic equipment. Composers like Robert Erickson have used prerecorded instrumental sounds with live performance. In *Ricercar à 3* (1967), Erickson employs two prerecorded contrabasses along with one contrabass performing with and against the tape creating unusual combinative effects.

David Cope's *Arena* (1974, cello and tape) is a classical studio composition that incorporates a dialogue between instrument and tape. Figure 7.20 shows a passage in which the tape exchanges pitches with the cello, in turn creating vertical sonorities. The rhythm and pitch of the cello must synchronize well or the passage (including the quarter-tone inflection indi-

cated by the arrows attached to the accidentals) will fall short of the desired result. The last system reflects more interplay—the harmonics on the tape represent only partial notation here—answered by the artificial harmonics on the cello. This score reflects the contrasting exact and graphic notations used by composers for tape in such situations.

Richard Felciano has composed many works for a variety of combinations of traditional instruments and tape. *God of the Expanding Universe* and *Litany* are excellent examples of works for organ and tape. His *Crasis* and *Lamentations for Jani Christou* represent examples of chamber music with tape.

John Watts's *WARP* (1972) includes electroacoustic sounds on tape with brass quintet. The four-channel quadraphonic speaker setup heightens both the balance and the effective humor and drama of this work. Interest in large ensemble composition with accompanying tape increased during the 1960s and 1970s. Works for tape and band include Donald Erb's *Reticulation* (1965) and Herbert Bielawa's *Spectrum*. Vladimir Ussachevsky's *Creation-Prologue* (1961) is for tape and choir.

John Eaton combines the compact Synket and full orchestra in his *Concert Piece for Synket and Symphony Orchestra*, effectively utilizing visual concerto performance techniques with specially designed electronic equipment (see Figure 7.22). Merrill Ellis includes

Figure 7.20. From David Cope's *Arena* for cello and tape (1974). Used by permission of the composer.

soprano, live synthesizer, and orchestra in his *Kaleidoscope* (1979).

A number of groups dedicated to the live performance of electroacoustic music (most now disbanded) formed in the 1960s: The Sonic Arts Union (1966), with Gordon Mumma, Robert Ashley, Alvin Lucier, and David Behrman; Musica Elettronica Viva (1967, in Italy), with Frederic Rzewski, Allan Bryant, and Alvin Curran; the Once Group (Michigan), with Robert Ashley, Gordon Mumma, and others. Festivals of live electroacoustic music at Davis, California (1967), Buffalo (1968), and Los Angeles (1968 and 1969), among others, have proved significant. A live electronics group, "It takes a year one earth to go around the sun," formed in 1970 by David Rosenboom (originator and director of New York's Elec-

tric Circus until 1969) with Jon Hassell, Gerald Shapiro, and Terry Riley, spent the summer of that year performing on electroacoustic instruments designed by the members of the group on "mesas in Wyoming, ghost towns in Death Valley, and lava caves in New Mexico."

Alvin Lucier's *North American Time Capsule* (1967) involves a Sylvania vocoder, an instrument designed to digitally encode speech sounds. The performers' voices act as the electroacoustic source material in live performance. Gordon Mumma's *Mesa* (1966) uses electronic sound modification as well. He uses a bandoneón (an accordion-like instrument) instead of voices. Work with tape-delay techniques have been used in live performance by Pauline Oliveros (*I of IV*, 1966, and *Lightpiece for David Tudor*, 1965).

Figure 7.20.   *(Continued)*

Figure 7.21.   Richard Felciano. Photo ©
Copyright Michelle Vignes. By permission.

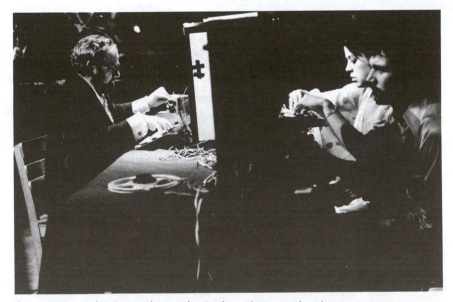

Figure 7.22.   John Eaton playing the Synket. Photo used with permission.

Figure 7.23.   Alvin Lucier. Photo
by Mary Lucier.

Several composers in the 1960s explored the possibilities of interactive electroacoustical, process-oriented composition (Appleton and Perera 1974; Schwartz 1972; Vercoe 1968). Representative works of this time include David Behrman's *Wavetrain* (1964), John Cage's *Variations V* (1965), Gordon Mumma's *Hornpipe* (1967), and Alvin Lucier's *Queen of the South* (1972). Behrman's *Wavetrain* involves the acoustical resonances of grand pianos or zithers. Cage's *Variations V* uses the movements of dancers on the stage translated by photoelectric cells and capacitance sensors into electroacoustic articulations for accompaniment. Lucier's *Queen of the South* (discussed in chapter 4) uses large plate surfaces resonated with special loudspeaker-like transducers.

Gordon Mumma was among the first composers to employ circuitry of his own design in composition and performance. A prolific composer and a virtuoso performer on French horn, his work is known for the integration of advanced electroacoustic principles. Mumma has termed his approach "cybersonic" and has applied it to a wide range of compositions including *Hornpipe*, electroacoustic music for cybersonic French horn, and *Ambivex*, a surrogate myoelectronic telemetering system with pairs of performing appendages.

Mumma discusses his *Hornpipe* in detail:

> *Hornpipe* is an interactive live-electronic work for solo hornist, cybersonic console, and a performance space. The hornist performs with various techniques on a valveless waldhorn and a standard "French horn." These techniques include a traditional embouchure, and the production of multiphonics with special double-reeds.
>
> The cybersonic console, attached to the hornist's belt, has microphones with which it

"hears" the sounds made by the hornist and the acoustical resonances of the space. The electronic circuitry of the console analyzes the acoustical resonances of the space, and responds interactively with the hornist. The console is connected by an umbilical cable to a stereophonic sound system, so that its responses are heard from loudspeakers (see Figure 7.24).

The cybersonic console has several functions. First, it makes an electronic map of the acoustical resonances of the space. This is achieved during the first few minutes of the performance by eight electronically resonant circuits that become automatically tuned to the acoustical resonances of the space. Second, each circuit has a memory that accumulates information about its resonant condition.

Technically, this condition is determined from the frequency (f) and the resonant efficiency (Q) of the circuit (see Figure 7.25). Third, when sufficient information is obtained, a VCA (voltage

Figure 7.24. Gordon Mumma performing *Hornpipe* (1967). Photo by Narrye Caldwell, 1974.

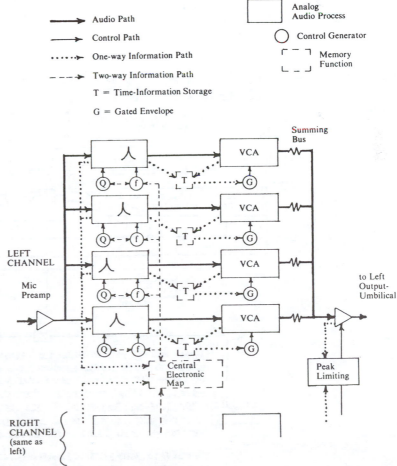

Figure 7.25. Functional diagram of Gordon Mumma's *Hornpipe*.

controlled amplifier) for each circuit is gated on, sending its electronically resonant response through the umbilical to the loudspeakers. Because each of the eight resonant circuits is somewhat independent, and has different memory and gating characteristics, these responses can occur in many different combinations.

A performance of *Hornpipe* begins as a solo, without electronic sound. When the responses of the cybersonic console are heard from the loudspeakers, the hornist can then interact with the electronic map of the cybersonic console. By playing sounds which reinforce the electronic map, the hornist can increase the responses of the cybersonic console. By playing sounds which are anti-resonant (opposed) to the resonances of the electronic map, the hornist can decrease the responses of the cybersonic console.

The performer's choice of anti-resonant sounds strongly influences the continuity of a performance. Without the reinforcement of its original electronic map, the cybersonic console gradually makes a new map representing the hornist's anti-resonant sounds. In other words, having interacted with the responses of the cybersonic console, and learned the electronic map of the acoustical resonances of the space, the

hornist can choose sounds which deceive the console into thinking it is in a different performance space. After the cybersonic console has developed a new map (of the hornist's anti-resonant sounds), it no longer responds to the natural acoustical resonances of the space. The performance of *Hornpipe* has evolved from an introductory solo, through an ensemble between hornist, cybersonic console and performance space, to a concluding solo section for horn. (Mumma 1967)

The score to Allen Strange's *Music of DOD* (1977), for virtuoso instrument and one player, plots the design for an electronic instrument with a short description of dissonance and resolution (see Figure 7.26).

Part of the score to Stockhausen's *Studie II* (1956) appears in Figure 7.27. The lower portion indicates dynamics (envelope) and the upper portion denotes pitch (100 to 17,200 Hertz, or cycles per second) based on a scale of 81 equal-tempered steps at a constant interval ratio of $^{25}\sqrt{5}$ (piano at $^{5}\sqrt{2}$). The middle portion of the score indicates an electroacoustic tape moving at 76.2 centimeters per second. This excerpt represents less than seven seconds of performance time (Cole 1974).

Figure 7.26. From *Music of DOD* by Allen Strange (1977).

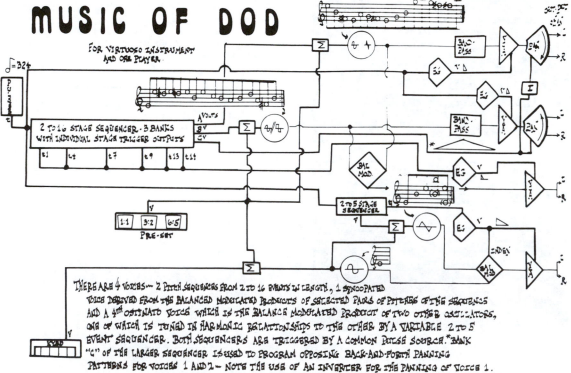

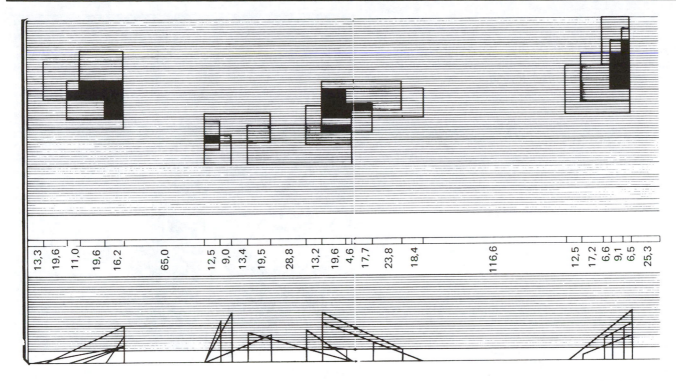

Figure 7.27. From Karlheinz Stockhausen's *Studie II. Die Reihe* No. 1, copyright 1968 by Theodore Presser Company, Bryn Mawr, PA.

POÈME ÉLECTRONIQUE

Poème électronique (1956–58) by Edgard Varèse was composed in the Philips Studio at Eindhaven, having been commissioned for performance in the Philips Pavilion at the 1958 Brussels Worlds Fair (Treib 1996; Varèse 1967, 1972). The pavilion itself was designed by the French architect Le Corbusier, who was assisted, interestingly, by then-architect Iannis Xenakis. The design of the pavilion included 400 or more loudspeakers, most of which were hidden in the walls or above the ceilings. David Ernst speaks of the elaborate setup:

> The taped sounds were distributed by telephone relays among various combinations of loudspeakers. These "sound paths" were determined by a fifteen-channel control tape, each track of which contained twelve separate signals. Therefore 180 (15 X 12) control signals were available to regulate the sound routes, lighting effects and a variety of light sources which consisted of film projectors and projection lanterns, spotlights, ultraviolet lamps, bulbs, and fluorescent lamps of various colors. (Ernst 1977, p. 42)

Nearly 16,000 people per day for six months provided the audience for the performance of this primarily *musique concrète* work. The projected images, consisting of various photographs of paintings, were not synchronized with the sound in any particular manner (the projections were chosen by Le Corbusier to fit the elaborate and complex internal design of the pavilion).

Varèse often referred to his work as "organized sound" rather than traditional composition. Clearly *Poème électronique* is very highly organized sound. Figure 7.29 shows one possible analysis of *Poème électronique* and represents a timeline of the piece (left-to-right). Numbers within the diagram indicate repetitions. Assorted sketchings between connections represent important but nonformal materials. When one symbol becomes an offshoot of another symbol, it represents a counterpoint, with the first material being more significant. Occasional use of words as in "low voice solo" identifies important characteristics that are varied during the course of the work.

Varèse uses two basic sound sources: *concrète*—instrumental and vocal; electronic—sine-type tones and complex noise. Varèse uses subtle techniques to vary these timbres. For example, the sixth iteration of the gong-type motive appearing at the beginning of the work is filtered so that it sounds nearly an octave lower in pitch. The reverberation as well as timbre of each of the bells is clearly different in the succeeding appearances of the motive.

Most techniques in *Poème électronique* result from the classical processes discussed earlier in this chapter. Most notable are the tape speed changes. For example,

Figure 7.28.   The Philips Pavilion at the Brussels Exposition World's Fair built by Le Corbusier where *Poème électronique* was first performed in 1958.

Figure 7.29.   Diagrammatic formal analysis of Varèse's *Poème électronique*.

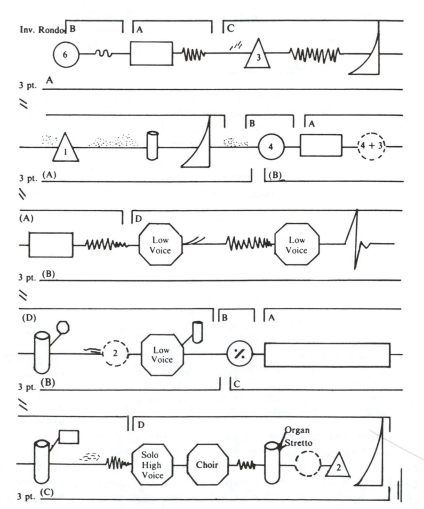

the solo female voice extends well beyond human range as a result of tape speed alterations. Varèse uses envelope control to cut off the opening long-note section. The fast switching between drums and organ in the final stretto provide good examples of synchronization.

Poème électronique represents an important work (along with Stockhausen's *Gesang der Jünglinge*, 1954) using hybridization of electroacoustic and recognizable sounds such as a jet airplane, drums, temple bells, and human voices. Along with the often humorous squeaks and squawks, this work presents a dynamic and linear design not unlike the composer's instrumental works (Schuller 1964; Wen-Chung 1966).

DIGITAL ELECTROACOUSTIC MUSIC

The electroacoustic music just discussed derives from analog or continuous, non-interrupted magnetic information. Sound—singing, speaking, and so on, most of the activities of life—is analog. The term digital, on the other hand, refers to information in digits or numbers: discrete, non-continuous bits of information. Unlike analog sound, computers use only numbers (Baggi 1992; Bateman 1980; DeFurio 1985; De Poli 1983; von Foerster and Beauchamp 1969).

The digits that digital refers to are binary, containing but two elements: *0* and *1*. These numbers indicate whether a column in an exponential series (e.g., 1, 2, 4, 8, etc. but appearing right-to-left) has a value or not. A *1* in any column trips the value of that column, while a *0* has zero value. The number 0100 equals *4* (since only the "4" slot has a value) and the number 1100 equals *12*. Binary numbers can be added and subtracted with one example of each shown below:

addition:
0 0 0 1
1 0 0 0
———
1 0 0 1

subtraction:
1 0 0 0
0 0 0 1
———
0 1 1 1

Note here that addition exists in much the same way it does in decimal mathematics (i.e., 0 + 0 = 0; 1 + 0 = 1, 1 + 1 = 0 carry the 1, etc.). Here the number 1 adds to the number 8 with the result equaling 9. In subtraction, 0 – 1 equals 1 carry the 1 and 1 – 1 equals 0, thus 0011 – 0001 equals 0010. Since binary elements require only two states, the operations can be quick—often less than a trillionth of a second—and occupy little storage space. The speed at which computers operate and the amount of material they can process offer

important attractions for composers exploring new approaches to sound (Brinkman 1990; Loy 1981).

Figure 7.30 demonstrates how computers produce sound. Typically between 20,000 and 55,000 samples per second must be produced for quality sound (Strawn 1985a, 1985b; Roads 1996; Mathews 1969; Morgan 1980; Pohlmann 1985). These numbers are converted into voltages and then smoothed and filtered in order to cancel the rate numbers themselves that can sometimes be read as an extra frequency, an effect called aliasing. This conversion then produces analog electronic sound through a high-fidelity system.

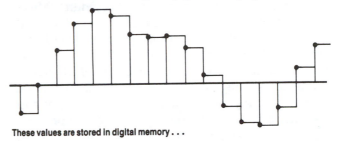

These values are stored in digital memory . . .

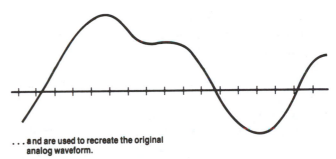

. . . and are used to recreate the original analog waveform.

Figure 7.30. How digital numbers are computed and used to create waveforms.

Since sound in digital electroacoustic music exists in the initial state as numbers, composers can control extremely small and often very precise data (Abbott 1978; Darter 1984). Editing, for example, can be accomplished quickly without the often complicated physical splicing common to classical electroacoustic music. Careful control of tuning and dynamics is also possible and practical. In these ways, computers offer composers more control and precision (Moore 1978, 1981, 1990; Roads 1997).

Analog to digital (A/D) aspects of computer operation often prove as valuable as digital to analog. Instead of sound being initiated in terms of numbers, it can begin as analog sound and then be translated into numbers for recording, editing, manipulation, or composition (Dodge and Jerse 1985; Haus 1993; Hiller and Isaacson 1959; Laske 1977).

Composers (primarily in the early and mid sixties)

such as Lejaren Hiller, Max Matthews, James Tenney, J. K. Randall, and Hubert Howe were among the first to create computer music (Davis 1988; Roads 1985, 1989). Work at the Bell Laboratories (beginning in 1959) proved enlightening and led to the first MUSIC series of programs including MUSIC IVB. MUSIC IVB was a culmination of MUSIC IV designed by Matthews using the IBM 7090 computer, eventually becoming MUSIC V for the GE 645 computer. These programs, as well as a host of programs designed since, allow composers extensive control over the elements of composition.

Other early programs include the Music Simulator-Interpreter for Compositional Procedure (Musicomp) developed for the IBM 7090 by Hiller and Robert Baker, MUSIGOL developed by Donald MacInnis for the Burroughs 5500, and the Transformational Electronic Music Process Organizer (TEMPO) developed by John Clough at Oberlin College. Each of these programs deals explicitly with composer control and uses computers as high-speed performers to produce magnetic tape recordings of works as output (Howe 1977; Lincoln 1970; Mathews and Pierce 1989; Moorer 1964, 1972, 1977).

Research into computer-generated sound continues at many centers, most notably at the Center for Computer Research in Music and Acoustics (CCRMA) at Stanford University. There, John Chowning and Leland Smith studied digital recording techniques, digital signal processing, psychoacoustics, advanced synthesis techniques, and the automatic production of musical scores. CCRMA continues today as a multidisciplinary facility where composers and researchers work together using computer-based technology both as an artistic medium and as a research tool. Software developed at CCRMA includes Common Music, an object-oriented music composition environment that produces sound by transforming high-level representations of musical structures into a variety of control protocols for sound synthesis and display including MIDI, Csound, Common Lisp Music, Music Kit, C Mix, C Music, M4C, RT, Mix, VRML, and Common Music Notation.

John Chowning's research and compositions have received considerable acclaim (Chowning 1971, 1973). His early work centered on mod-

Figure 7.31. John Chowning. Photo courtesy of the Stanford University News and Publications Service.

ulation processes. MUSIC V techniques called for instrument definition in terms of building complex tones. Called Fourier or additive synthesis, each overtone is added separately—a tedious and time-consuming process, though the results often are highly controllable. Chowning, on the other hand, worked primarily with frequency modulation (FM) and developed techniques using program and carrier waves. FM produces highly complex tones including inharmonics that frequently sound like bell tones. FM has become so important to the development of certain computer programs that the term *Chowning FM* is often used to designate the technique. As well, Chowning's research of musical space and discoveries correlating reverberation, dynamics, direction, and doppler to spatial modulation have contributed to the development of many new programs and works. Both reverberant space and FM principles are apparent in his *Turenas* (1972) and *Stria* (1977), both computer-generated quadraphonic tape compositions.

Chowning speaks of the former work in an interview:

> In *Turenas*, I used only the FM technique for generating the tones, I used it in both a harmonic series mode and a noisy inharmonic series mode, with transformations between the two. One of the compositional uses of FM was in timbral transformation. This was often coupled with spatial manipulation. As the sounds crossed the space they underwent a timbral transformation. (Roads 1985, p. 21)

The Center for New Music and Audio Technologies (CNMAT) founded at the University of California at Berkeley (1988) also has investigated important aspects of digital technologies. CNMAT is an interdisciplinary research center, drawing participants from physics, mathematics, electrical engineering, psychology, computer science, cognitive science, and music.

IRCAM (Institute of Research and Coordination in Acoustics and Music) in Paris (see also chapter 4) was founded for collaborative artistic and scientific research, development of related technologies, and contemporary music production. One of the primary links between research and music involves the development of software environments for composition that integrate models and prototypes. These integrations originate from research teams working in various fields related to music: computer science (languages, human-machine interfaces, real-time database management), digital signal processing, acoustics, psychoacoustics, and cognitive psychology of audition.

IRCAM has created a number of important software programs for composition. OpenMusic, a highly visual environment based on the earlier PatchWork software, uses the computer language Lisp. OpenMusic is an Object Oriented (OO) environment with objects symbolized by icons that may be dragged and dropped. Users drag objects and interconnect them in order to build musical algorithms.

Max is a graphical programming environment for developing real-time musical and interactive applications (Winkler 1998). Many composers use Max in order to generate musical structures using mathematical or random models. Max offers musicians the possibility of exercising direct control over music during performance. Also, performances on traditional instruments can be analyzed in real time. Max is particularly well suited to dynamic control of networks of complex programs combining not only musical signals but also video, lighting effects, and so on.

Morton Subotnick used live electroacoustic processing for his work *Ascent Into Air* (1981). Written for the powerful 4C computer at IRCAM, this piece involves many of the techniques that Subotnick had developed in his ghost scores (see reference earlier in this chapter). In addition to the processing normally used with his ghost boxes, Subotnick spatially locates sounds in a quadraphonic field and modulates timbres of the instruments. The performers, in effect, serve as control voltages to influence where a sound is placed, how it is modulated, by how much, and so on—the reverse situation of Subotnick's ghost score compositions. The instruments then control computer-generated sounds. Since 1985, Subotnick has used standard MIDI (soon to be discussed) gear in works such as *The Key to Songs*, *Return*, and *all my hummingbirds have alibis*. Subotnick's staged tone poem, *The Double Life of Amphibians* (1984), is a collaboration with director Lee Breuer and visual artist Irving Petlin utilizing live interaction between singers, instrumentalists, and computer.

Elody is a music composition environment based on a functional language developed at the GRAME Research Laboratory in Lyon, France. Elody is written in Java and uses the real-time MIDI services of MidiShare. Elody allows algorithmic descriptions and transformations of musical structures and compositional processes promoting Internet collaboration. Working with Elody comprises the building of new musical expressions by combining or composing other musical expressions. The user interface is based on drag and drop visual functionalities. Each action results in immediate sound and graphical feedback.

The Center for Research in Computing and the Arts (CRCA) is an Organized Research Unit of the University of California, San Diego. CRCA fosters collaborative working relationships among artists and scientists by identifying and promoting projects in which common research interests "may be advanced through the application of computer-mediated strategies." CRCA was established in 1991, to provide an environment for the exploration and research of issues pertaining to computing and the visual arts, music, media arts, literary and theatre arts, and architecture.

The Center for Research in Electronic Art Technology (CREATE) at the University of California, Santa Barbara focuses on developing software tools for signal synthesis and processing, spatial sound projection in virtual and physical spaces, distributed media signal processing, sound and music databases, multimedia telepresence systems and interfaces, new notation editors, and particle synthesis and processing. CREATE research in multimedia telepresence and virtual reality interfaces centers around its real-time *telepresence* software. The Distributed Real-time Interactive Virtual Environment (DRIVE) telepresence system uses new aural renderers for spatial sound and innovative input/output devices for creation of new virtual environments for applications such as acoustical simulation, musical performance, and art installation. CREATE also serves as a center for the SuperCollider language. SuperCollider is a flexible programming language for sound and image synthesis and processing. It was developed by James McCartney of Austin, Texas, and is the result of more than five years of development. SuperCollider's development environment includes a program text editor, rapid turnaround compiler run-time system, and a graphical user interface builder.

Many composers work almost exclusively with digital media. These composers have created new "classics" of the genre. For example, *Dreamsong* (1977/1978), a highly regarded computer composition by Michael McNabb, integrates synthesized sounds with digitally recorded natural sounds (McNabb 1981). The title derives from the work's vaguely recognizable sounds (as in a dream). This work, unlike most in the genre, has relatively simple harmonic and melodic structures enabling the composer (and hence the audience) to focus on the more important elements of texture and timbre. Figure 7.32 shows the two modes from which most of the pitch material in *Dreamsong* derives. This work, considered by many a classic of the field, has revitalized a sense of the lyric in the world of electroacoustic music.

Alfredo del Monaco, born in Caracas, Venezuela in 1938, has pioneered electroacoustic music in his country at the former Estudio de Fonologia and in

Figure 7.32. Modes used in Michael McNabb's *Dreamsong* with synthesized and digitally recorded sounds.

1968 founded the Venezuelan branch of the ISCM. His works have been performed extensively by distinguished performing ensembles and soloists at concerts and festivals around the world.

Eduardo Reck Miranda has degrees in music, data processing technology, and philosophy from his native Brazil, a Master's in music technology from the University of York (England), and a Ph.D. in music and artificial intelligence from the University of Edinburgh (Scotland). His work *Electroacoustic Samba X* (1995) makes very effective use of electroacoustic resources.

Salvatore Martirano's *Sal-Mar Construction* (1973), a semiportable live-performance computer with retrieval and storage capabilities, brought much attention to the potential of the microprocessor computer-synthesizer combination. Many other composers have used microprocessors in live performances. David Behrman has worked extensively in this area. His *On the Other Ocean* (1977), for example, involves flute, bassoon, and the Kim-1 microcomputer-controlled polyphonic analog synthesizer. Performers choose pitches according to the synthesizer's accompaniment and the synthesizer chooses its accompaniment according to the performers' pitches. Behrman has been active as a composer and electroacoustic artist since the 1960s and has created many works including sound installations. Most of his work since the late 1970s has involved computer-controlled music systems operating interactively with audiences. Behrman designs and writes much of the software for these systems.

Figure 7.33. David Behrman. Photo by Mary Lucier.

Paul de Marinis has created numerous performance works, sound and computer installations, and interactive electronic inventions. Much of his recent work involves speech processed and synthesized by computers. A recent series of installation works, *The Edison Effect*, uses optics and computers to make new sounds by scanning ancient phonograph records with lasers.

Leland Smith at CCRMA was among the first to create a computer program for traditional music nota-

tion (Smith 1972, 1973). Figure 7.34 shows an example of this notation. Advantages of using computer notation programs include:

(1) readability: scores approach engraved quality;

(2) editing: simple to make corrections;

(3) flexibility: easy to rearrange measure distribution for page turns and score layout;

(4) extractions: parts can be extracted in seconds in transposition (if necessary);

(5) versatility: pages can be rearranged quickly in a variety of ways for readability.

Smith's program, *Score*, creates engraved-quality music printing rivaling the best of traditional methods.

Many computer notation programs now exist, each with varying degrees of success in terms of user interface and quality of output (Yavelow 1993). Typically, musical symbols are placed on staves in one of three ways: from the standard ASCII keyboard, by use of the mouse, or by using a synthesizer keyboard. In the first two modes, users indicate which duration should be added to the staff at the pointer position. Tempo, meter, and so on can be added in a similar manner. Figure 7.35 shows a menu that allows a diverse number of pitches to occur within a beat or division of the beat and adds the appropriate number above or below the set.

Music also can be notated by performing music on a piano-style keyboard connected to computers through MIDI interfaces. This process typically produces quite ugly results since humans are not rhythmically accurate. Quantizing is often used to round off the rhythmic complexities. This quantizing often produces a more notable representation of performances.

Figure 7.36 shows a drawing of the Yamaha *Disklavier*, a computer-controlled piano, as well as an otherwise traditional grand piano. This instrument may be used for playback and/or recording. In the latter case it matches in playback the notes, rhythms, dynamics, and articulation of performances it has previously recorded. This process can be quite useful for teachers, performers (particularly accompanists), and composers. The control wagon uses Musical Instrument Digital Interface (*MIDI*, discussed later in this chapter).

With the advent of inexpensive personal computers, classroom applications have increased (Bartle 1987; Bowen 1994; Rudolph 1996; Webster and Williams 1996). Theorists and teachers such as Arthur Hunkins (University of North Carolina), Dorothy Gross (University of Minnesota), Fred Hofstetter (University of

Figure 7.34. *Intermezzo and Capriccio* for Piano by Leland Smith. Example of computer notation. Computer Music Graphics, San Andreas Press, 3732 Laguna Ave., Palo Alto, CA.

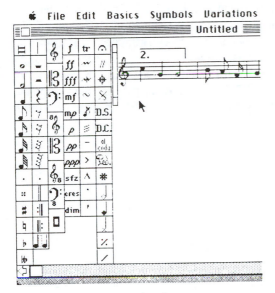

Figure 7.35. A screen shot from a computer notation program.

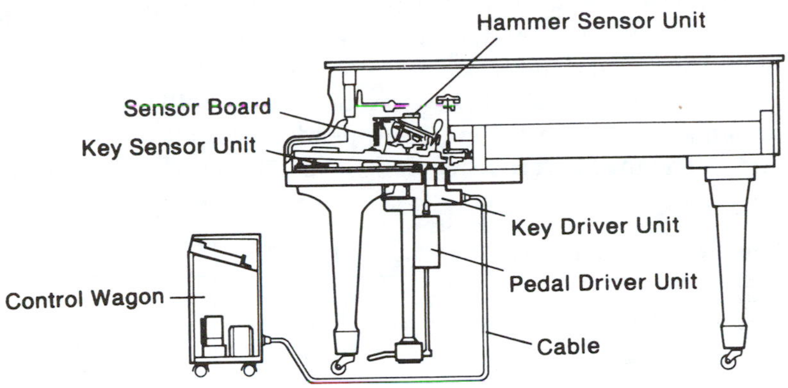

Figure 7.36. Yamaha's Disklavier.

Delaware), Rosemary Killam (North Texas State University), Gary Wittlich (Indiana University), Wolfgang Kuhn (Stanford University), Paul Lorton (University of San Francisco), and Herb Bielawa (San Francisco State University), have all developed sight-singing and ear-training programs. The advantages that the computer offers include immediate feedback to students, storage and retrieval of scoring, timbral versatility, speed, and long-term correlation of instructional viability of materials used. Recent commercial programs such as *Listen*, *Perceive*, and *Practica Musica* make effective tools for studying ear training and theory on computers.

Figure 7.37. Synclavier II by the New England Digital Corporation.

With the exception of the extraordinary New England Digital Corporation's Synclavier (see Figure 7.37), synthesizers have decreased in price and are available to the layperson (Appleton 1989). Since synthesizers in no way influence musical style, they have become widely popular in the music industry (see Appendix IV).

MIDI

MIDI (acronym for Musical Instrument Digital Interface) is the industry standard for communication links between synthesizers, drum machines, and other digital music equipment (Baird 1986; DeFurio and Scacciaferro 1986; Friedman 1985; Loy 1985; Massey 1987). MIDI was intended to create a cooperative standard for what had become, by the mid-1980s, a nightmare of different equipment with almost no opportunity to develop compatible combinations (Anderton 1985, 1986). Figure 7.38 shows a typical MIDI-chained network of synthesizers. Allowing synthesizers to interconnect in this way enables composers to mix the various advantages of one unit with another during composition without having to create completely separate (and highly redundant) setups. Figure 7.39 provides a summary of MIDI commands.

Virtually all major synthesizer manufacturers have adopted MIDI. The advantages of MIDI include (1) digital control of many instruments simultaneously; (2) the ability to add complementary equipment; (3) tapeless recording since works can be saved to disk using little space; (4) cost-efficiency since additional synthesizers do not require redundant equipment; (5) less obsolescence in that new equipment may simply be added as modules to systems (Moore 1987; Noll 1994; Otsuka and Nakajima 1987; Rothstein 1991).

The International MIDI Association and the MIDI Manufacturers Association (see Appendix IV) update and extend the MIDI code regularly. The IMA includes

users as well as manufacturers. SMPTE (Society of Motion Picture and Television Engineers) time code is the industry standard for linking multi-track digital recording and video. Several MIDI/SMPTE synchronizers now exist. Synchronizers operate by translating SMPTE time code into the number of MIDI elapsed beats. Since video production has made inexpensive what was, with film, an extremely costly process, these synchronizers profoundly impact many forms of contemporary music.

Digital information is inherently cleaner than its analog counterpart. Analog recordings suffer generation noise (added machine hum during copying). Copies of digital recordings, however, remain as clear as the original since digital information exists as discrete bits of information. CD (compact disc) players read only the bumps in the grooves of the recording. Dust and other

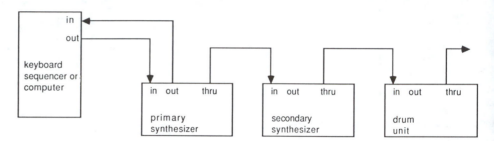

Figure 7.38.   A MIDI chain of synthesizers and drum unit.

	Compact Disc	LP Record
Disc diameter (mm)	120	300
Disc thickness (mm)	1·2	1·5 2·3
Disc playing time (min)	60	50– 60
Rotation speed (rpm)	200-500	33⅓ or 45
Scanning velocity (m/s)	1·2 - 1·4	0·4 approx.
Width of grooves or tracks (μm)	1·6	100 approx.
Diameter of center hole (mm)	15	7·24
Number of channels	2	2
Frequency range (Hz)	20-20,000 (±0·5dB)	30-20,000 (±2dB)
Typical dynamic range (dB)	90	55
Signal-to-noise ratio (dB)	90	60
Channel separation (dB)	90	25-35
Total harmonic distortion	0·005%	0·2%
Wow-and-flutter	Quartz accuracy	0·03%
Disc material	Transparent PVC with aluminum reflective coating and lacquer protective layer	Black vinyl
Life expectancy (disc)	Indefinite (no physical contact)	100 playings approx.
Life expectancy (laser/ stylus)	5,000 hours	400 – 800 hours
Effect of dust, scratches, and static charges	Largely ignored by the laser beam	Causes increasing background noise and mistracking

Figure 7.39.   A summary of MIDI commands.

potentially distorting material are ignored. This results in excellent playback with very long lifetime. CDs, which can hold up to 74 minutes and 33 seconds worth of music, show virtually no sign of wear since no direct contact occurs when played. DAT (digital audio tape) has become the industry standard recording process. DAT technology, unfortunately, suffers the same lack of random access that analog cassettes do (i.e., requires fast-forward and reverse for finding material whereas CDs allow random access). DAT recording nonetheless provides inexpensive and high quality low-noise recording.

As mentioned earlier, digital recording requires sampling. In turn, sampling requires an immense amount of memory, typically 1 megabyte per every 21 seconds at 48k/sec. However, once music has been digitally recorded, users can access each harmonic in every sound. Figure 7.40 shows a typical editing screen. This figure represents 110 milliseconds and shows harmonics between 0 and 55 kHz and their envelopes. The display on the left provides playback (the speaker icon), select (inverted sine wave with white box), and so on. Sounds may also be viewed as waveforms. Figure 7.41 shows how sine waves can be extended in both amplitude and time using digital software.

Figure 7.42 shows the editing of a section of sound by capturing a repeating loop. Here the recording of a D on a piano has been selected as source material. Note the single millisecond clicks at the bottom of the window. By controlling the pointer, one can alter and invent envelopes for many different elements. Figure 7.43 shows filter and amplitude envelopes. Grabbing any segment or line with the pointer, holding down the mouse's button and pulling creates a new node.

Figure 7.44 shows how the tempo for a segment of music can be digitally altered, rhythmically varied, and so on. A single sampled sound can be duplicated and projected to different pitch levels for assignment to a keyboard (for example). Composers then can create an entire choral composition from a single sampled voice. Music thus created may also be re-edited and varied.

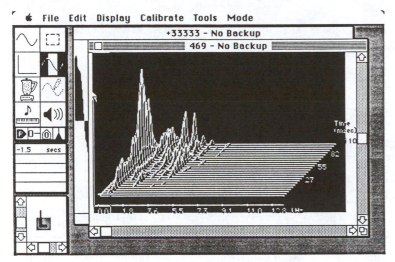

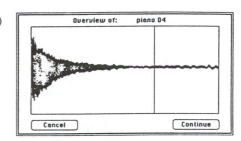

a)

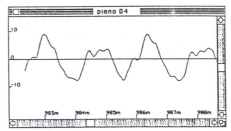

b)

Figure 7.40. Visual diagram of the amplitude characteristics of various harmonics of a sampled sound on the EMAX using Sound Designer software by Digidesign, Inc. All rights reserved.

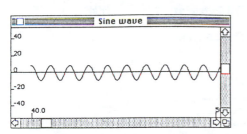

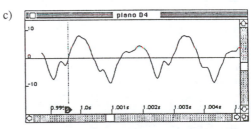

c)

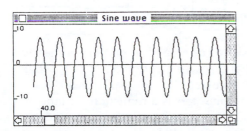

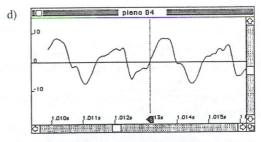

d)

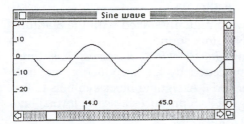

Figure 7.41. Various scaling adjustments including normal (top), amplitude axis stretched (middle), and time axis stretched (bottom).

Figure 7.42. These screens demonstrate how to make a digital sound loop using Sound Designer software by Digidesign, Inc.: a) an overview provides location of stable sustain; b) scaling the waveform displays one of two periods; c) placing a loop marker; d) placing loop end marker at zero crossing ends in the loop. All rights reserved.

Figure 7.43. Filter and amplifier envelope-adjusting process using the EMAX and Sound Designer software by Digidesign, Inc. All rights reserved.

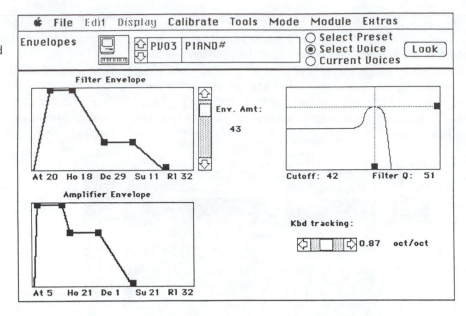

Figure 7.44. The arpeggiator module of Sound Designer software by Digidesign, Inc. All rights reserved.

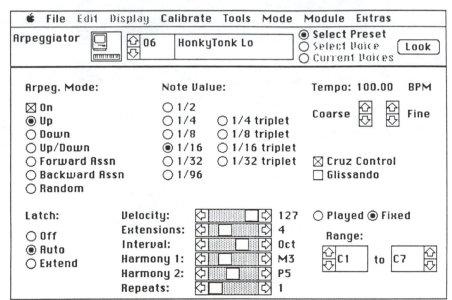

VECTORAL ANALYSIS
JEAN-CLAUDE RISSET: *INHARMONIC SOUNDSCAPES*

(For information on vectoral analysis and procedures, see Preface.)

1. Historical Background: Jean-Claude Risset (b. 1936, France) studied piano with Robert Trimaille and composition with Suzanne Demarquez and André Jolivet. He earned the Doctorates-Sciences Physiques in 1967 at the Ecole Normale Superieure. Risset spent three years working with Max Matthews at the Bell Laboratories in the early sixties researching sound synthesis and imitation of timbres and has served as head of computer research at IRCAM (Institut de Recherche et Coordination Acoustique/Musique) in Paris. He published a catalog of computer-synthesized sounds in 1969 and set up a computer music installation in Orsay, France in 1971.

Inharmonic Soundscapes is a reduction for tape of a larger work titled *Inharmonique* for soprano and tape (first performed in April, 1977, at IRCAM). The computer synthesis for this work was completed at IRCAM with a MUSIC V-type program (Risset 1985). Some sections were digitally mixed with the Stanford program MIXSND (mix-sound).

2. Overview: *Inharmonic Soundscapes* has three main sections preceded by an introduction and followed by a brief coda. Assigning block symbols to the sounds as in Figure 7.45 produces a useful formal layout as shown in Figure 7.46.

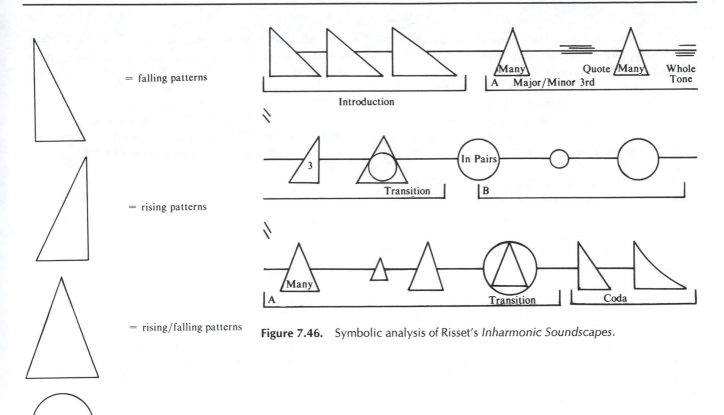

= falling patterns

= rising patterns

= rising/falling patterns

= bells

Figure 7.46.   Symbolic analysis of Risset's *Inharmonic Soundscapes*.

Figure 7.45.   Symbology for analysis of Risset's *Inharmonic Soundscapes*.

The quote, three-fourths of the way through line one, indicates a timbral and pitch reference to the work analyzed previously—*Poème électronique* by Edgard Varèse. Though possibly unintentional, this reference becomes apparent with familiarity of both works. The two overlapped symbols representing transitions at the end of the first A and the end of the second A help integrate the work.

3. Orchestration: The bell-like sonorities of both basic materials (the bowed glass of *A* and the rung bells of *B*) reflect the inharmonicity expressed in the work's title. The spectrum of these types of sounds characteristically includes partials that do not conform exactly to the tuning specifications of the overtone series. This, combined with bell-like envelopes, provides the work's basic consistency. The small amount of material here, and its slight variations, nonetheless results in a diverse and extraordinary work.

Risset speaks of his timbral studies in an interview:

Instrument-like tones can be transformed in subtle ways. For example, it is possible to construct an inharmonic bell-like tone with a more or less distinct pitch in a fashion similar to

building up a chord. That is, the amplitudes of selected frequency components all follow the same amplitude envelope (for example, an abrupt attack and a long decay). However, in contrast to a standard chord, the amplitude envelope of each component is given a different duration. Then one can take the same frequency components and apply a different amplitude envelope—one that builds slowly. As a result, the character of the tones changes. Because of the different lengths of the components, they do not swell in synchrony. Hence, instead of fusing into a bell-like sound, the components are diffracted, although the underlying harmony remains the same. Thus, by changing a single function in the score, one can change the internal structure of a sound. (Risset 1980)

4. Basic Techniques: The most notable technique in *Inharmonic Soundscapes*, aside from the timbral explorations, is rhythmic diversity. The composer provides controlled improvisation to direct the music to subtle points of arrival.

5, 6. Vertical and Horizontal Models: The harmonic sonorities of this work result from the extended durations of the melody. The suggestions of pitch content at two points in the top line in Figure 7.46 indicate such durational sonorities. In the first instance, a major/minor third appears in varying guises (e.g., E♭, E, C). The second appearance involves a whole-tone scale (i.e., E, D, C, B♭, with a G below). Both of these sections suggest a relatively consonant vocabulary with tuning logically derived from the inharmonic materials.

7. Style: Risset has used a consistent vocabulary of inharmonic timbral material to create *Inharmonic Soundscapes*. The form, while simple, supplies balance and direction to a work constructed from subtle variations of glass and bell-like timbres. The composer speaks of his use of the computer:

> The computer, a powerful tool, makes new sound sources available. However, it is necessary to learn how to use these new possibilities to produce the desired results . . . in order to take full advantage of the vast potential of direct digital synthesis of sound, one needs a deep understanding of the nature of sounds and of the correlations between the physical parameters and the aural effects of sound: this psycho-acoustic science is still in its infancy, but its present growth is promising. (Risset 1980)

This work exemplifies some of the major technological developments of the past thirty years and yet, strangely, very few new paradigms for composition. *Inharmonic Soundscapes* explores new sounds but remains traditional in design, resembling the works presented in the vectoral analyses of chapters 3 and 4. *Inharmonic Soundscapes* contrasts the Webern analysis of chapter 2, though influenced by its pointillism, and the Xenakis analysis of chapter 8. *Inharmonic Soundscapes* bears little relation to Glass's *Einstein on the Beach* of chapter 9.

ANDREW R. BROWN: AN INTERVIEW WITH PAUL LANSKY

Originally expecting to be caught up in the search for new sounds, Paul Lansky instead became much more interested in human sounds and the noise of the world around him. Since the early 1970s Lansky has been using the computer as a kind of microscope on this noise. His *Six Fantasies on a Poem by Thomas Campion*, widely regarded as a landmark work in computer music, takes us on a journey to the inner world of poetry and speech. *Idle Chatter* and its sister pieces, *just more idle-chatter* and *Notjustmoreidlechatter*, make music from the noise of synthesized speech. *Values of Time*, *Stroll*, and *Talkshow* all involve performers in a

kind of musical reality play. Recent works have made use of ambient noises such as those of shopping malls and highways, and he continues to explore the implicit music in the way people speak.

This interview with Lansky, as is the case with the interview with Steve Reich in chapter 9, was contributed by Andrew R. Brown from a series of interviews he has conducted with major figures of contemporary music.

> Brown: Composing involves an engagement with the musical materials. How do you build audience engagement into your computer-generated works?

> Lansky: The most important thing in my electronic work, which basically consists of creating sounds on tape or on compact disc, is the idea that there is not going to be a traditional performance of the piece, there is not going to be anything more than a tape or CD. So, it's very important to build as much engagement into the experience of listening as possible. The listener won't have a score to follow, or performers to watch. All he will ever have is a recording, and it will sound the same every time. Therefore, a lot of the work that I've done involves designing a certain level of complexity that engages the listener in a new way. In these pieces there are often many things going on and it's frequently not clear what it is that you should let your ears follow. You have to make a conscious decision about how to listen and what to listen to. I often use the analogy of painting, where the viewer designs his experience as his eyes wander around. The "chatter" pieces are a good example of this. In some other of my pieces the complexity lies in more conceptual realms, however. In *Things She Carried*, the burden of the complexity is in a relatively abstract story line. We get a list of attributes of a woman's life but we don't get very much that is explicit. So, in order for the listener to engage the piece, he has to thread together his own story out of the lists, apply his own template to the experience. Another analogy that I often make is that it's not unlike reading a book. When you read you build images in your mind of places and people based on your experiences. What I'm trying to do is similar. That is, construct music which encourages the listener to engage different kinds of imaginative and cognitive activities. In a way, in order to substitute for the absence of performers, I'm making the listener into a performer. The bottom line here is that I would like these pieces to invite repeated listenings. Just as a traditional piece invites repeat performances, I would like the listener to be encouraged to listen again and

Figure 7.47.   Paul Lansky.

again. Even though the sounds will be identical each time, I hope that the music will sound different, depending on the route the listener takes.

Brown: When writing about your work you use visual metaphors such as being a photographer with sound and sonic landscapes. However, you compose with computer code that is a textural representation of the sound. Do you use any visualizations as you work?

Lansky: Imagination always involves working with internal images and ideas. Just imagine what a composer of an opera has to go through. Computer code is about as far from the actual sound as the score an opera composer writes is from a performance. Part of the training of any composer is to learn to imagine music where there is very little to hold on to.

Brown: Do you see a big difference in the way you compose with a computer from the way someone using an off-the-shelf sequencing package might compose?

Lansky: Until a few years ago this was certainly the case. Most commercial software was pitiful, not only in the views of music it expressed, but also in terms of the straight jackets it put the user in. Today, however, things are considerably better. There are some software packages like MAX/MSP and SuperCollider that enable work at a very low level. If you want to work at a professional level, I think it is best to think of yourself as somewhat analogous to a professional driver. You ultimately want to design your own car, and when it breaks you want to be able to pull over to the side of the road, lift the hood and fix it yourself.

Brown: Do you find the computer an ideal instrument for that because it is so malleable?

Lansky: Absolutely. A computer is, ideally, perfectly dumb. Software is an attempt to give it some intelligence, and that intelligence is always going to be a translation of human intelligence of one sort or another. This is what computers do, automate intelligence (and work fast). The danger in designing software for creative purposes, however, is that the author will invest it with his own artistic predilections. There are two ways to go here. One is to imbed so many predilections that it becomes a virtual piece, that is, using it results in music that is highly congruent with the author's music or view of music. The other way to go is to attempt to make it as neutral as possible. Anything in between is going to be weak in one way or another. A long time ago I decided that I wanted the software I use to tell me as little as possible about how music should go, and at the time the only way to do this was to write my own software. In other words, my software has little intelligence, and using it means investing more of my own intelligence in the process.

Brown: Do you think there would be similar signatures in your music from the medium you deal with? Where it was obvious that this was done with that software?

Lansky: I can see this very clearly, although I hope that it is less obvious to others. On the other hand, there are a lot of other things which go into the compositional process that will ensure that the results are quite different, even if the tools are the same. We certainly don't think of all engravings as different versions of the same image, for example, even though the tools used were the same.

Brown: How do you alter sounds?

Lansky: There are a large number of techniques that are available to composers today. My preferences lean towards using processes that allow the sounds to retain some of their more recognizable characteristics while imbedding them in a musical context. There are techniques which many composers use which alter the sounds beyond recognition, but I tend to shy away from these.

Brown: Do you think you have an element of what might be considered John Cage's approach to challenging perceptions of what sounds are in a musical context?

Lansky: Possibly, although I tend to think of my approach as the inverse of Cage's. While he wants to teach us to hear all sounds as "music," I want to explicate the implicit music in so-called "unmusical" sounds, and by "music" I mean something much more traditional than Cage does, i.e., the "melodies" of informal speech, or the "rhythm" of traffic patterns, and so on.

Brown: Do you normally start with sounds or with processes?

Lansky: Both. At the moment, for example, I'm working with piano sounds. I've written several pieces which use very clearly defined piano sounds, but in different ways and contexts. In one case, I actually improvise on the piano, in another I build a model of a piano player, and in yet another I study the envelope and decay of single notes on the piano. In each case, the piano remains relatively unaltered, and the working process provides a unique perspective. (Several of these pieces are on my CD, *Conversation Pieces*.) Some might say that I'm more interested in algorithmic than spectral composition.

Brown: It seems that you try to stretch the envelope on things, but not too wide, to see things in a new light, moments where you could be convinced that it was live then other times not.

Lansky: I like to think of loudspeakers as windows into virtual worlds. The point of a virtual world is that the landscape will have familiar and unfamiliar dimensions, and it is the interaction of the two which provides a new experience. We use familiar things as doors into unfamiliar realms. Many composers, such as Xenakis, for example, regard loudspeakers as sound sources rather than windows. My interest is in using the experience many of us have with recording as an image of reality in which the loudspeakers recapture a past musical event. It is very important for a composer of electroacoustic music to be sensitive to the nature of loudspeakers. The sound coming from them is not the same as the sound coming from a live instrument. But we've learned to suspend disbelief and invest loudspeaker sounds with physical qualities. I often like to try to imagine what Mozart would think if he could hear his music coming from a loudspeaker. I bet it would sound quite strange to him and that he wouldn't like it very much. One has to learn how to hear music this way.

I like to think of my music as tinkering at the boundaries of the believable. You may hear a piano or a voice, for example, and it will be very familiar, but it will be doing things which no pianist or speaker could ever do in real life. In this way I think I'm creating a kind of virtual space in which we use the familiar to explore new realms.

Chapter 8

ALGORITHMIC COMPOSITION

BACKGROUND

Since most algorithmic music created during the past forty years has been accomplished with the use of computers, it is important to differentiate between this approach and computer-generated synthesis, the subject of the last chapter. The work covered in this chapter does not relate to the manner in which sound is actually produced. Rather it is related to the ordering of sounds in a composition. Some have distinguished the latter by using the term computer-assisted composition (CAC).

In a generic sense, algorithmic music has a rich and varied tradition (Ames 1987a, 1987b; Hiller 1970, 1981; Hiller and Isaacson 1959; Lincoln 1970; Loy 1989). Aeolian harps (algorithmic string instruments played by the wind) and wind chimes, for example, date back to ancient China. As mentioned in chapter 5, actual algorithmic composition appeared as early as the eighteenth century when Mozart and many other composers created *Musikalisches Würfelspiel* or "musical dice games." Mozart's K. 516f, for example, consists of two 8 by 11 matrices containing the numbers 1 through 176 (2 x 8 x 11), one of which appears in Figure 8.1. The eight vertical columns here represent the measures of an eight-bar phrase (traditional to classical period forms) and the eleven horizontal columns represent all possible outcomes of the throws of two dice. These numbers are then keyed to 176 measures of music some of which appear in Figure 8.2. Figure 8.3 shows one of the forty-six thousand billion possible combinations (according to $N = D^r$, where R = rank and D = vertical dimension of the 176 measures) of this work that creates viable music in Mozart's style. A second matrix produces a contrasting second theme. This type of music, often referred to as *ars combinatoria*, also was practiced by Haydn and other classical composers. Such machinations match well with what computers do best and *Musikalisches Würfelspiel* have been the subject of many software programs.

In the twentieth century, Joseph Schillinger, a mathematician, created designs for the composition of new works by machines (Schillinger 1948, 1978). Leon Theremin built Schillinger's *Rhythmicon*, which performed rhythmic patterns. Theremin also created Schillinger's *Musamaton* (an automatic instrument that varied previously composed music). Both of these instruments represent good examples of complex mathematical models intended for untrained musicians.

One of the first true composing machines was built by H. F. Olson and H. Belar (1951). This machine included two random number generators and a sound generating system. Pitch and rhythm were controlled by weighted probabilities during the composition process. Some of Olson and Belar's first attempts involved biasing composition toward Stephen Foster melodies.

The first serious algorithmic computer music studies took place in 1955–56 at the University of Illinois when Lejaren Hiller and Leonard Isaacson used

	I	II	III	IV	V	VI	VII	VIII
2	70	121	26	9	112	49	109	14
3	117	39	126	56	174	18	116	83
4	66	139	15	132	73	58	145	79
5	90	176	7	34	67	160	52	170
6	25	143	64	125	76	136	1	93
7	138	71	150	29	101	162	23	151
8	16	155	57	175	43	168	89	172
9	120	88	48	166	51	115	72	111
10	65	77	19	82	137	38	149	8
11	102	4	31	164	144	59	173	78
12	35	20	108	92	12	124	44	131

Figure 8.1. A table of measure numbers from Mozart's *Musikalisches Würfelspiel*, K. 516f.

Figure 8.2.   Measures of music from Mozart's *Musikalisches Würfelspiel*.

Figure 8.4.   Lejaren Hiller. By permission.

Figure 8.3.   An example of music created from Mozart's K. 516f.

the Illiac high-speed digital computer to program data and stylistic parameters (Hiller and Isaacson 1959). Hiller and Isaacson's program chose numbers from musical note tables. The result of their work, the *Illiac Suite for String Quartet* (1957), was published in the April 1957 edition of *New Music Quarterly*. This work was composed algorithmically, but transposed to traditional music notation by the researchers for live performance. The score of this work and a chronicle of the research that led to its composition are described in Hiller and Isaacson's *Experimental Music* (1959).

Also in 1956, Martin Klein and Douglas Bolito of

Burroughs, Inc. used a DATATRON computer to create a popular tune called *Push Button Bertha* (Syncopation by Automation 1956). An anonymous Burroughs publication describes the compositional process as follows: "The operator inspires DATATRON by first keying in a 10-digit random number. This causes the machine to generate and store 1000 single digits, each representing one of the eight diatonic notes in the scale with two allowable accidentals. The program then motivates DATATRON to pick notes at random, testing each for melodic acceptability as it goes along" (from *Syncopation by Automation, Data from ElectroData*, August 1956, Pasadena, CA: ElectroData Division of Burroughs, Inc.). *Push Button Bertha*, while musically trivial, represents one of the first completely machine-composed pieces of music.

About this same time, Iannis Xenakis began work based on stochastic probability techniques. Using the FORTRAN programming language on the IBM 7090, he produced what he termed *free stochastic music* (detailed in his book *Formalized Music*, 1971). Works such as *Metastasis* (1954), *Pithoprakta* (1956), and *Achoripsis* (1957) resulted from such calculations.

In 1960, Pierre Barbaud began studying the potential of algorithmic composition. Barbaud worked principally with random permutational methods applied to traditional harmonies and twelve-tone processes (Barbaud 1969). In the late 1960s, Barbaud developed an aesthetic that compared algorithmic music with music composed by humans. "It [algorithmic music] is 'human' inasmuch as it is the product of rational beings" (Barbaud 1969). Barbaud and Roger Blanchard completed a number of important papers on the subject during this period.

Harriet Padberg (1964) assigned notes to letters of the alphabet. She then created meaningful phrases in English using computer programs to transform the results into music using transformations of group theory. John Myhill composed his *Scherzo a Tre Voice* in 1965. This work is based in part on the previously described techniques of Joseph Schillinger. Myhill's *Scherzo a Tre Voice* resulted from a program following graphically-depicted sinusoidal waveforms that created three simultaneously-sounding contrapuntal voices.

Gottfried Michael Koenig's work at the Institute of Sonology in Utrecht beginning in 1964 focused on algorithmic composition (Koenig 1970, 1983). His work *PROJECT 2* (1969) demonstrates an effective use of statistical procedures that assemble in combinations. His *Übung für Klavier* (Study for Piano), written in 1970, uses this program as well. Other experiments during this time included computer generation of hymn tunes based on the statistical analysis of 37 hymns up to the eighth-order approximation. These experiments were carried out by F. Brooks, A. Hopkins, P. Neumann, and W. Wright.

Robert Baker's *CSX-1 Study* was created by the MUSICOMP (MUsic Simulator Interpreter for COMPositional Procedures) at the University of Illinois. Baker and Hiller then collaborated in the creation of the *Computer Cantata*, completed in 1963, one of the most interesting of the early pioneering works in algorithmic composition. This highly serialized work includes various tempered tuning systems of from nine to fifteen notes per octave.

In this same year, Herbert Brün completed *Sonoriferous Loops* for instrumental ensemble and tape using MUSICOMP. This work and his *Nonsequitur VI* (1966, tape and ensemble) are based on probability distributions, one of the most popular of the early processes for algorithmic composition. These two works stand alongside the *Illiac Suite* of Hiller and Isaacson as preeminent early computer compositions.

Cage and Hiller's dynamic *HPSCHD* (1969) utilizes a subroutine of MUSICOMP called *ICHING*. Through the use of highly sophisticated random numbers, they created the first recording with published indeterminate performance instructions. Listeners manipulate the various output controls on their playback systems according to instructions containing different sets of numbers for loudness and treble/bass control for each speaker. With both Xenakis and Cage, the computer serves (though for different ends) to achieve results impossible otherwise. In neither case has the computer actually produced sound; it has only aided composers by virtue of its high-speed computations (Hiller 1967).

Hiller speaks of his work with automated music in an interview:

> Nowadays I think that my computer pieces possess more expressive content than I would have first guessed. In other words, I hear in the pieces more of a reflection of my general approach to music than I would have supposed at the beginning. I don't find even the *Illiac Suite* that far disjunct from the other things I do. I suppose that my programming contains biases that are subjective.

Hiller's three *Algorithms* (I, 1968; II, 1972; and III, 1981) employ various stochastic and random elements. Each of Hiller's steps of composition are clearly laid out and described to produce what Hiller calls "change ringing." Hiller's program called PHRASE produced the orchestral work *A Preview of Coming Attractions* (1975).

James Tenney's work at Bell Laboratories produced a number of important works involving algorithmic composition including *Four Stochastic Studies* (1962), *Stochastic String Quartet* (1963), and *Dialogue* (1963). The results Tenney obtained are significant not only in their inherent musical worth but also in how they contrast with the works produced stochastically by Iannis Xenakis (Garland 1984).

Since these initial experiments, many other composers have been directly involved with algorithmic music (Balaban, Ebcioglu, and Laske 1992; Kelly 1996). They include, among others, Barry Truax, William Buxton, Thomas DeLio, Scot Gresham-Lancaster, Allen Strange, Larry Austin, Petr Kotik, Denis Lorrain, Horacio Vaggione, David Zicarelli, Clarence Barlow, Charles Dodge, Peter Gena, Kevin Jones, and Laura Tedeschini Lalli.

EXPERT SYSTEMS

Algorithmic composition programs can be created in a variety of ways. Traditionally, programs derive from a top-down structure. That is, programmers begin with a basic algorithmic overview and then break it into smaller and smaller elements until no further subdivision is possible (Dowling and Harwood 1985). However, a bottom-up approach also may be employed. For example, work-section-period-phrase-subphrase-pitch could be one way to model a traditional top-down composing process with pitch-subphrase-phrase-period-section-work representing the bottom-up approach.

Expert systems can be used to create algorithmic composing programs (Charniak, Riesbeck, and McDermott 1979; Charniak and McDermott 1984; Cope 1987a). Expert systems employ user-defined rules that govern their behavior. One good example of an expert system involves using succession rules for tonal music to create new progressions of chord functions (Hiller and Baker 1963; Hiller and Isaacson 1956; Meehan 1980; Winograd 1968). For example, new realizations of the chord protocols found in Figure 8.5 can be created by first analyzing music (upward direction in the fig-

ure to the left) and determining the explicit protocols or succession rules in the music. These protocols then can produce machine composition (downward direction in the figure to the right). Again, these examples are simple and the results trivial. However, the logical *processes* used serve as good models. More complex results can be achieved by sophisticating the program. Lerdahl and Jackendoff, for example, call their analytic approach a "generative grammar for tonal music," which incorporates a number of linguistically associated approaches to certain musical styles (see also Baroni and Callegari 1984; Cope 1991; Holtzman 1981). Figure 8.6 presents their "well-formedness" rules based on musical surface features, and possible underlying analyses based on linguistic principles. Figure 8.7 demonstrates their hierarchical approach to Beethoven's "Tempest" Sonata, Opus 31, No. 2. Here, only the most important and critical material survives to the top layer of the analysis. Primary material appears in the top-level parsing as initial splinters from main lines while secondary and tertiary material appear as angular lines (Lerdahl and Jackendoff 1977).

Figure 8.8 shows a simple expert program for the computer creation of twelve-tone rows. Written in the BASIC computer language, this small program provides a good example of *if/then/else* clauses (Winsor 1987). Line 80 here can be read as: "IF I = 1, THEN go to line 130, else go to line 90." This program is not a particularly complex expert system. It simply produces random twelve-tone rows. However, complexity and sophistication result from extending the program with further rules in much this same manner. For example, this program could next form a twelve-tone matrix or compose music following strict serial procedures.

Expert systems also can use pattern matching for composing music in particular styles (Cope 1987b, 1990, 1996; Desain 1992). Since musical motives or patterns occur in many styles both tonal and non-tonal, pattern matching notes and associated durations for motive recurrences and reusing such patterns in output occasionally can produce convincing results. These patterns include melodies and ornaments, harmonic sequences, and so on that repeat in various guises and remind listeners of a particular composer's style. With some composers these patterns occur as ostinati such as the Alberti-bass, walking bass, um-pah-pah, and so on which usually help to reference a period, but not a particular composer. Subtler pattern matching can help create music in a particular composer's style. In the author's work with Experiments in Musical Intelligence, these patterns are called signatures. A signature is a motive that is used by a composer in more than one work.

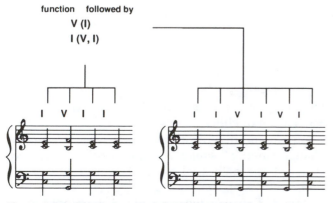

Figure 8.5. Generating new chord progressions from succession rules created by analyzing extant music.

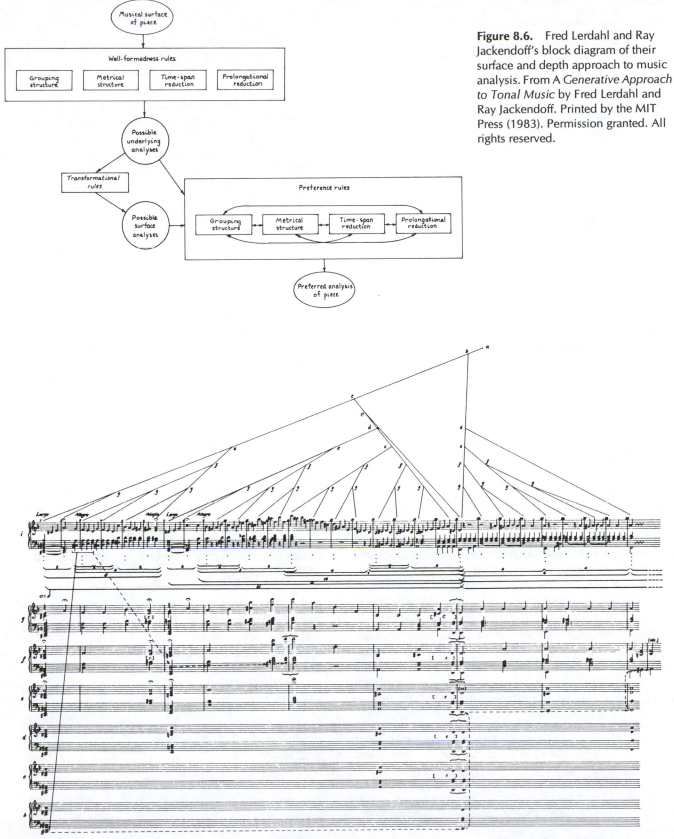

Figure 8.6. Fred Lerdahl and Ray Jackendoff's block diagram of their surface and depth approach to music analysis. From *A Generative Approach to Tonal Music* by Fred Lerdahl and Ray Jackendoff. Printed by the MIT Press (1983). Permission granted. All rights reserved.

Figure 8.7. Fred Lerdahl and Ray Jackendoff's analysis of Beethoven's *Tempest Sonata*, Op. 31, No. 2. From *A Generative Approach to Tonal Music* by Fred Lerdahl and Ray Jackendoff. Printed by the MIT Press (1983). Permission granted. All rights reserved.

```
0 RANDOMIZE
10 DIM N(12), M(12), N$(12)
20 DIM A(12, 12)
30 N$(1)="C ": N$(2)="C# ": N$(3)="D ": N$(4)="D# "
40 N$(5)="E ": N$(6)="F ": N$(7)="F# ": N$(8)="G "
50 N$(9)="G# ": N$(10)="A ": N$(11)="A# ": N$(12)="B "
60 FOR I = 1 TO 12
70 N(I) = INT (1 + (12 * RND))
80 IF I = 1 THEN 130
90 I1 = I - 1
100 FOR J = 1 TO I1
110 IF N(I) = N(J) THEN 70
120 NEXT J
130 NEXT I
140 FOR K = 1 TO 12
150 IF K = 1 THEN M(1) = N(1)
160 IF K = 1 THEN 230
170 Q = K - 1
180 P = N(K) - N(Q)
190 R = M(Q) - P
200 IF R < 1 THEN R = R + 12
210 IF R > 12 THEN R = R - 12
220 M(K) = R
230 NEXT K
240 FOR A = 1 TO 12
250 G = N(A)
255 PRINT N$(G)"  "
260 NEXT A
390 END
```

Figure 8.8.   A program written in the computer language BASIC for creating random twelve-tone rows.

Figure 8.9 shows a pitch and duration pattern found in Mozart. The first excerpt presents the basic structure—the leap of an octave upwards followed by chromatic motion a half-step down with successive occurrences of the pattern here widening to a major second. The second example differs in its use of eighth notes and the immediate occurrence of a lower chromatic major second. The third example delays the motion from minor to major by many repetitions but still represents the same signature. The fourth example ignores the downbeat octave, but nonetheless clearly resembles the original pattern. The fifth example does not resolve to the major second at all. The final example does not resolve and has less embellishment. These motives differ from one another and yet have aural similarities distinguishing them as a stylistic signature. The dates of these compositions span fourteen years with the last two showing less resemblance than those of 1778.

Figure 8.10 presents an algorithm of one possible expert system used for music composition based on the two models presented thus far: succession rules and pattern matching (Cope 1987a; Duisberg 1984; Gill 1973). Note how melody and harmony are treated separately according to their different roles. The part-writing rules section to the right of the figure could be eliminated if the actual data of the music analyzed originally were to accompany the functions as they moved down the right-hand side of the algorithm.

Modeling analytical and compositional processes in these ways creates better understanding of the musical intelligence required to replicate reasonable facsimiles of given styles or to create wholly new styles based on mathematical formulas, statistics, and/or random processes (Dowling and Harwood 1985; Forte 1967; Smoliar 1980). Expert systems may thusly be applied to a wide variety of different musical styles and constraint systems.

Expert systems also have renewed interest in natural language approaches to music composition (Lisle and Longuet-Higgins 1989; Holtzman 1981; Roads 1978, 1984, 1985; Steedman 1984). This interest often results from the desire for programmers to base their programs on some kind of natural process. Since language uses sound, and order proceeds by analogous protocols in music, natural language approaches have received much attention in recent years.

Figure 8.11 shows a parser developed by K. S. Fu for syntactic analysis of programming languages. Its top-down parsing algorithm consists of generation and backtracking sub-algorithms that systematically trace the programmed grammar of strings paralleling motives in music.

Interactive composition provides another opportunity for composers to engage in expert-system algorithmic composition. For example, George Lewis, a composer, trombonist, computer installation artist, and programmer of interactive computer music systems, includes aspects of artificial intelligence, improvisation, and interactivity in his compositional approach. Lewis's program *Voyager* analyzes aspects of an improvisor's performance in real time, and uses that analysis to guide an automatic composing program to generate complex responses to a musician's

Figure 8.9.   From Mozart's (1) Sonata 10, mvt. 3, m. 131, 1778; (2) Sonata 13, mvt. 3, m. 24, 1778; (3) Piano Concerto 23, mvt. 1, m. 131, 1786; (4) Sonata 16, mvt. 1, 1778; (5) Sonata 6, mvt. 1, m. 90, 1778; (6) Sonata 5, mvt. 3, 1774.

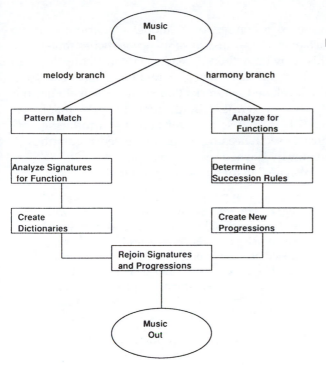

Figure 8.10.   An algorithm for automated music composition.

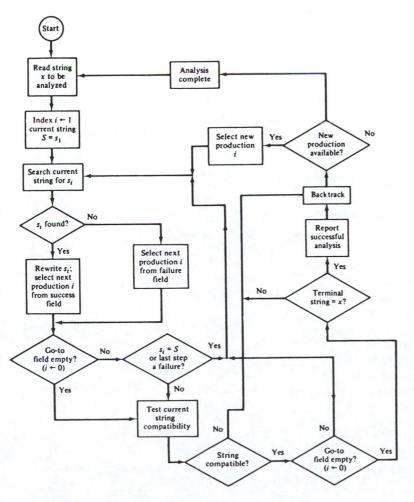

Figure 8.11.   A programmed grammar with a syntax of programming languages. King Sun Fu, Syntactic Pattern Recognition and Applications. Copyright 1982.

playing. Lewis's interactive installations have appeared in the Musée de la Villette (Paris), Randolph Street Gallery (Chicago), and the DeCordova Museum (Boston). He also has performed with Anthony Braxton, Count Basie, John Zorn, Anthony Davis, Derek Bailey, Richard Teitelbaum, and Steve Lacy.

NEURAL NETWORKS

Neural networks, often called parallel distributed processing or PDP connectionist models, function by reinforcing and diminishing connections between internal nodes and how successfully they back-propagate data (Todd and Loy 1992; Todd 1988, 1989). By sweeping—often hundreds of times—through a neural net, a set of data (which could be musical representations) can be "learned." This simplistic explanation of a very complex phenomenon demonstrates that neural nets operate differently than expert systems. Peter Todd makes the distinction between expert systems and neural nets even clearer in the following comments:

> One of the major features of the PDP approach is that it replaces strict rule-following behavior with regularity-learning and generalization. This fundamental shift allows the development of new algorithmic composition methods that rely on learning the structure of existing musical examples and generalizing from these learned structures to compose new pieces. These methods contrast greatly with the majority of older schemes that simply follow a previously assembled set of compositional rules, resulting in brittle systems typically unable to appropriately handle unexpected musical situations. (Todd 1989, p. 27)

Current research suggests that with enough melodies a net can create new works in the style of learned music. This can be accomplished in a number of ways. One method interrupts the net at some point prior to fully learning its input data, thus producing similar but not duplicate results. Another method combines two or more input data in a given style (Todd 1989).

Figure 8.12 shows a very simple net consisting of inputs and outputs separated by hidden units. Such networks begin with numerical weightings in each of the hidden units set randomly or, less often, to zero. When note representations enter this net, the hidden units make an initial attempt to replicate the input at the output level. When the output, initially random, recursively propagates back through the network after a comparison with the original input, the hidden units that perform well increase in weight and those that perform poorly decrease in weight.

Jamshed Bharucha (Bharucha and Todd 1989) has proposed a connectionist model of harmony where each event in a musical sequence activates tone units. This activation then spreads via connecting links to parent chords and then to parent key units. Peter Todd has developed networks that create new melodies out of what he terms "composition by plan manipulation." This process involves networks producing new musical sequences based on perceived regularities in previously learned sequences.

Wayne Bateman has observed that:

> Even if a compositional algorithm is stylistically "tight" enough to engender its output with readily identifiable stylistic features, the resulting music sounds mechanical and boring. Indeed one can offer no assurance that it is even possible to compose music according to an explicit, inflexible, formalized procedure that in the long run is artistically satisfying to most people. (Bharucha 1982, p. 238)

At MIT's Media Laboratory, hard-wired neural-net-learned accompaniments follow nuances of tempo indicated by human performers connected to the net via contact microphones attached to their instruments. The ability of hard-wired neural nets to respond almost instantaneously makes them quite useful as real-time musical tools.

The future of musical neural nets appears promising (Lischka 1987; Scarborough and Jones 1989). The connectionist concept is sophisticated and especially suited to music. Once problems of representation are resolved, neural networks should create interesting new music analogous to human composition.

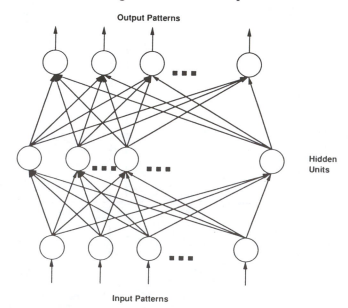

Figure 8.12.   A simple neural net.

MATHEMATICAL SOURCES

Any mathematical formula can be translated into an algorithm capable of producing music (Schillinger 1948, 1978; Winsor 1987). For example, the simple formula $z = \cos x^2 y^2$, shown in three-dimensional graph form in Figure 8.13, can produce a series of numbers resulting from inserting progressively larger linear numbers for x creating a non-linear output in the form of y. The simple Lisp function shown in Figure 8.14 accomplishes this transformation easily. The output of this function translates to the music shown in Figure 8.15 where the numbers produced by the mathematics have been transferred to pitches.

Stochastics (Xenakis 1954, 1956, 1971), genetic algorithms, Markov chains, generative grammars (Lerdahl and Jackendoff 1983; Baroni and Callegari 1984), and various other artificial intelligence techniques (Dodge 1970) also have been used to successfully compose music. For the most part, these techniques produce fairly random-sounding results that nonetheless can provide composers with a rich vocabulary of source materials for composing. In some instances, stochastics in particular, the process produces predictable results at the macrocompositional level by using random or quasi-random events at the micro level.

Fractals (so named by their creator Benoit Mendelbrot) also offer useful possibilities for modeling musical composition (Ames 1982, 1990; Bolognesi 1983). Fractals can be roughly defined as recursive structures that imitate themselves at succeedingly larger and smaller levels [by $X_{k+1} = \lambda X_k (1 - X_k)$]. Self-similar by nature, fractals are found in many real-world objects. Branch and root structures of trees, for example, have implanted recursive vein structures. Shorelines also can be defined in terms of fractals (Dodge and Bahn 1986; Dodge 1988).

INTERACTIVE COMPOSITION

Interactive composition occurs when humans and computers collaborate during composition (Rowe 1993). Interactive compositional software usually incorporates modules for analyzing music already composed. Such software also provides an interface between composers and programs, often appearing as notation or as graphic objects (Puckette 1991). Interactive composing programs typically stay abreast of their human partners and produce relevant music whenever need or curiosity arises.

Figure 8.13. A graph of the formula $z = \cos x^2 y^2$.

```
;(run-midi-cosine-function 20 10 10)
;(61 61 61 79 78 70 74 69 80 78 74 65 69 80 80 70 78 74 80 78)

(defun run-midi-cosine-function (limit x y)
  (if (zerop limit)()
    (cons (+ 60 (round (* 10 (+ 1 (cos (* (expt (random x) 2)
                                          (expt (random y) 2)))))))
      (run-midi-cosine-function (1- limit) x y))))
```

Figure 8.14. A LISP function to create MIDI pitch numbers from the formula $z = \cos x^2 y^2$.

Figure 8.15. Musical output and resultant scale derived from multiple runs of the function shown in Figure 8.14.

Figure 8.16 shows a diagram of an interactive composition environment. The composing engine here consists either of a rules-based or neural net core. The user need not know anything about programming or how the program functions in order to use this system. Figure 8.17 shows an interactively composed composition created with a program similar to that shown in Figure 8.16. Note how the music—composed equally by human and computer—fits seamlessly together here. Some feel that this process, that of sharing composing responsibilities with computers, has great potential as a model for future composers.

The Internet offers composers and artists of all types an opportunity to create interactively with various computational devices and collaboratively with other users. In what some term "module music," composers can create music for a particular module of a work being collaboratively designed by a group of composers linked through the Internet. Computers then contribute not only their hardware and software networks, over which living composers compose, but make intrinsic contributions themselves (see also the discussion under Virtual Reality and the Internet in chapter 6).

CURRENT PROGRAMS

At the present time, many algorithmic or computer-assisted (CAC) music programs are emerging. Most are based on straightforward random functions rather than demonstrating true intelligence. Of these, M, written by David Zicarelli, Joel Chadabe, John

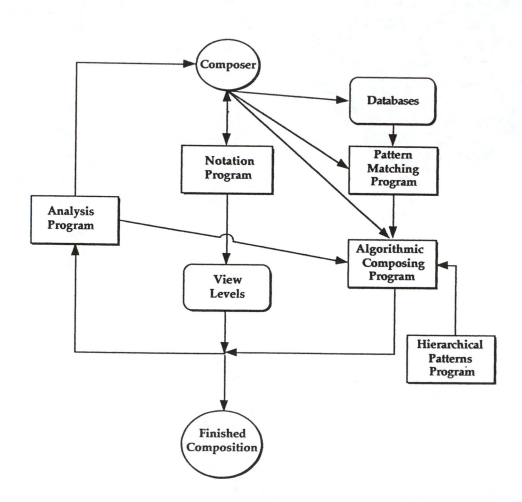

Figure 8.16. An interactive composition flowchart.

Figure 8.17. A work created using the algorithm shown in Figure 8.16.

Offenhartz, and Antony Widoff, has proven successful. Called "the intelligent composing and performing system," *M* stores composer-defined musical material as patterns and varies these according to such characteristics as orchestration and density. Figure 8.18 shows a sample screen from the *M* program.

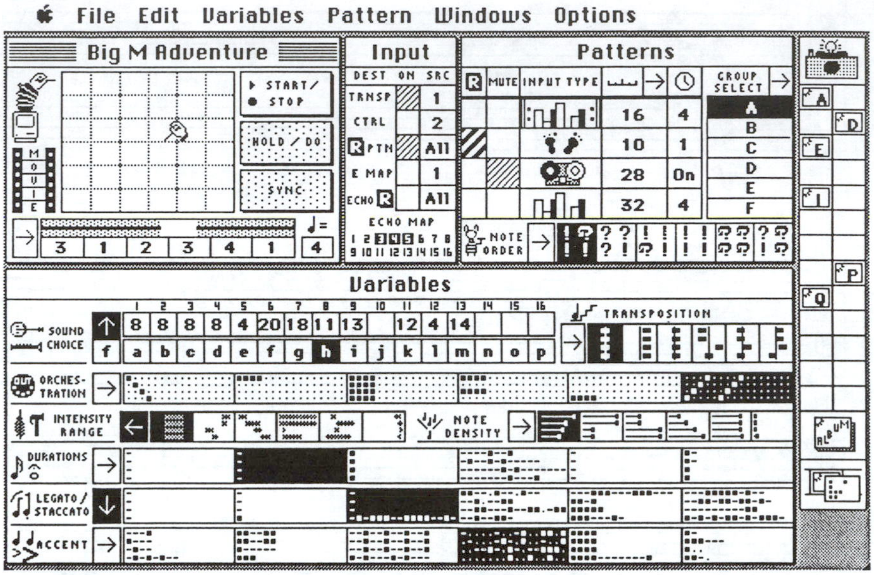

fit divergent examples together with some semblance of order, the program transposes the melody to fit with the harmonies. Because composing does not proceed randomly, the same choices always produce the same results. Different arrangements of parameters, however, create significantly different music. *Music*

Figure 8.18. Screen from *M* by Intelligent Music. Permission granted by Intelligent Music, Albany, NY.

Jam Factory, another program from Intelligent Music, follows more of an improvisatory structure based on an interactive sequencer-type system. Billed as a "real-time improvisation enhancement and performance system," users may work in real time with the program while it performs. Neither *M* nor *Jam Factory* has any real AI application. However, both have powerful algorithms that could serve as algorithmic music engines.

Music Mouse, created by Laurie Spiegel, transforms a Macintosh into what she calls "an intelligent instrument." The program allows users to control a variety of sequencing possibilities by moving the mouse during performance. The keyboard then can be used to control volume, tempo, tone, pitch, transposition, and various MIDI parameters. *Music Mouse* represents an example of computer-assisted improvisation, automating parts of the process and leaving other parts free for users to shape and direct the flow of the music.

Yaakov Kirschen's *Music Creator* software combines elements of different works in order to create new music. The program separately stores the chords, melodies, and rhythms of the works to be used for combination. Composing involves three different works. By combining the rhythm of one with the melody of another, and the chords of yet another, the program creates novel combinations of styles. In order to

Creator often "composes" nonsensical pastiches. Occasionally, however, the chosen works blend styles into novel and interesting new musical results.

Experiments in Music Intelligence creates music in the styles of the music in its database. Figure 8.19 shows the workstation on which *Experiments in Music Intelligence* operates. The program on the left side of the graph produces timbres and the lower right portion represents the computational section of the workstation.

Figures 8.20, 8.21, 8.23 and 8.24 show output from the *Experiments in Music Intelligence* program. In Figure 8.20, the textures, harmonic protocol, and general melodic shape suggest Mozart's style. Note the Mozart *signature* in the last measure, the result of pattern matching similar to that described earlier in this chapter. Figure 8.21 shows an example of machine-composed Debussy. Note the relation of this example to one of the works of Debussy in the program's database: *Clair de lune*, shown in Figure 8.22.

Figure 8.23 resembles Stravinsky's chorale style, not unlike that which appears at the end of his *Symphony in C*, one of the works used for pattern matching. Figure 8.24 shows an *Experiments in Music Intelligence*-created imitation of a Scott Joplin rag. Note the syncopation and other characteristics of Joplin's style. The motion to a minor subdominant chord (here in bar 3), unusual for Joplin, may be an anomaly cre-

THE WORKSTATION

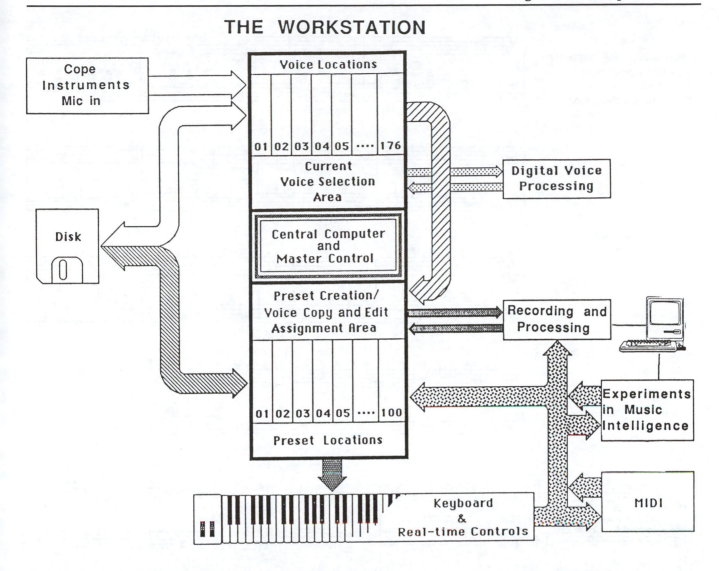

Figure 8.19. One possible workstation involving AI, sampling, and MIDI.

ated by the expert system's own originality. For other and more extensive examples created by *Experiments in Music Intelligence* refer to the author's books listed in the chapter bibliography.

The League of Automated Composers (Jim Horton, Tim Perkis, John Bischoff, and Rich Gold) has used mathematics and random sources to create ensemble works that have electronic output. In *Network Piece* (1980), each member of the group develops materials independently, communicating the results to other group members through digital-to-analog converters. Since one composer's work influences another, the outcome results from a dialogue. Figure 8.25 shows the ensemble before a 1980 performance of *Network Piece*.

Bischoff and Perkis, along with Chris Brown, Scot Gresham-Lancaster, Phil Stone, and Mark Trayle, have formed the international computer-music group *The*

Hub. The members design and build their own hardware and software instruments. The group electronically coordinates the activities of their individual systems through a central microcomputer, the Hub itself. Their performances in 1987 at the Clocktower and the Experimental Intermedia Foundation received wide acclaim. Perkis notes, "I see the aesthetic informing this work perhaps counter to other trends in computer music: instead of attempting to gain more individual control over every aspect of the music, we see more surprise through the lively and unpredictable response of these systems and hope to encourage an active response to surprise in hearing" (from program notes).

Joe Jones has created many algorithmic composing instruments. These instruments range from mechanical percussion orchestras to his percussion machine shown in Figure 8.26. While the image here

Figure 8.20.   The beginning of a machine-composed movement in the style of Wolfgang Amadeus Mozart.

Figure 8.22.   The first two measures of Debussy's *Clair de lune*, on which Figure 8.21 is based.

Figure 8.21.   The beginning of a machine-composed movement in the style of Claude Debussy.

Figure 8.23. Part of a machine-composed movement in the style of Igor Stravinsky.

Figure 8.24.   Part of a machine-composed movement in the style of Scott Joplin.

Figure 8.25.   The League of Automated Music Composers in performance in San Francisco on November 15, 1980. From the left: Jim Horton, Tim Perkis, and John Bischoff. Photograph by John Grau from Curtis Roads's 1985 book, figure 335, p. 596.

Figure 8.26.   Percussion Machine by Joe Jones, performed first at the Pocket Theatre in NYC on August 8, 1963.

may seem more theatrical than musical, such instruments have produced novel and musical results.

Tod Machover's music breaks traditional artistic and cultural boundaries, offering a synthesis of acoustic and electronic sounds, operatic arias, and rock. Machover's opera *VALIS* was commissioned by the Centre Pompidou in Paris to celebrate its tenth anniversary in 1987. He composed an unusual mini-opera,

Media/Medium, in 1994 for the magicians Penn and Teller, who toured it throughout the United States. Machover invented Hyperinstruments, a technology that uses computers to augment musical expression. Some of these hyperinstruments have been designed for such diverse virtuosi as Yo-Yo Ma and Prince, and the *Hyperstring Trilogy* is one of the culminating points of this development.

The Tsukuba Musical Robot, presented for the first time at the 1985 International Exposition in Tsukuba, Japan, is a fully implemented pianist capable of performing works either from sight or from its limited repertoire (Roads 1986a). Figure 8.27 shows this technical marvel during performance. Seated at a Yamaha digital organ, the robot scans scores with a video camera and speaks with bystanders about its performance. Tsukuba's control system consists of sixty-seven computers interconnected by fiberoptic data links. The

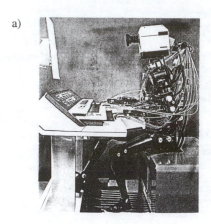

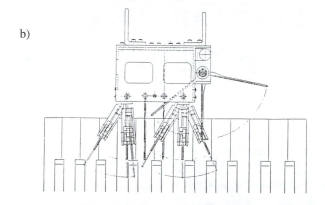

Figure 8.27.   The Tsukuba Musical Robot.

robot's eyes utilize a charge-coupled device (CCD) camera and frame buffer with a resolution of 2000 by 3000 pixels. The limb design follows human models and consists of two-joint thumbs and four three-joint fingers moving at a speed of 1.5 m/sec. The robot is designed to accompany a human who sings into a microphone attached to the system. If the live performer sings out of tune, the robot adjusts the synthesizer/organ accordingly to match the singer's pitch. Figure 8.27 also shows the robot's fingers at the keyboard.

Charles Ames developed his *Automated Music Composer* for stylistic imitation of jazz, Latin jazz, and rock. The *Automated Music Composer* composes and performs unique compositions faithful to the conventions of these styles (Ames 1987a). Ames's system uses a Kurzweil 250 digital sampling keyboard and sound system. *Automated Music Composer* was exhibited along with many other original music products for computers on tour with Digital Equipment Corporation's *Robots and Beyond: The Age of Intelligent Machines*. Ames also has developed a number of significant constraint-based programs for the development of algorithmic music. Ames uses mechanisms that maintain pitches in statistical balance by favoring the least-used

pitch in any decision. Ames's *Crystals*, in particular, exemplifies his use both of artificial intelligence processes and contextual sensitivity (Ames 1982).

Otto Laske, one of the major proponents of musical intelligence as related to computers and algorithmic music over the past two decades, sums up many current views when he states:

> The question is: How can we transfer human musical expertise to a computer and represent it within the machine? How can we construct musical knowledge bases incrementally? How can we get the machine to explain its musical reasoning to a human being? There is nothing peculiar about musical expertise that would force us to use different methods from those used in artificial intelligence applications today to solve these very legitimate problems. (Roads 1986b, p. 56)

VECTORAL ANALYSIS
IANNIS XENAKIS: *ATRÉES*

(For information on vectoral analysis and procedures see Preface.)

1. Historical Background: Iannis Xenakis was born in Braïla, Romania on May 29, 1922 of Greek parentage (Bois 1980; Fleuret 1981; Matossian 1990). He lived for ten years near the Danube before he moved with his family to Greece and obtained an education at a private college in Spetsai. Xenakis entered the Athens Polytechnic School majoring in engineering but soon became heavily involved with the Resistance. On January 1, 1945, he was badly wounded and blinded in his left eye. In 1947, Xenakis met Honegger, Milhaud, and Messiaen in Paris with the latter encouraging him to go into music. He also met Le Corbusier, the architect, who accepted him as a collaborator. The two worked closely together on many projects including the Baghdad stadium and the convent of La Tourette (Varga 1996). In 1958, Xenakis helped design the Philips pavilion at the Brussels Exposition (discussed in chapter 7) that further developed his ideas on architecture, acoustics, and music, ideas he finds inexorably linked. In 1966, he founded EMAMu (Equipe de Mathématique et d'Automatique Musicales) in Paris. He also taught at Indiana University (Bloomington) in 1967–72, during which time he founded the Center for Musical Mathematics and Automation (similar to EMAMu).

Xenakis's works result from the use of mathematical models and often are composed, at least partially, using computers (Xenakis 1971a, 1971b, 1976, 1985a, 1985b). His writings (particularly *Formalized Music*) represent standard reference relating to the early developments of computer composition. He has used

Figure 8.28. Iannis Xenakis

probability laws, stochastics, Markovian chains, game theory, group theory, set theory, Boolean algebra, and Gaussian distributions as formalizations. His music typically contains thick textures with many diverse elements sounding simultaneously. Some of his works contain extended silences punctuated by apparently random sounds.

2. Overview: Xenakis's stochastic and mathematical approach to music seems deeply rooted in indeterminacy. His works are, however, written out in traditional notation for predictable results. Xenakis describes his concepts and procedures in his book *Formalized Music*:

> As a result of the impasse in serial music, as well as other causes, I originated in 1954 a music constructed from the principle of indeterminism; two years later I named it "Stochastic Music." The laws of the calculus of probabilities entered composition through musical necessity. But other paths also led to the same stochastic crossroads—first of all, natural events such as the collision of hail or rain with hard surfaces, or the song of cicadas in a summer field. These sonic events are made out of thousands of isolated sounds; this multitude of sounds, seen as a totality, is a new sonic event. This mass event is articulated and forms a plastic mold of time, which itself follows aleatory and stochastic laws. If one then wishes to form a large mass of point-notes, such as string

> pizzicati, one must know these mathematical laws, which, in any case, are no more than a tight and concise expression of chains of logical reasoning. Everyone has observed the sonic phenomena of a political crowd of dozens of hundreds of thousands of people. The human river shouts a slogan in a uniform rhythm. Then another slogan springs from the head of the demonstration; it spreads toward the tail, replacing the first. A wave of transition thus passes from the head to the tail . . . The statistical laws of these events, separated from their political or moral context, are the same as those of the cicadas or the rain. They are the laws of the passage from complete order to total disorder in a continuous or explosive manner. They are stochastic laws. (Xenakis 1971, p. 9)

Some have argued that Xenakis's music is not indeterminate at all. Bernard Jacobson has written:

> He uses chance, but his music leaves nothing to chance. This is not the paradox it might seem. To Xenakis—as indeed, to most philosophers—chance itself is a scientific concept. Central among the scientific laws he has applied to music is Bernoulli's Law of large numbers, which provides that as the number of repetitions of a given "chance" trial (such as flipping a coin) increases, so the probability that the results will tend to a determinate end approaches certainty. (liner notes to Nonesuch 71201)

Xenakis's uses of probability theory include *ST/10-1, 080262* (1962, with first performance on May 24 of that year at the headquarters of IBM in France), *ST/48-1, 240162* (for large orchestra), *Atrées* (for ten soloists, 1962), and *Morsima-Amorsima* (for violin, cello, bass, and piano, 1962). Pitches for many of these works were calculated by a 7090 IBM computer in Paris following special probabilistic programs devised by Xenakis. These probabilistic programs derived from his thesis of "Minimum Rules of Composition," which he formulated in 1958. The computer program defines all of the sounds of a previously calculated sequence, including the time of occurrence, kind of timbre (arco, pizzicato, glissando, etc.), instrument, pitch, gradient of glissando, duration, and dynamic.

Atrées ST/10-3, 060962 (the last six digits of the full title represent the date 6 September, 1962) was completed in 1962 using the computer program ST (for stochastic—the same program used for *Morsima-Amorsima, Achorripsis,* and *ST/48-1*). This 15-minute work for 10 performers follows a dramatic and formidable form. Pitches are determined by the mean density of notes occurring during preconceived sequence lengths. Dynamics derive from a chart of 44 values based on the dynamics *ppp*, *p*, *f*, and *ff*, with all other levels occurring only briefly within crescendi and diminuendi giving the work the feel of movement toward or away from the listener. Figure 8.29 provides an example of some of the mathematical theory behind this work.

$$(0 \leq x \leq x_0) = \int_0^{x_0} f(x)\, dx = 1 - e^{-cx_0} = F(x_0),$$

$$F(x_0) = \text{prob.}\ (0 \leq y \leq y_0) = y_0$$

$$1 - e^{-cx_0} = y_0$$

$$x_0 = -\frac{\ln\,(1 - y_0)}{c}$$

$$f(x)\, dx = ce^{-cx}\, dx.$$

Figure 8.29. Some of the mathematical theory behind Xenakis's work (p. 142 of *Formalized Music*).

The primary formula in Figure 8.29 represents an elementary law of probability with the other formulas providing the distribution logic. Xenakis ran these programs on an IBM 7090 computer using punch cards, a process that could at the time take up to six months. Xenakis further ran many tests for errors before actually translating his work into music notation. Figures 8.30 and 8.31 show examples of the FORTRAN IV language instructions and the results obtained.

Atrées, like *Metastasis*, aptly demonstrates Xenakis's penchant for glissandi in his music. This work also emphasizes the fact that Xenakis uses statistics separate from musical meaning (i.e., the computer simply processes numbers). Xenakis comments, "There exists in all the arts what we may call rationalism in the etymological sense: the search for proportion" and "Now everything that is rule or repeated constraint is part of the mental machine" (Reichardt 1971, p. 124). Xenakis further refers to his use of science and art, "Computers resolve logical problems by heuristic methods. But composers are not really responsible for the introduction of mathematics into music: rather it is mathematics that makes use of the computer in composition" (Reichardt 1971, p. 124).

3. Orchestration techniques: *Atrées* is scored for clarinet, bass clarinet, two French horns, percussion, two violins, viola, and cello. The percussionist uses maracas, suspended cymbals, gong, five temple blocks, four tam-tams, and vibraphone. Determination of which instruments play together at any given time is achieved by breaking them into timbre classes. For example, classes exist for flute/clarinet, brass, struck strings (col legno), bowed strings, and glissando. Effects are treated similarly as instruments. As an example, the texture densities provided by the chart in Figure 8.32 show eight classes, four of which are instruments played normally, with the other four classes being effects.

The vertical columns in Figure 8.32 refer to percentages—each column summing to 100—of each of the eight categories of timbres that contribute to the overall textural shape of *Atrées*. The harp and clarinet have the least and most deviation—2 and 26 percent respectively. Patterns tend to imitate one another with only the percussion moving somewhat independently at times.

4. Basic techniques: Much of Xenakis's work with probability derives from a given line's memory of a preceding pitch. Choices then take place from a prescribed set of semitones. One formula appears in Figure 8.33, where P_z is the probability of the interval z chosen from the compass s. Lengths of notes and glissandi speeds are similarly determined. Part of an early flowchart in the ST series provides an example of the composer's process (see Figure 8.34). The formula creates values as a result of system-defined determinants.

5. Vertical models: Figure 8.35 shows the first two measures of *Atrées ST/10-1, 080262*. All twelve pitches appear here but clearly there are no tone rows or established protocol for their use. Key or mode centers (e.g., G♯ and E near the beginning) pass very quickly. Pitch itself seems elusive and often unimportant owing to the rapidity of the changing harmonic rhythm. The texture varies on a microscale—that is, changes from instant to instant. Polyrhythms abound. Contrasting effects occur simultaneously or in near proximity. Dynamics are mixed and subject to change on every note. At times instruments cannot be heard. This level of complexity abounds in this and other of Xenakis's works, no doubt a reflection of the mathematical processes that contributed to their creation.

6. Horizontal models: Figure 8.35 also provides an example of melodic order in *Atrées*. Only two melodic intervals are seconds (A-G♯ in the clarinet and C-C♯ in the viola), with most intervals larger than an octave. Even using pitch classes, one finds few seconds or thirds. The pointillism, however, often is clouded by the complex counterpoint taking place. Few lines can be followed independently from the others. Since each

```
C        PROGRAM FREE STOCHASTIC MUSIC   (FORTRAN IV)                    XEN    6
C                                                                        XEN    7
C        GLOSSARY OF THE PRINCIPAL ABBREVIATIONS                         XEN    8
C                                                                        XEN    9
C        A - DURATION OF EACH SEQUENCE IN SECONDS                        XEN   10
C        A10.A20.A17.A35.A30 - NUMBERS FOR GLISSANDO CALCULATION         XEN   11
C        ALEA - PARAMETER USED TO ALTER THE RESULT OF A SECOND RUN WITH THEXEN 12
C        SAME INPUT DATA                                                 XEN   13
C        ALFA(3) - THREE EXPRESSIONS ENTERING INTO THE THREE SPEED VALUES XEN  14
C        OF THE SLIDING TONES ( GLISSANDI )                              XEN   15
C        ALIM - MAXIMUM LIMIT OF SEQUENCE DURATION A                     XEN   16
C        (AMAX(I).I=1.KTR) TABLE OF AN EXPRESSION ENTERING INTO THE       XEN  17
C        CALCULATION OF THE NOTE LENGTH IN PART 8                        XEN   18
C        BF - DYNAMIC FORM NUMBER. THE LIST IS ESTABLISHED INDEPENDENTLY  XEN  19
C        OF THIS PROGRAM AND IS SUBJECT TO MODIFICATION                  XEN   20
C        DELTA - THE RECIPROCAL OF THE MEAN DENSITY OF SOUND EVENTS DURING XEN 21
C        A SEQUENCE OF DURATION A                                        XEN   22
C        (E(I.J).I=1.KTR.J=1.KTE) - PROBABILITIES OF THE KTR TIMBRE CLASSESXEN 23
C        INTRODUCED AS INPUT DATA. DEPENDING ON THE CLASS NUMBER I=KR AND XEN  24
C        ON THE POWER J=U OBTAINED FROM V3*EXPF(U)=DA                     XEN  25
C        EPSI - EPSILON FOR ACCURACY IN CALCULATING PN AND E(I.J).WHICH   XEN  26
C        IT IS ADVISABLE TO RETAIN.                                      XEN   27
C        (GN(I.J).I=1.KTR.J=1.KTS) - TABLE OF THE GIVEN LENGTH OF BREATH  XEN  28
C        FOR EACH INSTRUMENT. DEPENDING ON CLASS I AND INSTRUMENT J       XEN  29
C        GTNA - GREATEST NUMBER OF NOTES IN THE SEQUENCE OF DURATION A    XEN  30
C        GTNS - GREATEST NUMBER OF NOTES IN KW LOOPS                     XEN   31
C        (HAMIN(I.J).HAMAX(I.J).HBMIN(I.J).HBMAX(I.J).I=1.KTR.J=1.KTS)    XEN  32
C        TABLE OF INSTRUMENT COMPASS LIMITS. DEPENDING ON TIMBRE CLASS I  XEN  33
C        AND INSTRUMENT J.  TEST INSTRUCTION 480 IN PART 6 DETERMINES     XEN  34
C        WHETHER THE HA OR THE HB TABLE IS FOLLOWED. THE NUMBER 7 IS      XEN  35
C        ARBITRARY.                                                      XEN   36
C        JW - ORDINAL NUMBER OF THE SEQUENCE COMPUTED.                   XEN   37
C        KNL - NUMBER OF LINES PER PAGE OF THE PRINTED RESULT.KNL=50     XEN   38
C        KR1 - NUMBER IN THE CLASS KR=1 USED FOR PERCUSSION OR INSTRUMENTS XEN 39
C        WITHOUT A DEFINITE PITCH.                                       XEN   40
C        KTE - POWER OF THE EXPONENTIAL COEFFICIENT E SUCH THAT          XEN   41
C        DA(MAX)=V3*(E**(KTE-1))                                         XEN   42
C        KTR - NUMBER OF TIMBRE CLASSES                                  XEN   43
C        KW - MAXIMUM NUMBER OF JW                                       XEN   44
C        KTEST1.TAV1.ETC - EXPRESSIONS USEFUL IN CALCULATING HOW LONG THE XEN  45
C        VARIOUS PARTS OF THE PROGRAM WILL RUN.                          XEN   46
C        KT1 - ZERO IF THE PROGRAM IS BEING RUN. NONZERO DURING DEBUGGING XEN  47
C        KT2 - NUMBER OF LOOPS. EQUAL TO 15 BY ARBITRARY DEFINITION.     XEN   48
C        (MODI(IX8).IX8=7.1)  AUXILIARY FUNCTION TO INTERPOLATE VALUES IN XEN  49
C        THE TETA(256) TABLE (SEE PART 7)                                XEN   50
C        NA - NUMBER OF SOUNDS CALCULATED FOR THE SEQUENCE A(NA=DA*A)    XEN   51
C        (NT(I).I=1.KTR) NUMBER OF INSTRUMENTS ALLOCATED TO EACH OF THE   XEN  52
C        KTR TIMBRE CLASSES.                                             XEN   53
C        (PN(I.J).I=1.KTR.J=1.KTS).(KTS=NT(I).I=1.KTR) TABLE OF PROBABILITYXEN 54
C        OF EACH INSTRUMENT OF THE CLASS I.                             XEN   55
C        (Q(I).I=1.KTR) PROBABILITIES OF THE KTR TIMBRE CLASSES. CONSIDEREDXEN 56
C        AS LINEAR FUNCTIONS OF THE DENSITY DA.                          XEN   57
C        (S(I).I=1.KTR) SUM OF THE SUCCESSIVE Q(I) PROBABILITIES. USED TO XEN  58
C        CHOOSE THE CLASS KR BY COMPARING IT TO A RANDOM NUMBER X1 (SEE   XEN  59
C        PART 3. LOOP 380 AND PART 5. LOOP 430).                        XEN   60
C        SINA - SUM OF THE COMPUTED NOTES IN THE JW CLOUDS NA. ALWAYS LESS XEN 61
C        THAN GTNS ( SEE TEST IN PART 10 ).                             XEN   62
C        SQPI - SQUARE ROOT OF PI ( 3.14159...)                         XEN   63
C        TA - SOUND ATTACK TIME ABCISSA.                                XEN   64
C        TETA(256) - TABLE OF THE 256 VALUES OF THE INTEGRAL OF THE NORMAL XEN 65
C        DISTRIBUTION CURVE WHICH IS USEFUL IN CALCULATING GLISSANDO SPEED
```

Figure 8.30. The main glossary of Xenakis's stochastic music written in FORTRAN IV (p. 145 of *Formalized Music*).

line changes timbres and pitches often, this further complicates the issue.

7. **Style:** *Atrées ST/10-1, 080262* represents a stochastically determined work based on probability calculations using the IBM 7090 computer. The complex processes of developing such programs seem as important as the resultant works. Creating the formulae, the resultant programs, and the charts of data from which the computer may choose possible notes requires intense scrutiny. Debugging the large functions properly is crucial for success. Translating the resultant data to music notation requires a significant amount of time and care to avoid mistakes. The resultant complex work demands incredible patience of its performers and audience alike. Some critics, confused by the pluralism of much new music, have dubbed

Xenakis the founder of *maximalism*. Certainly this work ranks high in this regard, if not in size of orchestration, then in terms of event numbers per performer.

This work, while similar to Webern's *Symphonie* of chapter 2 in terms of pointillism, varies with respect to texture and lack of premeditated pitch control. *Atrées ST/10-1, 080262* also differs from Oliveros's *Sonic Meditations XIII* in chapter 6, which, by virtue of its outspoken simplicity and lack of tangible movement, represents the opposite extreme from Xenakis's work here. Interestingly, however, *Atrées ST/10-1, 080262* holds some conceptual ties with Oliveros's work. For example, both Xenakis and Oliveros are concerned with a high degree of indeterminacy yet both are preoccupied in their individual ways with predictable results in performance. Comparisons to the vectoral

Figure 8.31. Provisional results of one phrase of analysis (p. 153 of *Formalized Music*).

N	START	CLASS	INSTRM	PITCH	GLISS1	GLISS2	GLISS3	DURATION	DYNAM
1	0.00	7	1	34.0	0.0	0.0	0.0	0.00	3
2	0.10	10	1	43.2	0.0	0.0	0.0	0.41	50
3	0.11	6	8	81.3	0.0	0.0	0.0	0.63	21
4	0.13	6	3	47.0	0.0	0.0	0.0	0.18	10
5	0.18	1	4	0.0	0.0	0.0	0.0	1.90	29
6	0.25	9	1	48.7	0.0	0.0	0.0	0.51	35
7	0.33	6	7	11.4	0.0	0.0	0.0	0.37	42
8	0.34	9	1	38.1	0.0	0.0	0.0	0.00	59
9	0.40	1	1	0.0	0.0	0.0	0.0	2.20	45
10	0.41	6	9	55.0	0.0	0.0	0.0	1.07	0
11	0.76	6	7	11.5	0.0	0.0	0.0	0.40	7
12	0.90	8	2	23.2	0.0	0.0	0.0	0.00	19
13	1.00	7	2	26.9	0.0	0.0	0.0	0.00	6
14	1.09	10	1	46.2	0.0	0.0	0.0	0.32	57
15	1.09	6	2	68.5	0.0	0.0	0.0	0.71	25
16	1.23	6	3	46.9	0.0	0.0	0.0	0.64	32
17	1.42	6	1	44.0	0.0	0.0	0.0	0.44	1
18	1.57	10	1	36.2	0.0	0.0	0.0	0.22	21
19	1.65	4	2	32.5	0.0	0.0	0.0	1.09	13
20	1.78	6	8	72.6	0.0	0.0	0.0	0.06	60
21	1.92	6	3	38.9	0.0	0.0	0.0	0.55	60
22	1.94	5	1	74.6	71.0	-25.0	-71.0	0.80	62
23	2.18	4	1	32.6	0.0	0.0	0.0	1.50	50
24	2.18	6	6	50.9	0.0	0.0	0.0	0.60	26
25	2.19	1	12	0.0	0.0	0.0	0.0	4.58	24
26	2.20	9	1	49.3	0.0	0.0	0.0	0.02	58
27	2.23	9	1	51.0	0.0	0.0	0.0	0.22	13
28	2.32	7	1	36.9	0.0	0.0	0.0	0.00	43
29	2.33	4	1	31.8	0.0	0.0	0.0	1.38	56
30	2.54	1	6	0.0	0.0	0.0	0.0	0.28	14
31	2.57	11	2	12.2	0.0	0.0	0.0	1.65	40
32	2.71	9	1	48.5	0.0	0.0	0.0	0.37	55
33	2.80	1	5	0.0	0.0	0.0	0.0	1.50	58
34	3.28	5	2	15.4	49.0	5.0	-31.0	0.52	21
35	3.33	1	7	0.0	0.0	0.0	0.0	1.38	8
36	3.38	5	2	47.3	-71.0	-17.0	46.0	1.05	4
37	3.55	10	1	37.6	0.0	0.0	0.0	0.14	24
38	3.56	1	9	0.0	0.0	0.0	0.0	1.30	0
39	3.60	9	1	64.3	0.0	0.0	0.0	0.19	13
40	3.64	12	2	52.2	0.0	0.0	0.0	3.72	9
41	3.65	6	5	59.0	0.0	0.0	0.0	0.83	28
42	3.71	5	3	38.8	25.0	2.0	-15.0	0.00	11
43	3.80	6	8	75.6	0.0	0.0	0.0	0.43	17
44	3.87	6	2	51.5	0.0	0.0	0.0	0.77	57
45	3.89	6	7	12.1	0.0	0.0	0.0	0.39	2
46	4.15	5	2	43.0	-71.0	24.0	71.0	1.16	2
47	4.15	5	1	80.3	36.0	4.0	22.0	0.85	50
48	4.25	9	1	59.9	0.0	0.0	0.0	0.10	10
49	4.31	12	2	40.1	0.0	0.0	0.0	2.49	33
50	4.33	1	10	0.0	0.0	0.0	0.0	0.46	34

Figure 8.32. Percents utilized in the creation of *Atrées* (from *Cybernetics, Art and Ideas*, ed. by Jadis Reichardt, p. 128).

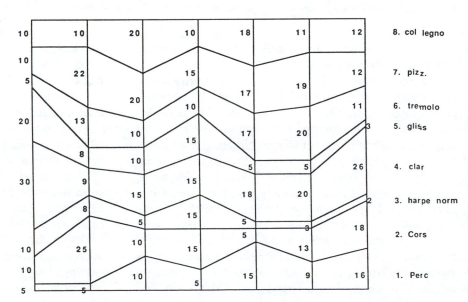

$$P_z = 2/S (1 - Z/S)DZ$$

Figure 8.33. One probability formula used by Xenakis.

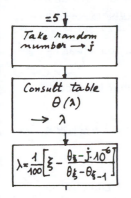

Figure 8.34. Examples of Xenakis's algorithm for random processes.

Figure 8.35. First two bars of *ST/10-1, 080262.*

analysis found in chapter 5 also proves very revealing, especially in the case where apparently opposite approaches to control reveal comparatively similar results.

JOHN CAGE, LUKAS FOSS, IANNIS XENAKIS: SHORT ANSWERS TO DIFFICULT QUESTIONS

This short three-way interview reveals interesting correlations between Foss (see chapter 5), Cage (see chapter 5), and Xenakis. In some ways, the questions and various responses seem tongue-in-cheek. However, note how many of the questions appear rhetorical and how often the responses skirt the real issues raised by the questions, yet cut right to the heart of many issues raised both in this chapter and in this book.

> The Buffalo Festival of the Arts Today was the occasion for a panel discussion that included three composers: John Cage, Lukas Foss, and Iannis Xenakis. Foss suggested a game: all three composers are on trial, each trying the two others. The questions had to be difficult, the answers short, well under a minute. An unidentified voice asked a final question.

Cage: Lukas, what is an idea?

Foss: A connection of parallels suddenly revealed.

Cage: What is a musical idea?

Foss: It would be a musical parallel which hadn't occurred to me before; something that makes things fit where before there appeared to be no connection.

Cage: The French speak of an *idée fixe*—can we now conceive of an *idée non-fixe*?

Foss: Well, an *idée fixe* is an obsession; an *idée non-fixe* would then be a free preoccupation, a non-obsessed, a non-fanatic, a non-single-minded one; that's what we work with most of the time.

Cage: Marcel Duchamp says that a work of art is not art until it becomes such in an observer or listener. What do you think?

Foss: Beauty in the eye of the beholder? An accepted truism. *"Je ne suis pas contre."*

Cage: Music is a form of government; a composer essentially tells others what to do. Thoreau says the best government would be no government at all; would the best form of music be no music at all?

Foss: I think there is an error here in the analogy. If we didn't *need* government we would, indeed, be better off, but if we didn't need music why would we be better off? Put that way the analogy between government and music no longer works.

Xenakis: Lukas, do you think that the public is necessary?

Foss: The public as such, no. Other people in the same boat, yes.

Xenakis: Are you interested in ancient, pre-medieval music?

Foss: Not yet.

Xenakis: How do you feel the influence of the future on you? Let me clarify my question. You say that we are influenced by the music of the past; I think that we are influenced by the future. How can you answer this?

Foss: There is a future and I don't know it. This not knowing something feels like an ominous presence; we can't quite see it but we know it's there—the only thing we know is that eventually we'll die. I think that if I didn't know that death is my ultimate future my work would be entirely different.

Cage: Mr. Xenakis, what compositions are you working on currently?

Xenakis: "Currently" means "now"?

Cage: Yes. What is the nature of your present work in composition?

Xenakis: For orchestra instruments and for technological means, computer, etc.

Cage: What do you think is wrong with the United States?

Xenakis: Too much power.

Cage: Is your music related to your political views?

Xenakis: I think my music was related to my political views, now less maybe. It was once like a reconversion of political things into music and there were events in my youth, sound events and form events which have influenced my music.

Cage: What do you think of the work of Buckminster Fuller?

Xenakis: I don't think that he can cover the earth.

Cage: I asked a Spanish lady scientist what she thought about the human mind in a world of computers. She said, "Computers are always right but life isn't about being right." What do you say to that?

Xenakis: The opposite—life has reason and computers are often wrong.

Cage: You have been an architect and now you are a musician. Are you going to go on to some other activity?

Xenakis: I'd like to but it is difficult.

Foss: Iannis, all the music of yours that I know is built on mathematical premise, mostly probabil-ity. Is there any aspect to chance that is not mathematical, that is, not probability theory?

Xenakis: All my music is not based on mathematics—there are parts of it which use mathematics. As to chance, it is not like dice or tossing a coin, this is ignorance, as if there were impossibility of predicting. What does chance mean to you?

Foss: Anything I cannot control. You left architecture for music—why?

Xenakis: Mostly because architecture was a business and music is less business.

Foss: In order to compose you need time, solitude—what else?

Xenakis: To live in a big city.

Foss: If someone imitates you (I know of an instance) does it flatter you or make you angry or both?

Xenakis: I am angry . . . angry and depressed.

Foss: What did you want to be when you were a child?

Xenakis: An elephant.

Foss: Has your native Greece shown interest in your music, and if not, why?

Xenakis: My people have but it is very difficult for them to hear my works because of the tyrannic grip of the actual government; they are practically never played in Greece. John, how do you consider the faculty of thought in respect to the whole full way of life that we have?

Cage: I think that if the activity of the mind, that is to say thinking, could flow from that point to any other point and could go *out* in the sense of sense perceptions, or could go *in* in the sense of dreams, then there is no real distinction or disconnection between those things.

Xenakis: What is your relationship to your own past and, in general, to the past of the rest of humanity?

Cage: My feeling about the past changes according to what I do; what I do is to bring to my attention things which I had not noticed in the past.

Xenakis: Do you think that a new era of mysticism is going to come for humanity? Christianity was a kind of era of mysticism which came at a period which was so much like ours now today (Alexandrian times). When science and all ways of life were so rich Christianity came like a sponge.

Cage: Comics, no?

Xenakis: Razor, no? As a sponge to erase fantastic ways of rich life and bring to humanity a certain degree of thought which was very, very different.

Cage: I believe that we are living in a period of change from competition; we're moving to a situation of overlap, interplay, where things which have seemed opposite and contradictory become part of a general cooperation; and I think that in that situation an attitude of mysticism could be entertained by individuals but that it would not be required—a period, in other words, of multiplicity of ways, all of which will manage to interpenetrate and not obstruct one another.

Xenakis: What sense do you make out of working with computers—what does it mean to you?

Cage: Well, I'm in the process of doing it and discovering what it does mean. It brings about the possibility of realization of projects so complex that I could not have approached the projects without the aid of the computer. I am heartened and delighted with the fact that there are no secrets in this field; that programs that are already available are shared; that what seems to be resulting is not music made by one person but rather music made by men, or many people.

Foss: John, what do you do with a composition of yours which you don't like—withdraw it?

Cage: No, I keep it.

Foss: Could you conceivably dislike a piece by someone else written totally in accordance with your own orientation, your own parti-pris? What would have to be wrong with it for you to dislike such a piece?

Cage: Some defect of it that would indicate that it was not done from belief.

Foss: Could you conceivably like a new piece of music totally opposite to your own music? If so, name one. And what would have to be right with it?

Cage: I think the work of La Monte Young is virtually opposite to mine, and I like it very much for the reason that it changes the way I hear.

Foss: Some years ago Stravinsky visited Pope John and the Pope said, "My son, is anything bothering you?" and Stravinsky said, "Yes, I cannot take criticism." The Pope said, "Neither can I." John, can you take criticism?

Cage: I pay very little attention to it.

Foss: My last question: Is it possible to ask a colleague a non-general, that is, a non-technical question which is not idiotic?

Cage: Yes.

Unidentified voice: As precisely as memory permits, retrace the history of music from 1910 to 1990; just the highlights, please.

Xenakis: I think that during the next ten years we will have a crazy mixture of music in everyday life. Then a kind of feedback will come in about fifteen to twenty years. It will probably be a decay if another world war does not happen.

Foss: Erickson says that there will be two kinds of people—those who know what they're doing (the technologists) and those who mean what they say. I suppose I belong to the latter group because I mean what I say and I don't know what I'm doing . . . I certainly don't know the music of the future. If I knew it I would write it.

Cage: I think we can expect in the future finer performances of classical music than we have now since societies will gather together to preserve things which we have the feeling might disappear if they didn't . . . just as we now have pro musica "Orchestra." I think we have yet to be surprised by further technological possibilities. At the same time there will be a greater and larger influence of cultures which have formerly been separated. I think that music will not swing back to something with which we are familiar— that it will include, not exclude, the past.

≈ Chapter 9 ≈

MINIMALISM

SOURCES

Nowhere does the influence of Eastern music on Western concepts appear so obviously and vigorously as it does in minimalism (Simms 1986; Schaeffer 1987). Both Terry Riley and Philip Glass visited India where they became fascinated by the ragas (melodies), talas (rhythmic patterns), gamaka (ornamentation), and tamburas (drone) they found there. Indian master sitarist Ravi Shankar influenced these and other minimalist composers producing a lasting effect on new music.

As with most new developments in the avant-garde (if indeed minimalism could be so defined), the influence of John Cage also must be acknowledged. While Debussy and others had crudely investigated the possible resources in the East, it was Cage who first began attending the lectures of D. T. Suzuki in 1947. Cage's studies of Zen and related Eastern philosophies greatly influenced him and hence the rest of the new music world. Those who worked directly with Cage, particularly Morton Feldman, whose often soft, effete works show significant Eastern influence, likewise created a stir. Lou Harrison (influenced by Henry Cowell) also has developed extensive Southeast Asian gamelans for the performance of his work.

Today, minimalism takes many forms and diversity abounds. In some cases (Steve Reich in particular), repeating materials shift in and out of phase. In other cases (namely Philip Glass), the bar line controls repeating sequences. Still other composers (especially Terry Riley) use slow expansions or contractions that occur over long and mesmerizing spans of time. Some composers (La Monte Young and Harold Budd) create terse works more conceptual than sonic. Still other composers adapt Indian and Eastern music techniques and apply them to triadic materials (Schwarz 1996; Strickland 1993).

Philip Glass comments, "[My music] is essentially concert music, which means inventing a new language as opposed to pop, which tends to be imitative. But the idea that concert music is only for a handful of people has only existed since the First World War. The language I've invented is not a purposely difficult one—it's a language of our time. I think people are beginning to hear that " (from an interview). Whether or not this new language has, in fact, been invented by him, that we are speaking of it as a language at all suggests the search for a common voice, a single mode through which composers can express their ideas without reinventing the wheel for each new work.

MINIMALISM

Frederic Rzewski (founder of the Musica Elettronica Viva) composed *Coming Together* in 1972. This work exemplifies minimalist techniques (Rzewski 1974). The score contains 394 measures of continuous sixteenth notes (no other rhythm occurs in the piece) over which a vocal line speaks the words of an inmate from the Attica Correction facility. Figure 9.1 provides an example of the repeating yet varied pulse. Figure 9.2 shows the second and third measures of the work. Here, the first two sixteenths frame the motive and pulse. The third, fourth, and fifth notes, however, extend the motive and cross the pulse at beat two. The

Figure 9.2. Measures 2 and 3 of Frederic Rzewski's *Coming Together*.

Figure 9.1. Measures 1 and 297 of Frederic Rzewski's *Coming Together* demonstrating the lack of significant variation in this minimalist work.

sixth and seventh notes repeat the initial note. This G can be considered the end of the extended motive or the beginning of a new version. While seemingly unimportant, these dual and even triple roles give the work diversity. Notes six and seven link to note eight in such a way that the opening motive repeats, but shifts with respect to beat. Notes nine, ten, and eleven repeat the first variant of the motive, metrically altered. Careful evaluation of these two bars (less than 1/100th of the piece) shows actions and reactions, cross accents and cross rhythms, all of which contrast the lack of pitch and rhythm development.

Steve Reich's career has spanned many different but highly related musical genres (Reich 1969, 1974; Schwartz 1981; Scott 1974). Most of Reich's early work involved phasing of different types. *It's Gonna Rain*, completed at the San Francisco Tape Music Center in January 1965 using the voice of Borther Walter on tape, and *Come Out* (1966) using the voice of Daniel Hamm on tape, are representative. *Piano Phase* (1967) for two pianos or two marimbas, *Pendulum Music* (1968) for three or more microphones, amplifiers, and loudspeakers, and *Four Organs* (1970) for four electric organs and maracas also belong to this important period. *Drumming* (1971) for two women's voices, piccolo, and percussion, and *Music for 18 Musicians* (1976) for four women's voices, two clarinets, bass clarinet, percussion, four pianos, violin, and cello involve more counterpoint and less phrasing. *Tehillim* (1981) for three sopranos, alto, flute, piccolo, oboe, English horn, six percussionists, two electric organs, and strings, *The Desert Music* (1984) for small chorus and large orchestra, *Different Trains* (1988) for double string quartet and tape, *The Cave* (1993) for percussion, voices, pianos, keyboards, strings, and winds, and *City Life* (1995) for two flutes, two oboes, two clarinets, percussion, keyboards, two violins, viola, cello, and bass belong to yet another period with longer material interlaced as in medieval isorhythm. *Hindenburg*—the first act of *Three Tales* (1998) for string quartet, four percussionists, two keyboards, and five singers—belongs to a more recent period that incorporates mixed media.

Minimalism also is apparent in the music of Harold Budd. In the early 1960s, under the influence of John Cage and Morton Feldman, Budd produced an indeterminate, improvisatory music, moving on, as the decade progressed, to a much more spare and minimalistic style—pieces consisting of quiet drones or simple instructions to performers. His *Lovely Thing (Piano)*, in which one chord softly repeats over a period of fifteen to twenty minutes; *One Sound* for string quartet; and *The Candy Apple Revision*, which

states simply, "D-flat Major," all classify as minimal compositions. About his approach, Budd remarks:

> Ever since (a long time ago) I've pushed and pushed towards zero: Running it all down, a kind of on-going process of removal. There's an enormous difference, by the way, between Monotony and Boredom. Boredom, it seems to me, is trying to make something interesting. Monotony is making nothing interesting. And insofar as I feel all art to be utterly worthless (no redeeming social values), I'm interested in that what I do is pretty—("Terrifying, " "Gripping, " "Sensitive, " "Relaxing, " "Hypnotic, " "Spiritual"—all to the side for a moment) an existential prettiness; a king of High-Art Uselessness . . . (personal letter)

Budd's turning point came with *Madrigals of the Rose Angel* in 1972, a gently hypnotic work for harp, electric piano, celeste, percussion, and chorus. His first record, *The Pavilion of Dreams* (1978), introduced an international audience to his works.

Brian Eno heard a tape of *Madrigals* and offered Budd the chance to record this and other pieces. In 1980, the two collaborated on *The Plateaux of Mirror*, the second record in Eno's *Ambient* series. Budd provided the electric and acoustic piano parts and Eno the crystalline studio treatments. This album was followed in 1981 by *The Serpent (In Quicksilver)*, a piano-based, solo mini-album, and in 1984 by *Abandoned Cities*, two brooding pieces, originally written for an art gallery installation. The same year, Budd and Eno worked together on *The Pearl*, refining their approach on *Plateaux* with 13 glimpses of enchanted landscapes and underwater domains.

Much minimal music is actually maximal in duration (Mertens 1983; Schwarz 1996; Strickland 1993). La Monte Young's New York City-based *Dream Houses* (1968) represent media works of long duration (Young and Zazeela 1969, 1970). Like most minimal works, these dream houses contain drones with slowly overlapping projections. These works derive from earlier experiments such as *The Tortoise, His Dream and Journeys* (1964), performed over extended periods of time by *The Theatre of Eternal Music*.

Erik Satie's *Vexations* is a 32-bar piece played softly 840 times. His *musique d'ameublement* (1920), co-composed with Darius Milhaud, was played during intermissions with the note: "We urge you to take no notice of it and to behave during the intervals as if it did not exist " (Templier 1969, p. 45).

Composers such as Charlemagne Palestine and Yoshima Wada create drones and/or slowly overlapping and evolving motives producing minimal works. Max Neuhaus's underwater work, *Water Whistle*, uti-

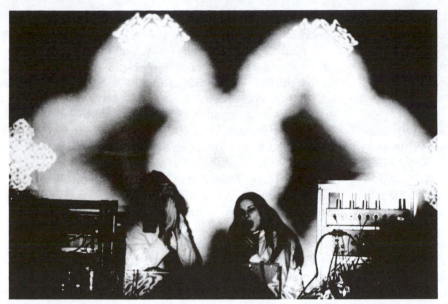

Figure 9.3. La Monte Young and Marian Zazeela performing *Dream Houses* in 1971. Copyright © La Monte Young and Marian Zazeela 1971. Photo courtesy Heiner Friedrich (photo credit Robert Adler).

lizes 8–10 water driven whistles that can be heard only if you are submerged in the same water as the whistles. Karlheinz Stockhausen's *aus den Sieben Tagen* (1968) has a verbal score containing very brief performance directions such as "play single sounds with such dedication until you feel the warmth that radiates from you—play on and sustain it as long as you can."

Philip Corner is noted for his minimal works often lasting evenings, or at other times only seconds. Corner's *One Note Once* is just that, the instrumentation being flexible. His *Metal Meditations* result from collaborations with others involved in the *Sounds out of Silent Spaces* series in New York City: Carole Weber, Julie Winter, Elaine Summers, Annea Lockwood, Alison Knowles, Daniel Goode, and Charles Morrow, among others. These evening-long events feature composer-constructed and traditional instruments struck softly but with intense aural expression. These meditations also involve slide projections and lights.

Many composers feel that the avant-garde as such is dead, and that minimal works in the 1960s point to a return to simplicity. These composers and their works no longer receive the notoriety that avant-garde works of the 1950s and 1960s characteristically received, nor do they have the pretentious complexities of systems and scientific paraphernalia so in evidence with more mainstream academic-based composers.

THE NEW TONALITY

During the late 1960s, many composers began to experiment with tonality (Kupbovic 1980). LaMonte Young's work in the very early sixties (mentioned earlier) influenced many composers. The simplicity of his design and materials, often based on justly tuned fifths, provided new ideas suggesting further development. James Fulkerson's *Triad*, for example, consists of a C major triad performed over a 12- to 20-hour period without variation. Robert Moran's *Illuminatio Nocturna* presents a C-rooted major thirteenth chord repeated slowly and softly for an extended period of time. This work and his subsequent trance music represent other manifestations of this drone-like approach to triadic materials.

Terry Riley's *In C* (1964) gave a needed impetus and visibility to this new school of composition. This work repeats and overlaps motives in the key of C moving, over a period of 45 to 90 minutes, to the key of E, back to the key of C, and then to the key of G around continuously repeating octave Cs. This is not the tonality one finds in late Romanticism, but rather represents a new kind of triadic minimalism. Two major works followed *In C*: *Poppy Nogood and the Phantom Band* (1968) and *A Rainbow in Curved Air* (1969). Both of these works continued the explorations begun with *In C*. Each work develops richer and more complex tonal interrelationships less associated with drones and rhythmic repetition.

Philip Glass began developing a similar kind of style in the late sixties with works like *Music in Fifths* (1969). This work evolves through expanding scalular cells in F-Dorian mode. Glass creates an additive structure common in his later works. For example, a three-note motive becomes four, then five, and so on with the initial motive repeated with each reoccurrence. His opera *Einstein on the Beach* (1976) is a massive tonal work that continues to receive wide acclaim. His audience is as eclectic as his music, with rock and pop followers as well as traditional and experimental admirers. His work with the Philip Glass Ensemble has contributed enormously to his success. Minimal tonal music can be very difficult to perform due both to its maximal length and to the attention to detail required to capture its often translucent textures. Glass's ensemble epitomizes the precision necessary for proper performance (Blass 1987).

Jon Gibson is a composer and visual artist who has taken part in numerous landmark musical events, performing in the early works of Steve Reich, Terry Riley, Philip Glass, LaMonte Young, Christian Wolff, Alvin Curran, and Peter Zummo. Gibson has performed in the Philip Glass Ensemble since its founding. He also has received commissions to compose music for the Merce Cunningham, Lucinda Childs (*Relative Calm*, an evening-length work with decor by Robert Wilson), Margaret Jenkins, Elaine Summers, Simone Forte, Nancy Topf, and Elisabetta Vittoni dance companies. Gibson more recently has created a video (*Interval*) that combines both his music and visual work, and has collaborated with theater director JoAnne Akalaitis on a music/theater work centered around Charles Darwin entitled *Voyage of the Beagle*.

John Adams's *Shaker Loops* for seven solo strings (1978) and *Phrygian Gates* for piano (1978) utilize triadic source materials. Both works create an atmosphere of self-regenerative energy while at the same time developing lyric melodies, traditionally associated with tonal music. The best known and most widely discussed of Adams's compositions is his opera *Nixon in China*, given its premiere by the Houston Grand Opera in 1987. With *Nixon in China*, the composer, along with director Peter Sellars, librettist Alice Goodman, and choreographer Mark Morris, brought contemporary history vividly into the opera house, pioneering an entire genre of postmodern music theater.

Adams's second opera, *The Death of Klinghoffer*, again a collaboration with Sellars, Goodman, and Morris, had its premiere at the Brussels Opera in 1991. Initially known as a minimalist, Adams has combined the rhythmic energy of minimalism with the harmonies and orchestral colors of late Romanticism. He also has referenced a wide range of twentieth-century idioms—both popular and classical. His eclectic orchestral piece *Fearful Symmetries* touches on the styles of Stravinsky, Honegger, and big-band swing music.

Other orchestral works by Adams include the two fanfares *Short Ride in a Fast Machine* and *Tromba Lontana*. One of Adams' most recent chamber pieces, *Chamber Symphony*, merges the virtuoso expressionism of Schoenberg with the manic world of cartoon soundtrack music. *I Was Looking at the Ceiling and Then I Saw the Sky* is described by Adams as a song play,

scored for seven singers and an onstage band of eight instrumentalists.

Paul Dresher, noted for his ability to integrate diverse musical influences into his personal minimalist style, pursues experimental opera and music theater, chamber and orchestral composition, live instrumental electroacoustic chamber music performances, and scores for theater, dance, and film. Other composers committed to similar types of minimal/tonal composition include Beth Anderson, Gavin Bryers, Stuart Smith, William Duckworth, and Phil Winsor.

In England, Cornelius Cardew's work with the Scratch Orchestra provided opportunity for both large-scale improvisation (performers were largely unskilled) and performances of simple tonal works. His enormous work *The Great Learning* (1971, particularly Paragraph 2) provides precedence for renewed tonal activity. Cardew was motivated by political beliefs and moved toward a more traditional tonal style with works such as *Soon*, based on Maoist-like texts and ideals. This music consists of single lines using chords similar to popular music, while at the same time unmistakably hinting at Cardew's inimitable rhythmic subtleties and twists of phrase.

Frederic Rzewski founded the MEV (Musica Elettronica Viva) group, which quickly became known for its pioneering work in live electronics and improvisation. Bringing together both classical and jazz avant-gardists (like Steve Lacy and Anthony Braxton), MEV developed an esthetic of music as a spontaneous collective process, an esthetic shared with other experimental groups of the same period (e.g., the Living Theatre and the Scratch Orchestra).

Rzewski's minimal compositions of the late 1960s and early 1970s combine elements derived equally from the worlds of written and improvised music (*Les Moutons de Panurge*, *Coming Together*—discussed earlier in this chapter). During the 1970s Rzewski experimented further with forms in which he treated style and language as structural elements. The best-known work of this period is *The People United Will Never Be Defeated!*, a 50-minute set of tonal piano variations. A number of pieces for larger ensembles written between 1979 and 1981 show a return to experimental and graphic notation (*Le Silence des Espaces Infinis*, *The Price of Oil*), while much of his work of the 1980s explores new ways of using twelve-tone technique (*Antigone-Legend*, *The Persians*). A freer, more spontaneous approach to composing can be found in more recent work (*Whangdoodles*, *Sonata*). Rzewski's *The Triumph of Death* (1987–88) is a two-hour oratorio based on texts adapted from Peter Weiss' 1965 play *Die Ermittlung* (*The Investigation*). His other works include *De Profundis* (1992, for a speaking pianist).

Lou Harrison's *Mass to St. Anthony* (1962) is modal-tonal in key and sixteenth-century in counterpoint. Traditional cadences balance and direct the lines that nonetheless have subtle twentieth-century influences. Harrison's work with the American gamelan has formed the basis for a number of new works that use rich modal materials but are less traditionally Western in cadence and phrasing.

Ingram Marshall's minimal and often tonal music emanates from an extremely personal source. However, attempts to lump him with the minimalists, New Romanticists, or the California School seem problematic. Marshall's music has a quality of dreamy evocativeness that derives from Indonesian influences. The gamelan gong forms also have influenced the way his music is structured.

With Marshall's interest in electroacoustic music and love of the traditions of Asia, it was not surprising that he developed, in the mid-1970s, a series of live-electronic performance pieces that employed the Balinese flute (gambuh), and analog synthesizers with elaborate tape delay systems. Marshall also maintains an interest in text-sound composition that resulted in a series of tape pieces based on the manipulation of the spoken voice. His most significant live-electronic performance work from this period, *The Fragility Cycles*, combines music from the gambuh series with experiments in the text-sound genre. Marshall has performed this work widely in Europe and America.

Marshall's main focus since 1985 has been ensemble music, both with and without electronics. His *Sinfonia 'Dolce far Niente'*, commissioned by Leonard Slatkin and the St. Louis Symphony, is his most ambitious orchestral work to date. This one-movement work juxtaposes gamelan-inspired textures and rhythms with music inspired by composers such as Bruckner and Sibelius. Based on a four-note motive, *Sinfonia 'Dolce far Niente'* gradually accumulates through subtle repetitions. Marshall's most recent work has been with the Kronos Quartet (*Fog Tropes II*) and singer/conductor Paul Hillier.

Robert Ashley's cryptic *Perfect Lives (Private Parts)*—an opera in seven episodes—uses tonal pitch materials. Its composer-created text has roots in 1960s nihilism as it surrealistically comments on Rodney's life. Ashley's voice and the keyboard performance of Blue Gene Tyranny in its recorded version represent an important achievement of the genre.

Meredith Monk, a composer, singer, filmmaker, director, and choreographer, pioneered what is now called "extended vocal technique" and "interdisciplinary performance." During a career that spans 30 years, she has been acclaimed by audiences and critics as a major creative force in the performing arts. Monk often uses very simple tonal materials as the basis for her minimalist compositions.

More and more composers seem interested in the potential of tonality. Even works that parody traditional tonality have gained a significant following in recent years. If any aspect of twentieth-century music seems providential, it is most surely this recent trend toward tonal consonance.

Arvo Pärt was born in Paide, Estonia in 1935 and grew up in Tallinn. From 1958 to 1967 he was employed as a recording director and a composer of music for film and television for the music division of Estonian radio. During this time he studied composition under Heino Eller at the Tallinn Conservatory. His early works, written while he was still a student (a string quartet and various neoclassic piano music) demonstrate the influence of Russian neoclassic composers such as Shostakovich and Prokofiev.

Pärt's first orchestral work, *Necrolog* (1960), was the first work in a new experimental phase and was also the first Estonian work to use Schoenberg's twelve-tone method. This composition, as well as other of Pärt's works of the early and mid 1960's, served as unfulfilling experiments with serialism and indeterminate techniques. However, two of Pärt's early choral compositions, the children's cantata *Meie aed* (Our Garden), and the oratorio *Maailma samm* (Stride of the World), won first prize in 1962 at the All-Union Young Composers' Competition in Moscow. A third important work from this period is a one-page composition called *Solfeggio* that consists of a series of major scales. *Solfeggio* looks like an exercise, but the manner in which the scales are voiced makes it a composition. Pärt's more recent works include *Cantus in Memory of Benjamin Britten for Bell and String Orchestra* (1977), *Fratres* (1983), *Summa* (1991), and *Berliner Messe* (1992), all minimal and quasi-tonal in nature.

Peter Garland was born in 1952 in Portland, Maine. He studied music with James Tenney and Harold Budd in addition to studies of Indonesian music, puppetry, performance, and video. From 1980–91, he lived in Santa Fe, New Mexico where he directed his own ensemble. Garland's first professional compositions date from 1972. He was one of the first minimalists of his generation. His music includes early percussion pieces inspired by Varèse and Cage, contrasting with mature lyrical works for harp, violin, and percussion influenced by Yaqui Indian and Mexican folk music. Garland is the author of two books on American music including *In Search of Silvestre Revueltas—Essays 1978–1990*. He is also a student of Native American music, especially of Mexico.

Orlando Jacinto Garcia's *Improvisation for Metallic Materials* slowly sets up patterns that ebb and flow in density, suggesting at times a futuristic carillon. His evocative *Sitio sin Nombre* (1990) uses computer manipulations of tapes of a singer's voice that often serve to alter it beyond recognition. Much of the tension of this multi-movement work comes from pitting minimalist solo lines against distorted backgrounds. The tape treatments of the percussionist in *Metallic Images* (1991) are relatively calm and benign, and evolve gently, almost meditatively, over twenty-one minutes.

Brian Eno composes ambient music (self-professed) for airports, businesses, and the home (notably *Ambiance I*). Ambient music includes the nonedited sounds of meadows, sailing, the sea, thunderstorms, heartbeats, the wind, Okefenokee Swamps, summer cornfields, and so on. Windham Hill and Natural States have developed ambient New Age videos with no plot and no direction. Some protagonists have termed the style *new impressionism* to indicate time suspension in many of the works. Keith Jarrett, Chick Correa, Pat Metheny, Ralph Towner, and others also produce music in this genre.

The works of Vangelis, noted for the film scores of *Blade Runner* and *Chariots of Fire*, exemplify the progressive side of New Age music. Vangelis uses long themes under which effects from a variety of found (cultural *musique concrète*) and synthesized sounds produce a significant catalog of interesting music. While Vangelis's works vary distinctly from much of New Age music, they conform to the concept of new impressionism. His *Earth* and *To the Unknown Man* particularly emphasize these characteristics.

Figure 9.4. Vangelis Papathanassious.

Vangelis notes, "You feel just like you have to start creating. It's like you feel when you have to go to the toilet. Then I just push the tape, and it happens when it happens. I don't know how it happens. I don't want to know. I don't try to know. It's like riding a bicycle. If you think, 'How am I going to do it?' you fall down. If you think about how to breathe, you choke. But when you do things dramatically they happen like that. "

VECTORAL ANALYSIS
PHILIP GLASS: *EINSTEIN ON THE BEACH*

(For information on vectoral analysis and procedures, see Preface.)

1. Historical background: Philip Glass was born in Baltimore, Maryland, on January 31, 1937. He received his bachelor's degree from the University of Chicago in 1956 and subsequently studied at Juilliard where he earned another B.A. (1959) followed by an M.A. (1961) working with William Bergsma and Vincent Persichetti (Duckworth 1995; Jones 1979). Glass also studied with Darius Milhaud at the Aspen Music Festival during the summer of 1960 and with Nadia Boulanger on a Fulbright scholarship during 1963–65. From 1961–63 he

Figure 9.5.   Philip Glass.

served as composer-in-residence for the Pittsburgh public schools under a Ford Foundation grant. Glass also worked with Ravi Shankar in Paris in 1965, teaching him solfège and taking lessons in tabla from Shankar's associate, Allah Rakha. Inspired by the rhythmic and metric centricity of this music, he spent six months in India during 1965–66.

On his return to America, Glass collaborated in performances with Steve Reich and Arthur Murphy, finally developing his own group, the Philip Glass Ensemble, in 1968. He and his ensemble toured extensively in 1970 both in America and abroad. Glass's film music includes *Koyaanisqatsi* (1983), *Powaqqatsi* (1988), and *Itaipu, The Canyon* (1993). *Einstein on the Beach* was completed in 1975 as a collaboration between Glass and noted mixed-media conceptualist Robert Wilson. Its first performances in Europe proved quite successful. On November 21, 1976, the American premiere brought immediate attention and acclaim.

Figure 9.6.   From a performance of *Einstein on the Beach*.

Glass has completed two other operas: *Satyagraha* (1980) and *Akhnaten* (1984). These and *Einstein* roughly form a trilogy, which Glass states is based on "historical figures who changed the course of world events through the wisdom and strength of their inner vision" (Gandhi and an Egyptian pharaoh in the latter cases respectively). Glass's work, especially since 1965, uses minimal repetitions layered over a varied rhythmic base.

Glass comments about his musical style in an interview: "I'm not interested in exotic and funny weird sounds. To me, that seems like an endless avenue; once you start on it, there's no telling where in the world it might lead. Maybe it's partly a generation thing, too. I'm a pencil-and-paper composer. That's how I was taught to write music, and it's easier for me to conceptualize with a paper and pencil than it is with a machine" (Glass, 1987).

2. Overview: *Einstein on the Beach* has four acts, nine scenes, and five kneeplays that occur at the beginning and end of each act (Glass and Wilson nd; Palmer and Glass 1979). *Einstein on the Beach* involves vocal and instrumental music, dance, and sets resembling traditional opera. However, no traditional plot exists here, no story to follow. Instead the work fol-

lows a sequence of events that develop the musical score more than follow a plot. The use of language, while expressive, is actually based on mathematical choices. For example, "I feel the earth move . . . I feel the tumbling down tumbling down . . . There was a judge who like puts (sic) in a court. And the judge have like in what able jail what it could be a spanking." Stage action follows similar discontinuity: Freud, Queen Victoria, Stalin, and Einstein (among others in the opera) enter and leave according to a mathematical schedule over the five-hour performance time (Duckworth 1995; Garland 1984).

The numbers 1, 2, and 3 figure heavily in the structural layout of this work. The first three acts have two scenes each, repeating twice the three elements of train, trial, and field. These elements appear in the final scenes of the last act as a building (for train), bed (in the trial scene earlier), and the interior of a time/space machine seen above the field in acts 2 and 3. The stage divides into three layers—foreground, middleground, and background (or downstage, centerstage, and upstage). These special areas then translate into sections called portrait, still life, and landscape and intensities termed skin, flesh, and bones.

3. Orchestration techniques: The ensemble for *Einstein* requires five to eight performers on electric organs, viola, cello, and soprano saxophones. Much of the work sounds in unison and at very fast and consistent tempi thus demanding high levels of technical proficiency from its performers. Effects are nonexistent and timbre exploration minimal. In fact, the music is so sparse vertically at times that when straightforward harmonies do occur they produce extraordinary results. Sparsity conditions listeners and Glass gets expansive results from subtle changes in his music.

4. Basic Techniques: Glass uses repetition, addition/subtraction, and modes to create an often hypnotizing effect. The number of repeats follows directions given during the course of performances. Figure 9.7 shows measures 3 and 4 of Act 4, Scene 2, organ solo. Repeats may be extensive. The second measure shows the additive procedure (7 to 8 notes), the filling in of structural detail (the E between D and G at the end of the second measure), and the harmonic variation (A-C-E instead of C-E-A). The drone of the octave C is

Figure 9.7.   From the score of *Einstein on the Beach*, mm. 3 and 4 of Act 4, Scene 2.

typical of Glass's style. Pedal tones, struck at the beginning of bars of constantly changing meters (though not explicitly shown), provide the underpinnings of the music's motion. The beat here—eighth notes—remains as fixed as possible providing a kind of locomotion that persists throughout the work.

5. Vertical Models: Figure 9.8 shows a typical harmonic progression from *Einstein on the Beach*. Common tones proliferate. While triadic, the music does not follow other traditional voice-leading practices though it does move stepwise (a Glass trademark). Virtually no contrary direction occurs in the voices and the 6/4 chord at the end of this passage suspends the cadence. The chromaticism follows that of Hovhaness and others by creating subtle key shifts between chords (i.e., difficult to explain the A major triad of measure 3 in the context of the key of F minor of measures 1 and 2). The non-triadic structure of measure 4 (A-D♯-B) outlines a dominant seventh of E major. Glass comments on this in an interview:

> In *Einstein*, the kind of cadential formula that runs through it, the I-VI-IVb-V-I progression that you hear in the Spaceship and the Knee Plays, the voicing and working out of that was done by somebody who knew very well how traditional harmony operated. I don't think that anyone who didn't have the training that I did could have written that. So even though my music seems so far away from her (Nadia Boulanger), it was only four or five years after studying with her that I began to find uses for the things that I had learned. (Gagne and Caras 1982)

Figure 9.8.   Harmonic progression from the second page of the score of *Einstein on the Beach*.

6. Horizontal Models: Measures 16 through 20 of the quoted section of *Einstein* provide an apt model as shown in Figure 9.9. Here, the measures show metric divisions of 4/3/4/5/6 with no two measures of the same length. Nothing else changes here. The repeating pulse of the pedal point and the left hand organ C

remain the same in each case. Given that each of these measures repeats many times during performance, the constantly changing appearance of these measures is somewhat deceiving. Once a pattern has begun, one can be reasonably confident that it will repeat often; first exactly and then with slight variations.

7. Style: Glass's *Einstein on the Beach* is an example of minimalism for non-literary theater. The discontinuity between the various musical sections, choreography, set, and action create a rich counterpoint at once mesmerizing and confusing. Repetitious and slightly varied fragments of music of different lengths, often performed in unison, suggest a more traditional vocabulary though with an exceptional lack of diversity. Glass continues to compose music for the theater, movies, and his ensemble.

This work compares favorably to the works analyzed in chapter 1 and chapter 6 (especially conceptualism). *Einstein* does not use technological developments or innovation. The repetitive nature of Glass's style, and that of most of the music reviewed in this chapter, contrasts sharply with the ideals expressed in chapters 2, 5, and 8. Indeterminacy, for example, suggests the exact opposite: a lack of repetition.

ANDREW R. BROWN: AN INTERVIEW WITH STEVE REICH

The following interview with Steve Reich, as is the case with the interview with Paul Lansky in chapter 7, was contributed by Andrew R. Brown from a series of interviews he has conducted with major figures of contemporary music.

> Brown: What is the order of commissioning and writing in your process?
>
> Reich: *The Cave* had seven co-commissioners. Basically *Three Tales* is Beryl Korot's and my second video opera and many of these same people were interested in it because they were interested in the previous work. With a few exceptions I have been writing for the last twenty odd years or so what I wanted to write and then trying to find people to commission it. I don't really write pieces I wouldn't otherwise write just because of a commission. If someone asks me for a piece I have no interest in, I simply don't accept the commission.

Figure 9.9.   From the second page of the score to *Einstein on the Beach*.

Brown: To what extent does your understanding of the commissioners' expectations guide the work you write?

Reich: If I write for the Kronos Quartet or Pat Metheny or Richard Stolzman, these musicians and their performing style inspire what I write for them. As to organizations and festivals, these are generally people who are going to trust me. I think I've got to the point where people will know what I've done and expect that hopefully I'll do something that they will like, although they're not going to know the details until it's finished. I've also become aware of how I work and how to keep my own fires burning. I want to keep those fires stoked because that's in everybody's best interest.

Brown: So you've developed a level of trust that you won't do something quite different from what you've previously done?

Reich: As a matter of fact, I always do something different from what I've previously done. I don't think that if you listened to *Piano Phase* that you would have predicted *Music for 18 Musicians*, and I don't think that if you listened to *Music for 18 Musicians* that you would have predicted *Different Trains*, and so on. As a matter of fact, commissioners hope for that. I'm not the only one. As an artist interested in other artists, I'm interested in them for their body of work. For instance, I want to hear whatever new piece Arvo Pärt or Michael Gordon does. I'm interested in their music and if one piece comes along that I don't like, well I'm interested to hear the next one.

Brown: Do you have a clear idea of the intended audience for your work?

Reich: I don't have any intended audience, I never had an intended audience. When I'm writing music I'm pleasing myself and I've always hoped that if I love it, you'll love it too, and thank heavens that's worked out to be the case. When I was very young I could have told you who my audience was. In 1967, I could have told you which people came to the Park Place Gallery to hear my first concerts there in New York City. They were mainly dancers, choreographers, painters, and sculptors, with very few composers, mostly jazz and downtown types. But now I can't possibly tell who is in the audience and I'm delighted that that's the case.

Brown: So you write to please yourself?

Reich: Any composer works from this basic principle. Are they going to do market research? In their studio they're doing what they're doing

Figure 9.10.   Steve Reich. Photo by Alice Arnold.

and if they're excited about it and they love it, and if they're fairly normal human beings and their receptors are in more-or-less working order, then hopefully there will be some other people who feel the same way.

Brown: Can you describe you compositional environment?

Reich: Well, I have two studios, one in New York and one in Vermont. They are both very similar and both small. I'm sitting in the one in Vermont now and there's a Baldwin Hamilton upright piano in each of them, and a vibraphone and marimba in each, a sampling keyboard in each. Then on the other side of the room is a Macintosh computer. Basically that's about it. I have a MIDI time piece AV that I use to keep synchronization when I'm working with Beryl. When I'm writing pieces of music by myself I don't need it. I also have a set of loudspeakers, amplifier, and mixer.

Brown: And you've been working with the Finale software for some years now.

Reich: Well, actually I still work with pencil and paper, I go back and forth between the computer and the piano where there is a music notebook. But the music notebooks take a lot longer to fill up now than before I started working with computer. I got my first Macintosh in 1986. A couple of years earlier, my son, who I guess was about eight years of age at the time, wanted an Apple II because all of his friends had one. So we finally broke down and got him one and it was the first computer that entered the house. When I was looking for software for him I noticed that there was a little music program that did four part notation and I bought it and fooled around with it and thought "Well, you know, it's pretty lame but it's interesting and maybe one day it will really be something. " I actually got to know Christopher Yavelow who was a kind of Mac fanatic and at the time wrote some articles about explaining what a Macintosh could do, and in those days there was Professional Composer.

I began in 1986 with Professional Composer to save money. I had just finished *Desert Music*, and the entire commission fee had gone from my bank account to the copyist's bank account. I didn't like losing all that money and I can't stand proofreading. He [Yavelow] said, "Look, if you get the score correct in Professional Composer, then when you're extracting the parts you don't have to proofread them." I could hardly believe that, but I printed out some parts for *Four Sections*. I used Professional Composer for *Four Sections*. In those days, the ties were so poor and the printing was so poor that I simply put the score in without any curved lines, no slurs, and no ties, and had my copyist fill those in by hand so it was a kind of hybrid. But when the San Francisco Symphony played it, the principal second violinist came up to me and said, "Man those are beautiful parts, who published them? No mistakes and gorgeous." Well I said, "That's it, I'm hooked."

At that point I was simply using the notation program, and then someone else said to me that the same company makes this terrific program called Performer which you can use like a tape recorder for MIDI. I'd been basically working with multitrack tape from the beginning. When I did *Piano Phase*, I was literally recording myself on piano, playing back a tape loop, and then playing with the loop, so it goes way back. So I became interested in Performer back around 1987 or 1988. Then, of course, one thing leads to another and I guess the real breakthrough was *Different Trains*, where I realized that if I worked on it on tape I'd still be working on it, my fingernails would be bleeding. It was really a piece to be done on computer, and I did that on a Mac

Plus running Professional Composer and occasionally Performer, and using these keyboard samplers that Casio had given me. So that was a real eye and ear opener. *Different Trains* gave me the idea of doing an opera that I actually believed in. Commissions for operas had been proposed to me in the late 70s and early 80s, first by the Holland Festival and later by the Frankfurt Opera. I was very flattered, but I didn't have an opera in me. I don't care for that form, and I have nothing to say there. Then I thought to myself, "This is insane, how come I don't at least have some alternative?" But I really had nothing, so I simply shrugged my shoulders and went about doing what I did those days. With *Different Trains* I thought, well if you could *see* the people that you were hearing, if it were on video tape instead of audio tape and you could see the musicians on stage playing the speech melody of what was being said, well then there would be the possibility of the kind of opera I would be extremely interested in. And since I knew this extremely good video artist Beryl Korot, and since she was willing, *The Cave* resulted. Syncing with video, of course, put me heavily into using Performer. At that point I switched from Professional Composer to Finale for scoring and I am still using it.

Brown: So it's clear that technology, both computers and video, has had an influence on your direction in terms of the possibilities they afford.

Reich: Yes. I came to be known to the public in the late sixties through two recordings, one was *Come Out*, a tape piece which came out on CBS Odyssey in 1967. Then they did a record of my music on Columbia Masterworks in 1969 which included *Violin Phase* and *It's Gonna Rain*, both of which involved tape. So my involvement with technology in the sense of tape goes back to the beginning of my public life. Obviously, when I was a music student I didn't know anything about tape recording. Then I was far away from technology. After the tape pieces I felt that I didn't want to spend my life making tapes and if the process of phasing didn't work with live human beings playing instruments, then it was merely a gimmick; which is something I still believe. So the result was *Piano Phase* and all the other pieces leading to *Drumming*, which was the last of the phase pieces. The whole phasing process was basically discovered with technology, taking the differentiation in speed between two tape recorders and transferring that to human beings, which is an unusual way of composing, a different direction than people mostly move.

Brown: There is more often a desire to have technology imitate a human action or process, but you have done the reverse with performed phase pieces.

Reich: I began to realize that the phasing process was just like "Row, Row, Row Your Boat" or "Frère Jacques," it's a round or canon except that the distance between voice one and voice two is flexible, constantly in motion. That then expressed itself in a lot of live pieces up to *Drumming* in 1971. I really felt that the only electronics I was interested in were microphones, amplifiers, and loudspeakers. Basically that's all I worked with from 1971 to 1988. I did *Four Organs* in 1970 for the four electric organs, and that was a pain in the neck when we were touring. We knew the marimbas would work, the glockenspiels would work, the drums were fine, but the electric organs were always broken. We carried five of them so we could get four that worked, but sometimes two of them would be broken. That kind of thing gets to you and I began to move further and further away from technology.

I have a dislike of synthesizers; there's not a synthesizer that's been built that I can stand. I would occasionally use a DX7 as a marriage of convenience to double the brass in *The Desert Music* so that when they were taking a breath there wouldn't be a hole in a long-held chord. I used them in *Sextet* because I knew I was going to tour the piece and if I used English horns and clarinets then I would have had four more musicians, ten instead of six, so I made do. It was a marriage of convenience not a marriage of love. If I want something that sounds like a violin I use a violin, I don't want to use an electronic imitation. The *sampler* is another whole world. The sampler allows you to bring your voice, my voice, the sound of slamming doors, or what-have-you into the music. Because the interface is a keyboard, it's easy to bring it in on the 'and' of three of the fifteenth bar by just playing. So that was tremendously exciting, and that resulted in *Different Trains*. *Different Trains* was like a line in the sand. *Different Trains*, in one sense, goes back to the early tape pieces, and at the same time, instead of it being speech that almost sounds like music, it was actually doubled and developed by string quartet. That piece was done at a time when I also decided I was not going to write for orchestra any more. Indeed I haven't and I don't plan to. That piece was a real turning point for me. In a sense I went back to a lot of the things I had been interested in when I was younger, with the sampling keyboard as the sort of open sesame.

Brown: In your work, there is still a performance going on, even when players trigger samples.

Reich: That's what interests me; performance. My music is written overwhelmingly for standard western acoustic instruments that are just amplified. But sometimes I write for a MIDI percussion pad which is an instrument which has no acoustical sound except a thud which sounds like a very metallic marimba or xylophone. That's still performance, but quite different than even *New York Counterpoint* played on clarinet.

Brown: You have an early history of purely electronic tape phase pieces that influenced later live performance works.

Reich: Well I did tape pieces in 1965 and 1966 and never again. I think what interests me is that electronic music can be seen as a kind of stream feeding into the live music river. There are a lot of new ideas that one would never have by pursuing the history of performed music east or west, which can be suggested by electronic equipment and then fed back into live performance.

Brown: How do you find working with sampled speech where timing is quite set, compared with a musical phrase which is unrestricted?

Reich: *Three Tales* is much more oriented to the music throughout. So even if I have some sampled material I change it to fit the key, and so on, even to fit the timing. The music comes first and the sampled material is made to fit the music. I slow down a radio announcer's voice in *Hindenburg* to 12 times its original length, and that floats over the music which stays in tempo. Now, I'm not letting the music be determined by the speech. Earlier, in *The Cave* and *Different Trains*, whatever the speech sample was, the music had to come out of that. In *Three Tales* it's just the opposite, music first.

Brown: In the same way that the tape machine influenced your work, would you say that the sampler influenced it in similarly powerful ways?

Reich: Without the possibility of sampling, I wouldn't have done *Different Trains*, and without doing *Different Trains* I wouldn't have thought of any solution to music theatre that *I* would have been interested in. So the idea of working with video was opened because of sampling. There can be a really tight synchronization between the sound and music. To put it in movie terms, when I go to movies I'm not interested in the mood music; I'm interested in the synchronized sound track—the traffic, the people talking, the clicking of heels of the pavement, that's my sound track—as to the movie music, that doesn't interest me at all.

Brown: So the computer is used for note-by-note

details and sound manipulations. How do you work with large scale structures and form?

Reich: Well, it depends. In *Three Tales*, Beryl and I had meetings and we sketched out the entire piece. Earlier on, I remember with *Music for 18 Musicians*, the macro level was done when the eleven initial pulsing chords were done, and I said "This is the basis for a short section of the piece. I'm going to take each one and make it a middle register drone." When I did *Desert Music*, I finally got the text extracts that I wanted and I literally arranged the text pages on the marimba until they were in an order I liked and I said "that's the form of the piece." Similarly with *Telhillim*, I took the psalm fragments and arranged them. Any piece of mine that is set to text uses an arrangement of the text as the form.

However, *Proverb* was different. But I wanted *Proverb* to be different. I wanted to go to something that would use a very short text that would be more musically developed; in the case of *Proverb*, a long augmentation canon. In the last few years I'm less interested in the discursiveness in a piece. I mean, *The Cave* was the extreme of discursiveness, and now I want to get back *Three Tales* to a more aphoristic, oblique treatment of text so that less is said and it is developed over a longer period of time and therefore more meanings come out of it.

Brown: So what are the techniques you are using for developing meaning in *Hindenburg*?

Reich: An augmentation canon as in *Proverb*. The first movement of *Hindenburg* is basically taking one short text, "it could not have been a technical matter," setting it one way, setting it another next way, then setting it a third way. The third way begins and ends by expanding rhythmically and I've found that to be enormously interesting. What happens with the augmentation canon in *Proverb* and in *Hindenburg* is a slowing down of the text. I knew very early on (in the 1970s) that slow motion sound was going to be interesting, but I've finally figured out exactly what that is: augmentation canon, and a parallel augmenting of the sound material to go with that. I'm very interested in that, and *Hindenburg* will end the way it began with a radio announcer's voice from those days saying something like, "*Hindenburg* is gone, but from her ashes will arise the knowledge." Which says a lot, you know, the tone of voice and everything. And the singers will probably be singing some part of that text as well. I'm very fond, as you know, of arch forms, and this piece will also be an arch.

Brown: Do you think of composing in terms of uncovering music or constructing music?

Reich: I am totally a composer in the traditional sense of the word: I mean, using my volition. But even when you're using your volition, for instance, the first thing that anybody does may have a lot going for it, and it may not. But the first shot, you never want to dismiss too easily.

There have been isolated instances of the other alternatives you were talking about, of discovering something, and making that be the "guiding light" as it were. That was true in *The Cave* in the sense in which the tonal center of the first two movements is in A minor, because of two happenstances. Number one, the drone inside *The Cave* space (that large empty Mosque space) is, because of its physics, its construction, reinforcing A and when you're in there has an A minor feel to it. Then after recording the chanted phrases from the Koran I got back to the piano and found out that the voice was, low and behold, in A minor. So I said, "Well that's it" because the aesthetic in *The Cave* and in *Different Trains* was, "Whatever people say I have to follow what they say." If I don't like it I can get something else, but I can't change its pitch. So that gave me the information since I knew that both first and second movements would take a trip to that place geographically. I figured that was my target, A minor.

That's the exception which proves the rule. I am not the Marcel Duchamp of music. Maybe John Cage is. The early tape pieces, *It's Gonna Rain* and *Come Out*, are they found objects? Yes they are. But I must have gone through ten hours of tapes to find "come out, to show them." At times it's like picking up a pebble on the beach. But it's like hours and hours on the beach to find exactly what you're looking for. Then once I found it, it went through a meticulous process and there were lots of rejects that went either too fast or too slow. So, yes, it's accepting some things and also working out a lot of things as well.

There was tension in the earlier pieces between letting it be and doing something to it, and there was more letting-it-be up to about *Music for 18 Musicians*. My composing gets more volitional with *Music for 18 Musicians* and after that. I'd say *Pendulum Music* was my piece closest to Cage, it's audible sculpture, it's whatever happens. But again the situation of the pendulums is highly set up.

Brown: How does the sampled material relate to the musical direction in *Three Tales*?

Reich: There are a lot of levels. What's really interesting me the most about this piece in a purely musical sense is that it is not like *Different Trains* and *The Cave*. In them, I worked as follows: I used either archive recordings of the Holocaust survivors or early recordings I made of my governess in *Different Trains*, and in *The Cave* all the recordings were made in Israel, on the West Bank, in New York, and in Dallas, Texas. Because of the nature of the pieces—*Different Trains* is kind of an homage to the living or the dead, and because *The Cave* deals with religious subject matter—I just accepted the speech melody of people as it was, and if it wasn't the right notes for what I needed, I had to go find another sample, that was the rule I set for myself. In other words, I was the faithful scribe. It also meant that, musically speaking, in *Different Trains* and *The Cave* every time you get a new speaker you get a new tempo, which was of course very different from the way I'd worked before that. I always had very long stretches of unbroken tempo.

In *Three Tales* I thought I'm not dealing with religious subject matter, I'm not making an homage to the living or the dead, I'm just dealing with radio announcers and all sorts of people who happened to be alive when the Hindenburg existed, and so on, and so forth. And I wanted to be able to structure the piece harmonically the way I would structure a piece which was not using samples, where the harmony would be worked out the way I wanted to work out the harmony independent of the sampled material. I wanted to set up a tempo and get a head of steam going rhythmically the way I did with my other pieces. So I decided that in this piece I will change, drastically if need be, any of the sampled material to fit the music. So I start off in three flats and if Herb Morrison is not in three flats, and he's not, then I'm going to change him to three flats, and when I want to stretch his voice out, then I just stretch it out. So the whole aesthetic is different and the whole technical means of working is different—it harkens back to the way I was writing before I was working with samples. I can make musical decisions. It's like having your cake and eating it too, I can use the samples and also write the music I want to write. It turns out that Digital Performer, the new incarnation of it, has this really superb pitch shifting which you can apply to spoken voice beautifully because it doesn't shift the formants when it shifts the pitch. You don't get the chipmunk effect, you don't get the Darth Vader effect, you really can move easily in thirds and sometimes more and neither I nor the speaker themselves is the least bit aware of it.

Brown: Would you say then that most of the larger-scale structural decisions are made away from the computer?

Reich: In general I would say that was the case. The computer is the scene of detailed working out. The larger things happen in discussion in dramatic work. Harmony and melody happens at the piano and then I bring my music notebook to the computer and start working out the details.

Brown: Would it be reasonable to characterize that as similar to a sort of orchestration-like process?

Reich: No, it's not at all the same as that. For a long time, my orchestration and my composition have been one and the same thing. A couple of the orchestra pieces were orchestrated, including parts of *Three Movements*, parts of the *Four Sections*, and *Desert Music*, but that is rare. Usually the musical ideas and the instruments that are going to be playing those ideas are one and the same thing. Because I composed from the very beginning by overdubbing on tape, I compose now using instrument samples so I can hear the timbre. Especially now with Sample Cell which I load with very good actual recordings of musical instruments, there's no need for orchestration later on. Occasionally in the old days I used to change some details, but I find now that if I'm writing for the percussion family and for keyboards, strings, and woodwinds, I rarely have to change anything.

One of the quintessential difficulties with orchestration was, do you put the clarinets above the oboes or the oboes above the clarinets? I found that in the early days I would simply have a woodwind player, who doubled, come over to my house and bring an oboe, English horn, and a B♭ clarinet and we would simply try it a number of different ways and record it. But then when I got Sample Cell for *City Life* I thought, "well let's see how good this thing really is. I'll see if what I come up with using Sample Cell will prove to be reality in rehearsal." I went ahead with Sample Cell and wrote it out that way and when I went into rehearsal with Ensemble Modern, bam, it was right there. So now I know I can trust the computer mock-up for even as subtle a question as that.

Brown: So the computer's feedback is close enough to the final product that you can make those fine judgments.

Reich: If it sounds good in the sampled mock-up, it sounds good in the instrumental performance, period. In fact it sounds better because in performance you have all those little extra added richnesses and irregularities. My rhythms in the MIDI mock-up are exact. An eighth note is a computer-accurate eighth note, but it's just a mock-up. When it's actually played it always feels better.

Brown: Do you have a favorite analogy for the composing process, such as painting on a blank canvas, or sculpting with sound?

Reich: It's very much like an architect, who makes drawings and then he makes a maquette, a model. It's almost exactly like an architect's model. You can call the client in and have them take a look at it, and you can alter it. I send my MIDI mock-ups to conductors with the score. It's very much analogous to an architect's model of a finished building.

Brown: How do you judge the success of the composition as you work on it?

Reich: By how I feel about it. If I think it sounds good and it moves me, then it's right. If it doesn't, then it's wrong. If it doesn't, I try to find out what the reasons for that are, and the reasons are technical, but "Das Affect" is what I'm looking for.

Brown: Who are your biggest influences and major influences?

Reich: We can start with Perotin, back in the 12th century, he's definitely up there. J. S. Bach, Béla Bartók, Igor Stravinsky, Ravel, and Debussy . . . I think those are the major ones. And on the jazz side, John Coltrane and to a lesser extent Miles Davis and the drummer Kenny Clark. Then African music, specifically that of Ghana, gamelan music specifically that of Bali, and Hebrew cantorlation with which I spent several years.

Brown: Do you see yourself as continuing the orchestral tradition?

Reich: People who write for orchestra generally are people I'm not interested in. Concertos, symphonies, and so on. I don't know anyone writing stuff like that, that I'm interested in.

Brown: Is that because you don't like the textural density of orchestras?

Reich: Well, there's a whole lot of things that go with the orchestra, with its traditions of the forms that were written for the orchestra. There's the fatness of the sound you talked about—I don't need 18 first violins, I need one which is amplified. There's the sociology that goes with it; the fact that those people themselves are preoccupied with Beethoven, Brahms, Mozart, and Haydn. I'm more interested in ensembles that when they play a piece of old classical music, they play a piece of Schoenberg or Stravinsky. Like the Ensemble Modern, or the Ensemble Intercontemporain. I am going to be in Belgium in March with the Ictus ensemble and in the same month I'm going to be in England with the London Sinfonetta. So my lot is cast entirely with those ensembles, which are similar to my own.

These are people who also, at least the better ones, have a member of the ensemble who is the sound engineer and runs the mixing board, and they are frequently or constantly amplified. They work with samplers and they work with computing equipment. People who don't do this at all I don't find their music very interesting. It isn't because I love the sound of any particular device, it's because people who aren't interested in those devices aren't very interesting people. Maybe it's because they aren't in touch with their own time, they're too preoccupied with a time in which they are not living. I think that's the key to it.

Brown: So where do you find your works most well received?

Reich: I would say in England, France, America, Belgium, and Japan. With the emphasis in Japan at the moment. It varies. I get an enormous amount of work in Germany. The German public likes it. The musical establishment, the critics, take me seriously even though I have no interest in German composers. In Holland Louis Andriessen has been influenced by my work. Pierre Boulez has sort of wiped out other composers in France. There's no one really who's strong. But there is a great deal of interest in what I do in France, as there is in England, too.

Chapter 10

INTEGRATION

BACKGROUND

The term *avant-garde* has become a designation for those composers or works displaying the boldest new technique or anti-technique (Cope 1974; Salzman 1988). This *raison d'être* of the avant-garde often seems to center around shock and newness. Certainly a movement begins its decline when an event so new, so shocking as to virtually negate anything surpassing it, occurs. Rudolf Schwarzkogler, a Viennese artist born in 1940, began his masterpiece in the late 1960s. It seems, as we pick up the story by Robert Hughes of *Time*, that Schwarzkogler, a prime mover of the avant-garde, had decided that *his* art, at least, depended not on the application of paint, but on the removal of his own flesh:

> So he proceeded, inch by inch to amputate his own penis, while a photographer recorded the act as an art event. In 1972, the resulting prints were reverently exhibited in that biennial motor show of Western art, Documenta 5 at Kassel. Successive acts of self-amputation finally did Schwarzkogler in . . . No doubt it could be argued by the proponents of body art . . . that Schwarzkogler's self-editing was not indulgent but brave, taking the audience's castration fears and reducing them to their most threatening quiddity. That the man was clearly as mad as a hatter, sick beyond rebuke, is not thought important; wasn't Van Gogh crazy too? But Schwarzkogler's gesture has a certain emblematic value. Having nothing to say, and nowhere to go but further out, he lopped himself and called it art. (Hughes 1972, pp. 111–12)

As this article states, Schwarzkogler is indeed dead, a victim of his own art. One often is reminded of Philip Corner's work entitled *One anti-personnel type CBU bomb will be thrown into the audience*—what kind of masochist would attend a program that had announced this work's performance? The composer thankfully sug-

gests that the performers not fulfill the title's promise. Nonetheless, the shock factor here is death and the newness that either of these works be considered art in the first place. Whether the act is real as with Schwarzkogler or imagined as with Corner, it seems difficult to conceive of anything more shocking appearing under the guise of *art*. For those of us who are aware of what has occurred in the arts, newness and shock have little meaning left, nor do many of the prime movers, the superstructure of the avant-garde movement.

Sensing the oblivion inherent in the implied rejection of the past, many composers have begun to accept the philosophy projected, but not carried out, by the avant-garde; that is, truly "anything goes." Not a statement of rejection, but of affirmation. Once composers again accept triads and tonality, consonance need no longer be avoided, dissonance need not be a requirement to be contemporary. Composers can use anything necessary to fulfill their creative needs, accepting all sounds and silences without limitations—listening to Bach, to Webern, to Cage, to rock and not rejecting any.

The works of this chapter, as different in sound and structure from one another as they may seem, have a distinctly recognizable common thread: integration (Cope 1972; Johnson 1980; Rochberg 1963). Ben Johnston comments that, "Awareness makes free choice possible. Freedom requires responsiveness: responsibility" (Johnston 1968, p. 35). Later, in the same article that appears after the Introduction to this book, his optimism grows more focused:

> It is as though we have to cross a chasm. If we are to build a bridge over it we will have to anchor its ends far in the past and far in the future. Tradition thoroughly assimilated will help us anchor in the past; only a sharp eye for where we are going can help us anchor in the future. Technology will help us build the bridge, which will not impose upon nature but will be

possible because we understand how things happen and cooperate rather than interfering. (Johnston 1968, p. 35)

There is no progress in music (or art). While an individual composer may improve with time, newer music with its complex new instruments for creating more diverse sounds has no greater significance than older music—or any less significance for that matter. No music can outdate Machaut's *Notre Dame Mass* (c. 1360) as a newer car can, for instance, outdate the horse and buggy.

SYNTHESIS

Igor Stravinsky said of *Le Sacre du Printemps*: "Very little tradition lies behind Le Sacre and no theory. I had only my ear to help me . . . I am the vessel through which Le Sacre passed" (Stravinsky 1955). Pierre Boulez, the director of IRCAM in Paris, has noted, "Since the discovery by the Viennese, all composition other than twelve-tone is useless" (Cope and Wilson 1969, p. 83). Both men are incorrect, yet each view retains that grain of truth on which theorists will argue for years. However, as we begin a new millennium, those who venture forth freely to take advantage of the evident skills of both tradition and innovation will brave an exciting new credible sensitivity into music.

György Ligeti's *Requiem* is a four-movement work for soprano and mezzo-soprano soloists, two choruses, and large orchestra. Composed during the years

Figure 10.1.   György Ligeti with permission of Universal Edition.

1963–65, the *Requiem* fuses *Klangflächenkomposition* (sound-mass which ebbs and flows through constant overlapping of timbres) and spatial modulations evident in the extreme in Ligeti's later *Lontano*. *Mikropolyphonie*—highly complex densities of polyphonic motion in which no single voice dominates—permeates the overall fabric of this work. Ligeti also creates a strong synthesis of traditional and avant-garde techniques (Griffiths 1983; Kaufman 1970; Ligeti 1960, 1968; Richart 1990). Conservative techniques are evidenced in the standard musical notation, text, determinate articulations, and rhythmic complexities. Avant-garde techniques include special effects such as muted bassoons with handkerchiefs and the *Langlois effect* of squeezing the string with thumb and forefinger rather than pressing it normally against the fingerboard. The score is accompanied by a 23-page booklet of incredibly exacting performance directions. Like his earlier *Aventures*, the *Requiem* occasionally moves from metered notation to *senza tempo* sections (especially in the third movement). Note particularly Ligeti's use of this effect for contrast in Figure 4.10. This effect is used quite differently in the *Requiem* with bar lines being, in the composer's words, ". . . purely a means of synchronizing the individual parts" (Ligeti 1965). Aside from its obvious synthesis of new and old, Ligeti's *Requiem* creates a controlled spatial movement. Ligeti remarks about this work, "You have a drawing in two dimensions and you give it perspective . . . I was constantly thinking of achieving this illusion of a musical space, which has only an acoustical existence in time" (Ligeti 1972, p. 19).

Witold Lutosławski's *Symphony No. 3* (1983) presents another good example of integration. Here, the composer injects sweeping gestures of glissandi and scales into quasi-tonal and recognizably contrapuntal music. The effect fuses avant-garde and more traditional styles (Stucky 1981; Varga 1976). Krzysztof Penderecki's *Cello Concerto No. 2* premiered during the same year (1983) and integrates his early gestural style (see the vectoral analysis of chapter 3) with neo-romantic counterpoint of a highly chromatic but nonetheless unmistakably tonal origin. These two works, along with those of Joseph Schwantner, Jacob Druckman, and others, demonstrate a serious attempt to meld avant-garde and more traditional styles of music into a new common practice (Burrows 1972; Cope 1973).

George Crumb's *Ancient Voices of Children* (1970), a 27-minute work for soprano, boy soprano, oboe, mandolin, harp, electric piano, and three percussionists, consists of five vocal movements separated by two instrumental dances. The texts, by Federico García Lorca, are sung in Spanish. The integration of this

Figure 10.2. George Crumb.

work becomes clear in the composer's own words about the piece:

> In composing *Ancient Voices of Children* I was conscious of an urge to fuse various unrelated stylistic elements. I was intrigued by the idea of juxtaposing the seemingly incongruous: a suggestion of Flamenco with a Baroque quotation ("Bist du bei mir," from the Notebook of Anna Magdelena Bach), or a reminiscence of Mahler with a breath of the Orient. It later occurred to me that both Bach and Mahler drew upon many disparate sources in their own music without sacrificing "stylistic purity." (Crumb 1970)

Crumb's style, beginning with his *Five Pieces for Piano* (1962), is characterized by five particularly distinct features: (1) extremely defined and thinly exposed textures often consisting of solo lines (solo lines constitute almost one-third of *Ancient Voices of Children*); (2) dramatic silences frequently integrated with square fermatas with duration in seconds (see Figure 10.3); (3) subtle motivic repetition and development; (4) equal use of instruments and voice for their special timbral qualities (Gillespie 1986) about which Crumb remarks:

> Certain special instrumental effects are used to heighten the "expressive intensity," e.g. "bending" the pitch of the piano by application of a chisel to the strings; . . . the mandolin has one set of strings tuned a quarter-tone low in order to give a special pungency to its tone. (Crumb 1970)

(5) musical imagery—a reflection of the texts without programmatic connotations.

I feel that the essential meaning of this poetry is concerned with the most primary things: life, death, love, the smell of the earth, the sounds of the wind and sea. These "ur-concepts" are embodied in language which is primitive and stark but which is capable of infinitely subtle nuance. (Crumb 1970)

Figure 10.3 shows the entire fourth movement of *Ancient Voices of Children* and exemplifies the synthesis referred to earlier. The use of the whole-tone scale in the opening vocal part beginning on C♯, the triadic harmonies, and the simple formal structure represent traditional resources. The marimba drones, the singing percussionists, and the Bach quote on toy piano suggest experimental origins. This movement, and indeed this work, has a high degree of continuity despite the contrasting material and styles.

Ellen Tsaffe Zwilich's *Double Quartet* convincingly demonstrates the composer's predilection for tight formal/modal structures and synthesis. This four-movement work begins and ends in the key of D. The opening, a dynamic and fast unison, defines the mode. The second movement begins in D minor with a transition to the third movement via a unison (leading tone) C♯ and concludes on a D dominant-seventh chord in 4/2 position. The fourth movement poses an F-F♯ contradiction with D again playing a very important role. The chromaticism without serialism balances well with the quasi-tonal harmonic vocabulary. Zwilich's orchestration makes effective use of spatial modulations.

George Rochberg's career spans three periods: rigorous serialism, Ivesian-like quotation, and his own brand of integration. His 23-minute *Trio* for piano, violin, and cello falls principally in the latter of these periods. The work begins and ends in E major. The nontonal syntax exploits the principle that successive chords contradict one another (chromatically) at least once with common tones providing continuity. The first movement spans the key signatures of E, B♭, E, C, D♭, C, D♭, G, and E major respectively, though clearly all of the music presented does not fall within these keys. In fact, Rochberg relentlessly avoids the C-major triad when in the signature of C major. Ostinato pedal tones on D and G in octaves provide tonal anticipation that serves as one of the most tasteful and successful aspects of this work. Ultimately, the composer provides the tonic pitch without the full triad. Much of this work belies the signature-implied key—a mid-movement section ends on a D♭ major triad with a signature of four sharps. The final movement propels the listener through the same key centers as the first movement, but with more bravura and direction.

Toshi Ichiyanagi's *Violin Concerto* is a three-move-

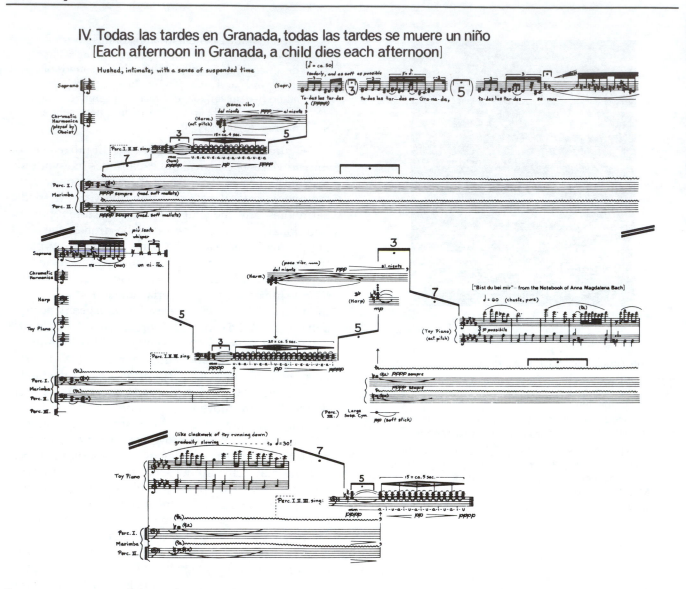

Figure 10.3.   From George Crumb's *Ancient Voices of Children*. Copyright © 1970 by C.F. Peters Corporation. Used by permission.

ment 26-minute tour de force. The soloist alternately converses with the orchestra and lapses into meditative soliloquies. Melodies typically ascend using primarily seconds and thirds or center on repeating figures that have little direction. Harmonically, roots change so quickly that they either lack distinction or remain steady, contrasting the melodic writing. This composition, with the exception of a few interchanges between orchestral soloists and the violin virtuoso, develops almost continually from the opening solo.

Henri Lazarof's *Second Concerto for Orchestra* (subtitled *Icarus*) uses serial techniques to create chromaticism. His harmonic vocabulary often includes panchromatic chords that occur on almost every page of the score. The opening of the *Second Concerto for Orchestra* reveals an all-exclusive twelve-note pitch set

that the composer varies freely throughout the work. His most frequently used technique involves presenting eleven notes of a row and then delaying the twelfth note until it appears dramatically. The principal motive of the work (C♯-F-G-A-B-C-E♭-G♭-A♭-B♭-D) announces each of the major sections. Vertical arrows and unevenly drawn stems without noteheads demonstrate notational integration.

György Kurtág's *Messages of the Late R. V. Troussova*, Op. 17, represents an integration of various traditional and avant-garde techniques. Elements of instrument exploration, time suspension, and use of a variety of notations create an atmospheric style similar to that of Crumb yet distinctly Kurtág's own. The composer uses a gestural approach to cadence that generates from extensive silence or soft concluding music.

Karel Husa's dynamic *Apotheosis of This Earth* (1970) for concert band has three movements—Apotheosis, Tragedy of Destruction, Postscript. Each movement has characteristic clusters built of repetitive composite motives (see Figure 3.11 in chapter 3) and cumulatively sustained panchromatic sound-mass. The final movement uses whispering ("this beautiful earth"). In *Apotheosis* one finds the synthesis of avant-garde and traditional techniques so integrated that neither is obvious.

Figure 10.4.   Karel Husa.

Other works of varying degrees of synthesis include Donald Erb's *Symphony of Overtures* (1964) and Richard Toensing's *Doxologies I*. Both composers have evolved personal styles integrated with avant-garde and traditional sources. These works do not espouse a particular process nor avoid the use of any sonic material. David Cope's *Threshold and Visions* (1979—a concerto for chamber orchestra) integrates a number of diverse avant-garde techniques including clusters, instrument exploration, and a free serial technique. This thirty-five-minute work is cast in five movements and centers around a basic arch-like form.

Walter Mays's *Icarus* for large orchestra (1976) incorporates sound-mass, new instrumental techniques, electronic tape, improvisation, proportional notation, and indeterminacy. Mays's large orchestration, well over one hundred players, includes musical saw, bowed crotales, and electric organ and develops large volumes of complex sonic textures. David Felder's *Rondàge*, on the other hand, involves only five performers, fusing live electronics, clusters, structured improvisations, and new instrumental techniques into a consistent vocabulary.

Barbara Kolb's *Soundings* has two forms of performance: chamber orchestra and tape prepared by the ensemble, or full orchestra divided into three groups directed by two conductors. Extensive program notes discuss the central conception of the work: "Soundings is a technique which makes it possible to ascertain the depth of water by measuring the interval of time between the sending of a signal and the return echo" with the resultant sounds developing "... a sea-change into something rich and strange" (Kolb 1981). A montage of triply overlaid contrapuntal textures results, with each mini-orchestra or tape channel, depending on version, being separate but often sounding simultaneous.

Soundings clearly divides into three major sections. The first section begins with an ostinato in the strings that slowly evolves into the first sounding and then its reflections. Tension results from thickening texture, increased chromaticism, and a rush of sound that slowly relaxes into a high tremolo in the solo violin and harp. The second section is soloistic and conversational, with a tightly woven interplay of musical gestures. The final section reverts to the thick textures of the first section, but contrasts it with long held notes in rising chromatic lines.

QUOTATION

Almost every composer at one time or another has quoted music from another composer or style within the framework of his or her music. The quotation of strikingly different styles in the twentieth-century avant-garde marks a decidedly different direction, however. The hymn quotes of Charles Ives, as well as his free borrowings of almost any material that suits his message (evident in such works as *Central Park in the Dark* and *Symphony No. 4*) often starkly contrast the dissonance of his own chromatic style (Ives 1962).

Reasons for such quoting vary from composer to composer and often from work to work by the same composer. George Rochberg speaks of his usage:

> The centerpiece of my *Music for the Magic Theatre* is a transcription, that is, a completely new version, of a Mozart adagio. I decided to repeat it in my own way because I loved it. People who understand, love it because they know it began with Mozart and ended with me. People who don't understand think it's by Mozart. (Rochberg 1969, p. 89)

Peter Maxwell Davies's use of Handel quotes in *Eight Songs for a Mad King* (1969) results in a strange periodization (of George III) as well as a superimposed collage effect especially in "Comfort Ye, Comfort Ye My People," of Song 7 (Harbison 1972). Michael Colgrass achieves an Ivesian-like montage in

As Quiet As (1966) for orchestra by using a multitude of varied quotes framed by a background of subtle clouds of modulating chords.

Mauricio Kagel superimposes many quotes from Beethoven in his *Ludwig Van* (1970) creating, like Lukas Foss in his *Baroque Variations* (1967) and Stockhausen in his *Opus 1970*, a surrealistic intertwining of stylistically consistent but rhythmically and texturally contrasting material.

The third movement of Luciano Berio's *Sinfonia* (1968), for eight soloists and orchestra, quotes extensively from Mahler and Debussy among others. Certainly more innocent, at least in its length and continuity, is George Crumb's use of a short Bach fragment (on a toy piano) in his *Ancient Voices of Children*, 1970, described earlier in this chapter. This work remains possibly one of the most powerful quotes in recent music (Cope 1986).

Phil Winsor's *Orgel I* (for pipe organ and prerecorded tape) consists almost entirely of quotes. Figure 10.6 shows page X, a page of choices from which performers may choose within a prescribed time frame. The accompanying tape, made by performers, contributes further overlays of the quotes resulting in crowded triadic clashes.

Varèse's comments seem apropos:

> My fight for the liberation of sound and for my right to make music with any sound and all sounds has sometimes been construed as a

Figure 10.5. Phil Winsor. Photo by Julia Winsor.

desire to disparage and even to discard the great music of the past. But that is where my roots are. No matter how original, how different a composer may seem, he has only grafted a little bit of himself on the old plant. But this he should be allowed to do without being accused of wanting to kill the plant. He only wants to produce a new flower . . . (Schwartz and Childs 1967, p. 201)

Figure 10.6. Phil Winsor's *ORGEL I* (page X). Copyright © 1975 by Pembroke Music Co., Inc. International Copyright secured. All rights reserved including public performance for profit. Used by permission.

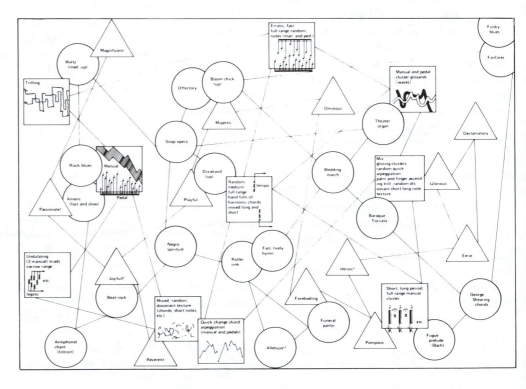

VECTORAL ANALYSIS
LUCIANO BERIO: *SINFONIA*

(For information on vectoral analysis and procedures, see Preface.)

1. Historical Background: Luciano Berio (b. 1925, Oneglia, Italy) cofounded (with Bruno Maderna) the electronic music studio in Milan (1955). He later taught at the Juilliard School of Music (until 1973), Mills College in Oakland, California, and has been director of the electronic music studio at IRCAM in Paris (Poissenot 1974; Santi 1958).

Berio's music separates into two major periods: (1) through the mid-fifties, a post-Webern serialism prevails with *Chamber Music* (1952) as a good example; and (2) from the 1960s to the present, an eclectic approach appears using electronics (e.g., *Visage*, 1961)

Figure 10.7.   Luciano Berio. BMI Archives. Used by permission.

and later using large instrumental forces (e.g., *Sinfonia*, 1968 and *Coro*, 1976 for voices and instruments). Other important works include *Circles* (for soprano, harp, and two percussion ensembles, 1962; see example in chapter 5), *Omaggio a Joyce* (1958), *Differences* (for five instruments and tape, 1959), and *Opera* (large opera, 1972 with a revised version completed in 1977).

Berio is best known for his extraordinary musical-theater works, many of which were influenced by Cathy Berberian, who for a number of years was married to Berio (Dalmonte and Varga 1985). Berberian's gymnastic vocal talents, fused with Berio's dramatic and lyric style, helped create *Recital* (1971), a singular study of a singer's mental breakdown. Other works dedicated to Cathy Berberian include *Circles* and *Epifanie* (1960).

2. Overview: *Sinfonia* was originally composed in four movements and later (in 1968) extended to include a fifth movement at a conductor's request for a flashy final flourish (Osmond-Smith 1985). *Sinfonia*, commissioned by the New York Philharmonic Orchestra and dedicated to Leonard Bernstein, is scored for large orchestra and eight voices, performed most notably by the Swingle Singers.

The first movement is cast in two large sections melded together with a smooth transition. The opening, ominously introduced by three tam-tams, sets repeated notes in motion. These repeated notes timbrally develop through a variety of homorhythmic and heterophonic rhythmic variants (e.g., slow vowel changes in the voices and use of mutes in the brass). This opening material is followed by similar groupings (i.e., initialization/pitch repetition development) of successively shorter and shorter duration. A second section emerges from this stretto with short bursts in the background from the piano. These outbursts increase in importance until they dominate completely, forming the nucleus of the second main section characterized by loud quick sounds followed by silences. Occasionally one or more of the notes rings after being set in motion by the quick bursts. This allows Berio (in the final few measures) to recollect the opening or first section briefly in an illusion of a three-part form.

The second movement, subtitled *O King*, centers on the simple text: "Martin Luther King." The idea from the first movement (excitation) continues in the piano, whose sudden attacks on certain notes initiate soft pitches held by the singers. This material surrounds the note F with a variety of chromatic scales emerging from this pivotal note. The end of the movement suggests a brief return to the end of the first movement, implying (as the first movement does to itself) a cyclical use of materials. At the outset of the movement, all melodic lines move upward from F, and at the end of the movement, melodic lines move downward from the same F.

The third movement of *Sinfonia* contains a thick overlay of quotations. Figure 10.8 shows a portion of this movement. The text here reads, "But now it's done, it's over, we've had our chance. There was even, for a second, hope of resurrection, or almost," which seems to encapsulate the stream-of-consciousness effect of this movement. Eclecticism abounds in both text and music. The text examples are drawn from such sources as Claude Lévi-Strauss's book *Du Cru et du Cuit* on Brazilian origin myths of water, Samuel Beckett, and Berio himself. Musical quotes appear often in this movement and include fragments from Debussy's *La Mer*, references to Berio's own *Epifanie*

Figure 10.8.   From Luciano Berio's *Sinfonia*, mvt. 3. © Copyright 1969 Universal Edition. All rights reserved.

and *Sequenza 4*, as well as quotations from Bach, Schoenberg, Ravel, Strauss, Berlioz, Brahms, Berg, Hindemith, Beethoven, Wagner, Stravinsky, Boulez, Stockhausen, Globokar, Pousseur, and Ives. The principal quote, however, from Mahler's *Second Symphony* scherzo, runs throughout the movement in one form or another. "As a structural point of reference, Mahler is to the totality of the music of this section what Beckett is to the text" (Berio 1968). Aside from the diverse juxtaposition of contrasting texts and music, the movement tends to revolve around a thrice-repeated centerpin: a short upbeat motion followed by a cluster chord. Between these three points flows a counterpoint of contrasting ideas for which the work has become so noted.

Berio refers to the expedition-like quality of this movement:

> This third part of *Sinfonia* has a skeleton which is the scherzo from Mahler's *Second Symphony*—a skeleton that often reemerges fully fleshed out, then disappears, then comes back again . . . But it's never alone: it's accompanied throughout by the "history of music" that it itself recalls for me, with all its many levels and references—or at least those bits of history that I was able to keep a grip on, granted that often there's anything up to four different references going on at the same

time. So the scherzo of Mahler's *Second Symphony* becomes a generator of harmonic functions and of musical references that are pertinent to them which appear, disappear, pursue their own courses, return to Mahler, cross paths, transform themselves into Mahler or hide behind it. The references to Bach, Brahms, Boulez, Berlioz, Schoenberg, Stravinsky, Strauss, Stockhausen, etc. are therefore *also* signals which indicate which harmonic country we are going through, like bookmarkers, or little flags in different colours stuck into a map to indicate salient points during an expedition full of surprises. (Dalmonte and Varga 1985, p. 19)

The fourth movement of *Sinfonia* returns to the reverie of the second movement and reaggregates materials of all three previous movements. The music climbs higher in range (as does the second movement) using major second/minor third intervals. The treatment of the vocal line in the first, second, and fourth sections of this movement resemble one another and the text cannot easily be understood. The words and their components undergo transformations integral to the musical structure. The varying degree of intelligibility of the text at different moments contributes to the overall experience of the work.

The fifth movement, a set of variations introduced

by a piano/voice/flute trio section, resembles the first movement, but seems more integrated and involves less contrast. The text continues as a collage with interlocking repeated clusters as accompaniment.

In its five movements, *Sinfonia* resembles an arch form with movement III—a striking compilation of materials—surrounded by two quiet, almost passive movements, further bounded externally by two agitated and dramatic movements.

3. Orchestration: *Sinfonia* requires an orchestra of eighty-one players and eight vocalists. The stage layout appears in the performance notes and includes a diagram of locations for each of the performing groups. The violins divide into three (not the usual two) sections spaced diagonally from left to rear right across the stage. The three percussionists are situated as far apart as possible, with percussion I in the center. The vocalists usually stand directly in front of the conductor and require amplification.

Berio gives the percussion (and particularly the piano) a large role. Orchestration involves some doubling but few solos. Effects—muting and harmonics—are rare and balance results from a careful handling of dynamics.

4. Basic Techniques: While quotation and texts play an important role in *Sinfonia*, the underlying core of materials ties the work together. These materials center rhythmically around additive and subtractive rhythmic units. These rhythmic techniques develop from two-note groupings shifting in regard to the beat. Pitch seems less important due to the thick textures consisting primarily of seconds and thirds. Figure 10.9 shows an example of these rhythmic techniques.

Figure 10.9. Examples of rhythmic development from Luciano Berio's *Sinfonia*.

5. Vertical Models: Harmonic structures in *Sinfonia* consist primarily of seconds and thirds. Figure 10.10 shows six of these vertical models in ascending order of complexity and dissonance.

The first example in Figure 10.10 represents a frequently repeated harmony found at the end of the first and fifth movements in the voices and in a number of other locations throughout the work. This harmony consists of a minor triad with a major seventh. The second example in Figure 10.10, like the first, is generally consonant but suggests a whole-tone scale derived from the opening of the second movement. Example 3 of Figure 10.10—from the fourth move-

ment—shows deepening complexity and illustrates the work's dependency on seconds and thirds. Example 4 of Figure 10.10—from the second movement—creates similar tension with slight variations, while example 5—from the beginning of the first movement—heightens the dissonance. The final example—from one of the large constructs of the third movement—has a near panchromatic (ten different notes) structure, again of stacked seconds and thirds. These chords show no clear systematic technique, but rather an imaginative and intuitive approach to intervallic development.

Figure 10.10. Examples of vertical sonorities from Luciano Berio's *Sinfonia*.

6. Horizontal Models: Most of the harmonies mentioned above arise out of slowly adding notes. All chord structures seen in Figure 10.10, except 1 and 6, result from adding notes in orders that incorporate no leap larger than a third. These are typical of the melodic style that pervades *Sinfonia*.

7. Style: *Sinfonia* is a highly contrapuntal work that integrates elements of quotation, clusters, and serialism. At one point the work talks about itself: "Keep going, going on, call that going, call that on. But wait. He is barely moving, now almost still. Should I make my introductions?"—at which point the singers are introduced by name while the music continues. The extensive quotation, exploring a wide variety of sonorities from major thirds, triads, and lush ninth chords to panchromatic clusters, and the use of dramatic bursts of sound within delicate textures, seem initially confusing. However, reflecting a society gone mad with self-preoccupation, *Sinfonia* forcefully drives its musical/dramatic point home, leaving few listeners with less than a profound sense of dislocation. *Sinfonia* has a kind of frightening continuity. While traditional in notation, material for quotes, form, and rhythmic flow, *Sinfonia* is nonetheless an avant-garde work in its use of text and its eclectic harmonic and melodic idioms.

This work, with its dramatics and often stream-of-consciousness text, resembles Peter Maxwell Davies' *8 Songs for a Mad King* analyzed in chapter 4. Both rely on quotation of various composers as well as freely using many different resources. *Sinfonia* also compares favorably with Penderecki's *Capriccio* of chapter 3, though not so explicitly.

David Felder: An Interview with Luciano Berio

The following interview with Luciano Berio took place on April 20, 1976, at Severance Hall, Cleveland, Ohio, following a rehearsal of his Calmo (*Homage a Bruno Maderna*), *Folk Songs*, *Differences*, and *Chemins IV* with the Cleveland Orchestra.

Felder: About 1951 you came to the United States to study serial techniques with Dallapiccola at Tanglewood on a Koussevitzky Foundation fellowship. In your early works you applied these techniques and since have abandoned them. Would you elaborate on your application of serialism and on your feelings concerning the use of serial technique?

Berio: My study with Dallapiccola was very short, was very limited. I loved him as a person, but certainly he was not a good teacher. In fact, musically speaking, it was not useful, but was very important culturally, spiritually. Especially being an Italian, Dallapiccola had an important influence, was a very important point of reference for me.

As for the serial technique, no, I don't believe in this type of strict label. I grew gradually, organically into this, and it was a kind of a natural developmental process for me. I didn't fall from the horseback of Saul on the way to Damascus and receive a revelation; no, long before I met Dallapiccola while I was still in the conservatory, I was aware of things, I was developing. Actually, the most important thing is constant growing, constant development. Then more specifically as serial technique goes, what is it? It is a way of thinking in terms of proportions. It's a relative proportion, a method of quantifying things; a quantification that is relevant for the perception, perception as you measure with your own ears. When you can have more abstract forms of quantification, which are also very useful because, dealing with abstract things, one walks in a kind of a "no man's land" in which trust is placed in certain abstract proportions, you can discover very important things.

So your question, strict application of serial technique, if you allow me, is a false question; it doesn't exist. For the moment that you make sense in what you do, it is strict by definition. I would say that in that respect Puccini's as strict as Anton Webern. Then if you go further, the world represented by Anton Webern is completely different than the world represented by Puccini. So you find, perhaps, a more strict, a more natural view of the world through Webern's music than, of course, that of Puccini.

The view is different because Webern's music is directed to the intellect, the most complex part of us, while Puccini is more directed toward the emotional, simpler part of us.

Felder: You've mentioned the simple and the complex, the emotional and the intellectual. Emphasis on the intellectual is suggested in your early serial works, but in some of your later works, emphasis seems to be on the emotional, the dramatic. Do you direct yourself consciously toward one or the other, the intellectual or the emotional?

Berio: I didn't know that in my later work I was involved more with emotional implications! No, I would say that I've refined my own instrument enough; now I can look at a wider range of expression. I can combine the most complex with the most simple. That's the point.

Felder: You began working with electronics sometime around 1954 with Bruno Maderna, whose work, sadly enough, is little known in this country. Could you elaborate regarding your interest in electronic music and your work at the Studio di Phonologie in Milan?

Berio: I started well before 1955. I must say that my interest for electronic music was triggered in New York, exactly 1952, when I went to the Museum of Modern Art and attended a concert conducted by Leopold Stokowski. He stepped out onto the podium and left a space for a loudspeaker, then played a work by Vladimir Ussachevsky and Otto Luening entitled *Sonic Contours*. It's a kind of elaboration, a transformation of piano sounds, which musically, of course, is absolutely irrelevant. Nevertheless, this was very shocking for me, the first time, in a concert-audience situation, to become aware of this possibility. In fact, just a few weeks later, I went to Milan, I was working for the Italian Radio putting together the first instruments, filters, oscillators, and so on. I started doing my first experiments with electronic sounds at the end of 1952–53. In 1953–54 the studio was more or less decided on, 1954 developed, and 1955 officially recognized and announced after two or three years of preparation. Bruno joined me in 1954. At that time the studio was a conventional electronic music studio, more or less like Cologne. That means comprised of equipment already available for other purposes, not for music; at that time there were no specifically designed instruments for realization of electronic music. Oscillators, filters, sinusoidal generators, pulse generators, echo chambers, tape recorders, these types of devices constituted the basic content of the studio. In the following years we developed more sophisticated filters, different types of other devices and so on.

Felder: A great deal of your electronic music involves manipulation and transformation of existing sonic material in the classical concrète fashion, for example *Visage* and *Differences*. Do you have a marked preference for permutation and extension of natural sounds electronically over those electronically generated sound sources?

Berio: I think the most important aspects, the most important results achieved thus far in electronic music, are not in the electronic product, but in the thinking involved in the work. As a musical possibility, electronic music is not self-sufficient yet. This is not to deny varied importance to many of the works that have been produced, but I see that as a very important exercise to a future that is not there yet. Electronic music even to this date, to a certain extent, is surrounded by silence; it doesn't connect with musical work, with man's work. When someone hears electronic music it doesn't reverberate to other levels of his experience, as instrumental music has and does. Up to now I feel electronic music has been developing, evolving as a bridge between what we know and what we don't know yet. It is not without reason that the best musical work that has been produced up until now (from the early 1950s to the present) are those that try to make this connection. For example, works such as *Gesang der Jünglinge* by Stockhausen, which is the first really meaningful work, and other works both in Europe and the United States. You use electronic music to explore a new type of bridge between known sound, known structural, acoustical situations and new ones. I think that the computer will be a great help in enlarging the bridge to the moment in which the musical mind might travel back and forth from known objects, old and new instruments, whatever it is, to synthetic sound, so the difference between so-called natural sound and so-called synthetic sound will be irrelevant. There will be no difference. With the computer, for instance, you can analyze sound very well. You know what's happening inside a sound, you can duplicate exactly the sound of a trumpet, for example, and combine the synthesized sound with that of a live trumpet, and you can imagine what kind of connection you can create—how far you can push the trumpet, how far away from you and how deep inside you can go with this natural sound.

Felder: You spoke briefly of Stockhausen. He dedicated the last section of *Hymnen* to you, and you have dedicated *Allelujah III* to him. Your relationship stems, I believe, especially from Darmstadt. Did Stockhausen influence your later compositional aesthetic in that you began exploring "chance" or "performer choice" operations?

Berio: No, we move in completely different directions, levels of expression. I have a great respect for him. We are very good friends, too. Nothing happens by itself, but I like to think that Stockhausen is there working and thinking about doing something, and I'm sure that he likes to think that I'm somewhere doing something. I'm aware of many things that he is doing, and he's aware also of those things others are doing. Even on the unconscious level there are influences, as sometimes a negative reaction to something. But any specific influence—none, I would say.

Felder: What was the significance of the Darmstadt experience to your compositional development?

Berio: Darmstadt was a necessary thing of the same gender as if one were speaking from a historical point of view. In that sense as Beethoven was necessary, Galileo Galilei was necessary, maybe in the smallest kind of a way one might state that Darmstadt was necessary. It was a kind of spontaneous, authentic meeting. In fact it had a relatively short life; the really good years lasted seven or eight years, ten at the most. After that, everybody went his own way. Yet it was important for the collective feeling, the give and take, mutual exchange of ideas, and reactions to each other. Darmstadt was an extremely intense type of exchange. It was responsible for, well, in looking back, many developments in what we can now call the "roaring fifties." Many things have been done, many roots have been planted, but I don't believe in the mystique of Darmstadt. Darmstadt cannot be repeated, as other events in history cannot be repeated. It was really a focal point of many different musical thinkers there, and yet, I look at Darmstadt as an extremely important experience for me.

Felder: In several of your works, notably *Epiphanie* and *Tempi Concertate*, you have employed indeterminate or performer choice operations. Seemingly, after works such as these you abandoned chance as an integral element. What has the composer to gain from chance elements?

Berio: Well it depends, I personally do not believe in chance, chance doesn't exist. In terms of performing technique, sometimes it is necessary to allow the performer a certain amount of freedom in order to achieve a certain objective which could not otherwise be obtained through, say, metrical notation; to remove obstacles between an ideal result and the performer. Of course, if the performer is good enough other psychological restrictions are placed upon him, but this is another matter.

In the case of *Epiphanie*, the chance element, I would say, doesn't exist. There's a limited number of organized strategies in the two cycles, one orchestral cycle, one vocal cycle, that can be interconnected in different ways. Depending on the ways in which you interconnect and superimpose them, you will take a different attitude toward the content of the text, text which goes from Proust to Brecht. In *Tempi Concertate*, which is a very rigid and severe work, there are instances in which the progression towards different types of harmonic categories is suspended. In these moments, a more loose type of activity is present to go beyond a certain harmonic norm, just for a brief moment. Otherwise everything is rather strict. You see, instead of having a 3/4 measure, if you have an organizational plan, perhaps with the conductor, that is equally strict, all that doesn't mean that there is chance present. Chance exists when your action in a musical sense can be completely responsible for the complete change of the structure, the form of the meaning. Your decisions are therefore so strong that you take the place of the composer, as a performer. As for compositional chance, as John Cage used it, it doesn't make any sense, especially now.

Felder: In a work such as *Circles*, you have directed that the singer should respond to audience reaction . . .

Berio: No! Respond to the other performers, yes, it's a very close secret between the three players and the singer. Perhaps you mean *Passagio*, another work, in which the singer attempts to provoke the audience to a certain type of behavior, but not in *Circles*.

Felder: Let me rephrase. Does the singer react musically to the perceived impact of the work as she feels it, on the audience? Is this an incorrect impression?

Berio: I think a performer is always aware of the audience. A passive audience can, of course, be very distressing to a performer. In the case of *Circles*, what you've heard is a studio recording with no audience interaction. Everything is completely written out.

Felder: *Passagio*, which you mentioned in passing a moment ago, has been labeled an anti-opera. Would you care to comment on that?

Berio: An anti-opera because it uses only one character. It is the story of one woman alone on the stage, addressing the audience at the end. It's a kind of letter to the audience itself, the typical audience of opera theater. In fact the audience itself is surrounded by a kind of "guerrilla group" inside, a speaking chorus scattered in the audience, which represents the audience itself. They are the "bad guys," and there is a constant conflict between the audience (composed) and the action on the stage. I wouldn't say anti-opera, but certainly it is a comment on opera. Because there is a refusal to employ scenography, only the minimal element is used to characterize every situation; and the real stage, in a way, is the audience. There are many political implications inherent in the work also.

Felder: In your later works you seem to have evolved a more eclectic, personal style in which the drama, especially psychological drama, is extremely important. Have you employed multimedia techniques; and if not, can you foresee this in your compositional future?

Berio: No, because I wouldn't be able to control those elements. I'm working currently for the theater. I'm preparing a very complicated work for La Scala. I know there is a fashion of so-called multimedia, but I think it's kind of amateurish, dilettante, because each of the separate media by itself is very complex. The result is usually a poor use of the media, instead of probing more deeply into one. So you have a kind of bouillabaisse, fish soup. Yes, you might have shocking effects, charming things, gags; but there is no overall, inner scope—at least up until now. I don't know of one.

Felder: Are collaborative efforts a distinct possibility in media works, for the creation of the artistic?

Berio: You mean like in San Diego. No, it doesn't make any sense. In fact, look at the results. They've been there for ten years. I don't know, it's kind of squalid. Many wishful thinkers go there, but they usually don't have the necessary technique. For example, Subotnick is an excellent musician and composer. When he works with music, okay, fine. But when he tries to combine laser and this and that, it's a curiosity, kind of nice for a Saturday or Sunday afternoon show, but no more than that.

Felder: Then it's too much of a task for the composer to master his craft and also the other component art forms?

Berio: No, it's not just that. Music as an art is very powerful; and through musical thinking, in fact, you can control many other elements besides just music. You can compose musically with many other things besides sound like the sound of a clarinet, so why not with lights or smell, etc. However, the grammar, the alphabet, the technique necessary to make this type of compositional control possible is not there yet. I don't believe this will be the discovery of an individual; rather, this type of a discovery is a result of slow social process. You don't invent a new grammar, you don't invent a new kind of situation. It's always a collective, very unconscious often, effort or direction. At least up until now the instruments that have been developed, the musical ideas that have been formulated, have been a result of gradual changes. Monteverdi was not a mushroom that suddenly sprouted. So many forces arrived there in his work and his thinking; so in Mozart, so in Beethoven, so in anything else of certain importance that happens. It's the focal point of many component directions, many factions. So development in media has a long way to go, I feel, because there's no way for a genius to have control, coordination of this.

Felder: You have, since 1968, added a fifth movement to *Sinfonia*, which of course is not present in the recording. What is the significance of this last movement in relation to the entire work?

Berio: The fifth movement is the most important movement. It is to the four previous movements as the third movement is to Mahler. Everything is included—for instance, the entire second movement is present as a skeletal framework. Also the text of the first movement is utilized to conclude the work. It's the most complex, and is the culmination of all that has happened before; therefore it's the most important.

Felder: The third movement employs an "information overload" type of technique with all its complexities and references. Are you planning to utilize this more frequently in forthcoming works?

Berio: No. Of course, I'm interested in layers of meanings, like the interweaving ideas used in the third movement. There's a lot of information, but each side of what you hear is meaningful in itself. There's a kind of indeterminacy of communication, if you want. Whatever you hear is complete in itself; it is not a fragment of a larger part.

Felder: Your *Sequenza - Chemins* works, for example *Sequenza VI* for viola and *Chemins II* and *III* for viola and different ensemble, are

closely interrelated. Does this constitute a larger, broader concept, namely, that a single work is incomplete in itself, and other works comprise a larger thought?

Berio: No, I think that perhaps in the life of a man, in the work of a man, the separate works can be viewed as segments of a larger work, which is your life. So why not go back, why not revisit a work to discover new things. It's a way of analyzing, educating yourself, and also thinking in terms of continuative processes. Everything which one does is never completed.

Felder: Is this analogous to the Boulez "work-in-progress" concept?

Berio: No, because his work-in-progress idea is that of open form, as in the *Third Piano Sonata*. No, this is completely different. He doesn't like to look back; and I like to look back—it's very ambitious.

POSTLUDE

At various points in this book, I have attempted to explore the various relationships between the arts and cultural trends in terms of the avant-garde. The comparisons hold true today. In obvious cases such as technology, the relevance appears so striking as to be impossible to refute. Eighty-six percent of all musical instruments sold in 1999 were at least partially electronic in construction. The accessibility of personal computers has provided technology to most first-world musicians. The economics of keeping up technologically has become critical for composers. The use of sampled sounds, digital editing, and storage will continue to be one of the most important challenges of the twenty-first century.

Musical style and instrumentation, however, show a distinct return to former aesthetics. One finds, for example, long tapering lines reminiscent of Mahler and quasi-tonal progressions in a variety of new music which only ten years ago would have seemed out of place. Effects, from the noises of Russolo to the early efforts in electronic music, have come full circle with sampling devices imitating traditional instruments. Lyricism, once fragmented by pointillism, has returned in the works of many composers. Meter has reappeared in many styles, sometimes even as motor-rhythms in the works of Philip Glass and Steve Reich. Interest in diverse tuning systems, combinations of various media, indeterminacy, and cluster chords have waned significantly since their inceptions in the 1940s and earlier. Even the challenge to tonal harmony seems exhausted.

While exact counterparts may stretch the point, some are irresistible. Glass and Satie, for example, or Crumb and Ives, new age and impressionism, while not presenting obvious parallels, do not stretch the point. Even techniques of artificial intelligence and music suggest the introspection so inherent in Schoenberg's self-studies in serialism and the work of Busoni and others. With technological advances expanding horizons in a multitude of directions, many composers have retrenched and reexamined the music of ages past where subtle hierarchies and nuances of musical structure predominated and individuality emanated from personal statements within styles, not from the shock of new styles.

Visionary Roberto Pavo (1987) has predicted the many changes he feels will take place during the next few decades: "The body will become cybernetic with all manner of contraptions attached to it including alpha-state Walkmen-like radio-tape-players and automatic massage units as well as the already extant electronic organs; talking machines everywhere, even toaster ovens; intelligent machines will run our houses, our businesses, even our lives—they will even tell our fortunes and our horoscopes (and we'll believe them). They will compose our music, write novels, create videos, fight our wars, run our space program and, generally speaking, our future. It's all fantastic" (Pavo 1987).

George Crumb attempts to sum it up succinctly in his article titled, "Music: Does it have a future?": "I am optimistic about the future of music. I frequently hear our present period described as uncertain, confused, chaotic. The two decades from 1950 to 1970 have been described as the rise and fall of the musical avant-garde, the implication being that nothing at all worthwhile was accomplished during those years. My own feeling is that music can never cease evolving; it will continually reinvent the world in its own terms" (Crumb 1986, p. 19).

As I look back over the thirty years and seven editions of *New Directions in Music*, I note that good music still requires the same dedication to create as it always has and the same patience on the part of its audience to understand it. New technologies and conservative or avant-garde styles do not guarantee quality—only good composers do that.

Appendix I

GLOSSARY OF TERMS

An asterisk (*) after a term within a definition signifies that the word so starred is itself defined within this glossary.

Additive Synthesis The electronic manipulation of timbre by plotting the amplitude envelopes of the fundamental and harmonics.

Algorithmic Music Music based on algorithms—a step-by-step process for solving a problem—usually involving a computer.

Amplifier An instrument used to increase the power of a sound or signal.

Amplitude The loudness or dynamic of sound.

Amplitude Modulation (AM) A periodic variation of amplitude* creating tremolo.

Antimusic A term denoting those works the concept or implication of which is opposed to the traditional meaning of music. In current terms, it refers to those compositions which either (1) include no direct or indirect reference to sound in their scores; (2) attempt to destroy one or more of the traditional composer/performer/audience relationships; or (3) are impossible to perform and exist only in concept.

Atonality Lacking tonality. Atonality seems impossible to achieve since any group of tones will have one or more strongest tone (tone center = tonality), just as they will have form, intended or not. *Pantonality**—inclusive of all tonalities—seems more appropriate than the term *atonality* in reference to serial music or dodecaphony*.

Augmentation Expanding durations without disturbing the relationships of the elements (e.g., doubling or tripling the value of each note).

Autonomous Music Xenakis's term for music that does not involve strategy or games in its performance. Autonomous music includes traditional music and all *indeterminate* music* that does not result from group conflict.

Avant-garde A French term literally meaning *advance guard* or *vanguard*. In the arts, this term applies to those who work at the cutting edge of creativity.

Band-reject Filter An electronic filtering device that eliminates a particular group of frequencies while allowing the remaining frequencies to pass.

Band-pass Filter An electronic filtering device which allows a certain group of frequencies to pass while rejecting all the remaining frequencies.

Bauhaus An art school in Germany founded in 1919 by Walter Gropius and closed in 1933 in which the various art forms and crafts were taught interdisciplinarily. Faculty included Paul Klee, Vasily Kandinsky, and Mies van der Rohe, among others, and was instrumental in encouraging the development of many of the extended media forms of today.

Binary A term used to denote a numbering system in base 2 (0,1). Binary numbers proceed from right to left by exponential increments. In this way, any number can be represented (0001 = 1; 0010 = 2; 0011 = 3; 0100 = 4; etc.).

Black Sound Used to denote silences, as opposed to white sound* (inclusive of all frequencies).

Brake Drum The brake housing of an automobile; also used as a percussion instrument.

Chance Music Often used synonymously with indeterminacy*, this term refers to any music that produces chance results.

Circular Bowing On string instruments, a procedure whereby the bow is kept in continuous motion by changing direction using a circular action of the bow across the string.

Circular Breathing On wind instruments, the ability of the performer to breathe in through the nose while

211

expelling air through the mouth, thereby requiring no rests to regain breaths. Performers practiced in this procedure can play continuously for great lengths of time.

Classic Electronic Music   Electronic music created primarily by splicing one sound to the next rather than by using keyboards or sequencers.

Cluster   A chord or sound containing two or more intervals of a second.

Combinatoriality   A serial technique wherein subset versions of a row can be exchanged to create new rows.

Computer-generated Sound   Timbres produced computationally using either additive* techniques or FM synthesis*.

Contact Microphone   A microphone requiring physical contact for sound reproduction.

Cross-coupling   A tape-recorder technique of attaching the playback of one channel to the record of another channel and vice versa to create a reiteration of attack with built-in decay*.

DAC   Digital-to-analog-converter. An instrument designed to translate digital* information into analog* sound.

Dada   International movement beginning around 1916 that originated with the poet Tristan Tzara. The dada movement included artists such as Man Ray and Marcel Duchamp among others, and challenged conventional standards and aesthetics of art.

Decay   The aspect of a tone's envelope* in which the amplitude decreases.

Digital Computer   A computer whose information is stored and processed in binary* numbers.

Dodecaphonic   A term commonly used to refer to twelve-tone music.

Drift   In electronic music, any unintentional shift of frequency due to equipment inaccuracy.

Envelope   The amplitude* characteristics of a signal. Most typically: attack, initial decay*, sustain, and final decay*.

Equal Temperament   Dividing the octave into twelve equal parts. Based on the twelfth root of two, this system represents to some composers an artificial solution to the problems encountered by just* intonation.

Feedback   A result of cross-coupling*. Literally, any electronic device in which sound feeds back through a system one or more times to produce echoes or, depending on gain* adjustment, an increase of sound to the limits of system tolerance.

Filter   An electronic instrument designed to allow selection of frequencies from a signal: band-pass* or band-reject*, for example.

Fluxus   A group of avant-garde* composers of the 1960s intentionally using danger and boredom as viable concepts of art.

FM Synthesis   The artificial creation of harmonics (sidebands).

Fractal   A self-similar object that regenerates at succeedingly smaller and larger levels.

Frequency Modulation (FM)   A periodic variation of frequency creating vibrato.

Futurists   Italian group of composers (1912–20) employing a wide variety of noise*-making instruments.

Gain   Amount of amplification. The loudness knob on any sound-producing device (e.g., amplifier) allows user control of gain.

Generator   Sound source of all types of electronic signals except sine waves*.

Gesamtkunstwerk   German term meaning literally complete art work. Used to denote the nineteenth-century view of opera (particularly Wagner's), the composer creating and controlling all aspects of a work—staging, music, lyrics, dance, and so on.

Graphic   In music, those scores that include visual graphics rather than musical symbols.

Hardware   A computer term used to denote actual instruments as opposed to program software*. Colloquially, hardware refers to physical instruments while software* refers to programs.

Heteronomous Music   Music that utilizes games and strategy during performance, producing *conflict* and indeterminate* results. Term primarily used by Xenakis.

Heterophony   Hetero = several; phony = sounds. This term identifies music that simultaneously uses many variations of a melody.

Hexachord   In its simplest form: a six-note chord. Commonly used in serial music to create related subgroupings of rows.

Improvisation   Music that involves performer freedom within a certain set of parameters* created by the composer. As opposed to indeterminate* music, improvisation asks that performers draw upon learned techniques and intuition within a set stylistic framework.

Indeterminacy   Act of a composer, performer, or both, in which the outcome is unpredictable. In general, unlike improvisation (where the performer is asked to draw upon previous experience and techniques), indeterminacy requires a completely free "letting of sounds be themselves" (as John Cage has put it). The term *aleatoric* is sometimes used in place of indeterminacy.

Interface Connection between two different instruments. In computer music, especially computer-generated sound*, the digital-to-analog (D/A) *interface* allows digital computers to produce analog sounds. A MIDI *interface* allows many different digital instruments to communicate.

Inversion Literally upside down. In serial music this refers to rearranging a row by calculating up intervals downward and vice versa.

Isorhythm A compositional technique of medieval music (c. twelfth to fifteenth century, primarily in Machaut) in which a set rhythm is repeated throughout a composition along with patterns of different numbers of notes (isomelos).

Just Tuning Tuning systems based on the overtone series*. The intervals of the fifth and the major third are calculated (ratios 3:2 and 5:4, respectively) from the series and projected into pitch series.

Klangfarbenmelodien German term denoting color pointillism*: individual but neighboring notes having distinctly different timbres further separated by register.

Klangflächenkomposition Sound-mass* that flows through overlappings of timbre* and spatial* modulations.

Laser An intense beam of light usually connected to a receiving device. When the beam is broken by a performer or other object, the receiver triggers an associated device.

Linear Literally meaning "pertaining to line." In traditional music, linear refers to melodic motion. In electronic terminology, linear refers to a straight line flow as opposed to exponential or other non-linear flow.

Live-electronic Sounds created by a performer using electronic instruments in a concert situation.

Matrix Rectangle of 144 squares that provides all versions of a twelve-tone row. The prime version appears across the top with the inversion top to bottom, retrograde right to left, and retrograde-inversion bottom to top. Matrices assist composers in the analysis and composition of serial music.

Microtone An interval that is less than an equal-tempered half-step. Quarter-tones* represent one example.

MIDI An acronym for Musical Instrument Digital Interface, the default standard in the music industry for digital instrument communication.

Micropolyphony Highly complex densities of polyphonic motion in which no single voice dominates.

Mixer An electronic instrument designed to combine signals by algebraically summing their amplitudes.

Modulation A process in which any aspect of a sound or signal is varied continuously as in amplitude modulation* and frequency modulation*.

Montage A visual overlapping of images.

Multimedia A work that uses two or more traditionally separate art forms. "Happenings" are multimedia events that are more or less indeterminate.

Multiphonics The technique, particularly on wind instruments, of creating two or more sounds simultaneously on an otherwise monophonic instrument. Multiphonics are typically produced by controlling the overtone* series so that one or more of the partials becomes prominent enough to be heard as a separate pitch. Another voice can be added by humming.

Musique Concrète Music that employs non-electronic sounds on tape. The tape recorder is most commonly the compositional tool with manipulation occurring after recording to achieve the desired effect.

Noise Traditionally defined as undesirable sound. Today, however, roughly meaning those sounds whose complexity disguises individual frequencies.

Oscillator An electronic instrument designed to create sine waves*.

Oscilloscope A device using cathode-ray tubes to show the characteristics of incoming signals (amplitude*, frequency, etc.).

Ostinato A repeated rhythmic grouping.

Overtone All sounds except sinusoidal forms contain secondary pitches called overtones, the alteration or filtering* of which alters timbre.

Panchromatic Inclusive of all chromatic tones. Usually used to refer to cluster* chords in which all or most of the twelve pitch classes occur.

Pandiatonicism Inclusive of all diatonic (or scale) notes. Pandiatonic clusters* include all scale notes.

Pantonality Inclusive of all tonalities. Like atonality*, impossible to achieve, and thus very loosely applied to serial music.

Parameter Any characteristic element of sound that can be controlled.

Pitch Class Pitches related to a given pitch by octave transposition (e.g., all Bs belong to the same pitch class).

Pointillism As applied to music, each sound becoming an entity in itself, separated distinctly from those before and after by frequency, register, and/or timbre.

Potentiometer (pot) A variable resistor used to control the output (amplitude) of a system. Most usually found as a volume control.

Prepared Piano   A piano the timbre of which has been altered by the placement of various objects between, on, or around the strings inside the instrument.

Program   Computer software* designed by programmers for particular tasks.

Process Music   Music created by overlaying short motives of different lengths. The "process" is as important as the resultant variations.

Psychoacoustics   The study of sound, its complexity, and its effects both physically and psychologically on humans.

Pulse Wave   Any waveform that instantaneously moves from a negative to a positive position or vice versa. This includes all square and rectangular waveforms.

Quarter-tone   One-half of a semitone.

Real-time   A term usually used to denote immediate rather than delayed actions.

Retrograde   Literally meaning backwards.

Ring Modulator   A signal multiplier circuit that combines signals to produce the sum and difference of their frequencies with only the resultant sidebands exiting.

Sampling   The ability of a computer to calculate the characteristics of a waveform as points. The higher the sampling rate, the better the resultant fidelity of sound.

Sequencer   A device capable of storing performance information in order to play it at any tempo.

Sine Wave   A pitch containing no overtones*.

Software   Computer programs* as opposed to hardware*. Software refers to programs and data.

Sound-mass   A block of sound in which individual pitches no longer have importance.

Spatial Modulation   The compositional technique of moving sound evenly and continuously from one physical location to another.

Square Wave   A pulse wave* with equal positive and negative energy.

Splicer   An instrument used to cut and paste together segments of tape for synchronization. It is used extensively in classic* electronic music.

Stochastic Music   Mathematician Jacques Bernoulli's term from the Greek meaning, literally, target. *Stochastic* laws state that the more numerous indeterminate* activities become, the more determinate their outcome.

Strategic Music   Heteronomous* music composed of "live-performance" games.

Synthesizer   An electronic device used to artificially create timbres.

Tetrachord   A group of four notes. Often used to designate one of three groups of four notes of a twelve-tone row.

Timbre Modulation   The compositional technique of moving sound evenly from one timbre to another.

Triangle Wave   Waveform that, when viewed on an oscilloscope*, takes the shape of a triangle. It contains every other overtone*.

Trichord   Any group of three notes. Often used to designate one of four groups of three notes of a twelve-tone row.

Vibrato   Frequency modulation*.

Vocoder   An instrument designed to code speech sounds into digital information for communication over cables or by radio—subsequently decoded upon reception. Some composers use vocoders to create new sounds by modifying traditional ones.

Voltage Control   The ability of one module in a synthesizer to control another allowing many processes (AM*, FM*, etc.) to take place without manual control.

White Sound   Sound that contains all possible frequencies, from white—inclusive of all colors—light. Often used in conjunction with various filters* to create a wide variety of timbres.

Wind Sound Sculptures   Sculptures designed to allow wind to create sound (e.g., wind chimes).

Appendix II

BIOGRAPHICAL DATA

A listing of many of the composers discussed in this book, with brief biographies and/or current information about each, appears here in alphabetical order. Omissions are due either to lack of definite information concerning the composer, and/or necessarily limited space. Only non-U.S. birthplaces are listed.

ANDRIESSEN, Louis (b. 1939, Utrecht, Holland) is a leading composer of Holland, where he has served as musical advisor to the Globe theater group of Amsterdam.

ANTHEIL, George (1900–1959) was noted as America's *Bad Boy of Music* (book by Antheil published in 1945) and became during the 1920s and 1930s one of the most confusing figures in the world of music. His *Ballet mécanique* (inclusive of airplane motors, doorbells, and the like) is considered by many as a milestone of the avant-garde.

ASHLEY, Robert (b. 1930) cofounded ONCE (at one time an annual festival of new music in Ann Arbor, Michigan) and coordinated the ONCE Group. He is active as both composer and performer of new music and holds degrees from the University of Michigan and the Manhattan School of Music.

AUSTIN, Larry (b. 1930) was the editor of *Source: Music of the Avant-Garde*, a biannual publication devoted to the music of the avant-garde. His works have appeared as part of a number of important festivals, including the New York Philharmonic 1964 Avant-Garde Series and the 1965 Rome Nuova Consonanza.

BABBITT, Milton (b. 1916) served for many years as professor of music at Princeton University and as director of the Columbia-Princeton Electronic Music Center. Educated in mathematics as well as in music, Babbitt composed using the Mark II Synthesizer. As one of the major representatives of American integral serialists, his work has received numerous performances throughout the world.

BEHRMAN, David (b. 1937) cofounded the Sonic Arts Group and produced recordings of new music for CBS and Odyssey Records. As a composer/performer, he has participated in many festivals of new music, including the Angry Arts Festival in New York and the Lincoln Center Library New Music Concerts. He continues to organize and support concerts and recordings of avant-garde music both here and abroad.

BERIO, Luciano (b. 1925, Italy) founded the electronic studio at the Italian Radio in Milan with Bruno Maderna in 1955. A prolific composer and conductor, he taught at Juilliard School of Music until 1973. He now conducts and composes in Europe and his music continues to rely on an intuitive dramatic approach.

BOULEZ, Pierre (b. 1925, France) is founder (in 1953) of the new music series Domaine Musicale, and continues to be active in his support of new music. In 1970, he took up duties as conductor of the New York Philharmonic, replacing Leonard Bernstein. A prolific composer and author, his music and approach continue to be a major influence in the European avant-garde. He founded IRCAM in Paris.

BRANT, Henry (b. 1913), whose first works appeared in the then avant-garde publication *New Music Quarterly* (early 1930s), contributed as both theorist and composer to spatial composing techniques.

BROWN, Earle (b. 1926) has been composer-in-residence at several universities including the University of California, the University of Southern California, and the Peabody Conservatory of Music. During the 1950s, his association with John Cage led to his use of indeterminate techniques. This, together with influences derived from Alex Calder's mobiles, led him further toward graphic and mobile-type structures, a composite of indeterminate and improvisatory techniques.

BUSSOTTI, Sylvano (b. 1931, Italy) is active as composer and promoter of avant-garde music, notably at the Cologne series Music of our Time, the Munich series New Music, and the Florence concerts Vita Musicale Contemporanea. His scores are primarily graphic with emphasis on live performing/composing situations.

CAGE, John (1912–1992) was unquestionably the world's leading exponent of the avant-garde. His writings (*Silence, A Year from Monday,* and *Notations,* among others) and music explore the basic concepts, techniques, and philosophy of all of the avant-garde forms presented in this book. His percussion concerts in early 1936 in Seattle, experiments about the same time with prepared piano techniques, and his first compositions on tape (1951), along with the inclusion of indeterminacy, culminated in a 25-year retrospective concert of his music in Town Hall in 1958. Very few concerts of new music have failed to include the name, music, or at least the influence of John Cage.

CARTER, Elliott (b. 1908), under the encouragement of Charles Ives, studied at Harvard with Walter Piston and in Paris with Nadia Boulanger. He has taught at Juilliard, Columbia, Cornell, Yale, and other schools and is particularly noted for his rigid views of rhythm (metric modulation) and harmonic space. He composes very slowly like Carl Ruggles (usually at the rate of one work every one or two years). His *Double Concerto* and the *Concerto for Orchestra* are considered by many to be the most difficult works in orchestral literature.

CHIARI, Giuseppe (b. 1926, Italy) coorganized (with Bussotti) the Musica e Segno and the Gruppo 70 in Florence. An active member of the European avant-garde movement, his works were performed at the 1963 Internazionale Nuova Musica at Palermo, the Festival of the Avant-Garde in New York, and several Fluxus festivals.

CHILDS, Barney (1926–2000) graduated from Stanford University (Ph.D.) and studied at Oxford University as a Rhodes scholar. His many awards include the Koussevitsky Memorial Award in 1954, and he was an associate editor of Genesis West. His works involve improvisatory and indeterminate techniques, often including audience participation.

COWELL, Henry (1897–1965) was editor of *New Music* from 1927 until the mid-forties (the periodical continued until the 1950s with Cowell on the executive board). His 1930 book *New Musical Resources* is devoted to the new possibilities of harmony and rhythm that would later form a cornerstone for avant-garde experimentation. Until his death, he promoted new music with great vitality and composed prolifically in countless styles and with considerable diversity, freely open to new and creative ideas.

CRUMB, George (b. 1929) studied at the University of Michigan with Ross Lee Finney and taught at the University of Pennsylvania in Philadelphia. His *Echoes of Time and the River* for orchestra won the 1968 Pulitzer Prize. His scores, unique both musically and in notation, exemplify many of the techniques discussed in this book.

CURRAN, Alvin (b. 1938) has been a recipient of both the Bearns Prize and BMI Student Composers award. An active member of Musica Elettronica Viva in Italy (live electronic performance group), his music is often theatrical and concerned with new sounds, both electronic and non-electronic in origin.

DAVIDOVSKY, Mario (b. 1934, Argentina) composes and teaches in New York City. His *Synchronisms No. 6* for piano and tape won the 1971 Pulitzer Prize. Like Carter and Ruggles, he composes very slowly and his electronic works are classical in construction. He was active for many years in the Columbia-Princeton Electronic Music Center.

DAVIES, Peter Maxwell (b. 1934, England) resides in England and has been active with The Fires of London and the Pierrot Players. His music, like that of Berio, is highly eclectic and dramatic.

DRUCKMAN, Jacob (b. 1928) teaches at the Yale School of Music and has been active in the Columbia-Princeton Electronic Music Center. His *Windows* for orchestra received a Pulitzer Prize in 1972. Much of his music, especially the *Animus* series, is for traditional instruments and tape.

DUCKWORTH, William (b. 1943) founded and was president of the Association of Independent Composers and Performers, a group dedicated to the performance of new music. He currently teaches at Bucknell University. His music often uses minimal techniques.

ERB, Donald (b. 1927) has received grants from the Ford and Guggenheim Foundations and from the National Council on the Arts. His music often uses both live and taped electronic sounds in combination with performers on traditional instruments. His works are performed widely both here and abroad.

FELCIANO, Richard (b. 1930) has taught at the University of California at Berkeley, and received grants from the Ford (two), Fulbright, and Guggenheim Foundations. His works, primarily for traditional instruments and tape, are published by E. C. Schirmer in Boston.

FELDMAN, Morton (1926–1986) was one of the major influences on young composers through both his music and his writings about music. His works generally require very soft dynamics and were influenced by painting (especially the works of Pollock and Kline) and dance (Merce Cunningham).

GLASS, Philip (b. 1937) studied at the University of Chicago and at Juilliard with Bergsma, Persichetti, and Milhaud. Known for his three major operas (especially *Einstein on the Beach*) and the film score for *Koyaanisqatsi*.

HAUBENSTOCK-RAMATI, Roman (b. 1919, Poland) studied at the University of Cracow and composes in a predominantly indeterminate style.

HILLER, Lejaren (1924–1991) studied with Milton Babbitt and Roger Sessions at Princeton while achieving his Ph.D. in chemistry. After 1955 he turned toward composition and with Leonard Isaacson began experiments in algorithmic music, first at the University of Illinois and later at SUNY, Buffalo.

HUSA, Karel (b. 1921, Prague) studied at the Prague Conservatory as well as at the Ecole Normale de Musique in Paris (composition with Arthur Honegger). Until recently he taught at Cornell University. His music fuses traditional and avant-garde techniques, and his *Music for Prague* and *Apotheosis of This Earth* have made the concert band a more viable ensemble for contemporary composers.

ICHIYANAGI, Toshi (b. 1933, Japan) formed a new music performing group called New Direction in 1963. His works have been performed both here and abroad, notably by David Tudor.

IVES, Charles (1874–1954) had major influence on almost every facet of avant-garde music, whether directly traceable to him or not.

JOHNSTON, Ben (b. 1926) taught for many years at the University of Illinois and received a Guggenheim Fellowship and grants from the University of Illinois and the National Council on the Arts and Humanities. His writings have appeared in *Perspectives of New Music* and *The Composer*. His music is highly structured and often utilizes unique sound sources and microtones.

KAGEL, Mauricio (b. 1931, Argentina) resides in Cologne, where he serves as composer/conductor for the Ensemble for New Music. Many of his works involve written directions rather than notes, employ some improvisatory and indeterminate elements, and rely primarily on theatrical concepts.

KNOWLES, Alison (b. 1933) is a visual/performance/graphic artist. Her work has been influential in environmental media (e.g., *The Hour of Dust*, 1968–71). She resides in New York City.

KRAFT, William (b. 1923) studied with Otto Luening, Vladimir Ussachevsky, and Henry Cowell, among others, and has written extensively not only for percussion, but for full orchestra as well. His *Contextures: Riots-Decade '60* represents a classic intermedia orchestral composition.

KRENEK, Ernst (1900–1991) began his composing career as a serial composer. His music is intellectual and complex with an approach directed towards individualizing each work both in concept and sound.

LENTZ, Daniel (b. 1942) has had numerous performances of his works both here and abroad. His music, generally graphic and dramatic, often expresses political messages, and his unusual use of colors to represent instruments and/or effects gives both the visual and aural image of his works a marked individuality.

LIGETI, György (b. 1923, Transylvania) worked from 1957 to 1958 in the Studio for Electronic Music of WDR in Cologne. Since 1961 he has been professor of composition at the Hochschule für Musik in Stockholm. Though largely non-electronic, his music explores the vast sonic possibilities of traditional orchestral and choral ensembles. Despite the fact that his ideas are extremely complex, he continues to employ traditional notation and composer control. He has attained wide acclaim as a leader of the avant-garde both through his recordings and exposure in the soundtrack of the motion picture *2001: A Space Odyssey*.

LUENING, Otto (1900–1996) was a foremost representative of electronic music in America. His ideas of the early 1950s continue to represent effective techniques and procedures for contemporary composers. His historical surveys of electronic music remain a primary source of information on the origins and development of this medium. He was co-director of the Columbia-Princeton Electronic Center. His music freely includes all sound sources available, especially *musique concrète*.

LUNETTA, Stanley (b. 1937) was a member of the New Music Ensemble and has composed many avant-garde works. His music is theatrical and uses many multimedia techniques. Through his association and performances with David Tudor and Larry Austin, he has been instrumental in advancing the cause of new music in America.

LUTOSŁAWSKI, Witold   (b. 1913, Poland) is both an active conductor and a composer. Most of his early works were destroyed in World War II, but showed a marked traditionalism. His works today fuse avant-garde and traditional techniques. He composes very slowly (a large work every two years or so) and has used indeterminate and improvisatory procedures. He attributes much of his style to a hearing of Cage's *Concert for Piano and Orchestra*.

MacKENZIE, I. A.   (1894–1969) was an early exponent of experimental ideas involved with novel instrument exploration and philosophical concepts. His music, though for the most part without notation or significant audience appeal, has philosophical importance.

MADERNA, Bruno   (1920–1974) was an active conductor of new music (testament are the large number of recordings and premieres of new works he conducted in both Europe and America), as well as a composer. In 1961 he founded the Darmstadt International Chamber Ensemble, which he conducted until his death.

MORAN, Robert   (b. 1937) is a freelance composer in New York City. His works often involve humor as well as drama. Primarily a composer of mixed-media compositions, Moran has also been active in performing a good deal of new music such as the puppet operas of Satie when he was director of the West Coast Music Ensemble, 1968–73.

MUMMA, Gordon   (b. 1935) was a member of the Sonic Arts Union (live-electronic music) and is a composer/performer actively concerned with the preservation of live performance and a controlled theatrical/gesture situation. His music is found on the Music of Our Time series and Lovely Music.

OLIVEROS, Pauline   (b. 1932) is a composer of electronic, live-electronic, and multimedia compositions and an articulate experimentalist. Her works have appeared on the Music of Our Time series and Columbia Records, and her articles appear in *Source, Composer,* and *Printed Editions*.

PARTCH, Harry   (1901–1974) received many grants, including those from the Carnegie Corporation, Fromm Foundation, and the University of Illinois. A virtually unknown experimentalist in new tunings and instruments for many years, his works and ideas have recently gained wide notice, consideration, and

success. His book *Genesis of a Music* serves as a storehouse of new concepts and performance techniques. He lived in San Diego and taught part-time at the University of California until his death.

PENDERECKI, Krzysztof   (b. 1933, Poland) has won awards from the Polish Union of Composers and UNESCO (1960) and is a graduate of the University of Cracow. His music explores the vast possibilities of sonic material available within orchestras, choirs, and so on. More recently his music follows neo-romantic techniques.

POUSSEUR, Henri   (b. 1929, Belgium) worked at the Brussels electronic music studio. He is a graduate of the Liége and Brussels Conservatories. Most of his music explores the numerous sonic and acoustical possibilities of tape with live performers (especially orchestra).

REICH, Steve   (b. 1936) founded (along with Terry Riley) the phase-music school of composition principally with the works *It's Gonna Rain* (1965) and *Piano Phase* (1967).

REYNOLDS, Roger   (b. 1934) cofounded ONCE and has received Fulbright, Guggenheim, and Rockefeller Foundation fellowships. He teaches at the University of California in San Diego. His works are available from C. F. Peters and are recorded on Nonesuch Records.

ROCHBERG, George   (b. 1918) has, until recently, taught at the University of Pennsylvania in Philadelphia. He uses quotes along with a liberal approach to serial techniques. Most recently his work has followed neo-classic stylistic principles.

SATIE, Erik   (1866–1925) was one of the most influential composers of the avant-garde. Composers such as John Cage, Robert Moran, and many others rate Satie highly in terms of his influence on new music. These influences take the form of ultra-simplicity, new time concepts (i.e., *Vexations*), and inter-media.

SCRIABIN, Alexander   (1872–1915) was influential in the use of media. Biographical information is available in almost any book on twentieth-century music.

STOCKHAUSEN, Karlheinz   (b. 1928, Germany) resides in Cologne. His experiments with electronic music in the mid-fifties, co-editorship of *Die Reihe*, and prolific compositions utilizing electronic sound sources on tape performed over numerous speakers placed acoustically and compositionally in and around audiences, rank him at the forefront of the European avant-garde. His life and works are discussed at length in

Kontrapunkte 6 (P. J. Tonger-Rodenkirchen/Rhein). His writings about music are prolific and complex.

SUBOTNICK, Morton   (b. 1933) teaches at the California Institute of the Arts in Valencia. He was one of the co-founders of the San Francisco Tape Center and has worked in the Columbia (New York) electronic studio.

USSACHEVSKY, Vladimir   (1911–1990) together with Otto Luening presented one of the first American tape music concerts in 1952, and was one of the foremost exponents of *musique concrète* in this country.

VARÈSE, Edgard   (1885–1965) spent the latter forty years of his life working in New York City. His early predictions and pioneering work with tape and electronic sounds, along with his original approach to concepts of music, mark him as one of the major experimentalists and creators of our time.

WOLFF, Christian   (b. 1934, France) teaches at Dartmouth University. His association in the early fifties with Cage and Feldman led to the development of very personal indeterminate procedures, often notated graphically but sometimes traditionally.

WUORINEN, Charles   (b. 1938) is an active composer and pianist. Most of his works require immense performer virtuosity and are explicit in notation.

XENAKIS, Iannis   (b. 1922, Romania) received his early training in science at the Ausbildung am Polytechnikaus in Athens, Greece. From 1947 until 1959 he worked with the famed architect Le Corbusier. His approach to composition focuses primarily on mathematical principles and explores fields of new sounds using traditional instruments and notation.

YOUNG, La Monte   (b. 1935) is one of the most highly original composers of the avant-garde. He studied briefly with Karlheinz Stockhausen in Germany, and is a free-lance composer in New York City. His Dream Houses and other mixed-media works, as well as the innovative compositions of 1960, have made him, along with John Cage, one of the most important exponents of new music both in America and abroad.

≈ *Appendix III* ≈

NOTATIONS

This appendix provides a skeletal outline of new music notations developed over the past fifty years which have become standard. It should help explain some of the examples in this book.

INTRODUCTION

Most scores over the past fifty years include performance instructions that describe the new symbols used by composers in their works. These symbols often conflict with similar symbols of other composers. Until the late 1960s, such symbols seemed as numerous as composers and works using them. Since the publication of the *Darmstädter Beiträge zur Neuen Musik* in 1965 there has been a slow but steady pull toward codification of symbology. The short bibliography that follows this introduction indicates a host of articles and books dedicated to this ever-changing subject.

One of the most important new concepts employed in new music is that of proportional notation. In most music since 1600 bar lines serve a variety of purposes:

(1) to keep performers together

(2) to provide (in some music) primary and secondary implied accents

(3) to make reading the music more feasible.

Contemporary composers often feel that meter conflicts with their ideas of freeing musical line, form, and rhythm from imposed constraints. While some of these composers have solved their problems within a metered structure (i.e., Elliott Carter—metric modulation; György Ligeti—involved and intricate rhythmic entrances, etc.), other composers have felt that the only solution was to dispense with meter entirely. Proportional notation is meter-less with rhythm derived from the performer proportioning left-to-right visual reading speed with the time allotted. Toru Takemitsu's *Voice*, as shown in Figure 4.4, uses small vertical slashes through the upper portion of the staff to indicate approximately 4½ seconds of playing time. Others, like Penderecki (see Figure 3.8—*Threnody*), use large blocks of space that equal certain durations. Performers then read at a speed proportional to the time given for performance (i.e., if an entrance begins about one-third through a 30-second section the performer waits 10 seconds before entering, etc.). This proportional approach eliminates the limits and implied accents of meter. At the same time, however, proportional notation introduces a certain degree of inexactness in that each performer will read a score differently, therefore giving more "chance" possibilities to their performance.

Some composers (like George Crumb, see Figure 10.3) use tempo marks without bar lines. At the same time most of these composers create very thin soloistic music so that the need for meter is minimal (less than, say, trying to perform *Le Sacre du Printemps* without meter). In any event, different composers use notations for different reasons. Many composers mix proportional and metered notations within the same work (see Figure 4.10—Ligeti's *Aventures*), thereby taking advantage of the benefits of both systems. While to the untrained eye these types of scores may appear unnecessarily difficult and/or obscure, they have become standard practice.

Following a short bibliography—completely annotated bibliographies on the subject are available in many other sources—is a list of somewhat standard new music notations. Again, this represents an outline only, and does not in any way suggest comprehensiveness.

BRIEF BIBLIOGRAPHY

Bartolozzi, Bruno. 1980. *New Sounds for Woodwind*. London: Oxford University Press, revised.

———. 1961. "Proposals for Changes in Musical Notation." *Journal of Music Theory, 5,* 297–301.

Behrman, David. 1965. "What Indeterminate Notation Determines." *Perspectives of New Music,* 58–73.

Brindle, Reginald Smith. 1970. *Contemporary Percussion*. London: Oxford University Press.

Cage, John. 1969. *Notations*. New York: Something Else Press.

Cope, David. 1976. *New Music Notation*. Dubuque, IA: Kendall/Hunt Publishing Company.

Cowell, Henry. *New Musical Resources*. 1930. New York: Alfred A. Knopf.

Darmstädter Beiträge zur Neuen Musik. 1965. Mainz: B. Schott's Sohne.

Eimert, Herbert, Fritz Enkel, and Karlheinz Stockhausen. 1956. *Problems of Electronic Music Notation*. Ottawa: National Research Council of Canada.

Howell, Thomas. 1974. *The Avant-Garde Flute: A Handbook for Composers and Flutists*. Berkeley: University of California Press.

Karkoschka, Erhard. 1972. *Notation in New Music*. New York: Praeger Publishers.

Kontarsky, Aloys. 1972. "Notation for Piano." *Perspectives of New Music*, 10, 72–91.

Pooler, Frank and Brent Pierce. 1973. *New Choral Notation*. New York: Walton Music.

Read, Gardner. *Twentieth-Century Music Notation* (unpublished).

Rehfeldt, Phillip. 1974. "Clarinet Resources and Performance." *Proceedings*, 7, American Society of University Composers, 12–24.

Salzedo, Carlos. 1921. *Modern Study of the Harp*. New York: G. Schirmer.

Stone, Kurt. 1974. "New Music Notation: Why?" *Musical America*, 24, 14–36.

———. 1980. *Music Notation in the Twentieth Century: A Practical Guidebook*. New York: W. W. Norton.

Turetzky, Bertram. 1974. *The Contemporary Contrabass*. Berkeley: University of California Press.

Yates, Peter. 1967. "The Proof of the Notation." *Twentieth-Century Music*. New York: Pantheon Books, 82–96.

NEW MUSIC NOTATIONS

A) Pitch meaning	Symbol	One composer among the many who use this type of notation
quarter-tones	↑ ↓ = (¼ up or down)	*Béla Bartók*
	♯ ♭ ♮ = (¼ up)	*Mauricio Kagel*
	(sharpen) (flatten)	
	↑ ↑↑ ♭ ┤ (¼) (¾) (¼) (¾)	*Krzysztof Penderecki*
highest and lowest pitch	↑ ↓	*Krzysztof Penderecki*
clusters	♩♮ or ♩♯	*Henry Cowell*
silent pitches	◇	*Arnold Schoenberg*
(to be held down on the piano for ring-off of overtones when other tones are struck)		

B) Rhythm		
half dot	•♩• = (♩ ♪)	*George Crumb*

repetition of whole groups of notes	• — • — • — • — •	*Krzysztof Penderecki*
slow/even speed-up of pitches		*Karel Husa*
slow/even decrease of speed of pitches		*Karel Husa*
long fermata with duration shown in seconds	5	*George Crumb*
irregular tremolo		*Krzysztof Penderecki*

C) Dynamics

refined dynamic changes		*Henry K. Gorecki*
ad lib dynamics and flux		*John Cage*

D) Articulation

articulation of ends of notes		*Richard Bunger*

E) Timbre effects

1. *Winds*

sing while playing		= play	*David Cope*
		= sing	
multiphonics			*Toru Takemitsu*

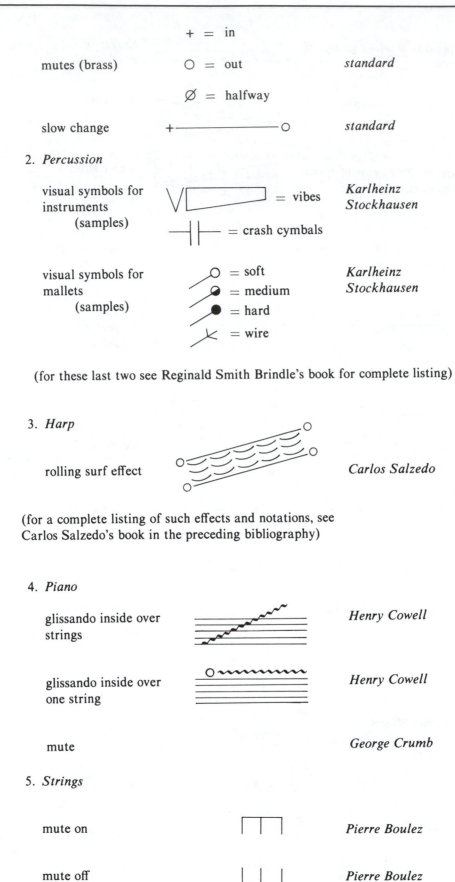

mutes (brass)
+ = in
O = out
Ø = halfway
standard

slow change
+————————O
standard

2. *Percussion*

visual symbols for
instruments
(samples)
= vibes
= crash cymbals
*Karlheinz
Stockhausen*

visual symbols for
mallets
(samples)
= soft
= medium
= hard
= wire
*Karlheinz
Stockhausen*

(for these last two see Reginald Smith Brindle's book for complete listing)

3. *Harp*

rolling surf effect
Carlos Salzedo

(for a complete listing of such effects and notations, see
Carlos Salzedo's book in the preceding bibliography)

4. *Piano*

glissando inside over
strings
Henry Cowell

glissando inside over
one string
Henry Cowell

mute
George Crumb

5. *Strings*

mute on
Pierre Boulez

mute off
Pierre Boulez

play between tailpiece
and bridge

*Krzysztof
Penderecki*

6. *Vocal*

falsetto

*Krzysztof
Penderecki*

spoken

György Ligeti

breath/inhale

György Ligeti

breath/exhale

György Ligeti

laughter

*Krzysztof
Penderecki*

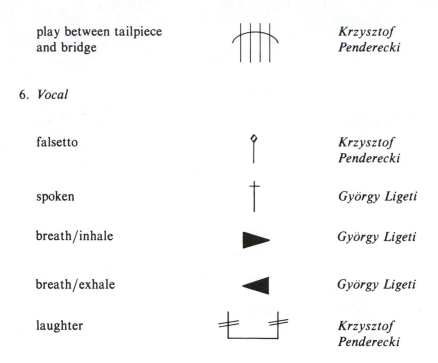

Note that a number of contemporary scores leave out staves of instruments with empty bars. This contributes to the avant-garde appearance of many of the scores of Crumb, Penderecki, and others shown in this book. Likewise, one-line staves are often used for non-pitch instruments (quite unfamiliar in appearance to those not familiar with percussion notation).

Appendix IV

SOURCE ADDRESSES

This appendix furnishes addresses of record companies, music periodicals, music publishers, software and hardware publishers, MIDI organizations, and websites that promote contemporary and avant-garde music. These lists should aid the reader in these ways:

1. to obtain works and equipment (hardware and software) for further study and research;

2. to become acquainted with the large number of sources not ordinarily found in music, record, and bookstores or even in many university libraries;

3. to help support the dissemination of new music by making the names and addresses of its supporters more available.

The lists are by no means complete for a variety of reasons:

1. lack of space (with apologies to all those companies who do support new music yet whose names, for one reason or another, do not appear in the list);

2. availability to the general public (i.e., many major labels do indeed support new music, but their names have not been included in this list as their recordings are available at any retail record store);

3. new music proportion to output: the emphasis here is on companies that devote a major portion of their production to new music;

4. emphasis on listing those companies that publish the examples in the book, thus giving the reader the opportunity to purchase scores, recordings, equipment, or books discussed here with comparative ease.

RECORD COMPANIES

Albany Records: P. O. Box 5011, Albany, NY 12205
Avant: c/o Crystal Records, 2235 Willida Lane, Sedro Woolly, WA 98284
Bridge Records: Box 1864, New York, NY 10016
CRI: 170 West 74th Street, New York, NY 10023
Crystal: 2235 Willida Lane, Sedro Woolly, WA 98284

Desto: c/o CMS Records, 4685 Manhattan College 120, Bronx, NY 10471
Deutsche Grammophone: 825 8th Avenue, New York, NY 10019
ECM: 825 8th Avenue, New York, NY 10019
Finnadar: 75 Rockefeller Plaza, New York, NY 10019
Flying Fish Records: 1304 West Schubert, Chicago, IL 60614
Folkways: c/o Rounder Records, One Camp Street, Cambridge, MA 02140
Golden Crest: 220 Broadway, Huntington Station, NY 11746
Harmonia Mundi: 3364 South Robertson Boulevard, Los Angeles, CA 90034
Hungaroton: 24-02 40th Avenue, Long Island City, NY 11101
Louisville: First Edition Records, 609 Main Street, Louisville, KY 40202
Mainstream: 1700 Broadway, New York, NY 10019
Music of the World: Box 285, Brooklyn, NY 11209
Nonesuch: 75 Rockefeller Plaza, New York, NY 10019
Now: 224 South Lebanon Street, Lebanon, IN 46052
Odyssey: 51 West 52nd Street, New York, NY 10019
Opus One: Box 604, Greenville, MA 04441
Owl: Box 4536, Boulder, CO 80302
Point Park: Wood and Boulevard of the Allies, Pittsburgh, PA 15222
Private Music: 1133 Avenue of the Americas, New York, NY 10036
Redwood: 6400 Hollis Street, Emeryville, CA 94608
Serenus: 9 Airport Drive, Hopedale, MA 01747
Smithsonian Folkways: 1250 W. Northwest Highway, Suite 505, Palatine, IL 60067
Trilogy: 723 7th Avenue, New York, NY 10017

PERIODICALS

Canadian Composer: 159 Bay Street, Toronto 1, Canada
Computer Music Journal: MIT Press, 28 Carlton Street, Cambridge, MA 02142

Darmstädter Beiträge zur Neuen Musik: B. Schotts Sohne, Weihergarten 12, Postfach 1403, 6500 Mainz, Germany

Interface: heerweg 347b Lisse, Netherlands

Interval: Box 8027, San Diego, CA 92102

Journal of Music Theory: Yale University, New Haven, CT 06520

Keyboard: 20085 Stevens Creek, Cupertino, CA 95015

Konzerte Mit Neuer Musik: Rundfunkplatz 1, 8 Munich 2, Germany

Melos: B. Schotts S/au/ohne, Weihergarten 12, Postfach 1403, 6500 Mainz, Germany

Musician: P.O. Box 701, 31 Commercial Street, Gloucester, MA 01930

Musical America: 10 Lake Drive, Hightstown, NJ 08520

Nutida Musik: Sveriges Radio, S-105, 10 Stockholm, Sweden

Perspectives of New Music: University of Washington, School of Music, Box 353450, Seattle, WA 98195-3450

Sonda: Juventudes Musicales, Madrid, Spain

Sonorum Speculum: Donemus 51, Jacob Obrechtstraat, Amsterdam, Netherlands

Soundings: 948 Canyon Road, Santa Fe, NM 87501

Tempo: c/o Boosey and Hawkes Ltd., 295 Regent Street, London, England W1A 1BR

There are a number of other periodicals that carry regular columns dealing with new music and/or magazines dealing with more mainstream musical trends. Names and addresses of such magazines can be found in either: *Directory of the Music Industry*, 1418 Lake Street, Evanston, IL 60204, or *Directory of the World of Music*, Music Information Service, 310 Madison Avenue, New York, NY 10017.

Music Publishers

It is very difficult to provide a complete list of publishers without filling several hundred pages with addresses. To avoid this, the author has listed only major U.S. music publishers, many of which handle the music of European companies dealing with new music (C. F. Peters, for example, aside from their own companies, represents many publishers of new music from around the world). These "umbrella" publishers are noted with an asterisk. Catalogs and lists of music available from many other new music publishers are available from these major companies.

Music distributors are also included in this list and designated by an asterisk. These companies distribute catalogs of publishers from around the world. The *Internationales Musikinstitut Darmstädt Informationszentrum für zeitgenössische Musik Katalog der Abteilung*

Noten (Druck und Herstellung: Druckerei und Verlag Jacob Helene KG., Pfungstadt, Ostendstrasse 10, Germany) provides a fairly comprehensive listing of new music publishers and is issued annually.

Along with the listing of major publishers and distributors are a number of smaller companies that deal almost exclusively with new and avant-garde music. These companies for the most part are not represented through distributors. Other such publisher addresses may be obtained from the *Directory of the World of Music*, Music Information Service, 310 Madison Avenue, New York, NY 10017, or *Directory of the Music Industry*, 1418 Lake Street, Evanston, IL 60204. The annual edition of *Musical America* also has listings of music publishers and their addresses.

ASCAP (1 Lincoln Plaza, New York 10023), BMI (320 West 57th Street, New York 10019), and Sesac (55 Music Square East, Nashville, TN 37203) all have publishers' names and addresses of their own affiliated "performance rights" publishers.

*Associated Music Publishers: 257 Park Avenue South, 20th Floor, New York 10010

Augsburg Fortress: P.O. Box 1209, Minneapolis, MN 55440

*Baerenreiter-Verlag: Heindrich Schutz Allee 35, 35 Kossel, Germany

*B. H. Blackwell Ltd.: 48–51 Broudstreet, Oxford, England OX1 3BQ

*Belwin Mills: Presser Place, Bryn Mawr, PA 19010

Brass Press: 140 Main Street, North Easton, MA 02356

*Alexander Broude, Inc.: 141 White Oaks Road, Williamstown, MA 01267

*J. W. Chester, Ltd.: Eagle Court, London, E.C.1, England

Dover Publications: 31 East Second Street, Mineola, NY 11501

*Carl Fischer, Inc.: 62 Cooper Square, New York 10003

*Galaxy Music: 138 Ipswich Street, Boston, MA 02215-3534

*Otto Harrassowitz: Postfach 349, 6200 Wiesbaben 1, Germany

*Edward Marks: Presser Place, Bryn Mawr, PA 19010

*Mills Music, Inc.: 1619 Broadway, New York, NY 10019

Moeck Verlag: D31 Celle, Postfach 143, Germany

*MCA Music: Presser Place, Bryn Mawr, PA 19010

*C. F. Peters: 373 Park Avenue South, New York, NY 10016

*Theodore Presser: Presser Place, Bryn Mawr, PA 19010

E. C. Schirmer Music Co.: 138 Ipswich Street, Boston, MA 02215-3534

G. Schirmer: 257 Park Avenue South, 20th Floor, New York, NY 10010

Seesaw Music Corp.: 2067 Broadway, New York, NY 10023

Smith Publications: 2617 Gwyndale Avenue, Baltimore, MD 21207

Universal Edition: P.O. Box 850, Valley Forge, PA 19482

Walton Music: 10585 Santa Monica Boulevard, Los Angeles, CA 90025-4950

*Wilhelm Hansen Group: Bornholmsgade 1, DK 1266 Copenhagen K, Denmark

HARDWARE

Akai: P.O. Box 2344, Fort Worth, TX 76113

Alesis Studio Electronics: P.O. Box 3908, Los Angeles, CA 90078

Analytic Systems Group Inc.: P.O. Box 621, Amherst, NY 14226

Axxess: Box 8435, Ft. Collins, CO 80525

Art Inc.: 215 Tremont Street, Rochester, NY 14608

Casio: 15 Gardner Road, Fairfield, NJ 07006

Clarity: Nelson Lane, Garrison, NY 10524

J. L. Cooper Electronics: 1931 Pontius Avenue, West Los Angeles, CA 90025

Decillionix: P.O. Box 70985, Sunnyvale, CA 94086

DigiTech: 5639 South Riley Lane, Salt Lake City, UT 84107

Drew Engineering: 35 Indiana Street, Rochester, NY 14609

D. Drum: 1201 U.S. Highway 1, Suite 280, North Palm Beach, FL 33408

Drum Workshop: 2697 Lavery Ct. 16, Dept. MI, Newbury Park, CA 91320

E-mu Systems: 1600 Green Hills Road, Scotts Valley, CA 95066

Europa Technology: 1638 West Washington Boulevard, Venice, CA 90291

Eventide Inc.: One Alsan Way, Little Ferry, NJ 07643

Fairlight Instruments: 2945 Westwood Boulevard, Los Angeles, CA 90064

Fender Musical Instruments: 1130 Columbia Street, Brea, CA 92621

Forte Music: Box 6322, San Jose, CA 95150

Garfield Electronics: P.O. Box 1941, Burbank, CA 91507

Gentle Electric: Dept. P, P.O. Box 132, Delta, CO 81416

Harris Sound, Inc.: 6640 Sunset Boulevard Suite 110, Hollywood, CA 90028

Hohner Inc.: P.O. Box 15035, Richmond, VA 23227

IMS: 1552 Laurel Street, San Carlos, CA 94070

Industrial Systems: 9811 Owensmouth, Suite 10, Chatsworth, CA 91311

Kawai: Dept. KM, P.O. Box 438, 24200 South Vermont, Harbor City, CA 90710

K-Muse: 18653 Ventura Boulevard, Suite 359, Tarzana, CA 91356

Kurzweil Music Systems: 411 Waverly Oaks Road, Waltham, MA 02154

Lexicon Inc.: 60 Turner Street, Waltham, MA 02154

Mellotron: 36 Main Street, Port Washington, NY 11050

Moog Electronics: 2500 Walden Avenue, Buffalo, NY 14225

New England Digital Corporation: Waltham, MA 02154

Oberheim Electronics: 2250 South Barrington Avenue, Los Angeles, CA 90064

Roland Corp.: 7200 Dominion Circle, Los Angeles, CA 90040

Sequential: 3051 North First Street, San Jose, CA 95134

Simmons Group Centre, Inc.: 23917 Craftsman Road, Calabasas, CA 91302

Standard Productions: 1314 34th Avenue, San Francisco, CA 94122

Syncordion: 117 Cedar Lane, Englewood, NJ 07631

Technics: 1 Panasonic Way, Secaucus, NJ 07094

TOA Electronics, Inc.: 480 Carlton Court, South San Francisco, CA 94080

Voyce Music: P.O. Box 27862, San Diego, CA 92128

Voyetra Technologies: 420 Mt. Pleasant Avenue, Mamaroneck, NY 10543

WERSI: 1720 Hempstead Road, P.O. Box 5318, Lancaster, PA 17601

Yamaha: Nippon Gakki Co. Ltd., Hamamatsu, Japan

SOFTWARE

Bacchus Software Systems: 2210 Wilshire Boulevard 330, Santa Monica, CA 90403

Blank Software: 2210 Wilshire Boulevard 330, Santa Monica, CA 90403

Decillionix: P.O. Box 70985, Sunnyvale, CA 95086

DigiDesign Inc.: 920 Commercial Street, Palo Alto, CA 94303

Digital Music Services: 23010 Lake Forest, Suite D334, Laguna Hills, CA 92653

Dr. T's Music Software: 66 Louise Road, Chestnut Hill, MA 02167

Electronic Arts: 2755 Campus Drive, San Mateo, CA 94403

Enharmonik: P.O. Box 22243, Sacramento, CA 95822

Great Wave Software: P.O. Box 5847, Stanford, CA 94305

Hayden Software: 18 Haviland, Boston, MA 02115

Hippopotamus Software, Inc.: 985 University Ave 12, Los Gatos, CA 95030

Hybrid Arts, Inc.: 11920 West Olympic Boulevard, Los Angeles, CA 90064

Imaja: P.O. Box 638, Middletown, CT 06457

Intelligent Music: P.O. Box 8748, Albany, NY 12208

Joreth Music: Box 20, Evansham, Worcs, WRII5EG, U.K.

Magnetic Music: P.O. Box 328, Rhinebeck, NY 12572

Mark of the Unicorn: 222 Third Street, Cambridge, MA 02142

McNifty Central (Impulse): 6860 Shingle Creek Parkway #110, Minneapolis, MN 12540

Jim Miller: P.O. Box 648, Honaunau, HI 96726

Mimetics: P.O. Box 60238, Station A, Palo Alto, CA 94306

Music Data: Box 28001, Crystal, MN 55428

Music Works: 18 Haviland, Boston, MA 02115

Note Worthy Software: 13119 Pleasant Place, Burnsville, MN 55337

Opcode Systems: 444 Romona, Palo Alto, CA 94301

Passport Designs: 625 Miramontes Street, Half Moon Bay, CA 94019

Roland Corporation: 7200 Dominion Circle, Los Angeles, CA 90840

SFX Computer Software: 1 Hunter Road, North Weldon Industrial Estate, Corby, Northhamptonshire, England

Southworth Music Systems, Inc.: Box 275 RD 1, Harvard, MA 01451

Syntech Corporation: 5699 Kanan Road, Agoura, CA 91301

Triangle Audio: P.O. Box 1108, Sterling, VA 22170

Voyetra Technologies: 51 Main Street, Yonkers, NY 10701

World Class Software: 1500 Valley River Drive, Suite 250, Eugene, OR 97401

MIDI ORGANIZATIONS AND PUBLICATIONS

International MIDI Association: 11857 Hartsook Street, North Hollywood, CA 91607

MIDI Manufacturers Association: 7200 Dominion Circle, Los Angeles, CA 90040

WEB ADDRESSES
(A FEW INTERESTING WEBSITES)

http://www.prs.net/midi.html (for classical MIDI files download)

http://www.ircam.fr/index1-e.html (IRCAM website)

http://www-ks.rus.uni-stuttgart.de/people/schulz/fmusic/symbolic/mainpage.html (Symbolic Composer website)

http://www.forwiss.uni-erlangen.de/~kinderma/musinum/wellcome.html (algorithmic composition website)

http://www.beatnik.com/ (playback software)

http://ccrma-www.stanford.edu/ (CCRMA website)

http://www.cnmat.berkeley.edu/index.html (CNMAT homepage)

http://www.music.sjsu.edu/Comp/cream.html (CREAM homepage)

http://www.mills.edu/LIFE/CCM/CCM.homepage.html (Center for Contemporary Music at Mills College)

http://www.create.ucsb.edu/ (Center for Research in Electronic Art Technology website)

http://www.music.unt.edu/CEMI/ (Center for Experimental Music and Intermedia website)

http://www.esm.rochester.edu/ (Eastman Computer Music Center)

http://crca-www.ucsd.edu (Center for Research in Computing and the Arts homepage)

http://cmp-rs.music.uiuc.edu/ (Experimental Music Studios, University of Illinois at Urbana-Champaign website)

http://www.cs.cmu.edu/afs/cs.cmu.edu/project/music/web/music.html (CMUC SD Computer Music Project)

http://www.music.princeton.edu:80/winham/PSK/ (Princeton Sound Kitchen)

http://www.emf.org/ (EMF - Electronic Music Foundation)

http://www.music.yale.edu/ (CSMT - Center for Studies in Music Technology)

http://music.dartmouth.edu/ (Bregman Electronic Music Studio at Dartmouth College)

http://www-mario.harvard.edu (Harvard Computer Music Center)

http://www.notam.uio.no/index-e.html (NoTAM - Norwegian network for Technology, Acoustics and Music)

http://www.bham.ac.uk/music/ea-studios/ (Electroacoustic Music Studios, University of Birmingham)

http://www.fen.bris.ac.uk/elec/dmr (DMR, Digital Music Research Group)

http://www.hut.fi/TKK/Yksikot/Osastot/S/Akustiikka/index.html (Acoustics Laboratory, Helsinki University of Technology)

http://www.iua.upf.es/ (Institut Universitari de l'Audiovisual)

http://ccrma-www.stanford.edu/LIPM/Welcome.html (LIPM - Musical Research and Production Laboratory, Buenos Aires, Argentina)

http://www.uottawa.ca/~gmartin/emusic/index.html (Electroacoustic Music at the University of Ottawa)

http://www.akin.ru/ (N.N. Andreyev Acoustics Institute)

http://music.dartmouth.edu/~icma (International Computer Music Association)

BIBLIOGRAPHY

CHAPTER 1

Further Readings

Aldwell, Edward and Carl Schachter. 1978. *Harmony and Voice Leading*. New York: Harcourt Brace Jovanovich.

Austin, William. 1966. *Music in the Twentieth Century*. New York: W. W. Norton.

Backus, John. 1969. *The Acoustical Foundations of Music*. New York: W. W. Norton.

Benade, Arthur. 1976. *Fundamentals of Music Acoustics*. New York: Oxford University Press.

Benward, Bruce. 1982. *Music in Theory and Practice*. 2nd ed. Dubuque, IA: Wm. C. Brown, Publishers.

Bernard, Jonathan W. 1977. *A Theory of Pitch and Register for the Music of Edgard Varèse*. New Haven, CT: Yale University Press.

———. 1987. *The Music of Edgard Varèse*. New Haven: Yale University Press.

Dallin, Leon. 1974. *Techniques of Twentieth Century Composition*. 3rd ed. Dubuque, IA: Wm. C. Brown.

Fink, Robert and Robert Ricci. 1975. *The Language of Twentieth Century Music*. New York: Schirmer Books.

Forte, Allen. 1955. *Contemporary Tone Structures*. New York: Columbia University Press.

———. 1979. *Tonal Harmony in Concept and Practice*. 3rd ed. New York: Holt, Rinehart and Winston.

Hall, Donald. 1980. *Musical Acoustics*. Belmont, CA: Wadsworth Publishing Co.

Harder, Paul. 1973. *Bridge to 20th Century Music*. Boston: Allyn and Bacon.

Hartog, H. 1957. *European Music in the Twentieth Century*. New York: Praeger.

Hindemith, Paul. 1937. *The Craft of Musical Composition*. New York: Associated Music Publishers.

Howat, Roy. 1983. *Debussy in Proportion*. Cambridge: Cambridge University Press.

Kostka, Stefan. 1990. *Materials and Techniques of Twentieth-Century Music*. Englewood Cliffs, NJ: Prentice Hall.

Lerdahl, Fred, and Ray Jackendoff. 1983. *A Generative Theory of Tonal Music*. Cambridge, MA: MIT Press.

Lester, Joel. 1989. *Analytic Approaches to Twentieth-Century Music*. New York: W. W. Norton.

Machlis, Joseph. 1979. *Introduction to Contemporary Music*. 2nd ed. New York: W. W. Norton and Company.

Martin, W. R. and J. Drossin. 1980. *Music of the Twentieth Century*. Englewood Cliffs, NJ: Prentice-Hall.

Mellers, Wilfred. 1969. *Romanticism and the Twentieth Century*. New York: Schocken.

Miller, Horace Alden. 1930. *New Harmonic Devices; A Treatise on Modern Harmonic Problems*. Boston: Ditson.

Myers, Rollo W. 1971. *Modern French Music from Fauré to Boulez*. New York: Praeger Books.

Narmour, Eugene. 1983. "Some Major Theoretical Problems Concerning the Concept of Hierarchy in the Analysis of Tonal Music." *Music Perception*, 1, 129–199.

Ouellette, Fernand. 1968. *Edgard Varèse*. Translated from the French by Derek Coltman. New York: Orion Press.

Persichetti, Vincent. 1961. *20th Century Harmony*. New York: W. W. Norton.

Roederer, Juan. 1974. *Introduction to the Physics and Psychophysics of Music*. London: The English University Press, Ltd.

Salzman, Eric. 1988. *Twentieth-Century Music: An Introduction*. 3rd ed. Englewood Cliffs, NJ: Prentice-Hall.

Schenker, Heinrich. 1933. *Five Analyses in Sketchform*. New York: David Mannes School of Music.

Schoenberg, Arnold. 1969. *Structural Functions of Harmony*. New York: W. W. Norton.

Schuller, Gunther. 1965. "Conversation with Varèse." *Perspectives of New Music*, 3, 32–37.

Simms, Bryan R. 1986. *Music of the Twentieth Century, Style and Structure*. New York: Schirmer Books.

Slonimsky, Nicolas. 1947. *Thesaurus of Scales and Melodic Patterns*. New York: Coleman-Ross.

———. 1971. *Music Since 1900*. 4th ed. New York: Charles Scribner's Sons.

Sternfeld, F. W., ed. 1973. *Music in the Modern Age. Praeger History of Music*, Vol. V. New York: Praeger Books.

Thompson, Oscar. 1973. *A Dictionary of Twentieth-Century Composers (1911-1971)*. London: Faber and Faber.

Varèse, Louise Norton. 1972. *A Looking Glass Diary*. New York: W. W. Norton.

Wehmeyer, Grete. 1977. *Edgard Varèse*. Regensburg: Bosse.

Wen-Chung, Chou. 1966. "Varèse: A Sketch of the Man and His Music." *Musical Quarterly*, 52, 157–170.

——. 1967. "The Liberation of Sound." *In Contemporary Composers on Contemporary Music*, Barney Childs and Elliott Schwartz, eds. New York: Holt, Rinehart and Winston, 308–315.

Yates, Peter. 1967. *Twentieth-Century Music*. New York: Pantheon.

Compact Discs, Recordings, and Publishers

Bartók, Béla. 1926. *Out of Doors Suite*. Universal Edition. Hungaroton 31051.

——. 1935. *Mikrokosmos*, Vol. V. Boosey and Hawkes. Hungaroton 31154.

Beethoven, Ludwig van. 1795. *Sonata* Op. 2, No. 3. C. F. Peters. Arcadia 903.

Busoni, Ferruccio. 1915. *Fantasia contrappuntistica*. Altarus 9044.

Debussy, Claude. 1894. *Prélude à "L'Après-midi d'un faune."* A. Durand. DG 35766.

——. 1903. *La Soiree dans Grenade*. International Music Corporation. Accord 200722.

——. 1907. *Pelleas and Melisande*. A. Durand. EMI Classics 49305.

——. 1910–13. *Preludes* Books I and II. A. Durand. Connesseur 4190.

Griffes, Charles Tomlinson. 1918. *Sonata*. G. Schirmer. Koch 7045.

Hindemith, Paul. 1939. *Chansons*. B. Schott's Soehne, Mainz. ACA Digital 20039.

Ives, Charles. 1884-1921. *114 Songs*. New Music Edition. Albany 306.

——. 1914. *Three Places in New England*. Mercury Music Corporation. Pro Arte 140.

——. 1915. *Concord Sonata*. Associated Music Publishers. Centaur 2285.

Mozart, Wolfgang Amadeus. 1782. *Theme and Variations: Ah! Vous Dirai-je, Maman*. (K. 265) Kalmus Edition. Laserlight 15877.

Ravel, Maurice. 1905. *Sonatine*. International Music Publishers. Centaur 2226.

——. 1913. *Daphnis et Chloe Suite 2*. A. Durand. RCA 68600.

——. 1917. *Le Tombeau de Couperin*. A. Durand. Columbia 63316.

Satie, Erik. 1888. *Trois Gymnopedies*. Kalmus Edition. EMI 56515.

Schoenberg, Arnold. 1911. *Sechs Kleine Klavierstücke* Op. 19. International Editions. Wergo 6268.

——. 1912. *Pierrot Lunaire*. Universal Edition. EMI 79237.

——. 1913. *Gurrelieder*. Columbia 48459.

Scriabin, Alexander. 1913. *Poème* Op. 69, No. 1. C. F. Peters. Calliope 9692.

Stravinsky, Igor. 1911. *Petrushka*. Edition Russe de Musique. Columbia 42423.

——. 1913. *Le sacre du printemps*. Dover. DG 35769.

Varèse, Edgard. 1922. *Amériques*. Colfranc Corporation. Mode 58.

——. 1936. *Density 21.5*. Colfranc Corporation. Erato 14332.

——. 1923. *Octandre*. Colfranc Corporation. Nonesuch 71269.

——. 1954. *Déserts*. Colfranc Corporation. Erato 14332.

Wagner, Richard. 1859. *Tristan und Isolde*. Eulenberg Scores. DG 13315.

Webern, Anton. 1913. *Six Bagatelles*. Universal Edition. Sony Classical 48059.

CHAPTER 2

Further Readings

Anderson, E. Ruth. 1976. *Contemporary American Composers: A Biographical Dictionary*. Boston: G. K. Hall.

Babbitt, Milton. 1958. "Who Cares if You Listen." *High Fidelity*, 8, 38–40.

——. 1961. "Set Structure as a Compositional Determinant." *Journal of Music Theory*, 5, 72–94.

Basart, Ann Phillips. 1961. *Serial Music: A Classified Bibliography of Writings on Twelve Tone and Electronic Music*. Berkeley: University of California Press.

Beach, David. 1979. "Pitch Structure and the Analytic Process in Atonal Music. An Interpretation of the Theory of Sets." *Music Theory Speculum*, 1, 7–22.

Beckwith, John and Udo Kasemets. 1961. *The Modern Composer and His World*. Toronto: University of Toronto Press.

Bell, Carla Huston. 1984. *Olivier Messiaen*. Boston, MA: Twayne Publishers.

Bent, Ian and William Drabkin. 1987. "Set-Theory Analysis." In *Analysis*. New York: Norton: 100–108.

Berg, Alban. 1952. "Why is Schoenberg's Music So Hard to Understand?" *The Music Review*, 12, 187–196.

Boatwright, Howard. 1961. *Essays Before a Sonata and Other Writings*. New York: W. W. Norton.

Boretz, Benjamin, and Edward T. Cone, eds. 1971. *Perspectives on American Composers*. New York: W. W. Norton and Co.

——. 1972. *Perspectives on Contemporary Music Theory*. New York: W. W. Norton and Co.

Boulez, Pierre. 1971. *Boulez on Music Today*. Cambridge, MA: Harvard University Press.

Brindle, Reginald Smith. 1975. *The New Music: The Avant-Garde since 1945*. New York: Oxford University Press, 8–15.

Cope, David. 1986. "George Crumb: Profile of a Composer." In *Biography of George Crumb*. New York: C. F. Peters Corporation.

——. 1997. *Techniques of the Contemporary Composer*. New York: Schirmer.

Cope, David and Galen Wilson, 1969. "An Interview with Pierre Boulez." *The Composer Magazine*, 1, 78–85.

Dallin, Leon. 1974. *Techniques of Twentieth Century Composition*. 3rd ed. Dubuque, IA: Wm. C. Brown Company Publishers.

Forte, Allen. 1955. *Contemporary Tone-Structures*. New York: Columbia University Press.

——. 1973. *The Structure of Atonal Music*. New Haven: Yale University Press.

———. 1978. *The Harmonic Organization of The Rite of Spring.* New Haven: Yale University Press.

———. 1985. "Pitch-Class Set Analysis Today." *Music Analysis,* 4, 29–58.

———. 1998. *The Atonal Music of Anton Webern.* New Haven: Yale University Press.

Gagne, Cole and Tracy Caras. 1982. *Soundpieces: Interviews with American Composers.* London: Scarecrow Press.

Griffiths, Paul. 1981. *Modern Music.* New York: George Braziller.

———. 1985. *Olivier Messiaen and the Music of Time.* London: Faber and Faber.

Hitchcock, H. Wiley. 1969. *Music in the United States: An Historical Introduction.* Englewood Cliffs, NJ: Prentice-Hall.

Jameux, Dominique. 1991. *Pierre Boulez.* Translated by Susan Bradshaw. Cambridge, MA: Harvard University Press.

Koblyakov, Lev. 1990. *Pierre Boulez: A World of Harmony.* New York: Harwood Academic Publishers.

Kolneder, Walter. 1968. *Anton Webern: An Introduction to His Works.* Berkeley: University of California Press.

Lang, Paul Henry, ed. 1960. *Problems of Modern Music.* New York: W. W. Norton and Co.

Lester, Joel. 1989. *Analytical Approaches to Twentieth-Century Music.* New York: Norton.

Lewin, David. 1987. *Generalized Musical Intervals and Transformations.* New Haven: Yale University Press.

Machlis, Joseph. 1979. *Introduction to Contemporary Music.* 2nd ed. New York: W. W. Norton and Co.

Messiaen, Olivier. 1950. *The Technique of My Musical Language.* Paris: Alphonse Leduc and Cie.

Neighbour, Oliver, Paul Griffiths, and George Perle. 1980. *The New Grove Second Viennese School.* London: Macmillan.

Perle, George. 1962. *Serial Composition and Atonality.* Berkeley: University of California Press.

———. 1977. *Twelve-Tone Tonality.* Berkeley: University of California Press.

Rahn, John. 1980. *Basic Atonal Theory.* New York: Longman.

Rossi, Nick. 1969. *Music of Our Time.* Boston: Crescendo Publishing Co.

Salzman, Eric. 1988. *Twentieth-Century Music: An Introduction.* 3rd ed. Englewood Cliffs, NJ: Prentice-Hall.

Schwartz, Elliott, and Barney Childs, eds. 1967. *Contemporary Composers on Contemporary Music.* New York: Holt, Rinehart and Winston.

Slonimsky, Nicolas. 1947. *Thesaurus of Scales and Melodic Patterns.* New York: Coleman-Ross.

Spinner, Leopold. 1960. *A Short Introduction to the Technique of Twelve-Tone Composition.* London: Boosey and Hawkes.

Straus, Joseph. 1990. *Introduction to Post-Tonal Theory.* Englewood Cliffs, NJ: Prentice-Hall.

Tremblay, George. 1974. *The Definitive Cycle of the Twelve-Tone Row.* New York: Criterion Music Corp.

Vinton, John, ed. 1974. *Dictionary of Contemporary Music.* New York: E. P. Dutton and Co.

Williams, J. Kent. 1997. *Theories and Analyses of Twentieth-Century Music.* New York: Harcourt Brace.

Wittlich, Gary, ed. 1975. *Aspects of Twentieth-Century Music.* Englewood Cliffs, NJ: Prentice-Hall.

Yates, Peter. *Twentieth Century Music.* 1967. New York: Pantheon Books.

Compact Discs, Recordings, and Publishers

Babbitt, Milton. 1947. *Three Compositions for Piano.* Boelke-Bonart. Harmonia Mundi 90516.

———. 1970. *Quartet No. 3.* Music and Arts MUA 707.

Berg, Alban. 1908. *4 Songs* Op. 2, No. 3. Robert Lienau Muskiverlag. Columbia 66826.

———. 1926. *Wozzeck.* Universal Edition. DG 23587.

———. 1935. *Concerto for Violin and Orchestra.* Universal Edition. Hungaroton 31635.

Boulez, Pierre. 1948. *Second Piano Sonata.* Heugel Publishers. Wergo 60121–50.

———. 1952. *Structures.* Universal Edition. Wergo 6011.

———. 1955. *Le Marteau sans Maître.* Universal Edition. Caprice 21581.

Crawford, Ruth. 1931. *Quartet.* New Music Edition. Gramavision R21S-79440.

Crumb, George. 1965–69. *Madrigals.* Peters. New World Records 357.

Dallapiccola, Luigi. 1941. *Canti di prigionia* (for chorus and orchestra). Carisch Publishers. Sony 68323.

Krenek, Ernst. 1939. *Twelve Short Piano Pieces Written in the Twelve-Tone Technique.* G. Schirmer. Gasparo Records 1016.

Messiaen, Olivier. 1940. *Quatuor pour la fin du temps.* Alphonse Leduc. DG 23247

———. 1960. *Chronochromie.* Leduc Publishers. Koch 311015.

Rudhyar, Dane. 1929. *Granites.* Published by Lengnick. (CRI 584).

Satie, Erik. 1920. *La belle eccentrique.* Sirene. Mandala 4882.

Schoenberg, Arnold. 1909. *Piano Pieces* Op. 11. Belmont Music Publishers. Wergo 6268.

———. 1911. *6 Little Piano Pieces* Op. 19. Belmont Music Publishers. Wergo 6268.

———. 1928. *Variations for Orchestra*, Op. 31. Universal Edition. Sony 48464.

Stravinsky, Igor. 1913. *Le sacre du printemps.* Dover. DG 35769.

Webern, Anton. 1909. *Movements for String Quartet* Op. 5. Universal Edition. Sony Classical 48059.

———. 1928. *Symphonie*, Op. 21. Universal Edition. DG 47431.

———. 1936. *Variations*, Op. 27. DG 419 202-2.

CHAPTER 3

Further Readings

Babbitt, Milton. 1962. "Twelve-Tone Rhythmic Structure and the Electronic Medium." *Perspectives of New Music*, 1, 49–79.

Boatwright, Howard, ed. 1962. *Essays before a Sonata, The Majority, and Other Writings by Charles Ives.* New York: W. W. Norton and Co.

Boulez, Pierre. 1971. *Boulez on Music Today.* Cambridge, MA: Harvard University Press.

Burkholder, J. Peter. 1985. *Charles Ives: The Ideas Behind the Music*. New Haven: Yale University Press.

Carter, Elliott. 1955. "The Rhythmic Basis of American Music." *Score*, 12, 94–102.

———. 1977. *The Writings of Elliott Carter*. Else Stone and Kurt Stone, eds. Bloomington: Indiana University Press.

Christiansen, Louis. 1973. "Introduction to the Music of György Ligeti." *Numus West*, 2, 5–10.

Cowell, Henry. 1930. *New Musical Resources*. New York: Alfred A. Knopf.

Cowell, Henry, ed. 1933. *American Composers on American Music*. New York: Frederick Ungar Publishing Co.

Creston, Paul. 1964. *Principles of Rhythm*. New York: Franco Columbo.

Dallin, Leon. 1974. *Techniques of Twentieth Century Composition*. 3rd ed. Dubuque, IA: Wm. C. Brown Company Publishers.

Edwards, Allen. 1971. *Flawed Words and Stubborn Sounds*. New York: W. W. Norton and Co.

Erickson, Robert. 1963. "Time Relations." *Journal of Music Theory*, 7, 174–192.

———. 1969. "Varèse: 1924–1937: Sound-Ikon." *The Composer Magazine*, 1, 144–149.

———. 1975. *Sound Structure in Music*. Berkeley: University of California Press.

Felder, David and Mark Schneider. 1977. "An Interview with Krzysztof Penderecki." *The Composer Magazine*, 8, 8–20.

Goldstein, Malcolm. 1974. "Texture." In *Dictionary of Contemporary Music*. John Vinton, ed. New York: E. P. Dutton and Co., 741–753.

Higgins, Dick. 1986. "Henry Cowell: Some Personal Recollections." *Soundings*, 14–15, 38–39.

Kramer, Jonathan. 1988. *The Time of Music*. New York: Schirmer Books.

Marquis, G. Welton. 1964. *Twentieth Century Music Idioms*. New York: Prentice-Hall.

Kagel, Mauricio. 1959. "Tone Clusters, Attacks, Transitions." *Die Reihe*, 5, 40–55.

Lewin, David. 1984. "On Formal Intervals between Time-Spans." *Music Perception*, 1, 412–423.

Ligeti, György. 1969. *Lontano*. New York: Schott Music Corp.

Messiaen, Olivier. 1950. *The Technique of My Musical Language*. Paris: Alphonse Leduc and Cie.

Persichetti, Vincent. 1961. *Twentieth Century Harmony*. New York: W. W. Norton Co.

Riegger, Wallingford. 1959. "John J. Becker." *Bulletin of the ACA*, 9, 2–7.

Robinson, Ray. 1983. *Krzysztof Penderecki: A Guide to His Works*. Princeton, NJ: Prestige Publications.

Rudhyar, Dane. 1986. "When Does Sound Become Music." *Soundings*, 14–15, 82–84.

Schwartz, Elliott. 1972. *Electronic Music: A Listener's Guide*. New York: Praeger Publishers.

Schwinger, Wolfram. 1994. *Krzysztof Penderecki: Begegnungen, Lebensdaten, Werkkommentare*. Mainz: Schott.

Stockhausen, Karlheinz. 1957. ". . . How Time Passes. . . ." *Die Reihe*, 3, 10–43.

Vinton, John, ed. 1974. *Dictionary of Contemporary Music*. New York: E. P. Dutton and Co.

Weisgall, Hugo. 1959. "The Music of Henry Cowell." *Musical Quarterly*, 45.

Xenakis, Iannis. 1955. "The Crisis of Serial Music." *Gravesaner Blätter*, 1, 23–66.

Compact Discs, Recordings, and Publishers

Bartók, Béla. 1926. *Sonata*. Universal Edition. Hungaroton HCD 31051.

———. 1934. *String Quartet No. 5*. Boosey & Hawkes. Hungaroton HCD-12502.

Becker, John. 1929. *Symphony No. 3*. C. F. Peters. Albany Records 27.

Blackwood, Easley. 1958. *Symphony No. 1*. Cedille 16.

Blomdahl, Karl-Birger. 1954. *Sisyfos*. Schott. Caprice 21365.

Boulez, Pierre. 1959. *Le Marteau sans Maître*. Universal Edition. Caprice 21581.

Britten, Benjamin. 1954. *The Turn of the Screw*. Boosey & Hawkes. Collins Classics 7030.

Carrillo, Julian. 1962. *Mass for Pope John XXIII in Quarter-Tones*. CRI 246.

Carter, Elliott. 1948. *Cello Sonata*. G. Schirmer. Nonesuch 79183.

———. 1951. *String Quartet No. 1*. AMP. Etcetera KTC 1065.

———. 1961. *Double Concerto*. Associated Music Publishers. Nonesuch 79183.

Cowell, Henry. 1911. *The Tides of Manaunaun*. Breitkopf & Härtel. Smithsonian Folkways 40801.

———. 1922. *The Hero Sun*. Breitkopf & Härtel. CRI ACS-6005.

———. 1922. *What's This*. Breitkopf & Härtel. Smithsonian Folkways 40801.

Crumb, George. 1970. *Black Angels*. C. F. Peters. Nonesuch 79242.

Dempster, Stuart. 1976. *Standing Waves*. New Albion 13.

Globokar, Vinko. 1969. *Ausstrahlungen*. Peters.

Helm, Everett. 1954. *Concerto for Five Solo Instruments, Percussion and Strings*. Schott.

Husa, Karel. 1968. *Music for Prague*. AMP. Sony 44916.

———. 1971. *Apotheosis of This Earth*. AMP. Louisville LCD 005

Ives, Charles. 1915. *Sonata #2*. AMP. New World 378.

———. 1921. *Majority*. AMP.

———. 1922. *Songs*. New Music Edition. Nonesuch 71325.

Kagel, Mauricio. 1964. *Sonant*. C. F. Peters.

Liebermann, Rolf. 1954. *Concerto for Jazz Band and Symphony Orchestra*. Universal Edition. Therofon 2331.

Ligeti, György. 1961. *Atmosphères*. Universal Edition. PGD-Phillips 46403.

———. 1962. *Aventures*. C. F. Peters. Sony 62311.

———. 1966. *Lux Aeterna*. C. F. Peters. BMG Catalyst 09026-61822-2.

———. 1965. *Nouvelles Aventures*. Neues. Sony 62311.

———. 1965. *Requiem*. C. F. Peters. Wergo 6045.

———. 1967. *Lontano*. Schott. Wergo 60045.

Lutosławski, Witold. 1954. *Concerto for Orchestra*. PWM. RCA 09026-61520-2.

———. 1975. *Les Espaces du Sommeil*. Published by Chester Music. Sony 42271.

Lybbert, Donald. 1968. *Lines for the Fallen*. C. F. Peters.

Messiaen, Oliver. 1934. *L'Ascension*. Leduc. Bis 409.

———. 1935. *La Nativité du Seigneur*. Leduc. Erato Bis 410.

———. 1949. *Quatre études de rythme for piano*. Durand.

Milhaud, Darius. 1916. *Piano Sonata*. Salabert. Discover International 920167.

Nono, Luigi. 1956. *Il canto sospeso*. Schott.

———. 1957. *La terra e la campagna*. Schott.

———. 1958. *Cori di Didone*. Schott.

Penderecki, Krzysztof. 1960. *Threnody for the Victims of Hiroshima*. Eulenberg. Vienns MM 3010.

———. 1965. *Passion According to St. Luke*. Moeck. EMI Harmonia Mundi 7 49313.

———. 1967. *Capriccio for Violin and Orchestra*. Moeck. RCA 60370.

Riegger, Wallingford. 1949. *Music for Brass Choir*. Mercury Music. CRI 572.

Rudhyar, Dane. 1926. *Stars* for piano. CRI 584.

———. 1929. *Granites*. CRI 584.

Ruggles, Carl. 1921. *Angels*. Curwen. Summit 122.

———. 1926. *Lilacs and Portals*. AME.

———. 1932. *Sun Treader*. London 443776.

Schuman, William. 1955. *Credendum*. Merion Music. CRI 308.

———. 1962. *Symphony No. 8*. Merion Music. Columbia 63163.

Schwartz, Elliott. 1966. *Texture*. A. Broude.

Stockhausen, Karlheinz. 1967. *Mixtur*. Universal Edition.

Stravinsky, Igor. 1913. *Le Sacre du Printemps*. Boosey & Hawkes. DG 31045.

Varèse, Edgard. 1923. *Octandre*. Ricordi. Nonesuch 71269.

———. 1933. *Hyperprism*. Columbia MG 68334.

———. 1934. *Equatorial*. G. Schirmer. Nonesuch 71269.

Woodbury, Arthur. 1968. *Remembrances*. CPE-Source.

CHAPTER 4

Further Readings

Amirkhanian, Charles. 1973. "An Introduction to George Antheil." *Soundings*, 7, 174–180.

Anhalt, Istvan. 1984. *Alternative Voices: Essays on Contemporary Vocal and Choral Composition*. Toronto: The University of Toronto Press.

Backus, John. 1969. *The Acoustical Foundation of Music*. New York: W. W. Norton and Co.

Balzano, Gerald J. 1980. "The Group-theoretic Description of 12-Fold and Microtonal Pitch Systems." *Computer Music Journal*, 4, 66–84.

———. 1986. "What are Musical Pitch and Timbre?" *Music Perception*, 3, 297–314.

Banek, Reinhold and Jon Scoville. 1980. *Sound Designs: A Handbook of Musical Instrument Building*. Berkeley: Ten Speed Press.

Bartolozzi, Bruno. 1967. *New Sounds for Woodwind*. London: Oxford University Press.

Baschet, Bernard and F. Baschet. 1987. "Sound Sculpture: Sounds, Shapes, Public Participation, Education." *Leonardo*, 20, 107–114.

Becker, John. 1950. "Finding a Personal Orchestral Idiom." *Musical America*, 126–127.

von Bekesy, Georg. 1970. "Musical Dynamics by Variation of Apparent Size of Sound Source." *Journal of Music Theory*, 14, 141–164.

Boatwright, Howard. 1965. "Ives' Quarter-Tone Impressions." *Perspectives of New Music*, 3, 146–166.

Boulanger, Richard. 1986. "Toward a New Age of Performance: Reading the Book of Dreams with the Mathews Electronic Violin." *Perspectives of New Music*, 24, 130–155.

Brant, Henry. 1967. "Space as an Essential Aspect of Musical Composition." In *Contemporary Composers on Contemporary Music*. Elliott Schwartz and Barney Childs, eds. New York: Holt, Rinehart and Winston, 222–242.

Brindle, Reginald Smith. 1970. *Contemporary Percussion*. London: Oxford University Press.

Bunger, Richard. 1981. *The Well-Prepared Piano*. 2nd ed. Sebastopol, CA: Litoral Arts Press.

Cage, John. 1961. *Silence: Lectures and Writings*. Cambridge, MA: The MIT Press.

Carrillo, Julian. 1972. "The Thirteenth Sound." Translated by Patricia Ann Smith. *Soundings*, 5, 62–79.

Chou Wen-Chung. 1974. "Asian Music and Western Composers." In *Dictionary of Contemporary Music*. John Vinton, ed. New York: E. P. Dutton and Co., 141.

Clough, Rosa Trillo. 1961. *Futurism*. New York: Philosophical Library.

Cogan, Robert and Pozzi Escot. 1981. *Sonic Design, Practice and Problems*. Englewood Cliffs, NJ: Prentice-Hall.

Cope, David. 1977. "Modulations." *The Composer Magazine*, 8, 25–30.

Cowell, Henry. 1933. *American Composers on American Music*. New York: Frederick Unger Publishing Co.

Cummings, Barton. 1974. "A Brief Summary of New Techniques for Tuba." *Numus West*, 5, 62–63.

———. 1984. *The Contemporary Tuba*. New London, CT: Whaling Music Publishers.

Davies, Peter Maxwell. 1969. *Eight Songs for a Mad King*. Boosey and Hawkes.

Dempster, Stuart. 1980. *The Modern Trombone: A Definition of Its Idiom*. Berkeley: University of California Press.

Finkenbeinger, Gerhard and Vera Meyer. 1987. "The Glass Harmonica: A Return from Obscurity." *Leonardo*, 20, 139–142.

Forsyth, Michael. 1985. *Buildings for Music*. Cambridge, MA: MIT Press.

Gagne, Cole and Tracy Caras. 1982. *Soundpieces: Interviews with American Composers*. London: Scarecrow Press.

Garland, Peter. 1982. *Americas: Essays on American Music and Culture, 1973–80*. Santa Fe, NM: Soundings Press.

Griffiths, Paul. 1982. *Peter Maxwell Davies*. London: Robson Books.

Griffiths, Paul. 1985. *New Sounds, New Personalities, British Composers of the 1980s in Conversation*. London: Faber Music Ltd.

Heiss, John C. 1966. "For the Flute: A List of Double-stops, Triple-stops, Quadruple-stops and Shakes." *Perspectives of New Music*, 5, 139–141.

———. 1968. "Some Multiple Sonorities for Flute, Oboe, Clarinet and Bassoon." *Perspectives of New Music*, 7, 136–142.

Hopkin, Bart. 1996. *Gravikords, Whirlies and Pyrophones: Experimental Musical Instruments*. Roslyn, NY: Ellipsis Arts.

Howell, Thomas. 1974. *The Avant-Garde Flute*. Berkeley: The University of California Press.

Johnston, Ben. 1966. "Proportionality and Expanded Pitch Relations." *Perspectives of New Music*, 5, 112–120.

———. 1970. "How to Cook an Albatross." *Source*, 7, 63–65.

———. 1974. "Harry Partch." In *Dictionary of Contemporary Music*. John Vinton, ed. New York: E. P. Dutton and Co., 555–556.

———. 1974. "Program Notes." University of Wisconsin, Milwaukee. April 28.

Junger, Miguel and David Feit, eds. 1986. *Sound, Structures and Their Interaction*. Cambridge, MA: MIT Press.

Lieberman, Fredric and Leta Miller. 1998. *Lou Harrison: Composing a World*. New York: Oxford University Press.

Livingston, Larry, and Frank McCarty. 1971. "Expanding Woodwind Sound Potential." *The Composer Magazine*, 3, 39–40

Mumma, Gordon. 1974. "Witchcraft, Cybersonics and Folkloric Virtuosity." *Darmstädter Beiträge zur Neue Musik*, 133–135.

Orga, Ates. 1968. "Alois Hába and Microtonality." *Musical Opinion*, 541.

Palm, Siegfried. 1972. "Notation for String Instruments." *The Composer Magazine*, 3, 63–66.

Partch, Harry. 1968. "And On the Seventh Day Petals Fell in Petaluma." *Source*, 2, 94–113.

———. 1977. *Genesis of a New Music*. New York: Da Capo Press.

Payton, Rodney J. 1976. "The Music of Futurism: Concerts and Polemics." *The Musical Quarterly*, 62, 25–45.

Pooler, Frank and Brent Pierce. 1973. *New Choral Notation*. New York: Walton Music.

Pound, Ezra. 1968. *Antheil*. New York: Da Capo Press.

Pruslin, Stephen, ed. 1979. *Peter Maxwell Davies: Studies from Two Decades*. London: Boosey and Hawkes.

Read, Gardner. 1953. *Thesaurus of Orchestral Devices*. London: Sir Isaac Pitman and Sons.

———. 1976. *Contemporary Instrumental Techniques*. New York: Schirmer Books.

Reck, David. 1977. *Music of the Whole Earth*. New York: Charles Scribner's Sons.

Reed, H. Owen, and Joel T. Leach. 1969. *Scoring for Percussion*. New York: Prentice-Hall.

Rehfeldt, Phillip. 1977. *New Directions for Clarinet*. Berkeley: University of California Press.

Robson, Ernest. 1987. "Research of the Sounds of Literature: Formant Music and a Prosodic Notation for Performance." *Leonardo*, 20, 131–138.

Rossi, Nick, and Robert Choate. 1969. *Music of Our Time*. Boston: Crescendo Publishing Co.

Sallis, Friedemann. 1996. *An Introduction to the Early Works of György Ligeti*. Colgne: Studio.

Salzedo, Carlos. 1921. *Modern Study of the Harp*. New York: G. Schirmer.

———. 1929. *Method for the Harp*. New York: G. Schirmer.

———. 1961. "Considerations on the Piano and the Harp." *Harp News*, 3, 10–11.

Schwartz, Elliott. 1970. "Elevator Music." *The Composer Magazine*, 2, 49–54.

Schwartz, Elliott and Barney Childs, eds. 1967. *Contemporary Composers on Contemporary Music*. New York: Holt, Rinehart, and Winston.

Slawson, Wayne. 1985. *Sound Color*. Berkeley: University of California Press.

Smith, Jeff. 1982. "The Partch Reverberations: Notes on a Musical Rebel." *Soundings*, 12, 46–59.

Steinberg, Michael. 1961. "Some Observations on the Harpsichord in Twentieth Century Music." *Perspectives of New Music*, 1, 189–194.

Turetzky, Bertram. 1969a. "The Bass as a Drum." *The Composer Magazine*, 1, 92–107.

———. 1969b. "A Technique of Contemporary Writing for the Contrabass." *The Composer Magazine*, 1, 118–135.

———. 1974. *The Contemporary Contrabass*. Berkeley: University of California Press.

Varèse, Edgard. 1967. "New Instruments and New Music." In *Contemporary Composers on Contemporary Music*. Elliott Schwartz and Barney Childs, eds. New York: Holt, Rinehart, and Winston, 195–208.

Verkoeyen, Jos. 1970. "String Players and New Music." *Sonorum Speculum*, 45, 19–26.

Vinton, John, ed. 1974. *Dictionary of Contemporary Music*. New York: E. P. Dutton and Co.

Winckel, Fritz. 1967. *Music, Sound and Sensation*. New York: Dover Publications.

Yates, Peter. 1959. "Lou Harrison." *ACA Bulletin*, 9, 2–7.

Compact Discs, Recordings, and Publishers

Albright, William. 1992. *Flights of Fancy*. Jobert. Albany 140.

Antheil, George. 1922. *Sonatas* (3). Weintraub. Albany 146.

———. 1924. *Ballet mécanique*. Templeton. Music Masters 67094.

———. 1929. *Transatlantic*. Universal Edition.

———. 1942. *Symphony No. 4*. Everest 9039.

Austin, Larry. 1965. *The Maze*. CPE-Source.

Becker, John. 1933. *Abongo*. Autograph Editions. New World Records 80285.

Berio, Luciano. 1968. *Sinfonia*. Universal Edition. Erato 2292-45228-2.

Brant, Henry. 1932. *Angels and Devils*. Centaur 2014.

———. 1970. *Kingdom Come for Orchestras, Circus Band, and Organ*. MCA. Phoenix 127.

———. 1973. *An American Requiem*. Henmar Press (Peters).

Cage, John. 1938. *Bacchanale*. C. F. Peters. Dorian 3002.

———. 1943. *Amores*. C. F. Peters. Wergo 6203.

———. 1944. *Perilous Night, Suite for Prepared Piano*. C. F. Peters. Dorian 3002.

———. 1948. *Sonatas and Interludes*. C. F. Peters. CRI 700.

———. 1951. *Concerto for Prepared Piano and Chamber Orchestra*. C. F. Peters. Mode 57.

Celli, Joseph. n.d. *Improvisations*. O.O. Discs 4.

Chavez, Carlos. 1942. *Toccata for Percussion*. Mills Music. Hungaraton 12991.

Chou Wen-Chung. 1957. *The Willows Are New*. C. F. Peters. CRI 691.

Cope, David. 1972. *Margins*. Carl Fischer.

———. 1976. *Rituals*. Smithsonian Folkways 33869.

Cowell, Henry. 1925. *The Banshee*. AMP. Smithsonian Folkways 40801.

Crumb, George. 1970. *Ancient Voices of Children*. C. F. Peters. Nonesuch 79149.

———. 1970. *Black Angels*. Peters. Nonesuch 79242.

———. 1970. *Songs, Drones, and Refrains of Death*. C. F. Peters. Bridge 9028.

Curtis-Smith, Curtis. 1973. *Rhapsodies*. Paris: Editions Salabert.

Dahl, Ingolf. 1949. *Concerto for Saxophone*. MCA. Crystal 655.

Davies, Peter Maxwell. 1969. *Eight Songs for a Mad King*. Boosey and Hawkes. Unicorn 9052.

———. 1978. *Vesalii Icones*. Boosey and Hawkes. Unicorn 2068.

Dlugoszewski, Lucia. 1973. *Fire Fragile Flight*. Vox 5144.

Druckman, Jacob. 1968. *Animus II*. MCA Music. CRI 781.

Erb, Donald. 1969. *Evensong for Orchestra*. Merion Music. Koch 7417.

———. 1992. *Concerto for Violin and Orchestra*. Merion Music. Koss 3302.

Fanshawe, David. 1973. *African Sanctus*. Proprius 9984.

Foss, Lukas. 1964. *Elytres*. Fischer and Schott.

Gaburo, Kenneth. 1985. *Antiphony IX*. Music and Arts 852.

Globokar, Vinko. 1969. *Discours II*. C. F. Peters.

Harrison, Lou. 1941. *Canticle No. 3 for Ocarina, Guitar and Percussion*. Music Masters 7051-2-C.

———. 1961. *Concerto in Slendro*. C. F. Peters.

———. 1963. *Pacifika Rondo*. Phoenix 118.

Haubenstock-Ramati, Roman. 1958. *Interpolations: a "Mobile" for Flute*. Universal Edition. Agora Musica 113.

Henze, Hans Werner. 1970. *Versuch uber Schweine*. Schott.

Holliger, Heinz. 1975. *Atembogen*. Mainz: B. Schott's Söhne.

Hovhaness, Alan. 1945. *Avak: The Healer*. C. F. Peters. Crystal C-800.

———. 1955. *Khaldis*. Op. 91. C. F. Peters.

Husa, Karel. 1971. *Apotheosis of This Earth*. AMP. Louisville LCD 005.

Ives, Charles. 1924. *Three Pieces for Two Pianos Tuned a Quarter-tone Apart*. C. F. Peters.

Johnson, Tom. 1992. *Music for 88*. Compact Discs 106.

Johnston, Ben. 1976. *Sonata for Microtonal Piano*. Koch 7369.

———. 1977. *Knocking Piece*. CPE-Source.

Kraft, William. 1968. *Triangles*. MCA. Crystal 124.

Kupferman, Meyer. 1968. *Infinities 22*. General Music. Crystal 669.

Leedy, Douglas. 1968. *Usable Music I*. CPE-Source.

Ligeti, György. 1961. *Atmospheres*. Universal Edition. Phillips 46403.

———. 1962. *Aventures*. C. F. Peters. Columbia 62311.

———. 1967. *Lontano*. Schott. Wergo 60045.

Lomon, Ruth. 1982. *Five Ceremonial Masks*. Arsis Press.

Mayuzumi, Toshiro. 1965. *Concerto for Percussion*. C.F. Peters.

McPhee, Colin. 1936. *Tabuh-Tabuhan*. AMP. Argo 44560.

Messiaen, Olivier. 1955. *Oiseaux exotiques*. Universal Edition. Sony 44762.

Meytuss, Julius. n.d. *Dnieper Dam*. Smithsonian Folkways 6160.

Moran, Robert. 1968. *Titus*. CPE-Source.

Mossolov, Alexander. 1928. *Steel Foundry*. Smithsonian Folkways 6160.

Nancarrow, Conlon. 1977. *Studies for Player Piano*, Vol. 5. Soundings, Book 4. RCA 61180.

Nogågrd, Per. 1969. *Waves* for percussion. Wilhelm Hansen. Camerata 313.

Partch, Harry. 1958. *Daphne of the Dunes*. Mode 33.

———. 1966. *And on the Seventh Day Petals Fell in Petaluma*. CPE-Source. CRI 752.

Pellman, Samuel. 1977. *Silent Night*. Alexander Broude Publishers.

Penderecki, Krzysztof. 1960. *Dimensions of Time and Silence*. Moeck. Polskie Nagrania PNCD 017.

———. 1960. *Threnody for the Victims of Hiroshima*. Eulenberg. Polskie Nagrania PNCD 017.

Reich, Steve. 1971. *Drumming*. Nonesuch 79170.

———. 1987. *Electric Counterpoint*. Nonesuch 79451.

Riley, Terry. 1964. *In C*. Sony 7178.

Salzedo, Carlos. 1921. *Chanson dans la Nuit*. Telarc 80418.

Scavarda, Donald. 1962. *Matrix*. Lingua Press.

Schoenberg, Arnold. 1909. *Five Pieces for Orchestra*. C. F. Peters. Koch 7263.

Schuller, Gunther. 1959. *Seven Studies on Themes of Paul Klee*. Universal Edition. Mercury 34329.

Scott, Stephen. 1985. *Minerva's Web for Grand Piano Bowed and Plucked by Ten Musicians*. New Albion 26.

Shankar, Ravi. 1971. *Concerto for Sitar and Orchestra*. EMI 69121.

Smith, William O. 1959. *Five Pieces for Clarinet Alone*. Ongaku 105.

Stockhausen, Karlheinz. 1963. *Gruppen*. Universal Edition.

———. 1950. *Zyklus*. Universal Edition. Camerata 202742.

Travis, Roy. 1968. *Collage for Orchestra*. CRI C259.

Varèse, Edgard. 1923. *Hyperprism*. G. Schirmer. Sony 68334.

———. 1925. *Intégrales*. G. Schirmer. Erata 14332.

———. 1933. *Ionisation*. G. Schirmer. Hungaroton 12991.

Xenakis, Iannis. 1994. *Dämmerschein for Orchestra*. Boosey & Hawkes. Mode 58.

CHAPTER 5

Further Readings

Behrman, David. 1964. "What Indeterminate Notation Determines." *Perspectives of New Music*, 3, 58–73.

Bosseur, Jean-Yves. 1993. *John Cage. Suivi d'entretiens avec Daniel Caux et Jean-Yves Bosseur*. Paris: Minerve.

Boulez, Pierre. 1964. "Alea." *Perspectives of New Music*, 3, 42–53.

———. 1990. *Pierre Boulez, John Cage, correspondance et documents, réunis, présentés et annotés par Jean-Jacques Nattiez; en collaboration avec Françoise Davoine . . . [et al.]* Winterthur, Schweiz: Amadeus.

Brecht, George. 1991. *George Brecht—Notebooks*. Edited by Dieter Daniels with collaboration of Hermann Braun. Köln: W. König.

Brinkman, R., ed. 1979. *Improvisation und Neue Musik*. Mainz: B. Schott.

Brown, Earle. 1964. *Program Notes*. New York: New York Philharmonic Society.

———. 1967. "Form in New Music." *Source*, 1, 48–51.

Bryant, Allan. 1968. "Groups." *Source*, 2, 14–27.

Cage, John. 1962. *The John Cage Catalog*. New York: C. F. Peters Co.

———. 1966. "History of Experimental Music in the United States." In *Silence: Lectures and Writings*. Cambridge, MA: The MIT Press.

———. 1966. *Silence: Lectures and Writings*. Cambridge, MA: The MIT Press.

———. 1967. *A Year from Monday*. Middletown, CT: Wesleyan University Press.

———. 1969. *Notations*. New York: Something Else Press.

———. 1973. *M: Writings '67–'72*. Middletown, CT: Wesleyan University Press.

———. 1976. *Pour les Oiseaux*. Paris: Pierre Belford.

———. 1979. *Empty Words: Writings '73–'78*. Middletown, CT: Wesleyan University Press.

———. 1979. *Writings through Finnegan's Wake*. New York: Printed Editions.

———. 1980. *Conversation without Feldman: A Talk Between John Cage and Geoffrey Barnard*. Kings Cross, N.S.W., Australia: Black Ram Books.

———. 1990. *I - VI: Method Structure Intention . . .* Cambridge, MA: Harvard University Press.

Cage, John, Lukas Foss, and Iannis Xenakis. 1970. "Short Answers to Difficult Questions." *The Composer Magazine*, 2, 39–43.

Cardew, Cornelius. 1968. "Groups." *Source*, 2, 14–27.

Cardew, Cornelius, ed. 1974. *Scratch Music*. Cambridge, MA: The MIT Press.

Childs, Barney. 1969. "Indeterminacy and Theory: Some Notes." *The Composer Magazine*, 1, 15–34.

Cope, David. 1973. "An Interview with Halsey Stevens." *The Composer Magazine*, 5, 28–41.

———. 1980. "An Interview with John Cage." *The Composer Magazine*, 10, 6–22.

Cope, David and Galen Wilson, 1969. "An Interview with Pierre Boulez." *The Composer Magazine*, 1, 78–85.

Copland, Aaron. 1968. *Our New Music*. New York: W. W. Norton and Co.

Corbett, John. 1994. *Extended Play: Sounding Off from John Cage to Dr. Funkenstein*. Durham, NC: Duke University Press.

DeLio, Thomas, ed. 1996. *The Music of Morton Feldman*. New York: Excelsior Music Pub. Co.

Duckworth, William and Richard Fleming, eds. 1989. *John Cage at Seventy-Five*. Lewisburg, PA: Bucknell University Press.

Erb, Donald. 1966. *Program Notes*. Turnabout TV-S 34433.

Feldman, Morton. 1966. "Predetermined / Indetermined." *Composer* (England), 3–4.

———. 1967. "Conversations without Stravinsky." *Source*, 1, 42–45.

———. 1969. "Between Categories." *The Composer Magazine*, 1, 73–77.

———. 1985. *Essays*. Kerpen: Beginner Press.

Foss, Lukas. 1963. "The Changing Composer-Performer Relationship: a Monologue and a Dialogue." *Perspectives of New Music*, 1, 45–53.

———. 1964. "Work-Notes for Echoi." *Perspectives of New Music*, 3, 54–61.

———. 1968. "Groups." *Source*, 2, 14–27.

Gagne, Cole and Tracy Caras. 1982. *Soundpieces: Interviews with American Composers*. Metuchen, NJ: The Scarecrow Press, Inc.

Higgins, Dick. 1964. *Postface*. New York: Something Else Press.

Hellermann, William. 1971. In "Questions and Answers." Tom Everett, ed. *The Composer Magazine*, 2, 79–92.

Hibbard, William. 1966. "Some Aspects of Serial Improvisation." *American Guild of Organists Quarterly*, 27–34.

Junkerman, Charles and Marjorie Perloff, eds. 1994. *John Cage: Composed in America*. Chicago: University of Chicago Press.

Kagel, Mauricio. 1979. *1898*. London: Universal Edition.

Kayn, Roland. 1966. "Random or Not Random." *Horyzonty muzyki*. Cracow, 14–28.

Kostelanetz, Richard. 1969. *Master Minds*. New York: Macmillan.

———. 1970. *John Cage*. New York: Praeger.

———. 1991. *John Cage: An Anthology*. New York: Da Capo Press.

———. 1996. *John Cage (ex)plain(ed)*. New York: Schirmer Books.

Landy, Leigh. 1991. *What's the Matter with Today's Experimental Music?: Organized Sound Too Rarely Heard*. Philadelphia: Harwood Academic Publishers.

Layton, Billy Jim. 1964. "The New Liberalism." *Perspectives of New Music*, 3, 137–142.

Logon, Wendell. 1975. "The Case of Mr. John Coltrane: A Compositional View." *Numus West*, 8, 40–45.

MacKenzie, I. A. 1971. "The Critique." *The Composer Magazine*, 2, 92.

McCarty, Frank. 1974. "An Interview with Stuart Dempster." *The Instrumentalist*, 28, 33–34.

Metzger, Heinz-Klaus and Riehn, Rainer, eds. 1981. *A Book about John Cage and His Music*. New York: C. F. Peters.

O'Grady, T. J. 1981. "Aesthetic Values in Indeterminate Music." *Musical Quarterly*, 67, 366–381.

Olson, Harry F., and Herbert Belar. 1961. "Aid to Composition Employing a Random Probability System." *Journal of the Acoustical Society of America*, 33, 1163–1170.

Paik, Nam June. 1978. *A Tribute to John Cage*. Hadano, Kanagawa, Japan: T. Okabe, Okabe Silkscreen Studio.

Pritchett, James. 1988. "From Choice to Chance: John Cage's *Concerto for Prepared Piano*." *Perspectives of New Music*, 26, 50–81.

———. 1993. *The Music of John Cage*. New York: Cambridge University Press.

Revill, David. 1992. *The Roaring Silence: John Cage, A Life*. London: Bloomsbury.

Reynolds, Roger. 1965. "Indeterminacy: Some Considerations." *Perspectives of New Music*, 4, 136–140.

———. 1968. "It (')s Time." *Electronic Music Review*, 7, 12–17.

———. 1976. *Mind Models*. New York: Praeger Books.

Satie, Erik. 1977. *Ecrits (réunis, établis et annotés par Ornella Volta)*. Paris: Editions Champ Libre.

Schwartz, Elliott and Barney Childs, eds. 1967. *Contemporary Composers on Contemporary Music*. New York: Holt, Rinehart, and Winston.

Schuller, Gunther. 1968. *Early Jazz: Its Roots and Development*. New York: Oxford University Press.

Shattuck, Roger. 1968. *The Banquet Years*. New York: Vintage Books.

Shultis, Christopher. 1998. *Silencing the Sounded Self: John Cage and the American Experimental Tradition*. Boston: Northeastern University Press.

Sumner, Melody, ed. 1986. *The Guests Go In To Supper*. New York: Burning Books.

Sutherland, Roger. 1994. *New Perspectives in Music*. London: Sun Tavern Fields.

Tomkins, Calvin. 1965. *The Bride and the Bachelors*. New York: Viking Press.

Xenakis, Iannis. 1971. *Formalized Music*. Bloomington: Indiana University Press.

Yates, Peter. 1967. *Twentieth Century Music*. New York: Pantheon Books.

Young, La Monte, and Jackson MacLow, eds. 1963. *An Anthology of Chance Operations*. New York: La Monte Young and Jackson MacLow.

Young, La Monte, and Marian Zazeela. 1969. *Selected Writings*. Munich: Heiner Friedrich.

Compact Discs, Recordings, and Publishers

Andriessen, Louis. 1968. *Contratempus for 22 Instruments*. Donemus 54.

———. 1965. *Paintings*. Belwin-Mills.

Ashley, Robert. 1963. *In memoriam Kit Carson*. Monroe Stree MSM 60101.

———. 1964. *Wolfman*. CPE-Source IV.

Austin, Larry. 1967. *Accidents*. CPE-Source.

Berio, Luciano. 1962. *Circles*. Universal Edition. Wergo 6021.

Boucourechliev, Andre. 1968. *Les Archipels*. MFA 216001.

Boulez, Pierre. 1954. *Improvisations sur Mallarmé*. Universal Edition. Hungaraton 11385.

———. 1952. *Structures II*. Universal Edition. Wergo 6011.

Brown, Earle. 1952. *December 1952*. C. F. Peters. New Albion 82.

———. 1954. *Four Systems*. Hat Hut 6146.

———. 1961. *Hodograph 1*. New Albion 82.

Bussotti, Sylvano. 1959. *Five Pieces for David Tudor*. Universal Edition.

———. 1959. *Brilliante*. Universal. Mode 65.

Cage, John. 1943. *Amores for Prepared Piano and Percussion*. Peters. Wergo 6203.

———. 1951. *Music of Changes*. C. F. Peters. Wergo 60099.

———. 1952. *4'33"*. C. F. Peters.

———. 1954. *34'46.776"* for a Pianist. C. F. Peters.

———. 1955. *26'1.1499"* for a String Player. C. F. Peters. Etcetera 2016.

———. 1958. *Aria for One Voice*. C. F. Peters. MD&G 6130701.

———. 1958. *Concert for Piano and Orchestra*. C. F. Peters. Wergo 6216.

———. 1958. *Fontana Mix*. C. F. Peters.

———. 1958. *Indeterminacy*. Smithsonian Folkways 40804.

———. 1958. *Variations I*. C. F. Peters. Hat Hut 6176.

———. 1960. *Cartridge Music*. C. F. Peters. Mode 24.

———. 1960. *Theatre Piece*. C. F. Peters.

———. 1961. *Atlas Eclipticalis*. Peters. Wergo 6216.

———. 1961. *Variations III*. C. F. Peters. Hat Hut 6176.

———. 1963. *Variations IV*. C. F. Peters. Hat Hut 6176.

———. 1969. *HPSCHD*. C. F. Peters.

Chiari, Giuseppe. 1965. *Quel Che Volete*. CPE-Source.

Duckworth, William. 1969. *Pitch City*. CAP.

Erb, Donald. 1985. *Concerto for Orchestra*. Merion Music. Koch 7417.

Feldman, Morton. 1953. *Intersection 3*. C. F. Peters. Hat Hut 6146.

———. 1961. *Durations*. C. F. Peters. CPO 999199.

———. 1962. *Out of "Last Pieces."* C. F. Peters. Mode 25.

———. 1963. *Christian Wolff in Cambridge*. C. F. Peters.

———. 1964. *King of Denmark*. C. F. Peters. Hat Hut 6146.

———. 1967. *In Search of an Orchestration*. C. F. Peters.

———. 1968. *False Relationships and the Extended Ending*. C. F. Peters.

———. 1970. *Viola in My Life*. C. F. Peters. CRI 620.

Foss, Lukas. 1960. *Time Cycle*. Sony 63164.

———. 1967. *Etudes for Organ*. CPE-Source.

Haubenstock-Ramati, Roman. 1958. *Interpolation: a "Mobile" for Flute (1,2,3), 1958*. Universal Edition. Hat Hut 6180.

———. 1968. *Mobile for Shakespeare*. Universal Edition.

Higgins, Dick. 1969. *Thousand Symphonies*. CPE-Source.

Kagel, Mauricio. 1962. *Improvisation ajoutée*. C. F. Peters.

———. 1973. *1898*. London: Universal Edition.

Kayn, Roland. 1962. *Calaxis*. Moeck.

Logothetis, Anestis. 1963. *Odyssee*. Universal Edition.

———. 1964. *Ichnologia*.

———. 1965. *Labyrinthos*. Universal Edition.

———. 1971. *Culmination*. Edition Modern/Munich.

Lutosławski, Witold. 1963. *Trois Poèmes d'Henri Michaux*. PWM.

———. 1968. *Livre pour Orchestra*. J. & W. Chester Ltd. Berlin Classics 9166.

Mizelle, John. 1967. *Radial Energy*. CPE-Source.

Moran, Robert. 1963. *Four Visions*. Universal Edition.

———. 1964. *Bombardments No. 2*. C. F. Peters.

Nilsson, Bo. 1960. *Reaktionen*. Universal Edition.

Pousseur, Henri. 1961. *Caractères*. Universal Edition.

———. 1973. *Phonèmes pour Cathy*. Universal Edition.

Rabe, Folke. 1984. *Shazam for Trumpet*. W. Hansen. Bis 287.

Schaffer, Boguslaw. 1963. *S'alto*. PWM.

———. 1963. *Violin Concerto*. PWM.

Schuller, Gunther. 1959. *Seven Studies on Themes of Paul Klee*. Universal Edition. Mercury 34329.

———. 1994. *Concerto for Organ and Orchestra*. New World 80492.

Stockhausen, Karlheinz. 1957. *Klavierstuck XI No. 7*. Universal Edition. Wergo 60135.

———. 1965. *STOP*. Universal Edition.

Winsor, Phil. 1975. *Orgel*. Carl Fischer.

Wolff, Christian. 1961. *Trio 2*. C. F. Peters.

———. 1962. *Duo II for Pianists*. C. F. Peters.

———. 1964. *For 1, 2 or 3 People*. C. F. Peters. Hat Hut 6176.

———. 1968. *Edges*. CPE-Source. Hat Hut 6181.

Xenakis, Iannis. 1965. *Akrata*. Boosey and Hawkes. Mode 56.

———. 1971. *Duel*. Boosey and Hawkes.

CHAPTER 6

Further Readings

Ashley, Robert. 1961. "Notes for Public Opinion Descends Upon the Demonstrators." *Asterisk*, 1, 49–51.

Austin, Larry. 1969. "Music is Dead, Long Live Music." *New York Times*, July 6.

Barfield, Woodrow and Thomas Furness, III, eds. 1995. *Virtual Environments and Advanced Interface Design*. New York: Oxford University Press.

Barnes, Clifford. 1972. "Music: Sent into Exile." *Cincinnati Post*, November 15.

Becker, Jurgen and Wolf Vostell, eds. 1965. *Happenings*. Hamburg: Rowohlt.

Beckwith, John and Udo Kasemets, eds. 1961. *The Modern Composer and His World*. Toronto: University of Toronto Press.

Born, Georgina. 1974. "An Interview with John Cage." *Asterisk*, 1, 26–32.

———. 1995. *Rationalizing Culture: IRCAM, Boulez, and the Institutionalization of the Musical Avant-Garde*. Berkeley: University of California Press.

Budd, Harold. 1969. *California 99*.

Burdea, Grigore and Philip Coiffet. 1994. *Virtual Reality Technology*. New York: John Wiley and Sons.

Byron, Michael, ed. 1975. *Pieces: An Anthology*. Vancouver: A.R.C.

Cage, John. 1957. "To Describe the Process of Composition 'Music for Piano 21-52.' " *Die Reihe*, 3, 23–32.

———. 1961. *Silence*. Middletown, CT: Wesleyan University Press.

———. 1967. *A Year from Monday*. Middletown, CT: Wesleyan University Press.

———. 1969. *Notations*. New York: Something Else Press.

———. 1973. *Empty Words*. Middletown, CT: Wesleyan University Press.

———. 1973. *M. Writings '67–'72*. Middletown, CT: Wesleyan University Press.

———. 1982. *Themes and Variations*. New York: Station Hill Press.

Cope, David. 1970. *Notes in Discontinuum*. Los Angeles: Discant Music.

———. 1980. "An Interview with John Cage." *The Composer Magazine*, 10, 6–22.

———. 1969. "Chronicles of a Cause: I. A. MacKenzie." *The Composer Magazine*, 1, 35–42.

Corner, Philip. 1982. *I Can Walk through the World as Music*. New York: Printed Editions.

Cott, Jonathan. 1973. *Stockhausen*. New York: Simon and Schuster.

Cunningham, Merce. 1969. *Changes: Notes on Choreography*. Frances Starr, ed. New York: Something Else Press.

Davis, Bob and Rich Gold. 1986. *Break Glass in Case of Fire*. Oakland: Mills College, Center for Contemporary Music.

DeWitt, Tom. 1987. "Visual Music: Searching for an Aesthetic." *Leonardo*, 20, 115–122.

Duckworth, William. 1995. *Talking Music: Conversations with John Cage, Philip Glass, Laurie Anderson, and Five Generations of American Experimental Composers*. New York: Schirmer Books.

Duckworth, William and Richard Fleming, eds. 1996. *Sound and Light: La Monte Young, Marian Zazeela*. Lewisburg, PA: Bucknell University Press.

Everett, Tom. 1972. "Questions and Answers." *The Composer Magazine*, 4, 16–23.

Fetterman, William. 1996. *John Cage's Theatre Pieces: Notations and Performances*. Amsterdam, Netherlands: Harwood Academic Publishers.

Fontana, Bill. 1987. "The Relocation of Ambient Sound: Urban Sound Sculpture." *Leonardo*, 20, 143–147.

Gaburo, Kenneth. 1975. *Collection of Works*. San Diego: Lingua Press.

Gibb, Stanley. 1973. "Understanding Terminology and Concepts Related to Media Art Forms." *The American Music Teacher*, 22, 23–25.

Grayson, John. 1977a. *Sound Sculpture*. Vancouver: A.R.C.

———. 1977b. *Environments of Musical Sculpture You Can Build*. Vancouver: A.R.C.

Greenman, Ben. 1995. *Net Music: Your Complete Guide to Rock and More on the Internet and Online Services*. New York: Random House Electronic Pub: M. Wolff and Co.

Griffiths, Paul. 1981. *Modern Music*. New York: George Brazillen.

Gurley, Ted. 1996. *Plug In: The Guide to Music on the Net*. Upper Saddle River, NJ: Prentice-Hall.

Hansen, Al. 1968. *A Primer of Happenings and Time-Space Art*. New York: Something Else Press.

Heim, Mike. 1993. *The Metaphysics of Virtual Reality*. New York: Oxford University Press.

Henahan, Donal. 1970. "Music Draws Strains Direct from Brains." *New York Times*, November 25.

Higgins, Dick. 1964. *Postface*. New York: Something Else Press.

———. 1966. "Boredom and Danger." *Source*, 3, 14–17.

———. 1969. *FOEW and OMBWHNW*. New York: Something Else Press.

———. 1979. *A Dialectic of Centuries: Notes Towards a Theory of the New Arts*. 2nd ed. West Glover, VT: Printed Editions.

Hill, Brad. 1996. *The Virtual Musician: A Complete Guide to Online Resources and Services*. New York: Schirmer Books.

Hiller, Lejaren. 1968. "HPSCHD." *Source*, 2, 10–19.

Hoffman, Paul. 1973. "An Interview with Robert Moran." *The Composer Magazine*, 4, 46–48.

Huff, Jay. 1972. "An Interview with David Behrman." *The Composer Magazine*, 4, 29–32.

Jacobson, Bernard. 1970. *Stereo Review*.

Johnson, Roger. 1980. *Scores: An Anthology of New Music*. New York: Schirmer Books.

Johnson, Tom. 1974. *Imaginary Music*. New York: Two-Eighteen Press.

Kagel, Mauricio. 1961. "Uber das instrumentale Theater." *Neue Musik*, 14–17.

———. 1972. "On Match for Three Performers." *The Composer Magazine*, 3, 70–81.

Kaprow, Allan. 1966. *Assemblage, Environments and Happenings*. New York: Abrams.

Khatchadourian, Haig. 1985. *Music, Film and Art*. New York: Gordon and Breach.

Kirby, E. T. 1969. *Total Theatre*. New York: E. P. Dutton and Co.

Kirby, Michael. 1965. *Happenings*. New York: E. P. Dutton and Co.

Klüver, Billy, Julie Martin, and Barbara Rose. 1972. *Pavilion*. New York: Dutton.

Knowles, Alison. 1976. *More by Alison Knowles*. New York: Printed Editions.

Kostelanetz, Richard. 1967. *Music of Today*. New York: Time-Life Books.

———. 1968. *The Theatre of Mixed Means*. New York: Dial Press.

———. 1970. *John Cage*. New York: Praeger.

———. 1988. *Conversing with Cage*. New York: Praeger.

Landy, Leigh. 1994. *Experimental Music Notebooks*. Philadelphia: Harwood Academic Publishers.

Lentz, Daniel. 1972. "Music Lib." *The Composer Magazine*, 4, 6–15.

Machlis, Joseph. 1979. *Introduction to Contemporary Music*. 2nd ed. New York: W. W. Norton and Company.

MacLow, Jackson. 1970. *An Anthology*. New York: Heiner Friedrich.

McLuhan, Marshall. 1964. *Understanding Media. The Extensions of Man*. New York: New American Library.

Moore, Carmen. 1970. "The Sound of Mind." *Village Voice*, December 24.

Moran, Robert. 1973. *Composition for Piano with Pianist*. *Soundings*, 1.

Motherwell, Robert. 1951. *The Dada Painters and Poets*. An Anthology. New York: Wittenborn, Schultz.

Mumma, Gordon. 1967. "Four Sound Environments for Modern Dance." *Impulse, the Annual of Contemporary Dance*, 22–34.

Nougé, Paul. 1973. "Music Is Dangerous." *Soundings*, 1, 6–11.

Nyman, Michael. 1974. *Experimental Music*. New York: Schirmer Books.

Oliveros, Pauline. 1973. "Many Strands." *Numus West*, 3, 8–11.

———. 1982. *Software for People*. New York: Printed Editions.

Oliveros, Pauline and Becky Cohen. 1982. *Initiation Dream*. Los Angeles: Astro Arts.

Osterreich, Norbert. 1977. "Music with Roots in the Aether." *Perspectives of New Music*, 16, 214–228.

Painter, J., et al., eds. 1992. *Companion to Contemporary Musical Thought* (2 vol.). London: Routledge.

Palmer, Robert. 1981. "A Father Figure for the Avant Garde." *Atlantic Monthly*, May.

Partch, Harry. 1973. "Show Horses in the Concert Ring." *Soundings*, 1, 12–14.

Patterson, Jeff. 1998. *Audio on the Web*. Berkeley, CA: Peachpit Press.

Pellegrino, Ronald. 1983. *The Electronic Arts of Sound and Light*. New York: Van Nostrand Reinhold Company.

Prévost, Eddie. 1995. *No Sound Is Innocent: AMM and the Practice of Self-invention, Meta-musical Narratives, Essays*. Essex, UK: Copula.

Proceedings. 1968. *ASUC Proceedings*.

Rosenboom, David, ed. 1976. *Biofeedback and the Arts: Results of Early Experimentation*. Vancouver: A.R.C.

Salzman, Eric. 1974. "Mixed Media." In *Dictionary of Contemporary Music*, John Vinton, ed. New York: E. P. Dutton and Co., 489–492.

Schafer, R. Murray. 1974. *Ear Cleaning*. Vancouver: BMI Canada Ltd.

———. 1973. "A Brief Introduction to the World Soundscape Project." Vancouver, 1.

Shattuck, Roger. 1968. *The Banquet Years*. New York: Vintage Books.

Schroeder, Ralph. 1996. *Possible Worlds*. Boulder, CO: Westview Press.

Shore, Michael. 1987. *Music Video: A Consumers Guide*. New York: Ballantine.

Subotnick, Morton. 1968. "Extending the Stuff Music is Made of." *Music Educators Journal*, 55, 109–110.

Summers, Jodi. 1998. *The Interactive Music Handbook: The Definitive Guide to Internet Music Strategies, Enhanced CD Production, and Business Development*. New York: Allworth Press.

Tomkins, Calvin. 1965. *The Bride and the Bachelors*. New York: Viking Press.

Von Gunden, Heidi. 1983. *The Music of Pauline Oliveros*. Metuchen, NJ: Scarecrow Press.

Weidnenaar, Reynold. 1986. "Live Music and Moving Images: Composing and Producing the Concert Video." *Perspectives of New Music*, 24, 270–279.

Whitney, John. 1965. "Moving Pictures and Electronic Music." *Die Reihe*, 7, 61–71.

———. 1980. *Digital Harmony*. Peterborough, NH: Byte Books.

Wiggins, Jim. 1975. "Lily Sings the Blues." *Rolling Stone*. September 12.

Woolley, Benjamin. 1992. *Virtual Worlds: A Journey in Hype and Hyperreality*. Oxford: Blackwell.

Young, La Monte, and Jackson MacLow. 1963. *An Anthology of Chance Operations*. New York: NP.

Young, La Monte, and Marian Zazeela. 1969. *Selected Writings*. Munich: Heiner Friedrich.

Zahler, Noel. 1987. "Isomorphism, Computers and the Multi-media Work." *Proceedings of the International Computer Music Conference*. San Francisco: Computer Music Association, 228–229.

Zimmerman, Walter. 1976. *Desert Plants*. Vancouver: A.R.C.

Compact Discs, Recordings, and Publishers

Amirkhanian, Charles. 1979. *Lexical Music*. Starkland 206.

Ashley, Robert. 1972. *Wolfman*. CPE-Source 2, no. 2. Source Records 4.

———. 1977. *Private Parts*. Kontrapunct 1001.

Austin, Larry. 1967. *Bass*. CPE-Source.

———. 1967. *Accidents*. CPE-Source 2, no. 2.

———. 1988. *Sinfonia Concertante*. Centaur 2029.

Beerman, Burton. 1972. *Mixtures*. Media Press.

Berio, Luciano. 1965. *Laborintus II*. Universal Edition. Harmonia Mundi 190764.

Budd, Harold. 1991. *She is a Phantom*. Vox 21.

Cage, John. 1952. *Winter Music*. Hat Hut 6141.

———. 1960. *Theatre Piece*. Peters.

———. 1961. *Variations III*. Peters. Etcetera 2016.

———. 1963. *Variations IV*. Hat Hut 6176.

Cage, John and Lejaren Hiller. 1968. *HPSCHD*. Peters.

Colgrass, Michael. 1991. *Arctic Dreams*. MCA. Centaur 2288.

Cope, David. 1970. *BTRB*. Brass Press.

———. 1971. *Deadliest Angel Revision*. Seesaw Music Corp.

Corner, Philip. 1977. *Ear Journeys: Water*. Printed Editions.

———. *Rounds*. Soundings 3, no. 4:92.

Crumb, George. 1970. *Ancient Voices of Children*. Peters. Nonesuch 79149.

———. 1970. *Black Angels*. Peters. Nonesuch 79242.

———. 1971. *Voice of the Whale (Vox Balaenae)*. Peters. New World 357.

Davies, Peter Maxwell. 1969. *Eight Songs for a Mad King*. Boosey and Hawkes. Unicorn 9052.

Erb, Donald. 1970. *Souvenir*. Merion Music.

Glass, Philip. 1969. *Music in Fifths*. Nonesuch 79326.

———. 1969. *Music in Similar Motion*. Nonesuch 79326.

———. 1972. *Music with Changing Parts*. Nonesuch 79325.

———. 1974. *Music in 12 Parts*. Nonesuch 79324.

———. 1976. *Einstein on the Beach*. Nonesuch 79323.

Hassell, Jon. 1976. *Vernal Equinox*. Lovely Music 1021.

Ives, Charles. 1906. *Central Park in the Dark*. AMP. DG 23243.

Kagel, Mauricio. 1966. *Match*. Universal Edition.

———. 1967. *Variaktionen*. Universal Edition.

———. 1981. *Rrrrrrr . . . .* Montaigne 782003.

Knowles, Alison. 1980. *Natural Assemblages and the True Crow*. New York: Printed Editions.

Kraft, William. 1967. *Contextures: Riots—Decade '60*. Cambria 1071.

Martirano, Salvatore. 1968. *L'sGA*. MCA. Centaur 2266.

———. n.d. *Underworld*. MCA.

Monk, Meredith. 1983. *Turtle Dreams*. ECM 21240.

Moran, Robert. n.d. *Music from the Towers of the Moon*. Argo 436565.

Oliveros, Pauline. 1974. *Sonic Meditations*. Smith Publications.

———. 1987. *The Roots of the Moment*. Hat Hut 6009.

Reck, David. 1966. *Blues and Screamer*. CPE-Source.

Reich, Steve. 1965. *It's Gonna Rain*. Nonesuch 79451.

———. 1971. *Drumming*. Nonesuch 79170.

———. 1976. *Music for 18 Musicians*. Nonesuch 79448.

———. 1984. *The Desert Music*. Nonesuch 79101.

Reynolds, Roger. 1962. *Emperor of Ice Cream*. Peters.

———. 1968. *Ping*. CPE-Source. CRI 285.

Riley, Terry. 1964, *In C*. New Albany 71.

———. 1970. *Poppy Nogood and the Phantom Band*. Sony 7315.

———. 1970. *A Rainbow in Curved Air*. Sony 7315.

Rochberg, George. 1953. *Music for the Magic Theatre*. Theodore Presser. New World 80462.

Rosenboom, David. 1975. *Portable Cold and Philosopher's Stones for Brains in Fours*. A.R.C. ST-1002.

Rzewski, Frederick. 1972. *Coming Together*. Soundings 3, no. 4. Hungaroton 12545.

Satie, Erik. 1893. *Vexations*. Salabert.

———. 1924. *Relâche*. Salabert.

Schäffer, Boguslaw. 1960. *Non-Stop*. PWM.

———. 1964. *Audiences No. 1-5*. PWM.

———. 1966. *Incident*. PWM.

Scriabin, Alexander. 1910. *Poem of Fire* (Symphony No. 5). Balawe Publishers. Allegretto 8170.

Songs of the Humpback Whale. 1968. Columbia ST-620.

Stockhausen, Karlheinz. 1968. *Aus den Sieben Tagen*. Universal Edition.

Strange, Allan. 1969. *No Dead Horses on the Moon*. Media Press.

Subotnick, Morton. 1960. *Mandolin*. MCA.

———. 1962. *Play*. MCA.

———. 1970. *A Ritual Game Room*. MCA.

The Vancouver Soundscape. 1973. Sonic Research Studio, Canada. EPM 186.

Young, La Monte. 1971. *Dream Houses*. Shandar 83.510.

CHAPTER 7

Further Readings

Abbott, Curtis. 1978. "Machine Tongues II." *Computer Music Journal*, 2, 4–6.

Anderton, Craig. 1986. *MIDI for Musicians*. New York: Amsco.

———. 1985. *Digital Delay Handbook*. New York: Amsco.

Appleton, Jon. 1989. *21st-century Musical Instruments: Hardware and Software*. Brooklyn, NY: Institute for Studies in American Music, Conservatory of Music, Brooklyn College of the City University of New York.

Appleton, Jon, and Ronald Perera, eds. 1974. *The Development and Practice of Electronic Music*. Englewood Cliffs, NJ: Prentice-Hall.

Babbitt, Milton. 1964. "An Introduction to the RCA Synthesizer." *Journal of Music Theory*, 8, 251–265.

Baggi, D., ed. 1992. *Readings in Computer-Generated Music*. New York: IEEE Press.

Baird, Jock. 1986. *Understanding MIDI*. New York: Amsco.

Bartle, Barton. 1987. *Computer Software in Music and Music Education: A Guide*. Metuchen, NJ: Scarecrow Press.

Bateman, Wayne. 1980. *Introduction to Computer Music*. New York: John Wiley and Sons.

Bates, John. 1988. *The Synthesizer*. Oxford: Oxford University Press.

Berio, Luciano. 1956. "The Studio di Fonologia Musicale of the Milan Radio." *Score*, 15, 89.

Boschi, Carlo. 1989. *Karlheinz Stockhausen*. Milano: Targa Italiana.

Bowen, Jeff. 1994. *Becoming a Computer Musician*. Indianapolis, IN: Sams Pub.

Brinkman, A. 1990. *Pascal Programming For Music Research*. Chicago: University of Chicago Press.

Cage, John. 1966. *Silence: Lectures and Writings*. Cambridge, MA: The MIT Press.

Cary, Tristram. 1992. *Dictionary of Musical Technology*. New York: Greenwood Press.

Chavez, Carlos. 1937. *Toward a New Music: Music and Electricity*. New York: W. W. Norton, Inc.

Chowning, John. 1971. "The Simulation of Moving Sound Sources." *Journal of the Audio Engineering Society*, 2, 2–6.

———. 1973. "The Synthesis of Complex Audio Spectra by Means of Frequency Modulation." *Journal of the Audio Engineering Society*, 21, 526–534.

Coker, Cecil, Peter Denes, and Elliot Pinson. 1963. *Speech/Synthesis*. Farmingdale, NY: Comspace Corp.

Cole, Hugo. *Sounds and Signs*. 1974. London: Oxford University Press.

Cope, David. 1975a. "A View on Electronic Music." *db: The Sound Engineering Magazine*, August, 30–32.

———. 1975b. "An Approach to Electronic Music Composition." *The Composer Magazine*, 6, 14–16.

Cott, Jonathan. 1973. *Stockhausen*. New York: Simon and Schuster.

Cross, Lowell M., ed. 1967. *A Bibliography of Electronic Music*. Toronto: University of Toronto Press.

Darter, Tom. 1984. *The Art of Electronic Music*. New York: Quill.

Davies, Hugh. 1964. "A Discography of Electronic Music and Musique Concrète." *Recorded Sound*, 14, 205–224.

Davies, Hugh, ed. 1968. *International Electronic Music Catalog*. Cambridge, MA: MIT Press.

Davis, Deta. 1988. *Computer Applications in Music: A Bibliography*. Madison, WI: A-R Editions.

DeFurio, Steve. 1985. *The Secrets of Analog and Digital Synthesis*. New York: Ferro.

DeFurio, Steve and Joe Scacciaferro. 1986. *The MIDI Implementation Book*. Pompton Lakes, NJ: Ferro Technologies.

De Poli, Giovanni. 1983. "A Tutorial on Digital Sound Synthesis Techniques." *Computer Music Journal*, 7, 8–26.

Deutsch, Herbert. 1993. *Electroacoustic Music: The First Century*. Miami: Belwin Mills.

Dobson, Richard. 1992. *A Dictionary of Electronic and Computer Music Technology: Instruments, Terms, Techniques*. New York: Oxford University Press.

Dockstader, Tod. 1968. "Inside-Out: Electronic Rock." *Electronic Music Review*, 5, 15–20.

Dodge, C. and T. A. Jerse. 1985. *Computer Music Synthesis, Composition and Performance*. New York: Schirmer Books.

Douglas, Alan. 1973. *Electronic Music Production*. London: Pitman Publishing.

Eimert, Herbert and Karlheinz Stockhausen, eds. 1965. *Die Reihe*, 1.

Ellis, Merrill. 1968. "Musique Concrète at Home." *Music Educators Journal*, 55, 94–96.

Emmerson, Simon. 1986. *The Language of Electromagnetic Music*. London: Macmillan Press.

Ernst, David. 1977. *The Evolution of Electronic Music*. New York: Schirmer Books.

Felder, David. 1976. "An Interview with Luciano Berio." *The Composer Magazine*, 7, 9–15.

von Foerster, Heinz, and James W. Beauchamp, eds. 1969. *Music by Computers*. New York: John Wiley and Sons.

Friedman, Dean. 1985. *The Complete Guide to Synthesizers, Sequencers and Drum Machines*. New York: Amsco.

Griffiths, Paul. 1979. *A Guide to Electronic Music*. London: Thane and Hudson.

Haus, Goffredo, ed. 1993. *Music Processing*. Madison, WI: A-R Editions.

Hiller, Lejaren and Leonard Isaacson. 1959. *Experimental Music*. New York: McGraw-Hill.

Holmes, Thomas B. 1985. *Electronic and Experimental Music*. New York: Charles Scribner's Sons.

Howe, Hubert S., Jr. 1977. "Electronic Music and Microcomputers." *Perspectives of New Music*, 18, 70–84.

———. 1975. *Electronic Music Synthesis*. New York: W. W. Norton and Co.

Judd, F. C. 1961. *Electronic Music and Musique Concrète*. London: Neville Spearman.

———. 1972. *Electronics in Music*. London: Neville Spearman.

Krênek, Ernst. 1958. "A Glance over the Shoulder of the Young." *Die Reihe*, 15–21.

Laske, Otto. 1977. "Toward a Theory of Interfaces for Computer Music Systems." *Computer Music Journal*, 1, 53–59.

Leitner, Gerhard. 1978. *Sound: Space*. New York: New York University Press.

Lincoln, Harry. 1970. *The Computer and Music*. Ithaca, NY: Cornell University Press.

Loy, Gareth. 1981. "The Composer Seduced into Programming." *Perspectives of New Music*, 20, 184–198.

———. 1985. "Musicians Make a Standard: The MIDI Phenomenon." *Computer Music Journal*, 9, 8–26.

———. 1987. "On the Scheduling of Multiple Parallel Processors Executing Synchronously." *Proceedings of the International Computer Music Conference*. San Francisco: Computer Music Association, 117–124.

Luening, Otto. 1964. "Some Random Remarks about Electronic Music." *Journal of Music Theory*, 8, 89–98.

———. 1968. "An Unfinished History of Electronic Music." *Music Educators Journal*, 55, 42–49.

———. 1981. *The Odyssey of An American Composer: The Autobiography of Otto Luening*. New York: C. F. Peters.

Maconie, Robin. 1971. "Stockhausen's Mikrophonie 1." *Perspectives of New Music*, 10, 92–101.

———. 1990. *The Works of Karlheinz Stockhausen; with a Foreword by Karlheinz Stockhausen*. 2nd ed. Oxford: Clarendon Press.

Manning, Peter. 1985. *Electronic and Computer Music*. Oxford, England: Clarendon Press.

Massey, Howard. 1987. *The Complete Guide to MIDI Software*. New York: Amsco.

Mathews, Max. 1969. *The Technology of Computer Music*. Cambridge, MA: MIT Press.

Mathews, Max and John Pierce, eds. 1989. *Current Directions in Computer Music Research*. Cambridge, MA: MIT Press.

McNabb, Michael. 1981. "Dreamsong: The Composition." *Computer Music Journal*, 5, 36–53.

Meyer, Robert G. 1964. "Technical Basis of Electronic Music." *Journal of Music Theory*, 8, 5–21.

Moore, F. R. 1978. "An Introduction to the Mathematics of Digital Signal Processing." *Computer Music Journal*, 2, 38–47.

———. 1981. "The Futures of Music." *Perspectives of New Music*, 20, 212–226.

———. 1987. "The Dysfunctions of MIDI." *Proceedings of the International Computer Music Conference*. San Francisco: Computer Music Association, 256–263.

———. 1990. *Elements of Computer Music*. Englewood Cliffs, NJ: Prentice Hall.

Moorer, James. 1964. "Musical Composition with the Computer." *Journal of the Acoustical Society of America*, 34, 36–52.

———. 1972. "Music and Computer Composition." *Communications of the ACM*, 15, 104–113.

———. 1977. "Signal Processing Aspects of Computer Music—A Survey." *Proceedings of the IEEE*, 65, 1108–1137.

Morgan, Christopher. 1980. *The BYTE Book of Computer Music*. New York: BYTE.

Mumma, Gordon. 1967. "The ONCE Festival and How It Happened." *Arts in Society*, 4, 381–398.

Naumann, J. and James Wagner. 1986. *Analog Electronic Music Technologies and Voltage-Controlled Synthesizer Studios*. New York: Schirmer Books.

Noll, D. Justus. 1994. *Musik-Programmierung: MIDI, C und Multimedia*. Reading, MA: Addison-Wesley.

Nyman, Michael. 1974. *Experimental Music*. London: Studio Vista.

Oliveros, Pauline. 1969. "Tape Delay Techniques for Electronic Music." *The Composer Magazine*, 1, 135–143.

Otsuka, Akira and Akihiko Nakajima. 1987. *MIDI Basics*. New York: Amsco.

Pellegrino, Ronald. 1973. "Some Thoughts on Thinking for the Electronic Music Synthesizer." *Proceedings* (American Society of University Composers), 7, 47–55.

Pellman, Samuel. 1994. *An Introduction to the Creation of Electroacoustic Music*. Belmont, CA: Wadsworth Pub. Co.

Pohlmann, Ken. 1985. *Principles of Digital Audio*. Indianapolis: Howard W. Sams Company.

Pope, S. T., ed. 1990. *The Well-Tempered Object*. Cambridge, MA: MIT Press.

Prieberg, F. K. 1960. *Musica ex Machina*. Berlin: Verlag Ullstein.

Risset, Jean-Claude. 1980. *Document Paru*. Paris: IRCAM.

———. 1985. "Computer Music Experiments 1964–" *Computer Music Journal*, 9, 11–18.

Roads, Curtis. 1985. *Composers and the Computer*. Madison, WI: A-R Editions.

———. 1996. *The Computer Music Tutorial*. Cambridge, MA: MIT Press.

———. 1997. *Musical Signal Processing*. Lisse. Exton, PA: Swets and Zeitlinger.

Roads, Curtis, ed. 1989. *The Music Machine: Selected Readings from Computer Music Journal*. Cambridge, MA: MIT Press.

Rothstein, J. 1991. *MIDI: A Comprehensive Introduction*. Madison, WI: A-R Editions.

Rudolph, Thomas. 1996. *Teaching Music with Technology*. Chicago: GIA Publications.

Russcol, Herbert. 1972. *The Liberation of Sound*. Englewood Cliffs, NJ: Prentice-Hall.

Schaeffer, Pierre. 1952. *A la Recherche d'une Musique Concrète*. Paris: Editions du Seuil.

Schrader, Barry. 1982. *Introduction to Electro-Acoustic Music*. Englewood Cliffs, NJ: Prentice-Hall, Inc.

Schuller, Gunther. 1964. "Conversation with Varèse." *Perspectives of New Music*, 3, 117–121.

Schwartz, Elliott. 1972. *Electronic Music: A Listener's Guide*. New York: Praeger Publishers.

Smith, L. C. 1972. "Score, A Musician's Approach to Computer Music." *Journal of the Audio Engineering Society*, 7–14.

———. 1973. "Editing and Printing Music by Computers." *Journal of Music Theory*, 17, 292–309.

Stockhausen, Karlheinz. 1969. "Not a Special Day." *The Composer Magazine*, 1, 59–72.

———. 1972. "The Concept of Unity in Electronic Music." In *Perspectives on Contemporary Music Theory*. Benjamin Boretz and Edward T. Cone, eds. New York: W. W. Norton and Co., 214–225.

Strange, Allen. 1982. *Electronic Music*. 2nd ed. Dubuque, IA: Wm. C. Brown Company Publishers.

Stravinsky, Igor and Robert Craft. 1963. *Dialogues and a Diary*. Garden City, NY: Doubleday and Co.

Strawn, John, ed. 1985a. *Digital Audio Signal Processing*. Madison, WI: A-R Editions.

———. 1985b. *Digital Audio Engineering*. Madison, WI: A-R Editions.

Treib, Marc. 1996. *Space Calculated in Seconds: The Philips Pavilion, Le Corbusier, Edgard Varèse*. Princeton, NJ: Princeton University Press.

Trythall, Gilbert. 1973. *Electronic Music*. New York: Grosset and Dunlap.

Ussachevsky, Vladimir. 1960. "Note on a Piece for Tape Recorder." In *Problems of Modern Music*. Paul Henry Lang, ed. New York: W. W. Norton and Co., 64–71.

———. 1961. "Sound Materials in the Experimental Media of Musique Concrète, Tape Music and Electronic Music." *Journal of the Acoustical Society of America*, 29, 1181–1194.

Varèse, Edgard. 1936. "Lecture at Mary Austin House." Santa Fe.

Varèse, Louise Norton. 1972. *A Looking Glass Diary*. New York: W. W. Norton.

Vercoe, Barry. 1968. "Electronic Sounds and the Sensitive Performer." *Music Educators Journal*, 55, 104–107.

Webster, Peter Richard and David Brian Williams. 1996. *Experiencing Music Technology*. New York: Schirmer Books.

Wells, Thomas and Eric Vogel. 1974. *The Technique of Electronic Music*. Austin, TX: University Stores.

Wen-Chung, Chou. 1966. "Varèse: A Sketch of the Man and His Music." *Musical Quarterly*, 52, 151–170.

———. 1967. "The Liberation of Sound." In *Contemporary Composers on Contemporary Music*. Barney Childs and Elliott Schwartz, eds. New York: Holt, Rinehart and Winston.

Wilson, Galen and David Cope. 1969. "An Interview with Pierre Boulez." *The Composer Magazine*, 1, 78–85.

Winkler, Todd. 1998. *Composing Interactive Music: Techniques and Ideas Using Max*. Cambridge, MA: MIT Press.

Wörner, Karl. 1973. *Stockhausen, Life and Work*. Translated by Bill Hopkins. Berkeley: University of California Press.

Yavelow, Christopher. 1993. *The Macintosh Music and Sound Bible*. IDG Books.

Compact Discs, Recordings, and Publishers

Appleton, Jon. 1990. *Brush Canyon*. Centaur 2052.

———. 1990. *Degitaru Ongaku*. Centaur 2052.

Albright, William. 1967. *Organbook I*. Jobert.

Anderson, Ruth. 1980. *I Come Out of Your Sleep*. XI Compact Disks 118.

Austin, Larry. 1988. *Sonata Concertante*. Centaur CRC 2029.

Babbitt, Milton. 1963. *Composition for Synthesizer*. Columbia 6566.

———. 1964. *Philomel for Soprano and 4-track Tape*. New World 80466.

———. 1967. *Correspondences for String Orchestra and Synthesized Magnetic Tape*. DG 31698.

Baitz, Rick. 1985. *Kaleidocycles for Synclavier*. Centaur 2039.

Beerman, Burton. 1972. *Sensations for Clarinet and Tape*. ACA.

Behrman, David. 1977. *On the Other Ocean*. Lovely Music Records 1041.

Berio, Luciano. 1959. *Thema: Omaggio à Joyce*. Zerboni Editions.

———. 1961. *Visage*. BMG Ricordi 1017.

Beyer, Johanna. 1938. *Music of the Spheres*. Monroe Street MSM 60101.

Bolcom, William. 1967. *Black Host*. Nonesuch 71260.

Borden, David. 1970. *Mother Mallard*. Cunyform 16.

Boulez, Pierre. 1982. *Répons*. DG 0173.

Bresnick, Martin. 1987. *Lady Nells Dumpe*. Centaur 2039.

Cage, John. 1960. *Imaginary Landscape No. 4*. C. F. Peters. Madacy Records 6179.

———. 1961. *Imaginary Landscape No. 5*. C. F. Peters. Madacy Records 6179.

———. 1963. *Variations IV*. Hat Hut 6176.

Chadabe, Joel. 1984. *Follow Me Softly for Percussion and Synclavier*. Centaur 2310.

Chowning, John. 1972. *Turenas*. Wergo 2012-50.

———. 1977. *Stria*. Wergo 2012-50.

Cope, David. 1974. *Arena*. Carl Fischer.

———. 1979. *Glassworks*. Smithsonian Folkways 33452.

Dashow, James. 1982. *Second Voyage*. CRI 456.

Davidovsky, Mario. 1965. *Synchronisms 3*. Edward B. Marks Corp. Delos 1011.

———. 1969. *Synchronisms 5*. Edward B. Marks Corp. CRI 611.

———. 1969. *Synchronisms 6*. Edward B. Marks Corp. CRI 707.

Dodge, Charles. 1970. *Earth's Magnetic Field*. New World 80521.

———. 1973. *Speech Songs*. New Albany 43.

Druckman, Jacob. 1969. *Animas II*. MCA Music. CRI 781.

Eaton, John. n.d. *Concert Piece for Synket and Orchestra*. Turnabout 34428.

Ellis, Merrill. 1971. *Kaleidoscope*. Louisville 711.

Erb, Donald. 1969. *In No Strange Land*. Merion Music.

———. 1971. *And Then Toward the End*. New World 80457.

Felciano, Richard. 1971. *God of the Expanding Universe*. E. C. Schirmer.

———. 1976. *"and from the abyss."* E. C. Schirmer. Opus One 19.

———. 1976. *Crasis*. E. C. Schirmer.

Gerhard, Roberto. 1960. *Collages* (Symphony 3). Chandos 9556.

Harvey, Jonathan. 1990. *Ritual Melodies for Quadraphonic Tape*. Bridge 9031.

Henry, Pierre. 1987. *The Veil of Orpheus*. Musique D'abord 490 5200.

———. 1994. *Variations for Door and a Sigh*. Musique D'abord 490 5200.

Hiller, Lejaren. 1981. *Quadrilateral for Piano and Tape*. Presser. 2E2M 1014.

Hunt, Jerry. 1988. *Fluid for dual Synclaviers*. Centaur 2029.

Jaffe, David. 1986. *Silicon Valley Breakdown*. Well-Tempered Productions 5184.

Karpen, Richard. 1992. *Denouement for Electronics*. Centaur 2144.

Kupferman, Meyer. 1974. *Concerto for Cello, Tape and Orchestra*. VB2 5158.

Lansky, Paul. 1979. *Six Fantasies on a Poem by Thomas Campion*. CRI 456.

Ligeti, György. 1985. *Etudes*. Col Legno 31815.

Lockwood, Annea. 1975. *World Rhythms*. XI Compact Disks 118.

Lucier, Alvin. 1979. *Music on a Long Thin Wire*. Lovely Music 1011.

———. 1984. *Crossings for Small Orchestra with Slow-Sweep Pure Wave Oscillator*. Lovely Music 1018.

Luening, Otto. 1951. *Fantasy in Space*. Peters. CRI 611.

———. 1957. *Poem in Cycles and Bells, Orch and Tape*. CRI 6011.

Machover, Tod. 1990. *Flora for Computer-Generated Tape*. Bridge 9020.

Marshall, Ingram. 1982. *Fog Tropes for Brass Sextet, Foghorns, and Tape*. New Albany 79249.

McLean, Barton. 1974. *Dimensions II*. Capstone 8637.

———. 1979. *Song of the Nahuatl*. CRI 764.

McLean, Priscilla. 1980. *Invisible Chariots*. CRI 764.

McNabb, Michael. 1978. *Dreamsong*. Wergo.

———. 1989. *Invisible Cities*. Wergo 2015-50.

Melby, John. 1984. *Concerto for Clarinet and Synthesized Sound*. Zuma 105.

———. 1986. *Concerto for Violin and Computer-Synthesized Tape*. New World 80333.

Mimaroglu, Ilhan. 1972. *Wings of the Delirious Demon*. Atlantic 91305.

Morrill, Dexter. 1989. *Sketches for Invisible Man for Soprano Saxophone and Computer Music System.* Centaur 2214.

———. 1976. *Studies for Trumpet and Computer.* Centaur 2214.

Mumma, Gordon. 1963. *Megaton for Wm. Burroughs.* Lovely Music 1091.

———. 1967. *Hornpipe.* Mainstream 5010.

Oliveros, Pauline. 1966. *Alien Bog.* Pogus 210122.

———. 1967. *Beautiful Soop.* Pogus 210122.

Randall, J. K. 1964. *Quartets in Pairs.* Nonesuch 71245.

———. 1967. *Lyric Variations for Violin and Computer.* Vanguard 10057.

Risset, Jean-Claude. 1977. *Inharmonic Soundscapes.*

———. 1983. *L'Autre face for Soprano and Electronics.* Neuma 45073.

Stockhausen, Karlheinz. 1956. *Gesang der Jünglinge.* DG 138811.

———. 1960. *Kontakte.* Universal Edition.

———. 1966. *Telemusik.* Universal Edition. DG 17012.

———. 1968. *Stimmung.* Universal Edition. Hyperion 66115.

———. 1969. *Hymnen.* Universal Edition. DG 2707039.

Subotnick, Morton. 1967. *Silver Apples of the Moon.* Wergo 2035.

———. 1968. *The Wild Bull.* Wergo 2035.

———. 1970. *Touch.* Wergo 2014.

Teitelbaum, Richard. 1988. *Golem 1.* Centaur CRC-2039.

Thome, Diane. 1967. *Anais.* Centaur 2229.

———. 1986. *Levadi for Soprano and Tape.* Centaur 2229.

Truax, Barry. 1975. *Sonic Landscapes No. 3.* Melbourne 4033.

Ussachevsky, Vladimir. 1951. *A Piece for Tape Recorder.* CRI 611.

Ussachevsky, Vladimir and Otto Luening. n.d. *Concerted Piece for Tape Recorder and Orchestra.* CRI 227.

Varèse , Edgard. 1954. *Déserts.* G. Schirmer. Erato 14332.

———. 1958. *Poème électronique.* One Way Records 26791.

Vercoe, Barry. 1978. *Synapse for Viola and Computer.* CRI 393.

Wuorinen, Charles. 1969. *Times Encomium.* Music and Arts 932.

CHAPTER 8

Further Readings

Ames, Charles. 1982. "Crystals: Recursive Structures in Automated Composition." *Computer Music Journal, 6,* 46–64.

———. 1987a. "Automated Composition in Retrospect: 1956–1986." *Leonardo: Journal of the International Society for Science, Technology and the Arts.* Oxford: Pergamon Press, 169–185.

———. 1987b. "AI in Music." *Encyclopedia of Artificial Intelligence.* New York: John Wiley and Sons, 638–642.

———. 1990. "Statistics and Compositional Balance." *Perspectives of New Music, 28,* 80–111.

Balaban, M., K. Ebcioglu, and O. Laske, eds. 1992. *Understanding Music with AI: Perspectives on Music Cognition.* Cambridge, MA: MIT Press.

Barbaud, P. 1969. "Algorithmic Music." Paris: *Systems Bulletin.*

Baroni, Mario and Laura Callegari, eds. 1984. *Musical Grammars and Computer Analysis: Atti del Convegno (Modena, 4–6 Ottobre 1982).* Florence, Italy: L. S. Olschki.

Bharucha, Jamshed. 1987. "Music Cognition and Perceptual Facilitation: A Connectionist Framework." *Music Perception, 5,* 1–30.

Bharucha, Jamshed and Peter Todd. 1989. "Modeling the Perception of Tonal Structure with Neural Nets." *Computer Music Journal, 13,* 44–53.

Bois, Mario. 1980. *Iannis Xenakis: The Man and His Music: A Conversation with the Composer and a Description of His Works.* Westport, CT: Greenwood Press.

Bolognesi, Tommaso. 1983. "Automated Composition: Experiments with Self-Similar Music." *Computer Music Journal, 7,* 25–36.

Charniak, E., C. Riesbeck, and D. McDermott. 1979. *Artificial Intelligence Programming Techniques.* Hillsdale, NJ: Lawrence Erlbaum Associates.

Charniak, Eugene and Drew McDermott. 1984. *Introduction to Artificial Intelligence.* Reading, MA: Addison-Wesley Publishing Company.

Cope, David. 1987a. "An Expert System for Computer-Assisted Music Composition." *Computer Music Journal, 11,* 30–46.

———. 1987b. "Experiments in Music Intelligence." *Proceedings of the International Computer Music Conference.* San Francisco: Computer Music Association, 174–181.

———. 1990. "Pattern Matching as an Engine for the Computer Simulation of Musical Style." *Proceedings of the International Computer Music Conference.* Computer Music Association, 288–294.

———. 1991. *Computers and Music Style.* Madison, WI: A-R Editions.

———. 1996. *Experiments in Musical Intelligence.* Madison, WI: A-R Editions.

Desain, Peter. 1992. *Music, Mind and Machine: Studies in Computer Music, Music Cognition and Artificial Intelligence.* Amsterdam: Thesis Publishers.

Dodge, Charles. 1988. "Profile of a Musical Fractal." *Computer Music Journal, 10,* 10–14.

Dodge, Charles and Curtis Bahn. 1986. "Musical Fractals." *BYTE Magazine,* June, 185–196.

Dowling, W. J. and D. L. Harwood. 1985. *Music Cognition.* Academic Press.

Duisberg, Robert. 1984. "On the Role of Affect in Artificial Intelligence and Music." *Perspectives of New Music, 23,* 6–37.

Fleuret, Maurice. 1981. *Iannis Xenakis.* Paris: Salabert.

Forte, A. 1967. "Computer-implemented Analysis of Musical Structure." *Computer Applications in Music,* 20–34.

Garland, Peter. 1984. *The Music of James Tenney.* Santa Fe, NM: Soundings Press.

Gill, S. A. 1973. "A Technique for the Composition of Music in a Computer." *Computer Journal, 6,* 6–12.

Hiller, Lejaren. 1967. "Programming a Computer for Musical Composition." In *Computer Applications in Music.* Gerald Lefkoff, ed. Morgantown: West Virginia University Library, 65–88.

———. 1970. "Music Composed with Computers: A Historical Survey." *The Computer and Music.* H. Lincoln, ed. Ithaca, NY: Cornell University Press.

———. 1981. "Composing with Computers: A Progress Report." *Computer Music Journal*, 5, 7–21.

Hiller, Lejaren and Robert Baker. 1963. *Computer Cantata*. Bryn Mawr, PA: Presser.

Hiller, Lejaren and Leonard Isaacson. 1959. *Experimental Music*. New York: McGraw-Hill.

Holtzman, S. R. 1981. "Using Generative Grammars for Music Composition." *Computer Music Journal*, 5, 51–64.

Kelly, Owen. 1996. *Digital Creativity*. London: Calouste Gulbenkian Foundation.

Koenig, Gottfried Michael. 1970. "Project 1." *Electronic Music Reports*, 1, 32–44.

———. 1983. "Aesthetic Integration of Computer-Composed Scores." *Computer Music Journal*, 7, 27–32.

Lansky, Paul. 1990. "A View from the Bus: When Machines Make Music." *Perspectives of New Music*, 28, 102–111.

Laske, Otto. 1973. "In Search of a Generative Grammar for Music." *Perspectives of New Music*, 12, 351–378.

———. 1984. "KEITH: A Rule-System for Making Music-Analytical Discoveries." In *Musical Grammars and Computer Analysis: Atti del Convegno (Modena, 4–6 Ottobre 1982)*. Mario Baroni and Laura Callegari, eds. Florence, Italy: L. S. Olschki, 165–199.

Lerdahl, Fred. 1987. "Cognitive Constraints on Compositional Systems." *Generative Processes in Music*. J. Sloboda, ed. London: Oxford University Press, 229–244.

Lerdahl, Fred and Ray Jackendoff. 1977. "Toward a Formal Theory of Music." *Journal of Music Theory*, 21, 111–172.

———. 1983. *A Generative Theory of Tonal Music*. Cambridge, MA: MIT Press.

Levitt, David. 1984. "Machine Tongues X: Constraint Languages." *Computer Music Journal*, 8, 9–21.

Lincoln, Harry, ed. 1970. *The Computer and Music*. Ithaca, NY: Cornell University Press.

Lischka, Christoph. 1987. "Connectionist Models of Musical Thinking." *Proceedings of the International Computer Music Conference*. San Francisco: Computer Music Association, 190–196.

Lisle, Edward and Christopher Longuet-Higgins. 1989. "Modelling Musical Cognition." *Contemporary Music Review*, 3, 15–27.

Longuet-Higgins, H. Christopher. 1987. *Mental Processes*. Cambridge, MA: MIT Press.

Loy, Gareth. 1989. "Composing with Computers: A Survey of Some Compositional Formalisms and Music Programming Languages." In *Current Directions in Computer Music Research*. Max Mathews and John R. Pierce, eds. Cambridge, MA: MIT Press, 291–396.

Matossian, Nouritza. 1990. *Iannis Xenakis*. White Plains, NY: Pro/Am Music Resources.

Meehan, James R. 1980. "An Artificial Intelligence Approach to Tonal Music Theory." *Computer Music Journal*, 4, 60–65.

Puckette, Millard. 1991. "Combining Event and Signal Processing in the MAX Graphical Programming Environment." *Computer Music Journal*, 15, 68–77.

Reichardt, Jasia. 1971. *Cybernetics, Art and Ideas*. Greenwich, CT: New York Graphic Society Ltd.

Roads, C. 1978. "Composing Grammars." *Proceedings of the 1977 International Computer Music Conference*. San Francisco: Computer Music Association, 26–30.

———. 1984. "An Overview of Music Representations." In *Musical Grammars and Computer Analysis: Atti del Convegno (Modena, 4–6 Ottobre 1982)*. Mario Baroni and Laura Callegari, eds. Florence, Italy: L. S. Olschki, 7–37.

———. 1985. "Grammars as Representations for Music." in *Foundations of Computer Music*. Curtis Roads and John Strawn, eds. Cambridge, MA: MIT Press, 403–422.

———. 1986a. "The Tsukuba Musical Robot." *Computer Music Journal*, 10, 39–43.

———. 1986b. "Symposium on Computer Music Composition." *Computer Music Journal*, 10, 40–63.

Rowe, R. 1992. *Interactive Music Systems*. Cambridge, MA: MIT Press.

Ruwet, N. 1975. "Théorie et Méthodes dans les études Musicales." *Musique en Jeu*, 17, 11–22.

Scarborough, Ben Miller and Jacqueline Jones. 1989. "Connectionist Models for Tonal Analysis." *Computer Music Journal*, 13, 49–55.

Schillinger, Joseph. 1948. *The Mathematical Basis of the Arts*. New York: The Philosophical Library.

———. 1978. *The Schillinger System of Musical Composition*. New York: Da Capo Press.

Smoliar, Stephen W. 1980. "A Computer Aid for Schenkerian Analysis." *Computer Music Journal*, 4, 41–59.

Steedman, Mark J. 1984. "A Generative Grammar for Jazz Chord Sequences." *Music Perception*, 2, 22–34.

"Syncopation by Automation." 1956. *Data from ElectroData*. Pasadena: Electro-Data Division of Burroughs, Inc.

Todd, Peter. 1988. "A Sequential Network Design for Musical Applications." *Proceedings of the 1988 Connectionist Models Summer School*. San Mateo, CA: Morgan Kaufmann, Publishers, 196–204.

———. 1989. "A Connectionist Approach to Algorithmic Composition." *Computer Music Journal*, 13, 27–43.

Todd, P. M., and D. G. Loy, eds. 1992. *Music and Connectionism*. Cambridge, MA: MIT Press.

Varga, Bálint András. 1996. *Conversations with Iannis Xenakis*. London: Faber and Faber.

Winograd, T. 1968. "Linguistics and the Computer Analysis of Tonal Harmony." *Journal of Music Theory*, 12, 2–49.

Winsor, Phil. 1987. *Computer-Assisted Music Composition*. Princeton, NJ: Petrocelli Books, Inc.

Xenakis, Iannis. 1971a. "Free Stochastic Music from the Computer." *Cybernetics, Art and Ideas*. Jasia Reichardt, ed. Greenwich: New York Graphic Society Ltd., 111–123.

———. 1971b. *Formalized Music*. Bloomington: Indiana University Press.

———. 1976. *Musique. Architecture*. Paris: Casterman.

———. 1985a. *Arts/science, alliages. English. Arts-sciences, alloys: the thesis defense of Iannis Xenakis before Oliver Messiaen, Michel Ragon, Olivier Revault d'Allonnes, Michel Serres, and Bernard Teyssèdre*. Translated by Sharon Kanach. New York: Pendragon Press.

———. 1985b. *Arts/Sciences: Alloys*. New York: Pendragon Press.

Compact Discs, Recordings, and Publishers

Bischoff, John and Tim Perkis. 1989. *Artificial Horizon*. Artefact 1003.

Brown, Chris. 1989. *Snakecharmer—Obedience School*. Artefact 1001.

Brün, Herbert. 1964. *Gestures for Eleven*. CRI 321.

Cage, John and Lejaren Hiller. 1968. *HPSCHD*. C. F. Peters.

Chadabe, Joel. 1984. *Follow Me Softly*. Centaur 2310.

———. 1989. *Modalities for an Interactive Computer System*. Centaur 2047.

Cope, David. 1994. *Bach by Design*. Centaur 2184.

———. 1997. *Classical Music Composed by Computer*. Centaur 2329.

Dodge, Charles. 1970. *Earth's Magnetic Field*.

Hiller, Lejaren. 1964. *Machine Music*. Presser.

Hiller, Lejaren and Robert Baker. 1968. *Computer Cantata*. Theodore Presser.

The Hub: Computer Network Music (John Bischoff, Tim Perkis, Chris Brown, Scot Gresham-Lancaster, Mark Trayle, Phil Stone): Perry Mason in East Germany, Farabi, Rol'em, Borrowing and Stealing, Whackers, Hot Pig, Dovetail, The Minister of Pitch, Simple Degradation. Artefact 1002.

Jaffe, David. 1986. *Silicon Valley Breakdown*. Well-Tempered Productions 5264.

Lerdahl, Fred. 1978. *String Quartet No. 1*. CRI 551.

Nelson, Gary Lee. 1992. *Fractal Mountains*. Wergo 2030-2.

Scalatti, Carla. 1989. *sunSurgeAutomata*. Centaur 2045.

Xenakis, Iannis. 1954. *Metastasis*. Boosey and Hawkes.

———. 1956. *Pithoprakta*. Boosey and Hawkes.

———. 1960. *Atrées*. Salabert.

———. 1962. *Morsima-Amorsima*. Salabert. Accord 205652.

———. 1965. *Akrata*. Salabert. Mode 56.

———. 1971. *Mikka*. Salabert. Accord 205652.

CHAPTER 9

Further Readings

Duckworth, William. 1995. *Talking Music: Conversations with John Cage, Philip Glass, Laurie Anderson, and Five Generations of American Experimental Composers*. New York: Schirmer Books.

The Experimental Music Catalog. n.d. London, England.

Gagne, Cole and Tracy Caras. 1982. *Soundpieces: Interviews with American Composers*. Metuchen, NJ: The Scarecrow Press, Inc.

Garland, D. 1984. "Creating Einstein on the Beach: Philip Glass and Robert Wilson Speak to Maxime de la Falaise." *The Audience Magazine of BAM's Next Wave Festival*, 2, 1.

Glass, Philip. 1987. *Music by Philip Glass*. Edited and with supplementary material by Robert T. Jones. New York: Harper and Row.

Glass, Philip and Robert Wilson. n.d. *Einstein on the Beach*. New York: EOS Enterprises Inc.

Jones, Robert T. 1979. "Musician of the Month: Philip Glass." *High Fidelity/Musical America*, 29, 26.

Kupbovic, L. 1980. "The Role of Tonality in Contemporary and `Up-to-date' Composition." *Tempo*, 135, 15–19.

Mertens, Wim. 1983. *American Minimal Music*. New York: Kahn and Averill.

Palmer, R. and Philip Glass. 1979. *Einstein on the Beach*. Liner notes to the Tomato 4-2901.

Pavo, Roberto. 1987. *Future Now!* New York: Futurista Publications.

Reich, Steve. 1969. "Music as a Gradual Process." In *Anti-Illusion Catalog of the Whitney Museum*. New York.

———. 1974. *Writings About Music*. New York: New York University Press.

Rzewski, Frederick. 1974. "Prose Music." In *Dictionary of Contemporary Music*. John Vinton, ed. New York: E. P. Dutton and Co., 593–595.

Schaeffer, John. 1987. *New Sounds, A Listener's Guide to New Music*. New York: Harper and Row, Publishers.

Schwarz, K. Robert. 1981. "Steve Reich: Music as a Gradual Process." *Perspectives of New Music*, 20, 225–286.

———. 1996. Minimalists. London: Phaidon.

Scott, Stephen. 1974. "The Music of Steve Reich." *Numus West*, 6, 21–27.

Simms, Bryan R. 1986. *Music of the Twentieth Century, Style and Structure*. New York: Schirmer Books.

Strickland, Edward. 1993. *Minimalism—Origins*. Bloomington: Indiana University Press.

Templier, Pierre-Daniel. 1969. *Erik Satie*. Translated by Elena French and David French. Cambridge, MA: MIT Press.

Young, La Monte and Marian Zazeela. 1969. *Selected Writings*. Munich: Heiner Friedrich.

———. 1970. "Sound is God: The Singing of Pran Nath." *Village Voice*, April 30.

Compact Discs, Recordings, and Publishers

Adams, John. 1978. *Phrygian Gates*. Albany 38.

———. 1978. *Shaker Loops*. New Albion 14.

———. 1985. *Harmonielehre*. EMI 55051.

Ashley, Robert. 1977. *Private Parts*. Lovely Music 4917.

Budd, Harold. 1991. *She is a Phantom*. New Albion 66.

Corner, Philip. 1977. *Ear Journeys: Water*. Printed Editions.

Eno, Brian. 1980. *Ambient 2—The Plateau of Mirrors*. Editions EG.

Glass, Philip. 1969. *Music in Fifths*. Nonesuch 79326.

———. 1969. *Music in Similar Motion*. Nonesuch 79326.

———. 1972. *Music with Changing Parts*. Nonesuch 79325.

———. 1976. *Einstein on the Beach*. New World 80313.

Górecki, Henryk-Mikolaj. 1969. *Old Polish Music for Brass and Strings*. Argo 436835.

———. 1976. *Symphony No. 3 for Soprano and Orchestra*. RCA 68387.

———. 1990. *Good Night (Requiem)*. Nonesuch 79362.

Harrison, Lou. 1992. *Suite No. 2 for Guitar and Percussion*. Bridge 9041.

Pärt, Arvo. 1977. *Cantus in Memory of Benjamin Britten for Bell and String Orchestra*. RCA 68061.

———. 1977. *Tabula rasa*. Bis 834.

———. 1983. *Fratres*. Bis 574.

———. 1991. *Summa for Orchestra*. Bis 834.

———. 1992. *Berliner Messe*. Koch 7177.

Reich, Steve. 1965. *It's Gonna Rain*. Nonesuch 79169.

———. 1970. *Four Organs*. Nonesuch 79451.

———. 1976. *Music for 18 Musicians*. Nonesuch 79448.

Riley, Terry. 1964. *In C*. Sony 7178.

———. 1968. *Poppy Nogood and the Phantom Band*. Sony 7315.

———. 1969. *A Rainbow in Curved Air*. Sony 7315.

Rzewski, Frederick. 1972. *Coming Together*. Soundings, 3, no. 4, Hungaraton 12545.

Young, La Monte. 1981. *The Well-Tuned Piano*. Gramavision 79452.

———. 1985. *The Second Dream of the High Tension Line Stepdown Transformer for Trumpet Ensemble*. Gramavision 79467.

CHAPTER 10

Further Readings

Burrows, David. 1972. "Music and the Biology of Time." *Perspectives of New Music*, 11, 1–10.

Cage, John. 1974. "The Future of Music." *Numus West*, 5, 6–15.

Cope, David. 1972. "A Post Avant-Garde." *The Composer Magazine*, 3, 61–65.

———. 1973. "Footnotes." *The Composer Magazine*, 4, 52–54.

———. 1986. "George Crumb: Profile of a Composer." In *Biography of George Crumb*. New York: C. F. Peters Corporation, 8–15.

Cope, David and Galen Wilson, 1969. "An Interview with Pierre Boulez." *The Composer Magazine*, 1, 78–85.

Dalmonte, Rossana and Bálint András Varga. 1985. *Luciano Berio: Two Interviews*. Translated and edited by David Osmond-Smith. New York: Marion Boyars.

Gillespie, Don, ed. 1986. *George Crumb: Profile of a Composer*. New York: C. F. Peters Corporation.

Griffiths, Paul. 1983. *György Ligeti*. London: Robson Books.

Harbison, John. 1972. "Peter Maxwell Davies' Taverner." *Perspectives of New Music*, 1, 233–240.

Henze, Hans Werner. 1982. *Music and Politics*. London: Faber and Faber.

Hughes, Robert. 1972. "The Decline and Fall of the Avant-Garde." *Time*, December 18.

Ives, Charles. 1962. "Music and Its Future." In *American Composers on American Music*. Henry Cowell, ed. New York: Unger Publishing Co., 191–198.

Johnson, Tom. 1980. "Exotic Music: Borrowing Is Not So Bad." *Village Voice*, 25.

Johnston, Ben. 1968. "On Context." *ASUC Proceedings*, 3, 32–36.

Kaufman, Harold. 1970. "Ligeti's Zweites Streichquartet." *Melos*, 37, 181–186.

Kolb, Barbara. 1981. *Soundings*. New York: Boosey and Hawkes.

Ligeti, György. 1960. "Metamorphosis of Musical Form." *Die Reihe*, 7, 5–19.

———. 1965. *Requiem*. New York: Peters.

———. 1968. *Witold Lutosławski, and Ingvar Lidholm. Three Aspects of New Music* (from a composition seminar in Stockholm). Stockholm: Nordiska Musikförlaget.

———. 1972. "Conversations with Ligeti at Stanford." *Numus West*, 2, 5–8.

Osmond-Smith, David. 1985. *Playing on Words: A Guide to Luciano Berio's Sinfonia*. London: Royal Musical Association.

Pavo, Roberto. 1987. *Future Now*. New York: Futurista Publications.

Poissenot, Jacques M. 1974. "Luciano Berio." In *Dictionary of Contemporary Music*, John Vinton, ed. New York: E. P. Dutton and Co., 78–79.

Richart, Robert W. 1990. *György Ligeti: A Bio-Bibliography*. New York: Greenwood Press.

Rochberg, George. 1963. "The New Image of Music." *Perspectives of New Music*, 2, 1–10.

———. 1969. "No Center." *The Composer Magazine*, 2, 86–91.

Salzman, Eric. 1988. *Twentieth-Century Music: An Introduction*. 3rd ed. Englewood Cliffs, NJ: Prentice-Hall.

Santi, Piero. 1958. "Luciano Berio." *Die Reihe*, 4, 98–102.

Schwartz, Elliott and Barney Childs, eds. 1967. *Contemporary Composers on Contemporary Music*. New York: Holt, Rinehart, and Winston.

Stravinsky, Igor. 1955. "Apropos Le Sacre du Printemps." Los Angeles: Columbia Records 5179.

Stucky, Steven. 1981. *Lutosławski and his Music*. Cambridge: Cambridge University Press.

Varga, Bálint András. 1976. *Witold Lutosławski*. London: Chester Music.

Compact Discs, Recordings, and Publishers

Berio, Luciano. 1966. *Sequenza IV*. Universal Edition. MD&G 6130754.

———. 1968. *Sinfonia*. Universal Edition. Erato 2292-45228-2.

———. 1975. *Chemins IV for Oboe and Strings*. Universal Edition. Sony 45862.

———. 1991. *Continuo for Orchestra*. Universal Edition. Teldec 4509-66596-2.

Cope, David. 1977. *Threshold and Visions*. New York: Alexander Broude. Smithsonian Folkways 33452.

———. 1981. *Concert for Piano and Orchestra*. Opus One 82.

Crumb, George. 1970. *Ancient Voices of Children*. Peters. Col Legno 31876.

———. 1974. *Makrokosmos III*. Peters. Musique Suisses 6091.

Davies, Peter Maxwell. 1969. *Eight Songs for a Mad King*. Boosey and Hawkes. Unicorn 9052.

del Tredici, David. 1976. *Final Alice*. Collins Classics 1287.

Druckman, Jacob. 1972. *Windows*. MCA Music. CRI 781.

Husa, Karel. 1970. *Apotheosis of This Earth*. Associated Music Publishers. Louisville 005.

———. 1973. *Sonata for Violin and Piano*. New World 80493.

Ives, Charles. 1906. *Central Park in the Dark*. AMP. DG 23243.

Kokkonen, Joonas. 1961. *Symphony No. 2*. Bis 498.

Kolb, Barbara. 1981. *Soundings*. Boosey & Hawkes.

Ligeti, György. 1963. *Aventures*. Peters. Wergo 60045.

———. 1965. *Requiem*. Peters. Wergo 60045.

———. 1967. *Lontano*. Schott. Wergo 60045.

Nono, Luigi. 1962. *Canti di Vita e d'Amore*. Ars Viva. Wergo 6229.

Rochberg, George. 1984. *Concerto for Oboe and Orchestra*. New World 335.

Schnittke, Alfred. 1966. *Quartet for Strings I*. Bis 467.

Schwantner, Joseph. 1978. *Aftertones of Infinity*. New World 381.

Takemitsu, Toru. 1986. *Gémeaux for Oboe, Trombone, and Two Orchestras*. Peters. Denon 78944.

Toensing, Richard. 1985. *Angels for Winds, Strings, Piano, and Percussion*. North/South 1005.

INDEX